DESIGN DRAWING

WILLIAM KIRBY LOCKARD

DRAWING

REVISED EDITION

VNR **VAN NOSTRAND REINHOLD COMPANY**

NEW YORK   CINCINNATI   TORONTO   LONDON   MELBOURNE

Published by Van Nostrand Reinhold Company Inc.
135 West 50th Street, New York, NY 10020

Van Nostrand Reinhold Publishing
1410 Birchmount Road
Scarborough, Ontario M1P 2E7, Canada

Van Nostrand Reinhold Australia Pty. Ltd.
17 Queen Street
Mitcham, Victoria 3132, Australia

Van Nostrand Reinhold Company Limited
Molly Millars Lanes
Wokingham, Berkshire, England

16   15   14   13   12   11   10   9   8   7   6   5   4   3   2   1

For my students
    whose eager appearance, year after year, with the enthusiasm
    to learn how to design/draw a better world has allowed
    the development of the ideas in this book.

For my fellow teachers
    who have tolerated, supported and encouraged a non-traditional
    approach to teaching the introductory drawing courses
    at the University of Arizona.

    and most of all

For Peggy,
    without whose love this book would never have been written,
    and whose equal and essential contributions to every
    phase of the writing, production and publication
    make it *our* book in the deepest sense.

CONTENTS

ILLUSTRATIONS

The author wishes to thank the following publishers, institutions and individuals for permission to reproduce the illustrations, tables and photographs, as listed:

Page 3 - Picasso — Guernica. (c) SPADEM, Paris/VAGA, New York, 1982. By permission of VAGA, New York, 1982.

Page 3 - Gearbox Control Surface Lock Casting. From *Graphics - Analysis and Conceptual Design* by A. S. Levins. Copyright (c) 1968 by John Wiley & Sons, Inc., New York.

Page 3 - Le Corbusier - Sketches for the Chapel at Ronchamp. From *Le Corbusier 1946-52*. Copyright (c) 1953 Verlag fur Architektur (Artemis), Zurich. By permission from Artemis Verlag, Zurich.

Page 6 - A Victorian Drawing Class. From *Nelson's New Drawing Course* by J. Vaughan (Edinburgh 1903). By permission of Thomas Nelson and Sons, Ltd., Publishers, London.

Pages 15, 37, 64, 69, 93, 137 - Johnny Hart - from the cartoon strip, *B.C.* By permission of Johnny Hart and Field Enterprises, Inc.

Pages 22 and 23 - Photographs by Peggy Lockard.

Page 26 - Charles M. Schultz - Peanuts Cartoons from *Fly, You Stupid Kite, Fly* by Charles M. Schultz. Copyright (c) 1958 United Feature Syndicate, Inc. By permission of United Feature Syndicate.

Page 35 - Le Corbusier - Le Modulor. From *Le Corbusier 1946-52*. Copyright (c) 1953 Verlag Fur Architektur (Artemis), Zurich. By permission from Artemis Verlag, Zurich.

Pages 38 and 39 - Sidney Harris cartoons. By permission of Sidney Harris.

Page 43 - Two Diagrams of the Brain. From *The Dragons of Eden* by Carl Sagan. Copyright (c) 1977 by Carl Sagan. Reprinted by permission of Random House, Inc., and by permission of the author and the author's agents, Scott Meredith Literary Agency, Inc., 845 Third Avenue, New York, New York, 10022.

Page 46 - Schematic Representation of the Organismic Hierarchy from *Janus: A Summing Up* by Arthur Koestler. Copyright (c) 1978 by Arthur Koestler. Reprinted by permission of Random House, Inc., and by permission of The Sterling Lord Agency, Inc.

Page 51 - The Two Modes of Consciousness: A Tentative Dichotomy from *The Psychology of Consciousness*, Second Edition, Copyright (c) 1977 by Robert E. Ornstein. Reprinted by permission of Harcourt Brace Jovanovich, Inc.

continued . . . .

Page 51 - Michael S. Gazzaniga - The Split Brain in Man. From *Draw! A Visual Approach to Thinking, Learning and Communicating* by Kurt Hanks and Larry Belliston. Copyright (c) 1977 by William Kaufman, Inc. By permission of the publisher.

Page 60 - Express Text Cycle from *Experiences in Visual Thinking*, Second Edition, by R. H. McKim. Copyright (c) 1980 by Wadsworth, Inc. Reprinted by permission of the publisher, Brooks/Cole Publishing Company, Monterey, California.

Page 68 - Nancy Strube - Fig. 21-50, Scroll. From *Experiences in Visual Thinking*, Second Edition, by R. H. McKim. Copyright (c) 1980 by Wadsworth, Inc. Reprinted by permission of the publisher, Brooks/Cole Publishing Company, Monterey, California.

Page 73 - Piranesi - Illustration 28, Carceri: Plate 3. From *Giovanni Battista Piranesi. Drawings and Etchings at Columbia University*. Copyright (c) 1972 by the Trustees of Columbia University of the City of New York. By permission of Columbia University.

Page 73 - Canaletto - Piazza San Marco: Looking East from South of the Central Line. From *Canaletto: Giovanni Antonio Canal 1697-1768* by W. G. Constable, Second Edition, edited by J. G. Links. Copyright (c) Oxford University Press 1976. By permission of the publisher.

Page 73 - Leonardo da Vinci - The Costruzione Legittima as it was Drawn by Leonardo from *On The Rationalization of Sight: With an Examination of Three Renaissance Texts on Perspective* by William J. Ivins, Jr. Copyright (c) 1973 by Da Capo Press, Inc. By permission of the publisher.

Page 74 - Peter Eisenman - Axonometric Drawing. From *Five Architects: Eisenman, Graves, Gwathmey, Hedjuk, Meier* by Peter Eisenman, Philip Johnson, Colin Rowe & Kenneth Frampton. Copyright (c) 1975 by Peter Eisenman, Charles Gwathmey, John Hedjuk, Colin Rowe, Michael Graves, Richard Meier & Kenneth Frampton. Reprinted by permission of Oxford University Press, Inc.

Page 75 - C. Leslie Martin - Multi-view Orthographic Projections. Reprinted with permission of Macmillan Publishing Co., Inc. from *Architectural Graphics*, Second Edition, by C. Leslie Martin. Copyright (c) 1970 by C. Leslie Martin.

Page 78 - Richard Welling - Line Drawing. From *The Technique of Drawing Buildings* by Richard Welling. Watson-Guptill Publications. By Permission of Richard Welling.

Page 78 - Paul Stevenson Oles - Tone Drawing. From *Architectural Illustration: The Value Delineation Process* by Paul Stevenson Oles. Copyright (c) 1979 by Van Nostrand Reinhold Company. Reprinted by permission of the publisher.

Page 80 - Ted Kautzky - Pencil Drawing of Gate. From *The Ted Kautzky Pencil Book* by Ted Kautzky. Copyright (c) 1979 by Van Nostrand Reinhold Company. Reprinted by permission of the publisher.

Page 81 - Mark deNalovy-Rozvadovski - Tone of Lines Drawing. From *Architectural Delineation* by Ernest Burden. Copyright (c) 1971 by McGraw-Hill Inc. Used with permission of McGraw-Hill Book Company.

Page 81 - Helmut Jacoby - Line and Tone Drawing. From *New Architectural Drawings* by Helmut Jacoby. Copyright (c) 1969 by Verlag Gerd Hatje. Reprinted by permission of the publisher.

Page 104 - Projected Perspective Methods. From *Architectural Graphic Standards*, Sixth Edition, by Charles G. Ramsey and Harold R. Sleeper. Copyright (c) 1970 by John Wiley & Sons, Inc. By permission of the publisher.

Page 109 - Leonard da Vinci - Studio del Corpo Umano O "Canone di Proporzioni". By permission of Scala New York/Florence.

Page 127 - C. Leslie Martin - Shadows on Elevations. Reprinted with permission of Macmillan Publishing Co., Inc. from *Architectural Graphics*, Second Edition, by C. Leslie Martin. Copyright (c) 1970 by C. Leslie Martin.

Page 128 - C. Leslie Martin - Shadows on Plans and Elevations. Reprinted with permission of Macmillan Publishing Co., Inc. from *Design Graphics*, Second Edition, by C. Leslie Martin. Copyright (c) 1968 by C. Leslie Martin.

Page 163 - Ted Kautzky - Pencil Drawings. From *The Ted Kautzky Pencil Book* by Ted Kautzky. Copyright (c) 1979 by Van Nostrand Reinhold Company. Reprinted by permission of the publisher.

Page 207 - Paul Laseau - Problem Solving Diagrams. From *Graphic Problem Solving for Architects and Builders* by Paul Laseau. Copyright (c) 1975 by CBI Publishing Company. Reprinted by permission of the publisher, CBI Publishing Company, Inc., 51 Sleeper St., Boston, MA 02210.

Pages 223, 224, 228, 232, 233 - Paul Laseau - Drawings from *Graphic Thinking for Architects and Designers* by Paul Laseau. Copyright (c) 1980 by Van Nostrand Reinhold Company. Reprinted by permission of the publisher.

Page 225 - Edward de Bono - Entry Point Diagram from page 179 of *Lateral Thinking: Creativity Step by Step* by Edward de Bono. Copyright (c) 1970 by Edward de Bono. Reprinted by permission of Harper & Row, Publishers, Inc. and of the author.

Pages 226 and 227 - Edward T. White - Programming Diagrams. From *Introduction to Architectural Programming* by Edward T. White. Copyright (c) 1972 by Edward T. White. By permission of the author.

Page 232 - Francis D. K. Ching - Regular and Irregular Forms. From *Architecture: Form, Space and Order* by Francis D. K. Ching. Copyright (c) 1979 by Van Nostrand Reinhold Company. Reprinted by permission of the publisher.

Page 245 - Edward T. White - The Variables of Presentation. From *Presentation Strategies in Architecture* by Edward T. White. Copyright (c) 1977 by Edward T. White. By permission of the author.

Page 246 - Documents de L'Ecole Nationale Superieure des Beaux-Arts, Paris. From *The Architecture of the Ecole Des Beaux-Arts*, The Museum of Modern Art, New York, edited by Arthur Drexler.

All other drawings in *Design Drawing* are by the author.

NOTES ON THE REVISED EDITION

The first edition of this book was hastened by the urgency of providing the promised back-up text for the companion workbook, *Design Drawing Experiences* (1973), which was published the previous year and already in use in several design schools. The pressure and haste under which the first edition was produced was regrettable, and I have had eight not exactly leisurely years in which to repent.

I included a questionnaire with examination copies, seeking criticism from the drawing teachers to whom the first edition was mailed. I didn't anticipate the volume of the response or the care most respondents took in evaluating the book. The responses were so many and so unexpected that, at that time in my life, I was unable to respond, or even to thank all the teachers who sent back the questionnaire.

I deeply appreciate all that criticism, learned a great deal from it, and this revised edition is a belated response to that feedback of eight years ago. The present revision is so complete that the book perhaps should have been renamed, but the core of ideas and the argument remain, and *Design Drawing* is still the most appropriate title I can think of.

My original intent for this book, and even when I seriously began the effort to revise it six years ago, was to write the definitive book on design drawing—a book which would somehow collect all we know about this kind of drawing and extend that knowledge with new ways of thinking about and using drawing. Such a book is no longer possible, at least not from this author. There are now many good books on drawing, written with a healthy variety of viewpoints, and their appearance seems to be accelerating at such a rate that any sort of comprehensive synthesis would be momentary. I hope, however, that the second goal, that of making a contribution to the extension of knowledge about design drawing, is fulfilled in this revised edition.

In the present revision I have tried to eliminate much of the speculation of the original edition and stick more closely to what I am competent to write about. The sections on perspective and shadow-casting are completely revised and integrated into a single comprehensive system. I have also added a whole section on drawing's relationship to the design process and generally increased the illustrations, analogies and references to the related ideas of others, especially non-designers.

I have also tried to tone down the rhetoric, although I am aware that there remains a certain preacher-like advocacy, but that is an honest reflection of my teaching style. I am really not comfortable with what for me is the dishonesty of the cool pseudo-objectivity of academic discussion. I would rather risk simplistic analogies, redundancy and overstatement than have the reader miss the significance of the choices involved in thinking about and using drawing.

William Kirby Lockard
Tucson 1982

ACKNOWLEDGMENTS

The author wishes to thank the following publishers and authors for permission to reprint material copyrighted or controlled by them.

Brooks/Cole Publishing Company for permission to quote from *Experiences in Visual Thinking*, Second Edition, by R. H. McKim. Copyright (c) 1972, 1980 by Wadsworth, Inc.

Jerome S. Bruner for permission to quote from *A Study of Thinking* by Jerome S. Bruner, Jacqueline J. Goodnow and George A. Austin. Copyright (c) 1956 by John Wiley & Sons.

Edward de Bono and Harper & Row, Publishers, Inc. for permission to quote specified excerpts on pages 50, 52, 219, 224, 225, and 226 abridged from *Lateral Thinking: Creativity Step by Step* by Edward de Bono. Copyright (c) 1970 by Edward de Bono.

Edward T. Hall and Doubleday & Company, Inc. for permission to quote excerpts from *The Hidden Dimension* by Edward T. Hall. Copyright (c) 1966 by Edward T. Hall.

Houghton Mifflin Company for permission to quote from *The Perception of the Visual World* by James J. Gibson. Copyright (c) 1950 by Houghton Mifflin Company, *The Senses Considered as Perceptual Systems* by James J. Gibson. Copyright (c) 1966 by Houghton Mifflin Company, and *The Ecological Approach to Visual Perception* by James J. Gibson. Copyright (c) 1979 by Houghton Mifflin Company.

William H. Ittelson and Seminar Press, Inc. for permission to quote from *Environment and Cognition*, edited by William H. Ittelson. Copyright (c) 1973 by Seminar Press, Inc.

W. W. Norton & Company, Inc. for permission to quote from *Conceptual Blockbusting* by James L. Adams. Copyright (c) 1974, 1976 by James L. Adams.

Random House, Inc. and The Sterling Lord Agency, Inc. for permission to quote from *Janus: A Summing Up* by Arthur Koestler. Copyright (c) 1978 by Arthur Koestler.

Van Nostrand Reinhold Company for permission to quote from *Graphic Thinking for Architects and Designers* by Paul Laseau. Copyright (c) 1980 by Van Nostrand Reinhold Company.

Viking Penguin Inc. for permission to quote excerpts from *Karl Popper* by Bryan Magee. Copyright (c) 1973 by Bryan Magee.

Edward T. White for permission to quote from *Introduction to Architectural Programming* by Edward T. White. Copyright (c) 1972 by Edward T. White.

INTRODUCTION

This book is written for students entering the environmental design professions: architecture, landscape architecture and interior design. Most beginning environmental design students bring some understanding of drawing as art or drawing as drafting, and they each bring a different level of drawing ability. Compared to the beginning design students' understanding of English, mathematics or science, however, their understanding of drawing, their attitudes toward drawing and their ability to draw could hardly be more misleading, diverse or lacking. In the design schools, there is often no more than a polishing of whatever drawing abilities the student happens to have, accompanied either by an extravagant and undeserved appreciation of the students' supposed "talent" or an equally undeserved deprecation of their lack of it. For these reasons, learning to draw and to use drawing in design is often unnecessarily difficult, frustrating and humiliating for students who are well prepared for design education in every other way.

I have written a previous book on drawing called *Drawing As a Means to Architecture* (1968). The success of that book, and a deepening conviction that the confident ability to draw is indispensable to the design process, and should be taught by designers, has led me to undertake the present book. The main claims of this book are that:

• design drawing is a particular kind of drawing, clearly different from the more conventional and long formalized Art and Drafting in its purposes, methods and values.

• to limit environmental design students to the conventional attitudes and methods of Art or Drafting is to limit their understanding of the most valuable tool in the design process.

The greatest difficulty of which I am aware as an author is the Western intellectual tradition of linear, logical argument—how to categorize and relate what you have to say. Unfortunately stream of consciousness prose is only accepted in authors of fiction. This is particularly difficult when much of what you have to say involves the breaking and remaking of traditional categories. The new category of drawing which this book hopes to begin to establish is best understood by founding the argument for it in a consideration of its relationship to the two traditional kinds of drawing.

TRADITIONAL SPLIT. The differences between art and drafting begin to be evident to students from the time mechanical drawing is introduced in junior high school. This new kind of precisely accurate drawing, with its own special orthographic form, comes after a much earlier, and quite different introduction to drawing, as art, in elementary school, and is reinforced by a culturally indoctrinated split based on the students' gender. Although society's notion of the proper male and female uses of drawing is weakening, you will still find few boys in art classes and fewer girls in mechanical drawing classes after junior high school. Art and drafting are well established, useful traditions and for the draftsperson, the artist and the illustrator their attitudes, values and methods are adequate.

VISUAL COMPONENT OF REASON.
Unfortunately, the two poles represented by *drawing as art* and *drawing as drafting* overlook a way of thinking about and using drawing which is potentially more valuable than either of the conventional concepts. This third concept of drawing is as the visual or graphic component of reason. Vision is our best-developed sense, and the unique linkage of remarkable vision with a facile hand is the source of the intelligence which separates us from the animals. If we would develop this visual component of reason, our eyes could often "see," in representative drawings, the most correct or reasonable alternative more directly than our minds alone can sort through the semantics of reason. Our eyes are very wise and we trust them above our other sense organs. Anyone who has agreed to a verbally described blind date will know what I mean. Our language is filled with trite, but true, phrases which illustrate this: "I see"; "It looks good to me"; "Show me"; "Let me see"; "I can visualize"; etc.

The use of drawing during any creative process, to make graphic representations of parts of the problem, tentative solutions, or the process itself, allows the designer and all others involved in the design process to see and evaluate proposals in the deepest and most direct way possible. This kind of drawing is used or should be used by all those who design the built environment on which our convenience, safety, delight and sanity depend. We have known for some time now that we are irrevocably shaped by whatever environment we inhabit, but we have been slow to take seriously the responsibility for the design of that environment. Knowing what it will be like to be surrounded by a proposed environment is absolutely basic to this kind of design responsibility, first for the designer, and through the designer's drawing ability, for all others involved in the design process.

I am not prepared to make an argument here for the use of drawing in philosophic or scientific inquiry, although I am persuaded that drawing could be very useful in those endeavors. There is, unfortunately, a prejudice against graphics in most of the higher human endeavors. Any illustrated book suffers a certain stigma.

As our children mature, we take away their pictures and deliberately inhibit the strong evolutionary link between eye and mind. The use of graphics is degraded to selling or persuading some presumably intellectually inferior group: consumers, children, or some group whose approval is needed, but whose real understanding is presumed to be limited or undesired.

A related attitude holds that drawings or pictures are misleading and strike emotional responses which are not to be trusted in serious matters. My experience is that, on the contrary, drawings are much more dependable and honest than words.

Drawing is also mistrusted as either a mysterious intuitive activity or discounted as automatic and mindless by many of today's leading design methods theorists, exemplified by Christopher Jones' unexplained but consistently pejorative use of the phrase "design by drawing" in his book *Design Methods* (1970). Most designers who are confident of their drawing ability and use drawing consciously in the design process find such a paranoia of the supposed evils of drawing more irrational than the ritual it seeks to avoid.

DRAWING AS SEEING. An argument can be made that one of the great benefits of language, beyond its communicative use, is that it promotes more precise thought. There is a parallel argument for drawing. The mastery of drawing to the point of being able to reproduce the spatial environment accurately and make evaluations from such drawn representations, promotes a more precise "seeing" and experiencing of the environment. Such a drawing ability allows us to propose precise changes in the environment and "see" them in an evaluative way. The ability to draw complex objects and spaces leads to a deeper understanding and appreciation of the spatial structure of our environment.

THREE KINDS OF DRAWING. The best way I have found of illustrating the differences between design drawing and art or mechanical drawing is to compare them in terms of their uses, methods and value systems.

As *art,* drawing values self-expression, choice of subject, virtuoso technique, many levels of communications (often deliberately obscure), and, above all, the drawing itself as a unique one-of-a-kind original. The drawing itself is the product. Reality, in terms of color, perspective and subject matter, is often deliberately distorted, and this distortion is a part of the expressionistic value of the work. The act of creating a drawing as art is also often considered to be a complete, finite act, and any redrawing or change degrades that particular drawing, since it indicates a certain indecision or weakness on the part of the artist. Art places no demand for efficiency on drawing. It may, in fact, value the laboriousness of the drawing.

As *drafting,* drawing values mechancial accuracy and efficiency and relates to reality through a rigidly formal set of orthographic abstractions (plan, elevation, section and isometric), and is only a record of, or pattern for making, an existing or already determined object. Excellence in drafting or mechanical drawing is judged exactly as you would judge the excellence of a copying machine. There is no room for self-expression or creative thinking except perhaps in lettering style or choice and placement of the north arrow.

As *design drawing*, drawing should be tentative and exploratory, inviting change and including the context and the user. The drawings are of no value except as a means of externalizing and evaluating a tentative design proposal. They should be informally, but essentially, accurate and should have a careful, if abstract relation to the design process, and a direct relation to reality. Design drawings should be made primarily for the designer and only secondarily for the others to whom the designer must communicate the design. The drawings both lead and record conception and represent the essentially visual symbol system of the mind. They should be a transparent viewer through which designers can see what they are designing.

PICASSO, Pablo - *Guernica* - (1937, May-early June)

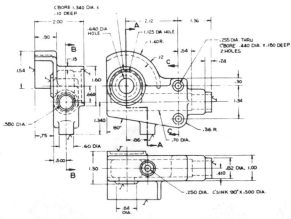

Fig. E-18.6   Gearbox control surface lock casting. (Adapted from a drawing by Convair Division of General Dynamics Corp.)

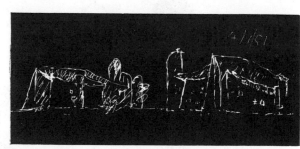

Le Corbusier: Sketches for the Chapel at Ronchamp

Drawing as *art* is the product of a single creative act valued by the dimension of its juxtaposition to reality and convention.

Drawing as *drafting* is an efficiently made pattern or record, mechanically accurate and obeying rigid formal rules.

The most valuable design drawings are those which extend and shape the design process and accurately represent the experiential qualities of the design.

These inherent differences in the uses, methods and value systems seem to leave room for *design drawing* to be established as a separate and quite different kind of drawing than either art or drafting.

The following table may clarify the differences between the three kinds of drawing. Design drawing shares certain characteristics with art or drafting, but in the total of all its characteristics it is clearly a different kind of drawing.

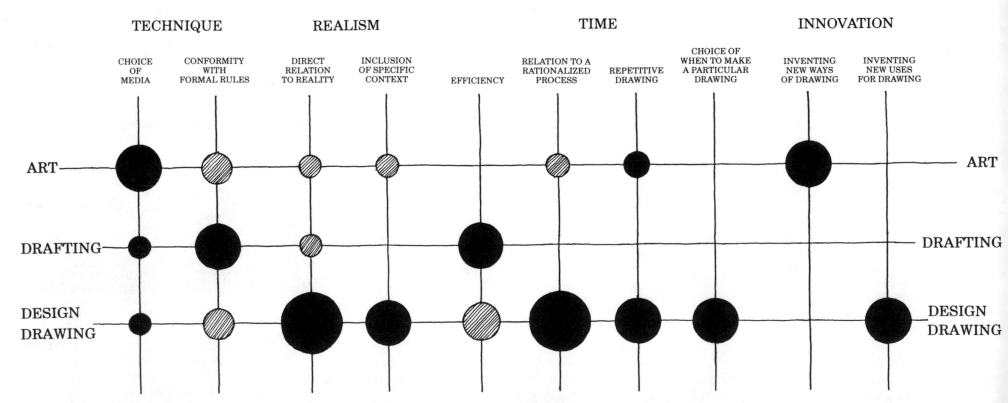

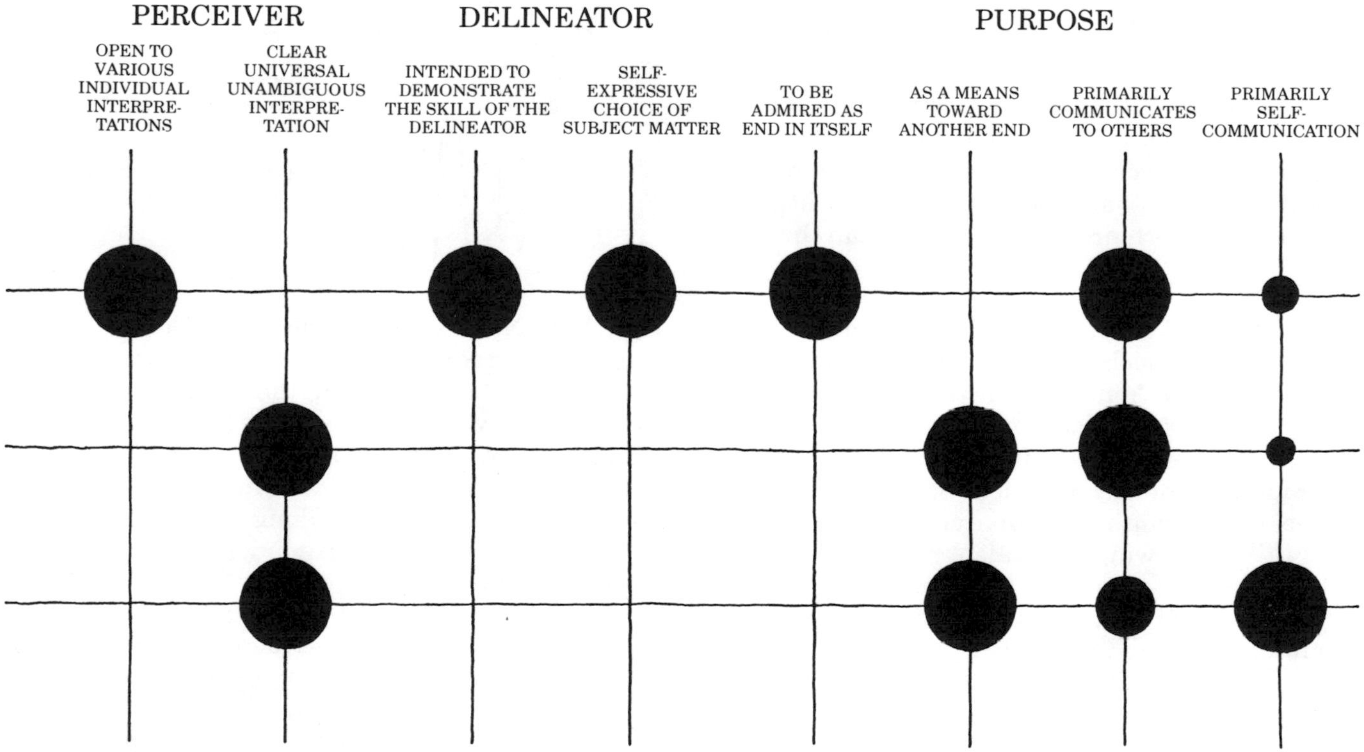

Perhaps the difference between the three kinds of drawing can be summed up in a triple analogy:

ART—*RESPONDING & EXPRESSING*

When artists draw they are *responding* to their environment, freely *expressing* their experience. When the drawing is finished they hope it will communicate a personal interpretation of something about their experience, variously interpreted in turn through the viewer's experience. Artists hang their drawings in galleries.

DRAFTING—*DESCRIBING & INSTRUCTING*

When draftspersons draw they are *describing* a predetermined object built or to-be-built. When the drawing is finished they must count on its *instructing* precisely, without any freedom of interpretation, how the described object is built or is to-be-built. Draftspersons duplicate their drawings as instructions and then file them as records.

DESIGN DRAWING—*GENERATING, EVALUATING & IMPROVING*

When designers draw they are designing an environment which does not exist and has not yet been determined. They are directly *generating, evaluating* and *improving* what they see in the crystal ball of the drawing. Their drawings may never be finished, but they count on them to accurately represent the experience of the proposed environment they are designing to themselves, and to those for whom they are designing. Designers may throw their drawings away.

PERCEIVER		DELINEATOR			PURPOSE		
OPEN TO VARIOUS INDIVIDUAL INTERPRETATIONS	CLEAR UNIVERSAL UNAMBIGUOUS INTERPRETATION	INTENDED TO DEMONSTRATE THE SKILL OF THE DELINEATOR	SELF-EXPRESSIVE CHOICE OF SUBJECT MATTER	TO BE ADMIRED AS END IN ITSELF	AS A MEANS TOWARD ANOTHER END	PRIMARILY COMMUNICATES TO OTHERS	PRIMARILY SELF-COMMUNICATION
●		●	●	●		●	•
	●				●	●	•
	●				●	•	●

The future of the three kinds of drawing will probably exaggerate their present differences. Drafting will be taken over more and more by machines or computers because of its repetitive mechanical nature. This future possibility seriously questions "mechanical" drawing courses. Their very name implies a machine-made ideal and it seems futile to continue to train a human to produce something which has mechanical perfection as its goal.

Drawing as art will certainly continue, but the realism which in the past demanded precise draftsmanship has been largely forsaken, and many artists may use drawing as a predictive representation with the final work being done by a painting process quite different from realistic representation.

Design drawing has perhaps the most potent future of the three. In his book, *Future Shock* (1970), Alvin Toffler suggests:

> Multiplying our images of possible futures is important; but these images need to be organized, crystallized into structured form. In the past, utopian literature did this for us. It played a practical, crucial role in ordering men's dreams about alternative futures. Today we suffer for lack of utopian ideas around which to organize competing images of possible futures.

A Victorian drawing class

TEACHING DRAWING. All concepts about teaching and learning drawing must be based on assumptions about the nature, origin and development of drawing ability. One of the few cases in which I agree with the behaviorist psychologists is that what appears to be drawing talent is actually the unrecognized product of years of reinforced behavior. Students who have not had drawing reinforced as a behavior may be discouraged in their first drawing or design class by noticing the comparison of their drawings with that of other students who, with little apparent effort, draw much better than they.

TALENT. The conventional copout is to assume that such effortless drawing skill is a God-given or "natural" talent. This is a comfortable assumption for students, since it excuses their poor drawings or, worse, their dropping the whole idea of becoming a designer because they apparently haven't the "gift" for drawing. The talent notion is also a convenient excuse for teachers, since they may assume that those students who draw clumsily are untalented and therefore unteachable. Little teaching or learning is possible where the assumption of innate or natural ability prevails. Talent is a myth,

comfortable perhaps, but surely untenable for those who teach and attend drawing courses.

When a student exhibits what commonly passes for talent, his fellow students and teachers do not see the ten or fifteen years of reinforced drawing behavior. In every case I know of, this so-called talent is the product of reinforcement by parents, teachers and friends, and has become very self-rewarding. The talent myth also takes away any credit for the hours and hours of concentrated effort it takes to learn to draw, which those who have made that effort deserve. And it similarly strips good drawing teachers of any credit they might claim for the drawing abilities of their students.

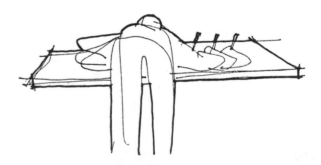

MOTIVATION. The development of drawing ability does require a great deal of actual drawing. There are not many shortcuts to learning to draw. One of the paradoxes in learning to draw is that you learn to draw quickly and confidently by drawing slowly and tentatively, over a long, long period of time. Clear, comprehensive explanation, graphic examples and a patient, supportive attitude are teaching essentials, but perhaps the greatest single influence on a student's learning to draw is the self-rewarding experience of success. The completion of a rather difficult drawing, that the student recognizes as successful and is proud of having drawn, will do more to help a student learn to draw than all the books and lectures in the world. It doesn't matter if the success was outrageously supported by beginning with a half-finished drawing, or having the teacher or a fellow student help with the actual drawing. As long as the student understands how to produce a similar drawing, the help will be forgotten in the glow of understanding that such a self-rewarding experience can be repeated, and improved. If a teacher can simply turn a student on to drawing as an enjoyable activity that teacher has done the most important thing any teacher can do.

The companion book of drawing exercises, *Design Drawing Experiences,* is intended to provide the kind of successful drawing experiences that support the success of students' efforts to learn to draw. Reasonable diligence and applied intelligence should always be rewarded by success in drawing courses.

COGNITIVE DRAWING. While learning to draw may begin with making drawing rewarding, as much of the learning as possible should be raised to the cognitive, verbal level. The ability to draw must be more than a mere physical routine that a well-coordinated animal or robot could be programmed to do.

While there are certainly levels of skill in drawing that seem to be beyond explanation and understanding, we need not fall back on the "talent" concept as a blanket explanation for abilities we cannot yet understand or explain.

There seems to be a certain romantic or mystic value in the idea of talent, giftedness and innate or natural ability. But how much more valuable for us all if these abilities could be learned by anyone; if we consciously made talent, as I think we can, rather than passively accepting the apparent whim of fate. Too many books and courses on drawing rush into drawing as you might in a physical education class, with little recognition that drawing ability somehow extends above the shoulder, and that there is a growing body of *knowledge* about drawing and its relationship to reality and to the design process. Most drawing mistakes are head mistakes not hand mistakes.

Because I am interested in the intellectual side of drawing, I have included more arguments and rationale than are normally found in a book on drawing. The arguments are intended to expose you—perhaps persuade you—to certain ideas concerning design drawing's uses, methods and values. But more than this, the arguments are intended to encourage you to think about the way you draw and make it conscious and communicable. The myth of talent or innate ability is of no service to the design disciplines or the design schools, or to the individual designer. It is much more valuable to know, insofar as possible, the alternative uses, methods and values of drawing, and consciously choose and develop them for yourself as a designer.

The establishment of design drawing as distinct from art or drafting has several implications for teaching design students to draw.
• design drawing courses should be taught by practicing designers who use drawing in the design process.

• design drawing tasks should always include design content—the ability is difficult to teach apart from the design process. There should always be something *beyond the drawing* for which the student is responsible and for which the drawing is only a representation. The design opportunity may be quite limited, but there must be some responsibility for the delineator beyond just acting as a copying machine. Otherwise the drawing becomes an end in itself and ceases to be a design drawing.

- design drawings should always include the context—pushing out the boundaries to include as much and as many kinds of context as possible.
- design drawing tasks should teach efficiency and quickness so the drawing can keep pace with the mind.

- drawing landscapes and still lifes has only limited potential for teaching design students how to draw, for what is needed in design drawing is the ability to draw what *doesn't* exist, except in the designer's mind. Drawing examples and details of well-designed environments, however, is extremely valuable in building a design vocabulary as well as drawing skills.
- design drawing should insist on essential but not mechanical accuracy.

- design drawing must have the correct focus—showing alternatives which must be selected in the decision-making process.

- design drawings should be direct, clear, honest self-communications.

- design drawing students should be aware of and should practice making choices of what and how to draw in various situations.
- design drawing students should be encouraged to develop both personal and broadly shared kinds of design drawings—and to make intelligent free use of whatever graphic representations might be helpful in a particular design process.

The understandings and skills involved in design drawing could be learned at junior high school level. I believe that the ability to represent the built environment, either as it exists or as it might be, and the ability to diagram various concepts graphically is at least as useful for the future as learning to make orthographic patterns of predetermined objects.

If we use writing as an analogy for drawing, *drawing as art* might be poetry, *drawing as drafting* might be a set of specifications, a scientific description or filling out a questionnaire, but *design drawing* would be the most basic of the three for it is no more than a vocabulary and syntax. Design drawing has little to do with what is said, or even how it is said, it is simply the vocabulary, the grammar or the voice. In this analogy, design drawing could even be thought of as preverbal, for whatever the designer wishes to say will be said and read in concrete and wood and steel and glass—not in drawings.

STRUCTURED FREEHAND DRAWING. The kind of drawing advocated throughout this book might be called structured freehand drawing. It is structured in four ways:

- by an understanding of the purpose and potential of any particular drawing in the design process, and an awareness of the alternative choices of what and how to draw.

- by a mastery of the spatial structure underlying perspectives and shadow-casting, drafted in critical cases as a basic framework.

- by a mastery of a perceptual and procedural structure in drawing certain graphic indications so that they may be dependably replicated.

- by the building up of an underlying structure of progressive studies so that the final drawing is always supported by previous drawings.

This way of drawing is influenced by years of trying to teach young people who have little drawing experience to use drawing as a design tool. I believe it is the best way to teach the majority of students to understand the underlying structure and rationale of the various drawings and techniques, and their relationship to reality and to the design process. Teaching this way of drawing does not raise the drawings of the best students to its highest peaks, but it supports and raises the average and weak students above a threshold which allows drawing not to be a handicap in communicating their proposals for the environment. I also believe the approach promotes the continued open ended learning *of* drawing and *about* drawing because it is knowledge based—based broadly on what is known about perception, conception and the design process; not limited to the *on the paper* technique or media application of art nor limited by the equipment and mechanical accuracy compulsions of drafting. It is in many ways a combination of art and drafting but I believe the combination is synergetic—unexpectedly different and in many ways more valuable for designers than either art or drafting.

One further characteristic of this way of drawing is the attempt it makes to separate the understanding and application of the underlying structure and essential accuracy of drawing from drawing tools. One of the mistaken ideas that students carry over from drafting is that the discipline and accuracy of drawing somehow resides in the T-square and triangle. This is not true of *design drawing*. There is an essential accuracy to be mastered, but it has nothing to do with tools. You can construct a perspective and cast the shadows on it freehand in the sand with your finger and make an essentially accurate, disciplined design drawing.

FREEDOM AND DISCIPLINE IN DRAWING

When students are given freedom in design or drawing classes they often ask, "You mean we can draw it any way we want?" The question poses a logical or semantic paradox, for the answer is, "No, for a long time you will be unable to draw it any way you want, unless you are prepared to have an experienced observer assume you wanted to draw it inaccurately, ineptly, naively, or crudely. You can only draw it the ways you *can* draw it." Freedom in drawing begins with the disciplined ability to make more than one kind of drawing in more than one technique. It is only then that a designer can be said to have any freedom at all. Freedom and discipline in drawing are two sides of the same coin, they cannot occur alone.

For those who have been indoctrinated into the disciplines of art or drafting this book may seem at first to offer a diluted or permissive approach to drawing. This is farthest from my intention. I do not believe today's environmental design students need less drawing skill or discipline—they need more—and a serious effort to learn or teach the skills presented here will find them at least as demanding as the traditional art or drafting courses normally offered to environmental designers. What I hope is added to the discipline of drawing method, and what environmental design students also need, is more *understanding* of how the drawing skills they are learning can be used in the design process.

THE FREE HAND. The free hand is the only fit companion to the free mind. The term has special significance because it is precisely because we walk upright, freeing our hands for more important tasks, that we have developed the intelligence called human. In the design process, we need to display tentative design proposals which we can continually compare to the restated design problem. These graphic representations will suggest restatements of the problem, and those restatements will in turn suggest more drawings. Design is essentially a stream of consciousness kind of thing, and the reliance on tools, even a sophisticated tool like a computer, is inhibiting. It is possible to sketch the diagrams, the doodles, and the graphic representations of tentative design proposals with a free mind, free hand, and any simple drawing tool.

THE FREE MIND. The goal in design drawing is the freedom that comes from being able to draw the environment as variously as possible, so that all drawing decisions are free. To make decisions out of a fearful, defensive incompetence is surely a miserable way to draw or design or live. To make a particular drawing in a particular way because you are afraid of perspectives, or ink, or color is the most regrettable of limitations in the design process.

The glory of design education is that it asks students to visualize a better environment than now surrounds us, and for which there are no answers at the back of the book. Environmental design students enjoy a unique form of education for life, which probably should be the general form of all education: to visualize, to propose and advocate, and to practice making the choices about our future, always with the possibility that you may be wrong. Drawing ability, like our environment or ourselves is not received as a gift, or discovered, or found, but must be consciously, deliberately, freely, joyously *made*. The purpose of this book is to help in that making.

THE VALUE OF LEARNING TO DRAW

Notes on the Graphic Revival

Recent conferences, exhibitions, publications and the sale of architects' drawings in galleries evidence a renewed interest in drawing and a returning awareness that drawing is still an essential skill for environmental designers. This graphic revival marks the end of a period of academic and editorial disinterest in the most basic traditional skill of the architectural profession. Drawing courses were crowded out of curricula by profound-sounding successors; and model-making and a wide range of analytical graphics replaced the traditional study and presentation drawings in our schools and in our professional publications.

Despite academic and editorial disinterest, most environmental designers kept right on using drawing as the best representational tool available to designers, and even in the professional schools there were teachers who continued to teach students how, and even why, to draw. We can come out in the open now and speculate as to why the teaching of drawing was mistakenly abandoned and how its neglect was caused partly by our own professional tradition, partly by our profession's more recent and misguided imitation of science and partly by much broader changes in our society and its values.

Traditionally environmental designers and environmental design educators have too often found it convenient to consider drawing ability as either a fortunate genetic result or some sort of providential gift. This myth of talent or giftedness relieved educators of any serious obligation to teach drawing, limiting their responsibility to encouraging those who had the right parents or the good fortune to be able to draw. This practice is just as vicious as any other form of discrimination and we should regret the humiliation suffered by the many people who have dropped out of the design professions because they apparently didn't happen to have a skill which, of all the abilities needed by a designer, is perhaps the most teachable.

Traditional design education could get away with merely selecting and encouraging students who could already draw, because until recently, a society which valued such hand skills as penmanship, needlework and whittling seemed to produce plenty of people with a supposed "talent" for drawing. Professional design schools often delegated the teaching of drawing to the engineering or art faculties, or when this support wasn't available, assigned drawing instruction to the most junior faculty, who abandoned the drawing courses the moment a newer faculty member appeared.

What many educators failed to understand was that their supposedly "talented" students had always been the products of twelve years of elementary and secondary education which valued hand skill as an integral part of education, and spent time teaching penmanship, drawing, woodworking and sewing. This attitude in the schools was solidly reinforced in the home, where skills like quilting and carpentry were valued for their necessity and their pleasure.

Both home life and education have changed profoundly in the last fifty years. The hand skills that once distinguished a mother or father in the eyes of a child or in the general estimation of our culture are today simply curious or perhaps even embarrassing. Time-consuming handwork has, until recently, been in a steady decline along with the value and dignity of all physical labor. To spend long periods of time alone, making anything by hand, particularly if the skill itself takes a long time to master, is generally considered to be eccentric, and certainly not associated with satisfaction and pleasure as it once was.

And in our schools we seem to have lost the will or the patience to teach abilities like handwriting—or even grammar or spelling for that matter—which require repetitive correction on an individual basis. It is much easier to show films or discuss ideas verbally than to take great stacks of papers home for correction. We also find teachers, even in high schools, insinuating, or in some cases insisting, that infrequent papers be typewritten, apparently for legibility.

With all these changes it is hardly surprising that so few students nowadays seem to have the "gift" of drawing. Our society and our schools have decided drawing is one of a group of gifts that are no longer worth giving, for it has always been a set of learned abilities and attitudes passed on by parents and teachers, and not only potential architects, landscape architects and interior designers but all our young people are much poorer without them.

Concurrently the last thirty years have seen a steady devaluation of drawing in the professional design schools. There are a number of reasons for this, all of them understandable and some justifiable. First there was the realization that the traditional emphasis on drawing ability was unfair to students who happened to have little previous drawing experience. Instead of trying to equalize these individual differences by taking on the responsibility for teaching everyone to draw, the equalization was attempted through the use of other forms of communication: verbal descriptions, analytical diagrams and models. These changes were rationalized by claims that drawings are misleading and generally less dependable than models or even analytical diagrams.

Drawing was also denigrated because it was associated with the academic formalism of the Ecole de Beaux Arts, and the overemphasis on elaborate presentation drawings was taken to be symptomatic of an overemphasis on formal visual qualities, which were held to be cosmetic and superficial. In its most extreme form this new view of architecture held that beautiful drawings were the first clue to design decadence, and the ability to make beautiful drawings and especially to enjoy their making was somewhere on a scale between the making of voodoo dolls and child-molestation.

The design methodologists found it easy to build on this devaluation of drawing and the misunderstanding of drawing's relationship to the design process. Most methodologists assume that drawing is or should be simply the neutral printing-out of decisions arrived at previously in the clear light of logical "problem solving." They generally mistrust drawing as some sort of irrational ritual, preferring various quantitative analytical models, and their influence has contributed to the general devaluation of what Christopher Jones has disparagingly called "design by drawing."

Underlying all these reasons for the deemphasis of drawing in design education is the persistent attempt to turn environmental design into a science. Scientism would replace the cultural certainty of tradition or the academic certainty of a particular style with the scientific certainty of method—what

Colin Rowe has called "physics envy." And this latest search for certainty is just as futile as the others. It has affected drawing by assuming that, like science, we need a series of metalanguages which will represent certain unseen but everpresent and all-important environmental qualities. Just like the neutrinos of sub-atomic physicists and the black holes of astronomers, scientism insists we must analyze, represent and calculate the effects of a proliferation of environmental "problems." We thus get matrices, graphs, decision trees, interaction nets, endless box and arrow diagrams and other pseudoscientific notations which supposedly represent critical, but invisible, characteristics of an environment or the process which designs environments. The analysis these various graphic tools allow is certainly beneficial, but it cannot replace the synthesis represented in the traditional design drawings. What the proponents of the various problem-solving languages seem to forget is that, unlike the explorations of science beyond the macro- and micro-scales of human vision, environmental design exists manifestly at human scale. Environmental qualities must be directly perceivable by human beings or not at all, and we have had the graphic means to represent such environmental qualities for a long time.

The speed with which all these changes in the teaching of drawing occured is perhaps unique to American academia. Bright young students who never learned to draw could, within a year or two, have earned a Master's degree and be telling a whole classroom full of slightly younger students that they really didn't need to learn to draw, because drawings are essentially misleading and when unavoidable can be produced by underlings or machines. The young teachers need never actually say anything about the value of learning to draw because their lack of respect for the ability will be very apparent in their design teaching, and as far as they know will be correct, since they may never have experienced the absolute necessity of drawing in practice.

Meanwhile, back at the office, the typical architect, landscape architect or interior designer kept right on drawing and wondering why recent graduates couldn't draw and generally weren't even convinced they needed to learn. In spite of the promises of over-enthusiastic computer salesmen who seemed to imply naively that computers would soon do most of a designer's drawing, any designer still had to produce, by hand, drawings that communicated to collaborators, clients and contractors.

The recent renewal of interest in drawing has made it clear that most designers continue, as they always have, to draw very well. While they may have said little about drawing's relationship to the way they design, one look tells us that their drawing ability and their design ability are interdependent.

It is not entirely clear, however, that the graphic revival brings with it any deeper understanding of the kind of drawing needed in design, and the interest in architects' drawings as gallery artifacts is even more self-conscious and superficial than the most overblown Beaux Arts presentations. What we should have learned is that drawing has a fundamental relationship to the design process and to its products, and the ability to draw is the best foundation of the self-confidence that every designer needs, and should be one of the goals of a culture and an educational system which values the skills of the hand and the eye as constituents of fully human intelligence.

During the design process, two different kinds of representational tools are needed. In the earlier analytical, conceptual stage designers need quick abstract representations of facts, precepts and concepts that can keep pace with their thought process and communicate it to others. Later, when the design is taking shape and being refined, it is best to have the freedom to choose representational modes which suit the developing solution. In both these phases of the design process, drawing is still the most flexible and efficient means of representation.

The ability to think visually or graphically is generally ignored in our educational system, and without a drawing ability which is a confident conceptual partner of our cognitive ability, we will be encouraged by our cultural indoctrination and much recent design methodology to translate all our design ideas into stiff and inappropriate mathematical or verbal statements. Such a translation is artificial and redundant because most environmental design ideas begin, and all must certainly end, if they are to be experienced at all, as physical, formal, visual ideas. To inhibit the conceptual process by forcing such an unnatural conversion to an alternate language is as awkward as attempting to draw a poem or sculpt a symphony.

The realistic representation of the developing solution which is necessary later in the process should be a matter of choice, and drawing offers more freedom of choice than model building or any other means of representation. There has always been a very intimate and interdependent relationship between the way architects design and the way they represent their designs to themselves and to others. The elegant pencil renderings of Schell Lewis and Otto Eggars were uniquely appropriate to the brick, stone, slate, shakes and shutters of which their buildings were made; just as the white Strathmore models of the neoCorbusians are so satisfyingly identical to the white geometries they build. To deliberately choose a particular way of representing a particular design, or after careful consideration, *all* your designs is to be desired, but *having* to represent your designs in a particular way because you don't have the ability to draw or model them any other way is quite another matter. Freedom of choice in representing your designs, as in other matters, comes from having first developed the disciplined ability that makes choice possible.

Modes of representation are never innocent. They all carry prejudices because they inevitably are, and should be, intimately related to the designs they represent. A balanced and confident drawing ability is the most neutral of representational tools, allowing a maturing designer to play all 88 keys of the representational piano, instead of pecking with one finger or playing as limited an instrument as a triangle. Drawing ability is the piano of environmental composers. It is difficult to imagine Beethoven composing his symphonies on a piccolo. After he had used the piano for many years he could compose without its sounds in the silence of his deafness, but while he was learning to compose I imagine that the range and flexibility of the piano as a representational instrument, like drawing ability to a designer, was indispensable.

The reason drawing ability is one of the foundations of self-confidence in designers, is that until we can believe and accept our own representations of the environment, we can never be very sure about the success of our proposed designs. It also helps if we can show these representations to those for whom we are designing and have them accepted as reliable. The correct perception of our environmental design proposals is as critical to designers as the correct perception of the effects of any other of one's actions in the environment. And we know how much human energy is spent in trying to accurately predict the effects of alternative courses of action. Such anticipation is one of humanity's hallmarks. The confidence to self-consciously design environments is dependent on our perception, through drawn or modeled representations of their success, and is a direct extension of the accurate perception of the simplest daily interactions with the environment, on which our confidence as human beings depends.

In order that the returning popularity of drawing have more meaning than merely the ebb and flow of fashion or the artificial editorial recycling of interest, we should use the graphic revival as an occasion to reconsider some of our attitudes toward drawing. We should begin by dropping the talent myth with which we have either dismissed drawing ability or excused its absence. By bringing the ability to draw out of the realm of giftedness and personal idiosyncrasy and acknowledging that it has a fundamental relationship to any designer's thinking process, we may initiate a serious dialogue. I believe such a dialogue would make clear the differences between design drawing and the traditions of art and drafting and soon establish an independent literature and body of theory to replace the hybrid collection of myths and inappropriate notions we have mindlessly accepted from artists and draftspersons. If we raised drawing to this level of serious discussion we might be less likely to lapse into forgetting that the ability to draw and the act of drawing are the foundation and the source of creative confidence.

We should also take this opportunity to review the curricula in our schools of environmental design to see if we can't find time in the early years of design education to make a serious attempt to teach drawing. The drawing courses should be taught by experienced designers, perhaps aided by student assistants, but with student/teacher ratios that allow the kind of personal attention such learning requires.

On a more basic level, as parents of today's school children, I believe environmental designers should lead the insistence that the writing and drawing skills once valued in our public schools should be restored as integral parts of elementary and secondary education and that the skilled hand and eye be recognized as indispensable partners of the skilled mind.

PERCEPTION

The transactional process by which we experience the world is called perception, and while, scientifically, perception is in the territory called psychology, the process is open to the experience of all of us as perceivers. It is particularly important for environmental designers since whatever intentions we have for the environments we design will only be responded to or understood through the perceptions of the inhabitants of those environments; and during the design process any representative drawings we make to study tentative designs will be comprehended by ourselves, our consultants and our clients by means of our individual processes of perception. As environmental designers our entire enterprise thus hinges on perception, and we should develop a deep and deserved confidence in our own perception as well as an understanding and appreciation of the accumulated theory and research on perception.

Psychology's concept of perception has changed over the years from a simplistic and passive stimulus/response model to a recognition that all perception occurs in concrete situations which are inevitably loaded with interdependent relationships; that we actively, even compulsively, seek perceptions as opportunities for action; and that the perception of the environment is fundamentally different from the perception of an object. There is not space in this book, nor do I have the credentials to consider perception comprehensively, but environmental designers should read the available literature on perception in order to understand themselves and the people for whom they will be designing, as perceivers.

Although perception includes the input from all our senses, I will concentrate on visual perception, not just because it is the most critical sense involved in drawing, but because our sense of vision is the dominant sense involved in our perception of and interaction with the environment.

A human being may be thought of as part genetic inheritance, part cultural indoctrination, and part conscious, self-directed experience. Of these three, genetic inheritance, or the legacy we are left by evolution is the most pervasive, and we can do little to change it in a lifetime; but by increasing our understanding of this ancient inheritance we may learn to respect its useful characteristics and somewhat mitigate its prejudices.

THE DOMINANCE OF VISION

All our senses have served our survival, but VISUAL PERCEPTION has been our most successful, though most recent servant and therefore dominates the perceptions of our other senses for several reasons:

- Vision operates at a greater distance than the other senses, and is thus our early warning system. Our evolutionary ancestors, once mauled by a sabretoothed tiger, undoubtedly found it valuable to recognize the species at a distance—without having to get close enough to smell, hear, feel or taste the second one. In *The Intelligent Eye* (1970), R. L. Gregory proposes:

  ...Eyes give warning of the future, by signalling distant objects. It seems very likely that brains as we know them could not have developed without senses—particularly eyes—capable of providing advance information, by signaling the presence of distant objects....

- Vision is our best developed sense. The visual world seems incomparably richer in information than the worlds which are available to our other senses, because the eye and the brain have evolved together. To quote Gregory again:

  ...As we shall see, eyes require intelligence to identify and locate objects in space, but intelligent brains could hardly have developed without eyes. It is not too much to say that eyes freed the nervous system from the tyranny of reflexes, leading to strategic planned behavior and ultimately to abstract thinking. We are still dominated by visual concepts....

Robert H. McKim, in *Experiences in Visual Thinking* (1972), explains the pervasiveness of visual thinking:

  Visual thinking pervades all human activity, from the abstract and theoretical to the down-to-earth and everyday. An astronomer ponders a mysterious cosmic event; a football coach considers a new strategy; a motorist maneuvers his car along an unfamiliar freeway: all are thinking visually. You are in the midst of a dream; you are planning what to wear today; you are making order out of the disarray on your desk; *you* are thinking visually.

From *Experiences in Visual Thinking*, Second Edition, by R. H. McKim. Copyright (c) 1972, 1980 by Wadsworth, Inc. This and all other quotes from the same source reprinted by permission of the publisher, Brooks/Cole Publishing Company, Monterey, California 93940

- Our minds have been built on an evolutionary linkage of vision and touch so strong as to make our other three senses secondary. Our world looks like it feels and feels like it looks and this correspondence is the foundation of our successful interaction with the environment.

- Vision is the feedback loop by which we manipulate our bodies, particularly our hands. All mental activity is visual/actual in the sense that we actually seek perceptions which promise some beneficial potential for action. Bronowski, in *The Ascent of Man* (1973), proposes:

  ...We are active; and indeed we know, as something more than a symbolic accident in the evolution of man, that it is the hand that drives the subsequent evolution of the brain....

  ...we can oppose the thumb precisely to the forefinger, and that is a special human gesture. And it can be done because there is an area in the brain so large that I can best describe its size to you in the following way; we spend more grey matter in the brain manipulating the thumb than in the total control of the chest and the abdomen.

For the preceding reasons vision has become our most trusted sense and our basic arbiter of value, and what we call *mind* would better be called *eyemind* as a reminder of this dominance of vision; or more correctly *eyemind-hand* because of the eye/hand linkage on which our brains are built, and because our perceptions and our conceptions are based on action and involve our whole body.

Although vision is the last sense to be developed in our evolution, its leading role in the development of the mind makes vision the source of most of our information about the world. As Gibson has pointed out, psychologists have seemed obsessed with the optical illusions which can trick our visual perception, forgetting that the main reason our vision can be tricked is that it is so dependable. Abstractly perverting the visual cues which serve us so well in the real world easily misleads us, not because our perception is faulty, but precisely because our vision is so trustworthy as to be beyond suspicion.

PERCEPTION'S PREJUDICES

Visual perception is never neutral and its prejudices can be traced to the evolution of the *eyemindhand* system we inherit.

- *Perception is selfish,* selectively perceiving information which promises survival, pleasure, personal gain or adulation.
- *Perception focuses,* using foveal vision to focus sharply on the center portion of our visual field at the expense of a fuzzy peripheral context.
- *Perception separates,* seeing a world of objects separated from one another in time and space.
- *Perception forms wholes* or gestalts, jumping to conclusions from partial evidence.
- *Perception discriminates,* seeking subtle differences in form and pattern.
- *Perception judges instantly,* in the first impression, and verbal explanation merely serves this visual choosing as a "rational" apology.
- *Perception chooses dominance over equivalence,* seeing one figure on a field at a time rather than seeing an object and background as equivalent.
- *Perception needs new input,* becoming jaded as in color perception or starved as in sensory deprivation.

While all these prejudices have served our evolutionary survival, they form our most persistent perceptual/conceptual blocks by making it difficult for us to comprehend, relate, include the context, withhold judgment or maintain balanced interest. Our compulsions to stereotype, discriminate, make premature decisions and endlessly sort and classify the world can be traced to the way we see.

PERCEPTION OF THE ENVIRONMENT

SPATIAL PERCEPTION

The visual cues by which we perceive space are particularly important for environmental designers, both in the environments they design and in the drawings they make to represent those environments to themselves and to their clients. Spatial perception depends on surfaces, edges, and various perspective cues.

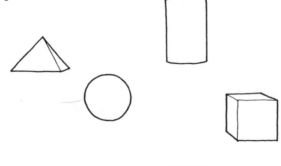

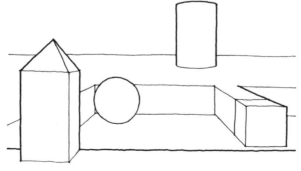

SURFACES

From its crude beginnings our visual perceptual system has always seen a visual field divided at the horizon. The upper half of this visual field has always been a bright sky, and the lower half the earth's surface, with a textural gradient of that horizontal surface from coarse to fine as it recedes into the distance. The perception of this surface and similar continuous background surfaces is essential to our perception of space. In *The Perception of the Visual World* (1950), Gibson argues:

> ...*there is literally no such thing as a perception of space without the perception of a continuous background surface....*

The basic idea is that visual space should be conceived not as an object or an array of objects in air but as a continuous surface or an array of adjoining surfaces. The spatial character of the visual world is given not by the objects in it but by the background of objects....

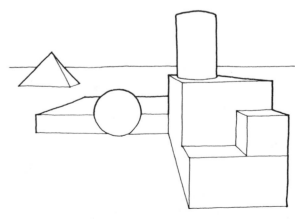

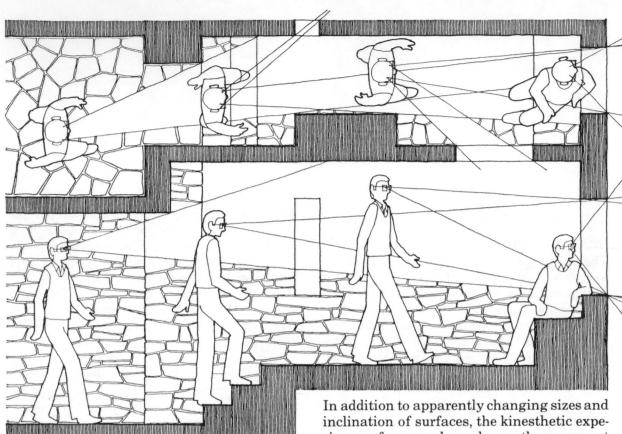

EDGES

The shape or conformation of the space and especially the kinesthetic experiences of space as we move through the environment is conveyed by the perception of edges. Gibson in *The Senses Considered as Perceptual Systems* (1966), explains what happens in our kinesthetic experience of the world:

> ...whenever an observer moves, the array changes. Every solid angle of ambient light— each one of the adjacent pyramids in the diagram—is altered. Every form that would be projected on a sphere centered at the eye is altered by a perspective transformation, and every form projected on the retina, of course, undergoes a corresponding transformation....
>
> ...Introspectively, the field is everywhere alive with motion when the observer moves....

In addition to apparently changing sizes and inclination of surfaces, the kinesthetic experience of space depends on the apparent movement of spatial edges against their backgrounds—the striptease of space, or what Gibson calls "Kinetic Optical Occlusion and Edge Information." To quote Gibson further:

> ...The *edge* of a surface in the room is specified by a discontinuity in the flow of optical texture, as at the table top. The *corner* of a surface in the room, the angle of two planes, is specified by another kind of discontinuity in the flow.... As I will phrase it, texture can undergo "wiping" or "shearing" at a margin. That is, one texture can be 'wiped out' by another or 'cut across' by another. This kind of optical discontinuity corresponds to a separation of surfaces in the world.... The motion perspective for an environment is theoretically loaded with information about its layout, and the experimental tests that have been made so far agree in showing that this information is effective for human perception.

One last series of quotations from Gibson's *The Senses Considered as Perceptual Systems* describes the extension of what we learn from the kinesthetic experience of space:

> ...When the individual goes from one place to another,...he has a different *vista*. What is the connection between one vista and another? The answer is interesting; the transition is another edge phenomenon, an "emergence-from-behind."

When the man in the room walks up to and through the door, the edge of the doorframe expands to uncover the new array of the next room. The same unwiping of the new array (or wiping out of the old one) occurs in reaching the corner of a street or the brow of a hill. If the man had panoramic vision, he could see the old array gradually being wiped out behind his back. The specification for a hole in the world, an aperture, window, or space between obstacles, is that it "opens up" on an optically denser array....

> ...One vista leads to another in a set of continuous connected sequences. Over time, as the individual moves about the house, the street, the town, and the country, the sequences come to be perceived as a scene, and the fact that the transformations all make a group becomes evident to him. The individual is then able to find his way from place to place, but more than that, he is able to *see one place behind another* on a larger and larger scale. He is then geographically oriented. Even when he is shut into the room he is able to apprehend the house, the street, the town, and the countryside in relation to the room....

The information provided by kinetic occlusion and its variants is extremely rich. It specifies the existence of an edge in the world, and the depth at the edge, but it does even more. *It also specifies the existence of one surface behind another, that is, the continued existence of a hidden surface....*

PERSPECTIVE

For too long philosophers and psychologists thought that the perception of space or depth was entirely the result of binocular vision. There are at least twelve other visual clues by which we perceive space. The list which follows, of which binocular vision is only one, was abstracted from James J. Gibson's *The Perception of the Visual World* by Edward T. Hall in the appendix to his book *The Hidden Dimension* (1969):

A. *Perspectives of Position*

1. TEXTURE PERSPECTIVE. This is the gradual increase in the density of the texture of a surface as it recedes in the distance.

2. SIZE PERSPECTIVE. As the objects get farther away they decrease in size. (Apparently not fully recognized by the Italian painters in the twelfth century as applying to humans.)

3. LINEAR PERSPECTIVE. Possibly the most commonly known form of perspective in the Western world. Renaissance art is the best known for its incorporation of the so-called laws of perspective. Parallel lines like railroad tracks or highways that join at a single vanishing point at the horizon illustrate this form of perspective.

B. *Perspectives of Parallax*

4. BINOCULAR PERSPECTIVE. Binocular perspective operates very much out of awareness. It is sensed because, owing to the separation of the eyes, each projects a different image. The difference is much more apparent at close distances than at great distances. Closing and opening one eye and then the other makes the differences in the images apparent.

5. MOTION PERSPECTIVE. As one moves forward in space, the closer one approaches a stationary object, the faster it appears to move. Likewise, objects moving at uniform speeds appear to be moving more slowly as distance increases.

C. *Perspectives Independent of the Position or Motion of the Observer*

6. AERIAL PERSPECTIVE. Western ranchers used to have fun at the expense of dudes unfamiliar with regional differences in "aerial perspective." Untold numbers of these innocents would awaken refreshed and stimulated, look out the window and, seeing what looked like a nearby hill, announce that it was such a nice, clear morning they were going to walk to the hill and back before breakfast. Some were dissuaded. Others took off only to discover that the hill was little closer at the end of half an hour's walk than when they started. The "hill" proved to be a mountain anywhere from three to seven miles away and was seen in reduced scale because of an unfamiliar form of aerial perspective. The extreme clarity of the dry, high-altitude air altered the aerial perspective, giving the impression that everything was miles closer than it really was. From this we gather that aerial perspective is derived from the increased haziness and *changes in color* due to the intervening atmosphere. It is an indicator of distance but not as stable and reliable as some of the other forms of perspective.

7. THE PERSPECTIVE OF BLUR. Photographers and painters are more likely than laymen to be aware of perspective of blur. This form of visual space perception is evident when focusing on an object held out in front of the face, so that the background is blurred. Objects in a visual plane other than the one on which the eyes are focused will be seen less distinctly.

8. RELATIVE UPWARD LOCATION IN THE VISUAL FIELD. On the deck of a ship or on the plains of Kansas and eastern Colorado, the horizon is seen as a line at about eye level. The surface of the globe climbs, as it were, from one's feet to eye level. The further from the ground one is, the more pronounced this effect. In the context of everyday experience, one looks *down* at objects that are close and *up* to objects that are far away.

9. SHIFT OF TEXTURE OR LINEAR SPACING. A valley seen over the edge of a cliff is perceived as more distant because of the break or rapid increase in texture density. Although several years have passed since I first saw a certain Swiss valley, I can recall clearly the bizarre sensations it produced. Standing on a grassy ledge, I looked down 1500 feet at the streets and houses of a village. Blades of grass were sharply etched in the visual field, while each blade was the width of one of the small houses.

10. SHIFT IN THE AMOUNT OF DOUBLE IMAGERY. If one looks at a distant point, everything between the viewer and the point will be seen as double. The closer to the viewer, the greater the doubling; the more distant the point, the less doubling. The gradient in the shift is a cue to distance; a steep gradient is read as close, a gradual gradient as far.

11. SHIFT IN THE RATE OF MOTION. One of the most dependable and consistent ways of sensing depth is the differential movement of objects in the visual field. Those objects which are close move much more than distant objects. They also move more quickly, as noted in Point 5. If two objects are seen as overlapping and they do not shift positions relative to each other when the viewer changes positions, they are either on the same plane or so far away that the shift is not perceived. Television audiences have become accustomed to perspective of this type because it is so pronounced whenever the camera moves through space in a manner similar to the moving viewer.

12. COMPLETENESS OR CONTINUITY OF OUTLINE. One feature of depth perception that has been exploited during wartime is *continuity of outline*. Camouflage is deceptive because it breaks the continuity. Even if there is no texture difference, no shift in double imagery, and no shift in the rate of motion, the manner in which one object obscures (eclipses) another determines whether the one is seen as behind the other or not. If, for example, the *outline* of the nearest object is unbroken and that of the obscured objects is broken in the process of being eclipsed, this fact will cause one object to appear behind the other.

13. TRANSITIONS BETWEEN LIGHT AND SHADE. Just as an abrupt shift or change in the texture of an object in the visual field will signal a cliff or an edge, so will an abrupt shift in *brightness* be interpreted as an edge. Gradual transitions in brightness are the principal means of perceiving molding or roundness.

Since surfaces, edges and perspective form the basis of our perception of space, they are especially important for the design drawings which represent kinesthetic space, but this will be discussed later in the chapter on REPRESENTATION.

PERCEPTION AS TRANSACTION

The scientific study of perception is the province of psychology, and while I believe that designers should never uncritically accept what others, even scientists, tell them about human behavior when it conflicts with the designer's own experience, psychologists have established a body of theory and research that has direct implications for anyone who would design or draw the environment.

I have mentioned Gibson's work on the perception of space and I will return to it again under REPRESENTATION, and I will talk about the application of Gestalt psychology to the drawings we show ourselves during the design process; but the psychologists whose work has the most direct bearing on environmental design are the *transactional* psychologists (not to be confused with *transactional analysis* which has recently become popular as a psychiatric therapy technique). Transactional psychologists trace their name to John Dewey and A. F. Bentley's 1949 book *Knowing and the Known* from which William H. Ittelson has abstracted the following collection of quotations in his 1973 book *Environment and Cognition.*

"Observation of this general [transactional] type sees man-in-action, not as something radically set over against an environing world nor yet as something merely acting 'in' a world, but as action *of* and *in* the world in which man belongs as an integral constituent [p. 52]." Under this procedure we treat "all of [man's] behavings, including his most advanced knowings, as activities not of himself alone, nor

even as primarily his, but as processes of the full situation of organism-environment [p. 104]." "From birth to death every human being is a *Party*, so that neither he nor anything done or suffered can possibly be understood when it is separated from the fact of participation in an extensive body of transactions—to which a given human being may contribute and which he modifies, but only in virtue of being a partaker in them [p. 271]."

The transactional psychologists have led the development of the emerging field of environmental psychology and their thought is indispensable for architects, landscape architects and interior designers. The transactionalists have made us aware that what appears to our prejudiced perception as a simplistic world of separate pieces is actually something much more complex. I will refer to the distinctions they make between object perception and environment perception in the chapter on REPRESENTATION because they are so critical to drawn representations of environments, but here, to introduce the range of richness and complexity they have identified in our perception of the environment, the best I can do is quote directly from *Environment and Cognition,* by one of the originators of the ideas, William H. Ittelson, with whom I teach at the University of Arizona:

The distinction between object and environment is crucial....

Environments surround....

The quality of surrounding—the first, most obvious, and defining property—forces the observer to become a participant. One does not, indeed cannot, observe the environment: one explores it. If the observation is the object then the exploration is the environment. The problem of exploratory behavior, its nature, function, and its relation to the individual's larger purposes, becomes central to the study of environment perception. The limits of the exploration, moreover, are not determined; the environment has no fixed boundaries in space

or time, and one must study how the explorer himself goes about setting boundaries to the various environments he encounters. The exploratory aspects of environment perception can thus extend over large spaces and long time spans, and require some process of spatial and temporal summation; both long- and short-term memory are essential.

Environments, in addition, are always multimodal. It may be possible to conceive of an environment which offers information through only one sense modality, but it probably would be impossible to build. In any event, it would be a curiosity. Perceptual experiments have been notably deficient in their study of multimodal processes, and yet these are essential for understanding environment perception. We need to know the relative importance of the various modalities, the kinds of environmental concepts, and sets of environmental predictabilities associated with each modality. But more important, we need to know how they function in concert: what processes are involved when supplementing, conflicting, and distracting information is presented through several modalities at once.

A third necessary characteristic of environments is that peripheral, as well as central, information is always present, peripheral in the mechanical sense—the area behind one is no less a part of the environment than that in front—and peripheral in the sense of being outside the focus of attention. Both meanings are important and raise questions concerning the process underlying the direction of attention.

Fourth, environments always provide more information than can possibly be processed. Questions of channel capacity and overload are inherent in environmental studies. However, the mere quantity of information does not tell the whole story. Environments always represent simultaneously, instances of redundant information, of inadequate and ambiguous information, and of conflicting and contradictory information. The entire mechanism of information processing in the nervous system, about which psychologists are only beginning to learn, is brought into play.

The four characteristics of environments which objects either cannot or usually do not possess (their surrounding quality; their multimodal property; the presence of peripheral stimulation; and the presence of too much information which is simultaneously redundant, inadequate, and contradictory) already suggests that findings in object perception can be applied only with great caution to environment perception. But these characteristics are nevertheless rather traditional in perceptual studies in that they refer to what can very broadly be called stimulus properties. Beyond these properties, however, there is another group of properties of the environment which must be taken into account in any study of environmental perception, and which are almost completely foreign to the field of object perception.

The first of these, or a fifth characteristic of the environment, is that environment perception always involves action. Environments, as we have seen, are not and cannot be passively observed; they provide the arena for action. They define the probabilities of occurrence of potential actions, they demand qualities which call forth certain kinds of actions, and they offer differing opportunities for the control and manipulation of the environment itself.

Environments call forth actions, but not blind, purposeless actions. Of course, what an individual does can be expected to be largely influenced by the particular purposes which he brings to the situation; at the same time, however, the environment possesses the property, a sixth characteristic, of providing symbolic meanings and motivational messages which themselves may effect the directions which action takes. Meanings and motivational messages are a necessary part of the content of environment perception.

Finally, and perhaps most important of all, environments always have an ambiance, an atmosphere, difficult to define, but overriding in importance. One can at this point only speculate on some of the features of the environment which contribute to this ambiance and which, thereby become of central significance for the study of environment perception. First of all, environments are almost without exception encountered as part of a social activity; other people are always a part of the situation and environment perception is largely a social phenomenon. Second, environments always have

a definite esthetic quality. Esthetically neutral objects can be designed; esthetically neutral environments are unthinkable. Last, environments always have a systemic quality. The various components and events relate to each other in particular ways which, perhaps more than anything else, serve to characterize and define the particular environment. The identification of these systemic relationships is one of the major features of the process of environment perception.

Thus, to the first four characteristics dealing roughly with stimulus properties, three others must be added: the role of action and purpose as defined, delimited, and called forth by the environment; the presence of meanings and motivational messages carried by the environment; and the concept of ambiance, related to the esthetic, social, and systemic qualities of the environment....

ENVIRONMENTAL INTEREST

The brains of human babies require a certain amount of visual stimulation from the environment for adequate development and, deprived of any sensory stimulation, the brain will actually manufacture visual patterns. There is a threshold to visual environmental interest below which we will judge the content as not being worthy of our attention. There is also an upper limit to visual environmental interest above which we will, after some effort, again judge it unworthy of our attention, but for the different reason that it is impossible or unrewarding to understand.

Between this minimum and maximum there is a wide variation in complexity of visual environmental interest which will hold a perceiver's attention, depending on the skill of the environmental designer and the sophistication and sensitivity of the viewer. The clue to holding and rewarding any perceiver's attention is to promise and deliver successive levels of visual interest or information which are discoverable.

I will try to categorize the information which

is available in the visual environment and arrange it in a hierarchy of such discoverable levels, beginning with basic sense data which any environment communicates to any perceiver and progressing through innocent and informed perception of natural and built environments, from the uninhibited interaction of a child with the environment to the perception by one human mind of the intentions of another human mind expressed in the built environment.

VISUAL INTEREST categories are covered in the chapter on REPRESENTATION and need only be mentioned here. These interest categories are the most basic level of visual information, if indeed they can be said to inform at all, and are really only different kinds of sense data, stopping well short of meaning. There seem to be three such visual interest categories which are integral to any environment:

SPATIAL, TONAL (light) and TEXTURAL and one category which people or nature add to any built environment. This ADDITIONAL category consists of furniture, plants and all those figural decorations which we add to our environments.

INNOCENT INTERACTION with the environment depends on another quality of the environment which demonstrates Ittelson's statement that one does not, indeed cannot, observe the environment: one explores it. Children at play are perhaps the best example of this uninhibited interaction with the environment.

I had the good fortune of growing up in a very small mid-western town and our house was perhaps half a mile from the grade school. Over the years of coming and going, the boys from my side of town made the most interesting route to and from school. This route

changed as our bodies and our sense of adventure strengthened and it had various options, depending on the time available, the time of year, and the mood and make-up of the group. But it was a deliberate synthetic making, not just a passive finding, putting the experience together from what was available each day and actually moving or relocating such things as we could.

The environmental values from which we made our route were almost entirely participatory interactions with our environment and had nothing to do with cleanliness, efficiency or safety, which society lays on us as we grow up. Rather, we valued getting dirty, spending great amounts of time, and taking physical risks as being valid ways of interacting with the environment.

If I went home with a playmate on the other side of town, we took his way home, which he was very proud to show me. His route was a different sequence of experiences that he and his friends had put together. The routes children choose to take are chosen on the basis of participatory environmental interest. Turn an active, uninhibited group of children loose in any environment and they will find the special interactive opportunities it offers in an instant.

22

Photograph by Peggy Lockard

SPATIAL INTEREST is the most dynamic interest category and the richest source of interest for most environmental designers. The spatial interest of any environment is potential kinesthetic interest and is simply the variety of exploratory experiences which can be anticipated in any environment.

Specifically, the sources of spatial interest in any environment are those edges, mentioned earlier, which hide various volumes of space. Interesting spatial environments exténd space ahead, to the sides, and up and down, and abound in partially hidden spatial volumes. The simplest measure of an environment's spatial interest would be its choice by a group of children as a place to play hide and seek.

Photograph by Peggy Lockard

TEXTURAL INTEREST is primarily tactile, a matter of touch or potential touching. Evolution has left us with a particularly close coupling of our eye and hand. In his book, *Man's Emerging Mind* (1965), N.J. Berrill explains:

Sight for us is vision in action, and memory of things seen is memory of visual images and of our own optic muscle movements. Close your eyes for a moment and picture a triangle: you can sense your eyes moving from point to point. And to all of this we add all the sensory impressions gathered from the skin and muscles of fingers and palms. The brain is enlarged between the regions set apart for vision and touch so that records of their past associations can be neatly stored. We have in fact a type of brain as highly distinctive as it can be, in which seeing and doing are in some ways indissoluble,...

We can sense how things will feel by looking at them and recalling what similar textures felt like. We can almost "touch" or "feel" a surface with our eyes because of the close link between hand and eye that evolution has given us. By looking at an environment and the textures of its surfaces, we can sense what it will feel like to stand barefoot on a sheepskin rug, lean against a stone wall or grasp an oak handrail. The experience of textures and the anticipation of their experience by our vision promises perhaps the most intimate potential for experiencing any environment.

Photograph by Peggy Lockard

TONAL INTEREST derives from the relative darkness or lightness of the various surfaces of a space or object. This variety may be the play of sunlight, shade and shadow, or the result of color or material selections. Tonal interest may be judged simply by squinting your eyes when viewing a space or object. If, when you squint, all the interest or definition is squinted out, you are probably looking at a space or object which has little or no tonal interest.

The tonal interest which comes from sunlight is the most dynamic because it changes as the sun moves, making the morning experience of a space much different than the late afternoon experience. A strong example of this is the casting of shadows by the grandstands on a baseball diamond as the afternoon lengthens. Another source of tonal interest caused by the sun is the difference in tone between a brightly lit exterior space and the relative dimness of an interior space which looks out on it. The tonal interest which comes from sunlight also contributes potential kinesthetic interest because the viewer can anticipate the sensual experience of moving out of shade into sunlight or from sunlight into the coolness of shade.

Material and color selections afford a static but worthwhile opportunity for tonal interest. This tonal opportunity is often used to exaggerate or correct the proportions of spaces on the assumption that light surfaces tend to recede and dark surfaces tend to advance. Another approach is to tone-code the space or object in such a way that all surfaces oriented similarly have the same relative tone—all ceilings light, all floors dark and all walls somewhere in between.

TONAL INTEREST is the category which is perceived at the greatest distance and under the poorest illumination, the last one squinted out and the last information we surrender as we lose our sight. While it is thus the grossest or coarsest category of environmental/visual interest, it is also perhaps the most basic.

Photograph by Peggy Lockard

ADDITIONAL INTEREST is perhaps a uniquely contemporary interest category. In past times, I doubt that it would have been thought of separately, but today's esthetic in many design disciplines has stripped this category of interest from the spaces and objects we design under the indictment of being cosmetic ornament. That it is still a valid category of environmental interest is suggested by the plants, sculptures and sculptural furnishings with which we decorate our stripped, sterile spaces; the latest of these being supergraphics. I suppose this category of environmental and drawing interest comes from the delight our eyes have always found in following a sinuous line in space or in comprehending a complex geometric pattern. Almost all natural forms have this category of interest in abundance. Perhaps there is a valid argument for leaving this category to nature; that for man or machine to make such forms is futile competition.

INFORMED PERCEPTION would seem to be the next level of perceived environmental interest until a moment's thought reveals that *all* perception after the first opening of our eyes is informed—informed by past perceptions, informed by purposes—even the purposes of innocent interaction from the previous category—and informed from our earliest moments by the indoctrination of our culture. So this begins an immediate retreat into all the personal and specialized adult ways of looking at the world, which will be discussed later under PERCEPTUAL EXPERIENCE.

NATURE. When we perceive nature we find it interesting or dull, beautiful or ugly, but whether we believe in a Creator God, or the natural selection of evolution, we accept what we see as necessary, beyond or above the assignment of design responsibility. We may perceive a tree of a certain species as being a mishapen specimen, but it would seldom occur to us to seriously criticize the entire species as being a bad design. And even if we did decide that hyenas or camels are unfortunate evolutionary results, it would remain a passive perception; we would hardly recommend their extinction based on that perception.

THE BUILT ENVIRONMENT. When we perceive the built environment, we must learn to assign design responsibility. One of the main reasons our cities are so ugly and unworkable is that the design responsibility is fragmented—traceable only to unquestioned and inflexible regulations. Because the design responsibility is thus obscured, we tend to accept the entire built environment as "natural" and inevitable—just as we accept the nature world. We forget that people deliberately wrote the regulations, set the utility poles, and erected the billboards.

We should be very careful what we call natural, for we allow that word to pull a protective mantle with it which allows no criticism or assignment of design responsibility. If we view either the natural or the built environment as irrevocable and inevitable, we will never perceive it critically or consider the possibility of acting to correct it.

INTENTION AND MEANING
Another side of our humanness, we are told, is our compulsive search for intention and meaning in the world. This is true on several levels when we perceive the built environment, and on the deepest level is probably why we are designers. We believe that the qualities of the environments we design will be perceived by those who inhabit them—that our intentions will be perceived in the environments we design.

Although certain environmental qualities are rather obvious and will be open to any observer, the deeper levels of meaning and intention in the built environment, as in the natural world are only available to those who have learned to see them.

THE FIRST IMPRESSION. The first level and perhaps the most important level on which the manmade environment communicates, is the level of the instantly pervasive first impression. This immediate reflex may be a visual habit once necessary in our evolutionary history to judge instantly the danger or safety of a situation. I'm not sure it serves us well in those situations which require in-depth study and evaluation, for the first impression prejudice dies hard. But the almost instant formation of an evaluative perception is a part of our perceptual legacy.

Exactly what is perceived in that first impression is difficult to define, but perhaps the immediate and dominant impression of

any built environment is one of human skill—not just brute effort, but the record of the ability, care and intelligent intention of the maker or designer.

The reason this first impression of human skill or intelligence is so important is that it determines, more than anything else, our willingness or interest in spending more time in the perception of any particular human product and the discovery of succeeding levels of communication.

DESIGN INTENTION. If, in the first impression of any visual perception, we perceive an intelligent intention on the part of the designer or maker, a gate is opened through which we will go in search on several levels. The perception of design intention is the key to all further perception and is one of the most exciting discoveries a human can make in perceiving any human product. This communication can occur across thousands of years. An archeologist can read the design intention of people long dead in what remains of their cities or artifacts. Musicians can appreciate Bach or Beethoven by playing their music and understanding their intentions as they composed it. Human products have the possibility of communicationg their maker's intentions long after they are gone. What follows is not so much intended as a complete list, as a demonstration of what can be read as design intention.

CRAFTSMANSHIP communicates the skill of the maker, and in that way differs from design intention if the designer and maker were different people. The appreciation of craftsmanship demands that you be familiar with the particular skill involved, either by having done it yourself or having watched it being done, or having seen other examples of similar work. The appreciation of design intention in craftsmanship depends on how well the design extends or demonstrates the craft. Does the aria extend and demonstrate a coloratura soprana voice? Does the brick wall extend and demonstrate a mason's skill? Does the design of the wall recognize what can be done with brick at openings, corners and cap, or does it simply use masonry as so much wallpaper?

CONSTRUCTION PROCESS can also be communicated in any design by leaving a record of the process in the finished work. An exception to this, such as the pyramids, may also be interesting and lead to endless speculation as to how they were made. The deliberate design of curiosities must be considered a luxury, however, and frustrating to the viewer or user in most cases. The motion of the potter's wheel, the formwork or tie holes for concrete, or the exposed trusses of a roof all add to the understanding of a construction process and tell us more about the intention and skill of the designers and builders.

FUNCTION can also be read in a well-designed place or object. The sense of how something is to be held, or opened, or moved through can be communicated by its form and material, and particularly by the designed articulation of its parts. A simple example is that most objects which are intended to set or stand are often impossible to place upside down or on their sides. In equipment which is to be held, a good design will articulate the handle. One test of anything designed for human use is that its use is visually predictable.

BUDGET is perhaps the best contemporary word I can find to name the information communicated regarding the economy or richness of the design of any human product. A definite sense of this quality is communicated, not only in the richness of the materials and ornamentation, but in the care and permanence or lasting quality of the design. Remembering that the budget is normally beyond the control of the designer, however, the sophisticated perceiver will never equate a fat budget with good design. Shaker furniture and farm implements are examples of excellent design, perhaps *because* of a severe budget limitation.

STRUCTURAL ORDER (INTERIOR RELATIONSHIPS) is communicated by the relationship or lack of relationship of a design's constituent parts. The relationships may be made by geometry, proportion, material similarity or contrast, joint articulation and arrangement, and many other ways. Other analogies for structural order might be the relationship of the skeleton and circulatory system to the human body, or the table of contents to a book. This internal ordering also always occurs in relationship to the entire design—the relationship of the parts to one another and to the whole.

CONTEXTUAL ORDER (EXTERIOR RELATIONSHIPS). Designs will also have a relationship to their context. The context into which anything is designed includes the immediate physical surroundings and climate, the cultural or regional tradition, the prevailing technology and the contemporary esthetic. Designers may choose to relate closely to some of these and contrast to others but an important part of what their designs communicate will be the combination of relationships they choose to make to the design's context.

UNITY is another way of thinking about structural and contextual order and can be achieved in at least two ways. The traditional concept of unity is closed or exclusive. The internal parts of a composition are designed to relate so strongly that they form a closure which excludes any contextual relationships and especially any additions or mutations. The form of a symphony, a Greek temple, or a limerick defy addition. The other form of unity is open or inclusive. It relies on an internal structure that has little to do with spatial or temporal boundaries and can easily be extended and added to. Either of these ways of obtaining unity may be valid for a particular design and the designer's choice will be communicated in the design.

REACTION may be thought of as a level of communication and is closely related to contextual order. By reaction, I mean the appeal of novelty for novelty's sake, or similarly the identification with a historic style for whatever that identification may add to the design. The perception of this communicative quality depends completely on the perceiver's prejudices and its inclusion in any design depends on the designer's prejudices.

CLASSIC PATINA is a final quality which most designers strive for, but is actually added to good designs by years of valued human use. It is the quality that some designers try to get cheaply at the reactionary level by recalling historic design styles, but can only come from designs which function for a long time as they were intended and which are found worth keeping.

If we will learn to look for them, there are probably many other levels of communication that could be added to this list which can be seen as a part of the information-richness of anything made by human beings.

CULTURE'S CATEGORIES.

Cultural indoctrination gives its members a set of operating instructions for the eyemindhand *system inherited from evolution. The instructions include an interpretation and categorical naming of the environment and experience, and a set of inhibitions and guilt structures designed to enforce a culturally correct way of using the* eyemindhand *system.*

PERCEPTUAL EXPERIENCE

In addition to the perceptual prejudices which we inherit from evolution, whatever culture we are born into and our individual experience quickly add to the selectivity of the experience network through which we perceive the world. These developing perceptual attitudes influence all our perceptions and are a compilation of cultural indoctrination, past perceptual experience and our individual personalities and self-consciousness. It is here, in what we expect to perceive, that perception and conception become indistinguishable. This correspondence of perception and conception will be discussed in the next chapter but, for perception, can be demonstrated in our referring to any conceptual framework in which we think or act as our *world view.*

Anthropologists have clearly established that different cultures inhabit different perceptual worlds. Edward T. Hall, in his book, *The Hidden Dimension* (1969), says:

> ...Space itself is perceived entirely differently. In the West, man perceives the objects but not the spaces between. In Japan, the spaces are perceived, named, and revered as the *ma,* or intervening interval.

Cultures with different world views explain the visual world differently and in languages which further reinforce their cultural differences. Bruner, Goodnow and Austin, in *A Study of Thinking* (1956), write:

> The categories in terms of which man sorts out and responds to the world around him reflect deeply the culture into which he is born. The language, the way of life, the religion and science of a people: all of these mold the way in which a man experiences the events out of which his own history is fashioned....

Because of the preceding arguments for the dominance and accuracy of vision, visual perception might seem to be beyond any kind of cultural censorship. Precisely because of its dominance, however, vision is our most carefully censored sense and carries most of our cultural prejudices.

Our visual indoctrination is doubled in that we are not only taught how to see the world but also what to show the world. Our manners are very much matters of appearance. We are taught to respond to certain visual cues and ignore others. Fortunately by adolescence there is a strong counter-cultural rebellion in matters of personal appearance; and the dominance of vision as a tool of cultural indoctrination is nowhere more clear than in the threat this adolescent personal appearance rebellion always seems to pose to the older generation.

PLURAL PREJUDICES

Cultures pluralize the prejudices which are built into the visual perceptual system we inherit from evolution.

- Perception's selfish tendency is extended into a group selfishness that serves the culture's longterm survival.
- Perception's focusing tendency is extended into a preference for simplistic causes and effects and a compulsive search for scapegoats and enemies.

- Perception's separating tendency helps us accept the endless inclusive/exclusive boundaries of the categories and hierarchies in which cultures would have us see the world.
- Perception's tendency to form wholes or gestalts gives us perhaps our most powerful cultural esthetic and ethic—UNITY—beginning with the family and ending with the nationalism of "United we stand, divided we fall."
- Perception's tendency to discriminate is extended into all the abuses of discrimination and privilege within a culture.
- Perception's instant judgment is extended into the demand for partisan loyalty on which cultures have thrived. "You are either with us or against us."
- Perception's choice of dominance is extended into all the forms of competition within and between cultures.
- Perception's need for new input becomes a culture's need for change, expressed superficially in fashion or entertainment and most deeply in conversion or revolution.

Perception reinforces, or perhaps is the source of, all these mechanisms of cultural indoctrination. We SEE a world which is differentiated, but culture's indoctrination assures that we PERCEIVE a world of categories structured in the hierarchies and polarized in the dualities that the culture has found useful.

Joseph Chilton Pearce, in *The Crack in the Cosmic Egg* (1971), sums up our cultural indoctrination:

> Our world view is a cultural pattern that shapes our mind from birth. It happens to us as fate. We speak of a child becoming "reality-adjusted" as he responds and becomes a cooperating strand in the social web. We are shaped by this web; it determines the way we think, the way we see what we see....

EXPERIENCE'S OPPORTUNITIES.

The variables that affect perception assure that unless the perceiver's cultural indoctrination, past experience, and the context in which the perception takes place are all identical, the perception will be different. A moment's thought discloses that identical perceptions are, therefore, impossible—since in any attempt at duplicate perception, even a single perceiver will have been changed by the first perception. This explains why valued experiences are never quite the same in attempted repetitions and why eye-witness accounts inevitably vary. Perception, knowledge and truth are transitory and different for each of us.

OPPORTUNITY SEEKING

Perhaps the most basic distinction in perceptual attitude is whether our experience leads us to anticipate success or failure in our interactions with the environment. A history of success will lead perceivers to see the world as a field of opportunities for further success, while a history of failures can cause perceivers to spend most of their perceptual energy in avoiding responsibility or perceiving potential excuses for their anticipated failures.

Anticipated success and opportunity-seeking are the keys to education. When either education or society fails to offer perceived opportunities, education and society fail together. The heightening of perception based on perceived opportunity accelerates learning. If an opportunity is perceived, it sharpens perception, and the sharpened perception itself promotes further opportunities and their perception.

On the other hand, children who fail to perceive any opportunity for gratifying their self-interests, in school or in society, will have their perception dulled, and this will foreclose other opportunities and their perception of them. The presence of perceived opportunity is exhilarating and the absence of perceived opportunity is debilitating, in education and in life. The basic goal of education and of society should be to make perceived opportunity abundant and equal for everyone.

Most designers are optimists and their optimism is usually sufficient to withstand several years of intensely critical design education. The traditional optimism in the design professions makes me wonder at the increasing use of the phrase "problem-solving" to describe what a designer does. Problem-solving sounds more like a motto for an exterminating company than for any creative activity.

Unlike mathematical problems, so-called design "problems" are never fixed or absolute. Experienced designers perceive design opportunities more comprehensively and more flexibly than designers with little experience. Experienced designer's solutions to design opportunities will be more sophisticated and creative because their experience has given them the ability to perceive both their responsibilities and their freedom more comprehensively and flexibly. They simultaneously see a much more complex "problem" and much greater flexibility in restating that "problem" to match a broader range of "solutions."

The self-education of experienced perception is important for designers. In designing for others designers must learn as much as possible about how perception works and develop a sensitivity for the perceptions of others. The main thing to remember about other perceivers is that while they share a similar evolutionary heritage and may share a similar cultural indoctrination, they come to perception selfishly prejudiced by their experiences and self-interests and their prejudices will never be the same as yours.

Our experience as free individuals is the last, but not necessarily the least of what we are as perceivers. From evolution, we inherit a common *eyemindhand* system, some relatively minor strengths and weaknesses from our immediate ancestors, and an indoctrination into a particular cultural view of the world. This legacy is not ours to choose, but, subsequently, we are free to choose much of our perceptual experience. If there is one thing I have learned as a teacher in trying to hold the attention of a group of students, it is that human beings exercise perceptual freedom. Our responsible use of this freedom to choose perceptual experiences, however, is not as apparent to me.

John Locke proposed that the mind is a blank slate, a *tabula rasa,* on which our senses write the experiences of our lifetime. It seems clear now that the slate can only accept certain messages because of the evolutionary *eyemindhand* system and the cultural world view we inherit; and it is equally clear that we actively hold the chalk as it writes, by choosing our perceptual experiences. Our grip on the chalk can be much stronger today than in the past when perceptions were forced on us by the responses necessary for survival; but our grip on the chalk is also uncomfortable because we are responsible for the perceptions we choose, and through them, all we learn in our lifetime.

The effect of the positive perceptual attitude involved in opportunity-seeking is clearly demonstrated in most designers. They eagerly seek perceptions in the confidence that they will have the opportunity to use them. Instead of the "problems" collected by negative perceivers, positive perceivers compulsively collect "solutions." Successful designers and creative people in any field tend to choose their perceptions carefully. They are perhaps more selective in what they show themselves, in where they travel, in what they read, in whom they listen to; and they find ways to relate more of what they perceive to their work.

A lifetime may be thought of as the sum of a person's consciousness, and today we are remarkably free in what we may choose to fill our consciousness. Just as dieticians or nutritionists claim, "You are what you eat," most designers know that as perceivers, "You are what you have seen."

RELATIVITY OF
PERCEPTUAL EXPERIENCE
All perception is relative, and there is perhaps an infinite range of variables which affect its relativity. Only three of the more obvious variables will be considered here, as demonstrations of how relative perceptions can be: past experience, role of the perceiver and context.

PAST EXPERIENCE establishes the relativity of subsequent perceptions. What is presented for perception would seem to be entirely objective, and in any specific case, is certainly invariable, but because of our past visual experience, and its cultural indoctrination, we see things as seeming to have inherent qualities. However, our perception of both quality and quantity are entirely relative to our past experience; like the question, "How's your wife?" and the answering question, "Compared to what?"

It is pointless then to consider either quality or quantity as inherent characteristics of whatever is presented to our perception. We can, however, examine some of the interest and information categories within which we perceive the relative characteristics of whatever is presented.

The perception of environmental quality is entirely dependent on the range of quality of the environments you have experienced, and perhaps your sophistication at the time. Thanks to color photography and the efforts of the publishers serving the environmental design professions we can know many environments, at least superficially, without actually experiencing them directly. The effort made by most great designers, however, to actually experience historic and contemporary buildings, and cities or gardens whose designers they admired, is well documented. There are few cases of creativity in a field without intense and prolonged perception of the existing accomplishments in that field.

The role in which perceivers find themselves is another potent variable in the relativity of perception. The perception of a bull is quite different for a bullfighter, a butcher and a tanner. The perception of a building is quite different for a contractor, a realtor, an owner or an architect. Our attitude in perception will also change in response to whether we are actively associated with the perception or just a passive observer. If we are the contractor for the building, then our perception of it is certainly heightened by that direct association and the fact that we expect to act on what we perceive, not just ponder it at our leisure. A baseball pitcher's high, fast one is something quite different to the batter, the catcher and the umpire, than to the Sunday afternoon bleacher fan.

Our attitude toward perception may also be affected by our confidence in our own perception. This is one reason many people commission designers—lacking a confidence in their own evaluative visual perception or "taste", they seek the comfort of a professional. Other people who are unsure of their own perception may need to rely on the opinions of friends and be very afraid of wearing, driving, or occupying anything which their friends might not approve. This can be seen in Design Education, when beginning students must ask frequently for their teacher's opinion or approval. Later, if they work at sophisticating their perception, they won't need to ask as often to assure approval, and much later, as they develop confidence in their own perception, they should not find the teacher's approval necessary.

CONTEXT. All perception occurs in a specific context and the context may strongly influence what is perceived. Because perceptual contexts vary widely, it seems worthwhile to consider and try to understand some of these variations.

PREPARATION for perception is one of the contextual variables. By contextual preparation, I mean the immediate circumstances that either may have prepared you or left you unprepared for a particular perception. Certain kinds of preparation can sharpen perception while others tend to dull it. Preparation depends primarily on how you come to a particular perception. Whether you come voluntarily or involuntarily can make quite a difference, while the only other possibility, chance perception, allows no preparation and so can carry no preparatory prejudice.

Voluntary perception, like the decision to see an exhibit of paintings, carries a certain preparation or expectation. The experience may have been recommended by a friend or by a favorable review, or you may have seen other paintings by the same artist. In most cases of voluntary perception, the decision to perceive carries with it a prejudice which

favors the perception.

On the other hand, involuntary perception in all its degrees is something to be endured and the perceiver is not likely to be sharpened by the same anticipation.

Preparation further prejudices perception by the anticipation of certain qualities to the exclusion of others. Reading a critical review before you see a movie may focus your perception on the movie's faults or strong points, and focused perception is always at the expense of other information which remains excluded by the focusing. Professional athletes and coaches well know that when they tell a football official to "Watch the tackle, he's using his hands on our end," he can hardly keep from it—to the exclusion of other infractions he might see.

At first, such prejudicing of perception may seem negative, but all knowledge is prejudicial and the very aim of education is to change your perception. There is no such thing as informed innocence. The important thing is to be careful of whom and what you allow to prejudice you and become as aware as you can of all your perceptual prejudices.

PRESSURES in any perceptual context vary dramatically and strongly influence perception. One kind of pressure is that which we feel when we are perceiving for others. This varies from the perception involved in selecting a gift for someone to the pressure a sentry might feel in wartime, when the security of an army might depend on his perception. In all cases, depending on the perceiver's relationship and sense of responsibility to those for whom he is perceiving, perception will be affected.

This second-hand perception wastes immense amounts of time in bureaucracies

and other management hierarchies where underlings are not acting on their own perception, but spend their entire perceptual effort in trying to second-guess what their superiors' perception will be. Perceiving for others also allows a kind of dishonest appraisal where the perceiver blames his rejection on his superior by saying, "Well, it looks good to me, but J.C. will never approve it because..." When a designer is kept from dealing directly with the user or decision-maker, this kind of second-hand perception is one of the most frustrating.

Another kind of pressure is that of convention or manners. This pressure doesn't influence perception so much as it inhibits what we say about our perception. The opinion of designers is often sought as expert in matters of visual "taste."

Persuasion is another pressure which may also influence perception. Saturated as we are today with advertising, persuasion may as easily turn our perception off as on. The quality of the persuasion—whether the "sell" is hard or soft—will also make a difference.

The author or presenter of anything we perceive will also influence our perception. "Look at the picture I drew Daddy," is a sure setup for favorable perception. The reputation or associations of the presenter may also heighten perception. Bosses, for instance, usually benefit from some perceptual pressure on their employees. Good teachers still enjoy a similarly heightened perception among their students.

Time and age also exert a pressure on perception. The leisurely, dawdling perception of childhood is too soon replaced with the hurried perceptions which must be made in order to cope with the adult world. Although we perceive visual information almost instantaneously, in-depth seeing requires time. One of the ways psychologists exaggerate optical illusions and perceptual errors is by cutting back on the illumination or the time allowed for visual perception.

What other people may think can also influence your perception. Strong, confident perceivers may be little influenced by other's opinions. Many people, however, are counterpunch perceivers; they need to know what someone else has perceived before they feel their perception is complete.

CONSEQUENCES which may follow from perception are perhaps the most important contextual influences on perception. The influence which consequences bring depends on the perceived self-interest which the context implies.

The consequences of perception may be extreme. The perception of tight-rope walkers, mountain climbers and gunfighters are of this variety. The testimony of burglars about the sharpening of their senses in a strange, darkened house with the owners asleep, is a witness to the effect of possible consequences on perception. Designers are introduced to this kind of heightened perception when they are commissioned to design a very prominent public environment.

The relativity of perceptual experience is what gives "experience" its meaning. Knowing that a brick wall is laid correctly depends on having seen or laid other brick walls. Knowing that a particular exterior space you are designing will have an intimate human scale depends on having "experienced" or designed similar spaces. Being confident that a drawing you are making will have an acceptable or exceptional professional quality depends on your having seen and made similar drawings.

PERCEPTION OF DESIGN DRAWINGS

BY THE DESIGNER

Perception, not hand skill, is the key to drawing ability, and designers' practiced perception of their own drawings is crucial in developing design ability.

Design students should learn to look at all design drawings critically—especially their own. You should respect a peer's or a teacher's opinion, and learn to perceive what they can perceive in a drawing, but you should never passively accept any evaluation of your design drawings except your own.

The development of this critical attitude toward your own work should be tempered with patience and understanding. Because your perceptual ability has been operating much longer than your drawing ability, you will always be able to perceive more flaws in your drawings than you can ever correct, but don't be too hard on yourself. Especially do not deprecate your drawing ability compared to a fellow student's drawing ability until you understand that student's drawing background. You will find that a fellow student who, with little apparent effort, draws much better than you, has been drawing a lot longer, or a lot more intelligently, or both. The differences in drawing ability can almost always be explained by variations in experience and motivation.

TRANSPARENCY. Design drawings represent successive attempts at drawing a congruence between the design problem and its solution. The drawings themselves are not the congruence, but are simply representative transparencies through which the real congruence can be judged. The importance of the transparency of design drawings cannot be overemphasized, and perhaps is best understood in comparison to a drawing intended as a work of art.

When we look at anything, the completion or meaning of the perception requires a synthesis in the perceiver's *eyemind*. When we view a painting, this perceptual synthesis is initiated at the plane of the canvas. There is nothing beyond the canvas.

In contrast, the design drawings designers make for themselves must be neutrally transparent representations of an attempted congruence between the problem and its solution. Unlike a painting, a design drawing forms a window through which the real environment it represents can be seen. Design drawings must be honest, direct and undistorted, and the perceptual synthesis must be consummated beyond the drawing— in the reality of the environment the drawing represents.

THE OPACITY OF DESIGN DRAWINGS is one of the major hangups in their use by designers. When a design drawing becomes opaque the designer is unable to see *through* the drawing to the reality of the environment being designed. The drawings a designer uses in the design process can become opaque in two quite different ways.

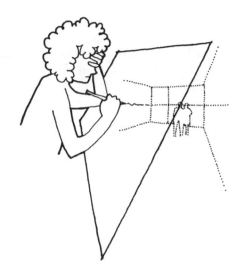

The first kind of opacity beginning designers usually encounter comes from a loathing of their own drawings. By the time most students enter professional design education, their past visual experience makes them rather sophisticated judges of "beauty" or "good drawing"; and their own first attempts at making design drawings are often so repulsive to them, or so poor in relation to some of their fellow students' drawings, that they are unable to look through them to the reality of what they are designing. You should be patient, though never satisfied, with your drawing ability. As your perception improves, so will your drawing, and you will be able to look through even the crudest sketches and see the design content they represent.

The opposite kind of opacity, while less painful, can be even more damaging to a designer. This kind of opacity comes not from a loathing, but from a love of the drawing *as a drawing*—at the level of drawing technique and cliche graphic cosmetics. Students who draw very well are most subject to this perceptual error. These students often become more interested in a virtuoso drawing technique and its superficialities then in communicating the real environment which the drawing represents and for which they are responsible.

Both kinds of opacity are often encouraged in drawing courses by assignments which have no design content, so that there really is nothing *beyond the drawing* for which the student is responsible. Both kinds of opacity stop designers' perceptions at the level of the drawing and keep them from perceiving the reality of what they are representing with the drawing. As long as designers see and think of their design drawings as only a relatively clumsy or elegant composition of lines on a piece of paper, and fail to look through them to the reality they represent, they will misunderstand and misuse drawing.

TWO-CIRCUIT CYBERNETICS. Another way of looking at the problem of getting hung up at the level of drawing is to remember that the *eyemindhand* system has two potential feedback loops. One feedback loop allows your *eyemind* to monitor and continually control your hand as you draw. This circuit helps us draw and could be called the drawing loop. The second loop allows your *eyemind* to monitor and continually evaluate the design as your hand draws it. This circuit may operate more slowly, but it is your main means of evaluating and potentially improving the design. Both circuits must be ON in making design drawings.

If designers can avoid either loathing or loving their own drawings and learn to look through them to their design content, they can learn to see design opportunities to be found nowhere else.

THE PERCEPTION OF DESIGN OPPORTUNITIES in design drawings is perhaps the central idea of this book. The perception of such opportunities depends on:

- the assumption of a participatory role for drawing in the design process;

- the anticipation of the appearance of design opportunities;

- the perceptual experience to recognize them when they appear;

- willingness and confidence to keep drawing until they appear.

If you believe that drawing is nothing more than the direct printout of full blown conception, you won't expect to gain much from the perception of your design drawings, except some sort of relative evaluation of them as products. If on the other hand, you have learned from experience that drawings are much more than just a conceptual print-out; that they are an integral part of conception, then you will perceive design opportunities as you draw. You will seldom finish a drawing without changing it or starting a new one based on opportunities you see in the drawing.

Design opportunities appear only to those who are prepared to recognize them. You must have saturated your perceptual experience with design solutions, with ways of making environments, however, if you hope to recognize similar potentials in your drawings. The opportunities aren't announced with fanfares and blinking neon signs. You must recognize them as potential patterns, and the recognition will only come from study and experience.

If design opportunities are to "appear" in your drawings you must also learn to enjoy drawing. This means that the activity of making the drawings and the drawings themselves must be a source of satisfaction. Designers who use drawing confidently in the design process surround themselves with their drawings and spend hours looking for opportunities in the drawings. The drawings themselves, although they may be rather mysterious multicolored patterns on buff tracing paper, inevitably develop a certain personal vitality and are also displayed with a certain pride *as drawings*. Although I have warned against overly self-conscious drawings because the superficial graphic cosmetics may obscure the design content, rough design study drawings are a different matter. The haste and intensity with which such design drawings are made will almost always make them immune to the evils of narcissism.

Design drawings are special examples of what Newell and Simon (*Human Problem Solving,* 1972) have called EMs (External Memories—as opposed to STM—Short Term Memory or LTM—Long Term Memory). And as external memories they deserve careful attention because they are drawn simultaneously in our consciousness and in the world. They are written on and written by our consciousness and once externalized they become part of what Karl Popper has called World 3—the product of minds (as distinguished from World 1—material things, and World 2—subjective minds). Design drawings have a life of their own and may contain more than we ever intended in making them. Brian Magee in his *Karl Popper* (1973) explains:

> ...In man, some of the biological characteristics which developed to cope with the environment changed that environment in the most spectacular ways: the human hand is only one example. And man's abstract structures have at all times equaled in scale and degree of elaboration his transformation of the physical environment: language, ethics, law, religion, philosophy, the sciences, the arts, institutions. Like those of animals, only more so, his creations acquired a central importance in the environment to which he had then to adapt himself, and which therefore shaped him. Their objective existence in relation to him meant that he could examine them, evaluate and criticize them, explore, extend, revise, or revolutionize them, and indeed make wholly unexpected discoveries within them....

Through our hand's drawing them, and our eye's seeing them, drawing also allows the participation of all the elements of human intelligence and includes through the eye and the hand the unconscious layers of our experience network. We may draw and recognize potentials in the drawing for patterns and relationships that we "know"—preverbally, intuitively, illogically.

Exploratory design drawings also legitimately offer the kind of random stimulation recommended for creativity by Edward de Bono (*Lateral Thinking,* 1970) and especially so because they are visual.

THE CHOICE OF DRAWINGS which designers make to represent their ideas to themselves should be made consciously and very carefully. Our perception can only work with what is presented to it and mindless habit or convention in the choice of drawings to show our *eyeminds* can critically inhibit the design process. The relationship of design drawings to *experience* and to the *design process* is discussed at length in the chapter on REPRESENTATION.

The order in which we perceive design drawings is critical because subsequent perceptions are limited by the information gained in initial perceptions. The habit of always beginning with a plan drawing should be questioned in relation to the particular design problem.

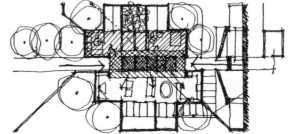

Another mistake is to underestimate the information processing potential of our *eyeminds*. Design drawings should be loaded with as much graphically encoded meaning as possible. The use of color, lineweight and texture to represent various functions or design qualities can all be perceived and interrelated. To draw and perceive less is to waste our potential.

OBJECT PERCEPTION vs. ENVIRONMENT PERCEPTION

OBJECT PERCEPTION is the traditional way of studying perception, and of making and perceiving design drawings. It is also the traditional way of evaluating the integrity and unity of a work of architecture, and perhaps to a lesser degree, of landscape architecture or interior design.

Environmental psychologists have pointed out that the more basic mode of perceptual experience is that of environmental perception, and if we are to understand what the experience of our designs will be like, and hope to improve that experience, we must perceive our design drawings as *environments*. Although, after years of experience, some sense of what an environment will be like can be perceived from the traditional plan, section and elevation drawings, the only way to directly represent and perceive environmental qualities is to draw and perceive eyelevel perspectives, especially interior perspectives.

DESIGN EDUCATION'S INDOCTRINATION

Design students can experience serious frustration in adapting to the indoctrination of the design discipline or particular school they have chosen. Most schools would deny as narrow an indoctrination as this might imply, but even the most liberal design or drawing education amounts to indoctrination. Students may discover that both the design discipline (architecture, landscape architecture or interior design) and the particular school or university they have chosen contradict their parents', friends', former teachers' and their own ideas of what constitutes good design or good drawing.

If students can weather the frustration, they will learn a great deal from this doctrinal shift. They will learn a new design and drawing discipline and more importantly, they will learn that there are many possible approaches to design and drawing and that they must make their own. Perceptually, such a shift in indoctrination can be shattering because the student must master a whole new set of visual cues. An example of this in architectural design education is the difficulty of getting students to look at the *space* and its shape, structure, surfaces, openings and relation to other spaces, rather than at the *things* in the space or on its surfaces.

Although few design schools today indoctrinate their students in any single style or esthetic, there will probably be an indoctrination from the teachers or advanced students in a general esthetic, which may be foreign to the student's previous experiences; lack of ornament, exposed structure, 45° geometry, or shed roofs may constitute a "style" as surely as the historic styles which were once taught. Unfortunately, such a style is the first thing students master because it is most easily perceived and they may take much

longer to understand the deeper levels of design indoctrination. Similarly in design drawing, the students first master the "school" method of drawing trees or figures and their understanding of design drawing may stay at this superficial level.

WHAT YOU SEE IS WHAT YOU GET THE COMMUNICATED QUALITIES OF A DESIGNED PRODUCT OR ENVIRONMENT

The validity of the design professions turns on the assumption that anything which is designed will be better, in some sense, for having been designed. This designed value relies on the communication of designed qualities to the viewer and user. When we look at a chair we may find it beautiful in its structure, workmanship, materials, or in relationship to its context. Then we sit in the chair and it communicates its physical comfort, which then colors our future visual appraisal of it and other chairs.

This communication takes place on several levels, but remains narrowly, though not exclusively, focused in the viewer's and user's visual sense. The direct experience of an object or place by the other senses tends to verify or modify our visual evaluations, but the visual sense remains dominant in succeeding evaluations of similar objects or places.

The fact that our evaluation of environments, even those past direct experiences of our other senses, comes to reside in the visual sense is then the primary reason for using drawing in designing an environment.

This argument demonstrates that the basic validity for learning and using drawing in the design professions, does not lie in their usefulness as patterns for construction or quantity take-offs. These may be happily turned over to a machine as soon as one is available. Neither should a designer learn drawing primarily to sell the design for an environment. This function may almost as happily be turned over to professional delineators. Drawing should rather be used by a designer to predict, evaluate and improve the visual communication of design quality. If these qualities aren't communicated by the drawings they probably won't be communicated by the environment.

I have heard arguments which put down drawings or three-dimensional models as misleading and deceptive. Such arguments undoubtedly have some validity. Drawings and models are misleading, but they are the best we have. Words, I think, are even more misleading. Our language is highly value-colored and I have found the eye to be much more trustworthy than either the ear or mouth.

James L. Adams argues for drawings over words in his *Conceptual Blockbusting* (1974):

> ...Visualization, as expressed through the use of drawings, is almost essential in designing physical things well. One reason for this is that verbal thinking, when applied to the design of physical things, has the strange attribute of allowing one to think that he has an answer when, in fact, he does not. Verbal thinking among articulate persons is fraught with glib generalities. And in design it is not until one backs it up with the visual mode that he can see whether he is fooling himself or not.

Language is more broadly understood and accepted as the almost exclusive media of intelligence and reason. Drawing and other nonverbal forms of expression, like music, have been denigrated as unreliable, warped by fashion, emotions and personal expression. However, the environments designed by the design professions are experienced directly and pervasively by the visual sense.

We cannot read a building or a garden, or an interior. The designer does not have the opportunity to give every user or viewer a guided tour or hand out a descriptive brochure in persuasive prose. The users for which the environment was designed experience it directly without benefit of language, and so any intentions of the designer must communicate directly, and primarily visually, to the user. The use of the environment over time will involve many other senses, but they are all secondary to vision.

The validity of using drawing in the design process then seems undeniable. Designers must be masters of visual/spatial communication, both as delineators and perceivers, for the visual qualities of their designs must speak for them, and the best means of predicting what will eventually be perceived from the designed environment is to draw accurately and perceive carefully what appears in design drawings.

DRAWINGS BY OTHER DESIGNERS can be a great source of frustration when you are learning to draw, but if you can get over seeing them as threatening, they are also perhaps the best source for learning to draw.

Many design students are discouraged early in their education by something like the following experience. You arrive at the design studio on time, well prepared, and with the proper equipment, having read the assigned material, and begin to work with great diligence and seriousness on the assigned design or drawing project. The person at the next desk arrives late, asks what the assignment is, borrows equipment from neighbors, sings or whistles, spends very little time actually drawing, but a great deal of time apparently admiring the drawing. After some time you cast a curious glance at the next desk to see what could possibly result from this less serious neighbor's behavior. The perception

is shattering, because the drawing which is emerging on that other person's drawing board is nothing short of miraculous. Much better than anyone ever made at Diligence High School or Sincerity Summer Studio. In that instant the unfairness of the world seems crushing, having extended beyond looks or social position, even into drawing ability.

This end of innocence concerning drawing is very crucial. You may invoke the talent myth and tell yourself that you were somehow excluded when drawing ability was distributed or you may begin to build a similar myth as to why drawings are misleading or unimportant and have little to do with design. What you should try to understand, however, is that what you saw was a performance. Your late neighbor was performing—just as anyone who really dances well, or plays tennis well, or tells stories well, enjoys doing it and having others watch. What you didn't see, and what is visible only in the miraculous drawing, is perhaps fifteen years of drawing, drawing, drawing, with steady encouragement from parents, teachers and friends, so that the drawing performance you saw had long ago become a self-rewarding activity.

There is an opposite but equally shattering experience for the diligent but naive design student. This usually happens when the first big design or drawing assignment is due. About a week before the due date the student on the other side of you disappears, to reappear a half hour before the project is due with twice the number of required boards, all rendered in the most breathtakingly meticulous technique. The student is clean-shaven, seems bright eyed and rested. Meanwhile, you have been working at school with the other students, stayed up all last night, haven't washed or eaten, and still haven't finished the required drawings.

Your prolific neighbor mentions that, "I was going to do one other board, but I knocked off last night and caught a movie." As in the first example, you're not seeing the whole story. Your second neighbor has been working steadily at home in every spare moment for the last three weeks and those drawings that look like they took hours and hours did take hours and hours. As in the first case, there is no magic involved, and the talent myth is only a comfortable cop-out. It you want to make beautiful drawings you must have the motivation to spend the time drawing—over many years or in intensely concentrated efforts, or both.

If you can survive such experiences with other designers' drawings and understand that drawing ability is learnable and worth learning, you will find the drawings of others to be the best of all schools. You should look at all drawing as the record of an activity over time and try to discover what was done first, second, third and what the controlling rules were. If you become a practiced perceiver of the drawings of other designers you will be surprised at how much you can learn just from looking, if you apply what you have seen to your own drawings the next chance you get. This actual application of what you have learned to see is crucial. No amount of casual admiring page-turning will help. Your perception must have the intensity of an undercover agent. You must look for ways of drawing which you can copy and begin to use immediately. We learn from one another. Accounts of the Renaissance, when painting and sculpture and architecture made such advances, abound in stories of how artists overtly or covertly made it a point to study one another's work. If you doubt this, check the sign-out slips for the books on drawing or rendering in your school's library. I think you will find the paradox that they have been checked out by your fellow students who already draw very well.

PERCEPTION OF DESIGN DRAWINGS

BY OTHERS

COMMUNICATIVE RESPONSIBILITY is the designer's and the failure to communicate is a failure of the designer's perception, not the perception of those with whom we must communicate. The drawings designers make to show teachers, bosses and clients their design proposals are an inseparable part of design responsibility. To blame the perceiver for not seeing the qualities in a design is to duck an integral part of design responsibility.

This is one of the most difficult responsibilities a designer has to accept. The responsibility for communicating your designs to others begins, however, in the development of your own perception. Designers must learn to perceive how their designs, and the drawings which represent their designs, will be perceived by others.

This communicative responsibility means that designers' drawing abilities may either promote or inhibit their ability to get their designs built. Someday you may be able to afford to have someone else make the drawings you present to a client, but junior designers are seldom assigned a delineator as their personal slave. This means that whatever YOU design YOU are going to have to draw, and draw in such a way that someone will want to build it.

LeCorbusier developed a system of proportions based on the dimensions of the human figure and his drawings of the system illustrate the point I am trying to make. If we take the vertical dimension as ability, then the designer's hand should be as good, or as high as his or her head, for it is the hand that will have to communicate the head's creativity.

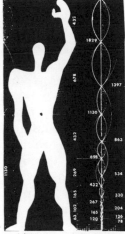

Le Corbusier - LE MODULOR

Actually, they are integrally connected and I believe that for the designer, the head must help the hand draw and the hand must help the head design.

The two possible imbalances of head and hand are equally frustrating. A facile hand which makes beautiful empty-headed drawings is comparable to a brilliantly creative mind that must communicate with a clumsy hand.

FIRST IMPRESSION. The fact that what is presented is obviously a human product will sharpen the immediate perception or first impression. In the first few seconds of perception, the perceiver will gain a rush of perceptual information which is difficult and sometimes impossible to change in subsequent perception.

Whatever is presented will communicate the amount of human effort and skill in an instantaneous rush. If the perceiver judges it to be adequate, or more than adequate, based on past experience and in the context in which it is presented, she or he will eagerly look further for design intention. If, on the other hand, the perceiver is put off by any inadequacy perceived in the first instants of perception, subsequent perception will already be negatively prejudiced.

TRANSPARENCY

In the first impression of design drawings, the actual drawing should have the same kind of transparency for the "other" perceiver as was discussed earlier for the designer. By transparent, I mean that the perceiver should immediately accept the drawing as realistic and competently drawn and look through it to the design content being presented. It is difficult to overemphasize this point and it deserves careful explanation.

If the drawing technique is clumsy and distorted or inaccurate, the perciever is put off by the ineptitude of the delineator and will be hesitant in accepting the drawing as a true representation of the design.

Most drawings which a designer uses to communicate to others, especially clients, will need to be drawn rather explicitly in order for the client to see the design. Design drawings can easily be overdrawn, however, to the point where an overworked or virtuoso technique, or a technique which is loaded with drawing cliches, actually inhibits the communication of the design the drawing was intended to communicate. If you make design drawings to demonstrate how well you can draw, you may obscure the intended transparency of the drawing in such a way that the design content is pushed into the background.

THE FORM OF DRAWINGS is important to their success as communications. Marshall McLuhans' insight, *The Medium is the Message* (1967), certainly applies to drawings. Just as the communicative form of books, radio, or TV communicates as much as their content, so does the form of drawing—conceptual diagram, rough sketch, working drawing or slick rendering—communicate as much as what is drawn.

During the stages of design when a designer is seeking the participation of teacher, consultant, boss or client in the design process, the choice of drawing form can invite or discourage participation. If the drawing is diagrammatic or tentative, and particularly if alternative designs are shown, the design process will appear open and participation will be invited. If the drawing is a working drawing or a slick "final" presentation, the design process will appear closed, asking only approval or rejection, not participation.

This impression is communicated entirely by the form of drawing used. It is related to the adequacy of effort mentioned before, but rough sketches can be adequate to invite perception and participation if they are well done. I have had the most success when clients are shown the first conceptual diagrams and invited to participate in the design process from its earliest conceptual stages.

This early involvement of the client and the opportunity it affords a designer to perceive the client's perception proves invaluable to the success of later communications.

PROFESSIONAL PERCEIVERS

Designers must be professional perceivers. They must learn to perceive their environment comprehensively and predict other's perception of the environments they design. Drawing is a primary means of developing this needed perceptual ability.

In architectural education, this function was traditionally served by the field sketch. Students and architects carried sketchbooks and recorded their experience of buildings and urban spaces. After years of such training, buildings and spaces can be recalled by this sharpened perception and drawn with remarkable accuracy, months later and miles away.

Photographers, painters, animal trackers, and archaeologists have similarly trained perception. This trained perception gives them a special kind of access to the visual world. The ability to draw, similarly gives perceivers a special structured way of looking at the world. They look at the world as a potential drawing with themselves as the delineators.

By permission of Johnny Hart and Field Enterprises, Inc.

CONCEPTION

The synthesis by which we relate and apply what we know is given various names: thinking, cognition, problem-solving, etc. I will call it CONCEPTION here because that name reinforces its relationship to perception.

Design drawing is, potentially, one of conception's most valuable tools. While the ability to draw helps perception indirectly, drawing directly promotes conception by externalizing concepts in graphic form, which may then be evaluated and manipulated with all the human tools of intelligence: EYE, MIND and HAND.

Our conceptual ability has gradually turned from the basic task of serving our immediate survival, to planning our futures, to the comparative luxury of thinking about our think-ing. This development of our conceptual ability has not been achieved without cost. The abilities and patterns which have allowed us to survive and on which our minds are built also form our deepest conceptual blocks.

We inherit the experience of the entire human race throughout its evolutionary history. Very early in life we are also subjected to a lengthy indoctrination by a prejudiced language into the collective experience of whatever culture happens to have produced us. To this massive legacy we add the experience of our lifetime, much of which is unconscious. The conscious experience which we can add to this largely inherited framework might seem of little value, but it is preeminently worth understanding and managing for it is, after all, all we can call our own.

SELF·CONCEPTION

Of all the variables involved in the use of the conscious experience of our lifetime, in the range, direction and depth of our thought, perhaps the most important is our own self-conception. Whether thought through and held consciously or adopted at an unconscious level, such a self-model can do more to influence the way we think about our lives or the way we design an environment than any other factor. Self models may be either inhibiting or liberating depending on what they assume as possible and proper use of the conceptual abilities we inherit from evolution.

The most crucial difference in the many various mindmodels that have been proposed and are currently held, is to what extent human conceptual functioning is free or determined: whether the mind is modeled as working in certain predetermined, inevitable ways or modeled as being free and largely under the control of the individual to whom it belongs. Because of our evolutionary inheritance and our cultural indoctrination, few would argue that we can ever have complete conceptual freedom, but the argument over the extent to which our thoughts are determined remains very much alive.

Determinism has many forms and much of the argument over the various mindmodels is actually between these conflicting forms of determinism. Determinism may be either *future-determined* by some plan or script for the future which we call fate, destiny, divine will or secular historicism; or it may be *past-determined* by the inevitable winding down of various deterministic natural laws set in motion by science's "big bang." The argument over the relative influence of heredity and environment is also between alternate forms of determinism. The various cause and effect explanations of the deterministic models, though seemingly open and debatable,

mask a common mechanical or mystical explanation which enforces the cultural status quo by holding that free, responsible, creative use of the mind is either an impossibility or a heresy.

Technology has given us the perfect analogy for the deterministic models—the robot. It may help to summarize the various deterministic models as various kinds of robots.

THE CULTURALLY PROGRAMMED ROBOT is the oldest of the deterministic models, and continues to serve the survival of most members of the animal world and many nominally human cultures. There are cultural and political systems in which the individual members are expected simply to memorize a set of rules and doctrines, live their lives by them, and pass them on to their children—unquestioned, unchanged, and unbroken. In animals and insects much of the programming is in fact carried by heredity as instinct, which is nature's most perfect form of pre-programming. Humans may have escaped a similar hard-wiring only because of their relatively premature birth and their necessarily long period of acculturation. Ants, bees, lemmings and some of the oldest and newest of human societies depend on this strict control of their members, whether by heredity or environment.

Contemporary humans have infinitely more flexibility and capacity in their programmable memory than earlier models or other animal models. It is not a question of *whether* to program the human child or not, for extensive programming is obviously necessary for survival. The question is *how* the programming should be done, and all cultures approach this responsibility with great care. There is little disagreement as to the awesome responsibility involved, because the culture's future clearly depends on how well

each new robot is programmed. What is arguable is the kind and extent of the programming as a relevant preparation for the individual's life in a changing world. Some cultures' programs consist of detailed specifications which attempt to cover every situation, while others rely on relative principles which the individual is expected to apply to varying situations. Julian Jaynes (*The Origin of Consciousness in the Breakdown of the Bicameral Mind,* 1977) makes a compelling argument for the failure of overly specific cultural programming as the origin of consciousness.

THE STIMULUS-RESPONSE ROBOT is an alternative automaton proposed by the school of psychology know as Behaviorism. This set of notions was initiated early in this century by John B. Watson, and its current spokesman is B. F. Skinner. Behaviorists deny or ignore such concepts as *mind* or *consciousness* and insist that the only basis for psychology is observable human behavior. Strangely, however, most of their theories are based on the observed behavior of rats or pigeons. They assume that the complex functioning of humans is nothing more than an additive collection of the simple stimulus/response/reinforcement patterns observable in much simpler animals.

"SO WHAT IF UNCLE BERTIE RAN AN IDENTICAL MAZE IN LONDON! I'M STILL LOST."

This deterministic model would restrict even the cultural programming discussed in the previous model to the kind of behavior modification demonstrated in various laboratory animals by reinforcing punishments and rewards and would completely rule out any self-modification or self-determined behavior. The stimulus-response robot is completely hard-wired inside a closed console and may only be "trained."

Howard Gruber (*Darwin On Man—A Psychological Study of Scientific Creativity*, 1974) describes and names this kind of determinism:

> A view of human life has arisen in which the individual is subject both to deterministic and probabilistic laws in such a way as to make the idea of free and purposeful creativity meaningless. To the extent that life is governed by deterministic laws, the argument runs, there is no way of affecting the future because it has all been determined by circumstances beyond personal control. Meanwhile, wherever probabilistic laws prevail, there is no way of intelligently influencing the future because things are chancy and unpredictable.
>
> It may help to give this view a name. Because it combines determinism and chance in a thoroughly materialistic way, and proceeds on this basis to deny any significance or reality to mental processes, we may label it *hypermaterialism....*

THE HISTORICALLY PROGRAMMED ROBOT is perhaps a very old deterministic model but has rather recently been given a very convincing form by Sigmund Freud. This robot is assumed to have been largely programmed by its earlier experiences, which it can do little about, especially since much of this programming occured below the level of consciousness. The robot's past experiences have programmed its future in a subtly different way than in the cultural robot, since this robot's history was not the deliberate work of cultural indoctrination but primarily the random experiences suffered in the relationships of the immediate family.

HEREDITY vs. ENVIRONMENT. The continuing controversy over whether our minds are predetermined by heredity or conditioned by environment obscures the underlying determinism of both these notions. Neither heredity nor environment, nor their compromised combinations can account for some of the human race's most creative individuals. Hereditary determinism and environmental determinism are simply alternate forms of a claim culture seems to need to make on the creativity of its individuals.

GIFTEDNESS is an even more remote deterministic explanation. Aside from its lack of proof it is not even a useful idea, especially in education, since it becomes a cop-out for student and teacher alike. The idea that our minds are largely predetermined at birth even seems to deny the usefulness of the cultural indoctrination of which it is a part.

Elsewhere in this book I have argued against the notion of giftedness and have taken the side of the environment or more specifically, experience, in explaining the "talent" or ability to draw. My quarrel with environmental explanations of abilities, including drawing ability, is that they often treat the environment as something which inevitably *happens* to individuals, leaving no room for their free choice of experiences and thus no responsibility for their own abilities.

SCIENCE promises the last and perhaps most threatening deterministic model of the mind. While some scientists have contributed to the arguments supporting various deterministic models of the mind, the scientific community has not agreed on any single paradigm for the mind and its functioning. Several branches of science have been busily collecting data for decades or centuries but their data and their discoveries are equally impressive in their diffuse detail and their lack of any comprehensive explanation of the mind.

Most scientists are quite candid about their distance from any comprehensive mind-model and some talk like they believe or hope that there may indeed by a "ghost in the machine" which will defy scientific explanation. But the popular understanding or *misunderstanding* of science and the faith we have bestowed on it as a culture, makes many of us believe that science will one day inexorably discover *exactly* how the mind works. This attitude holds that like the cancer cure we must just wait a little longer for the eventual triumph of this difficult but inevitable deterministic explanation—perhaps we won't live to see it, but in some more fortunate future generation...! Meanwhile we can only greet science's successive revelations with wonder and compliance.

Science's deterministic self-model is of course the general model we have been using—the robot. And the mindmodel of any robot is the triumph of modern technology, the computer.

The computer is poignantly appropriate both as the perfectly predictable laboratory animal, the obedient cultural descendant or dependable statistical cipher, and a graven cultural image beyond compare. Have you processed any interesting information lately?

The general adoption of the computer as analogous to the mind, and information processing as analogous to mental function makes it clear, however, that many of our traditional mindmodels have outlived their usefulness, especially as examples of what the human mind should be. The filing cabinet, the unquestioning believer, the infallible calculator, the obedient servant, the fanatic patriot, and the impartially objective analyst have all reached their ideal manifestation in the computer and have therefore become useless subhuman mindmodels. Human minds must find other, better things to do.

All deterministic models have some usefulness. They are not all wrong, but their common determinism leaves little room for the concepts of freedom, responsibility or creativity, which would seem to be the hallmarks of *designers*.

FREE MODELS of the mind are, conversely, not all right, but they would seem to be much more useful for the future of the species. Whatever model of the mind we hold probably has more potential for influencing our use of our minds than any other factor subject to our conscious control. If we model the mind as entirely predetermined by fate or external influences over which we have no control we are indeed doomed to be automatons. Choosing to conceive of at least the consciousness of the mind as free, capable of synthesizing its own values and answers, and accepting the responsibility commensurate with such a

conception of the mind, seems to be at once the proof of such a possibility and the only hope for the future of human intelligence.

Human intelligence and free will turns on an insistence that while there may be some generalized patterns which are our legacy from our evolution's and our culture's response to the environment, we are always in the process of changing these patterns—in our individual lifetimes and over the longterm evolution of our species. While most of our history has been outer-directed or environment-directed, we now have the precious possibility of making an increasing part of our future be inner-directed or *self-directed*.

We continue to look longingly over our shoulders for approval, or at the back of some book for the answers. We are slow to understand that both must be *made* and continually remade synthetically in our own consciousness. They are ours *only* for the making.

A METAPHORICAL MINDMODEL
In the absence of any definitive scientific description of how what we have come to call our "minds" work, we need some sort of owner's manual. I offer the following model as an example of the kind of analogue that each of us must make if we are to understand and begin to take conscious control of the complex system we call mind. I will call the total system *eyemindhand* as a reminder that it includes the body, is dominated by vision and functions best as a whole.

The model I will propose for the human *eyemindhand* system is free rather than deterministic. The system's basic structure is the inherited evolutionary result of our species' interaction with the environment and our use of the system is both promoted and inhibited

by our cultural indoctrination. Neither heredity nor environment, however, can completely determine or excuse our minds because of the freedom of our consciousness.

The proposed *mindmodel* consists of three parts:

• ENVIRONMENT

• EXPERIENCE

• CONSCIOUSNESS

ENVIRONMENT—the context.
This element in the model represents everything that is outside us. This includes the natural and built environments, other people, and all forms of communication, books, conversation and drawings.

EXPERIENCE—a network.
This element is the interrelated network of all our accumulated knowledge and experience: *what we know*. In the integrated model, this experience network surrounds, in fact *forms* the third part of the model, consciousness. The experience network is represented as an integrated system, the *eyemindhand* which includes our evolutionary heritage, our cultural indoctrination, the conscious and unconscious experience of our lifetimes and such concepts as emotion and will. The experience network is everything we are *except* consciousness.

All living organisms may be thought of as experience networks. In the lower or earlier forms of life this experience network is entirely the product of evolution and heredity. Each organism inherits its experience network from evolution with perhaps an infinitessimal potential for mutational change in each generation. Whatever mutational change is possible must be accomplished by transactions at the experience/ environment interface, as adaptations for survival.

In simple organisms, the structure of the inherited experience network is entirely and inevitably *given*. During any lifetime the organism is environmentally responsive, based on a pattern of successful survival responses to the environment inherited from its evolutionary history. These simplest organisms are completely environment-respondent and heredity-descendant. Their existence is dominated by a linear hereditary hierarchy. The sense of belonging to, and the tendency to think in linear hierarchies could be that deep in our evolutionary heritage.

Certain groups of organisms have added a social interdependence. This social interdependence is in some cases hard-wired into their evolutionary heritage and in some cases learned from parents and other members of society. Social interdependence is built on responses to other organisms who are members of the society and may be diagrammed as happening at the interface of the two experience networks.

Some human cultures are so strongly socially interdependent that they have never reached the next, tentative, fully human stage of development. Social interdependence consists of strict conformance to a narrow functional role in the society that is either instinctually programmed by evolutionary heredity or taught and enforced by other members of the society. This next level of social organisms is environment-resultant, heredity-descendent and socially interdependent. Social interdependence institutionalizes the linear hierarchies established by heredity. This is the level of the Cultural Robot discussed earlier.

CONSCIOUSNESS—a space.

In contrast to all nature's other forms of life, the hallmork of human intelligence and freedom is the development and free individual use of consciousness. C. G. Jung explained, "Consciousness is a very recent acquisition of nature and is still in an experimental state."

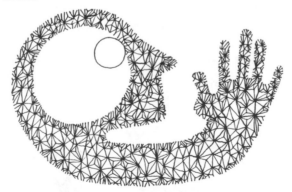

This element of the mind is represented as the space of our attention. Consciousness is the most uniquely human part of the mind and is limited in three ways: the quantity of information it can hold at any particular time, the extent to which it can be opened up or closed off to sensory input from the environment, and the length of time it can be held either fully open or fully closed.

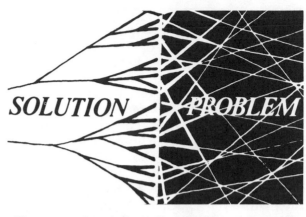

SOLUTION PROBLEM

The most characteristic use of human intelligence is the making of synthetic congruences between problem/solution, past/future, real/ ideal, etc. Our sense of reality, our identity and all our day-to-day conscious thoughts are the products of such syntheses, and in the present *mindmodel,* design drawing draws the attempts at these synthetic congruences along the interface of consciousness and experience, and simultaneously on the paper, in the environment. The forming of such synthetic congruences is both the highest and most common use of human intelligence, and the participation of the hand in drawing the congruences includes and legitimizes the final participant—the unconscious layers of our experience network. The model now represents and integrates the whole human being, and one of the central ideas of this book is that we function better whole—using all the tools of human intelligence. Drawing is an example and a symbol of that holistic functioning.

Models are very powerful in their paradoxical potential for both extending and limiting our thinking about whatever it is that they model. We will be best served by a *mindmodel* that is very carefully and individually made and remade: free, open, responsible and mature enough to be self-motivating and self-rewarding.

41

THE FREE MIND

The arch enemy of the free mind is determinism in all its forms. The determinism that was once advocated by religions has now largely been inherited by science. Science has also documented, however, that our inherited mental equipment is extremely flexible. The range and variety of conceptual worlds which have developed in diverse cultures suggests that the mind may be a do-it-yourself kit of near-infinite flexibility and undreamed-of potential. If this is true, or even partly true, then whatever models of the mind we adopt will do more to promote or inhibit the use of our minds than anything else.

The future of human intelligence depends on our insistence on such a model, and that model, or rather those millions of different models are what we should continue to call *mind*.

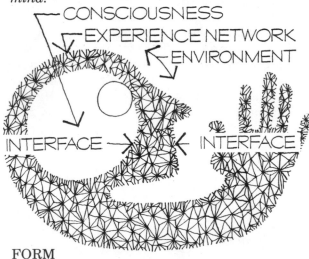

CONSCIOUSNESS
EXPERIENCE NETWORK
ENVIRONMENT
INTERFACE   INTERFACE

FORM

Models are never innocent and it is important to understand the prejudices which may be inherent in the form of any model. In addition to separating and naming the three constituents of environment, experience and consciousness, the present *mindmodel* establishes two interfaces: environment/experience and experience/consciousness.

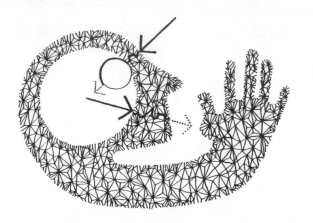

The spatial arrangement of the three elements and their two interfaces rules out any interface between consciousness and the environment except by a transition through our experience. This means that our perception of the environment is only possible through the mediation of our experience. It also means that any perceptions or conceptions that develop in our consciousness can only be communicated or acted out in the environment through the same experience network. The network of our experience thus translates or mediates both the input and output of the system.

The model thus correctly represents the difficulty we encounter in understanding ideas that are beyond our experience, or in saying what we think, or in doing what we intend.

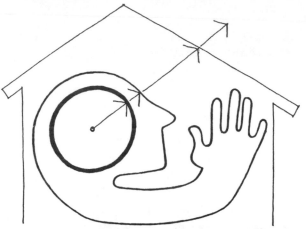

The model's other formal prejudice is that of successive concentric layers emanating from our consciousness with an emphasis on inner/outer spatial relationships. This formal prejudice seems to match experience and it corresponds to territoriality and to all the ancient taboos concerning entering or penetrating the body.

Inside/outside relationships and relative distance from some central point become much more important in this model than questions of up/down, right/left, front/back, or temporal sequence and any piece of the system will retain its orientation by its concavity/convexity, like a potsherd.

The present *mindmodel* retains, but avoids emphasizing, two traditional ways of subcategorizing the mind which may have outlived their usefulness.

The unfortunate articulation of the human form at the neck seems to be partly responsible for that most regrettable categorization of human function called the mind/body duality. This way of categorizing human functions into mental and physical, with those functions and desires of the mind being higher and purer while considering those of the body as lower and more base, has plagued us since Plato. Literally applied, this mind/

body dualism seems to locate drawing ability somewhere below the shoulder. It relegates drawing to being a physical skill having little to do with thinking. The present *mindmodel* insists that any model of the mind include the body as separate and integral, and the drawings of the model include the hands as representative of the whole body.

The second traditional categorization of the mind is Freud's conscious/subconscious or Jung's conscious/unconscious duality. Like the mind/body duality, the conscious/unconscious distinction is becoming recognized as an arbitrary distinction and the value judgments which traditionally have held that that part of the mind which was not conscious was inherently *evil* have been shown to be very questionable. In the *mindmodel* the enterface between consciousness and the unconscious experience network preserves the conscious/unconscious distinction, but the interface is movable and flexible, not fixed; and no value judgments are made as to whether consciousness or experience is the better side of the interface.

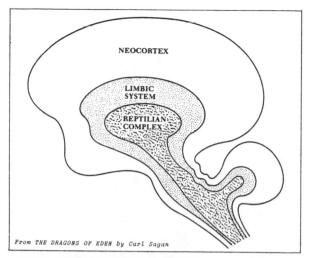

From THE DRAGONS OF EDEN by Carl Sagan

EVOLUTIONARY LAYERS

Paul MacLean has classified the brain as successive layers laid down by our evolutionary history. The oldest layer is reptilian, concerned with aggression, territoriality, ritual and social hierarchies. Next comes what can be thought of as the mammalian layer, which introduces the emotions, altruistic behavior and parental care. The last, and by far the largest layer of the brain is the neocortex and can be thought of as the human layer of the brain, which is concerned with anticipation and regulation, vision, bipedal posture and manipulation of the hand.

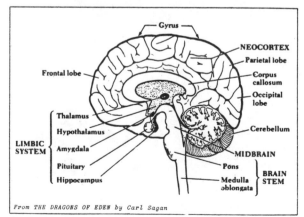

A schematic diagram of a side view of the human brain, dominated by the neocortex, with a smaller limbic system and brainstem or hindbrain. The R-complex is not shown.

While the reptilian brain is the deepest part of the brain, overlaid by the mammalian and "human" additions, in our analogical model the earlier brains are the most removed from consciousness or conscious control and their responses are, for the most part, direct reactions to the environment/experience interface.

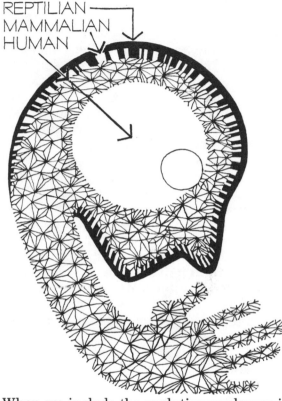

When we include the evolutionary layers in the mindmodel, the reptilian brain is the outermost layer in direct contact with the environment and least subject to conscious control. Next comes the mammalian layer, and last of all, surrounding consciousness and most controlled by it, comes the neocortex or "human" layer of the brain. This reversal of the layering in the model is backwards physiologically because of the central position given to consciousness in the model, and demonstrates the analogical nature of the model.

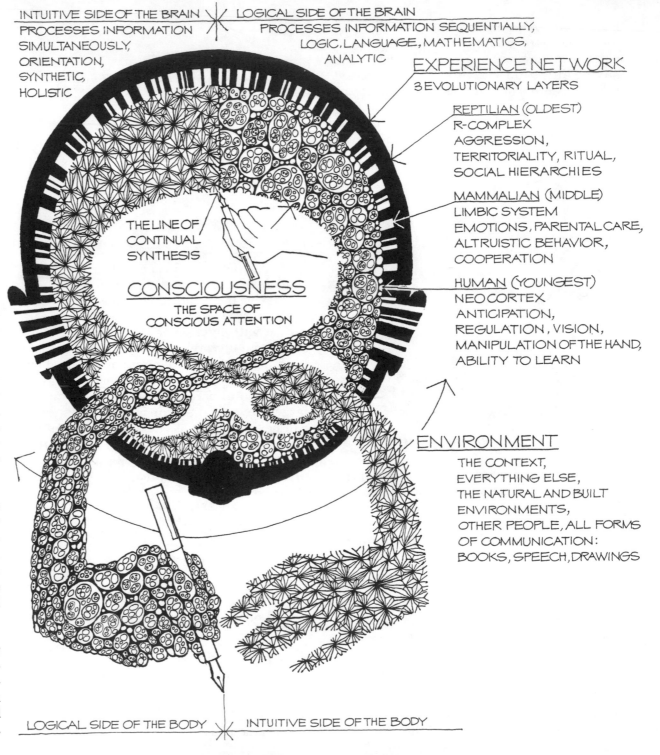

FUNCTIONAL SEPARATION

A further complication which the mindmodel attempts to indicate is that the left and right cerebral hemispheres of the neocortex are specialized in their functioning. The right hemisphere processes information instantaneously and is generally described as the intuitive or creative half of the brain, concerned with pattern recognition, spatial orientation and instant holistic judgments—*synthesis*. The left hemisphere processes information linearly or sequentially and is generally described as the rational or logical half of the brain, having the abilities of reason, language and mathematics—*analysis*. Interestingly, the right half of the brain is connected to the left side of the body, including the left eye, while the left half of the brain is connected to the right side of the body and the right eye.

The drawing of the *mindmodel* represents the patterning of the right hemisphere as being an open network that is completely and complexly interconnected—a unified relational pattern. The left brain, on the other hand, is represented as being organized in exclusive categories and hierarchies—a classified diversity.

The present model is not proposed as being physiologically correct or scientifically verifiable. Its value depends on the number of processes, relationships and experiences which can be explained in terms of the model, and the clarity and richness of the explanations.

INTUITIVE SIDE OF THE BRAIN
PROCESSES INFORMATION SIMULTANEOUSLY, ORIENTATION, SYNTHETIC, HOLISTIC

LOGICAL SIDE OF THE BRAIN
PROCESSES INFORMATION SEQUENTIALLY, LOGIC, LANGUAGE, MATHEMATICS, ANALYTIC

EXPERIENCE NETWORK
3 EVOLUTIONARY LAYERS

REPTILIAN (OLDEST)
R-COMPLEX
AGGRESSION, TERRITORIALITY, RITUAL, SOCIAL HIERARCHIES

MAMMALIAN (MIDDLE)
LIMBIC SYSTEM
EMOTIONS, PARENTAL CARE, ALTRUISTIC BEHAVIOR, COOPERATION

HUMAN (YOUNGEST)
NEOCORTEX
ANTICIPATION, REGULATION, VISION, MANIPULATION OF THE HAND, ABILITY TO LEARN

THE LINE OF CONTINUAL SYNTHESIS

CONSCIOUSNESS
THE SPACE OF CONSCIOUS ATTENTION

ENVIRONMENT
THE CONTEXT, EVERYTHING ELSE, THE NATURAL AND BUILT ENVIRONMENTS, OTHER PEOPLE, ALL FORMS OF COMMUNICATION: BOOKS, SPEECH, DRAWINGS

LOGICAL SIDE OF THE BODY

INTUITIVE SIDE OF THE BODY

CATEGORIES AND HIERARCHIES

In *A Study of Thinking* (1956), Bruner, Goodnow and Austin propose that "... virtually all cognitive activity involves and is dependent on the process of categorizing." Although we can never know any kind of perceptual/conceptual innocence, the world we perceive seems differentiated, made up of different kinds of things. Seeing differences in the world is perhaps part of perception's prejudice. The focus of our vision, our tendency to form gestalts or wholes, the *eyehand* correspondence which sees and feels separate objects and our ability to discriminate between subtly different patterns all promote seeing a differentiated environment.

Gibson points out that this differentiated world we see seems to be organized into parts and wholes by the nesting of some patterns or elements within others (*An Ecological Approach to Perception,* 1979):

> Now with respect to these units, an essential point of theory must be emphasized. The smaller units are embedded in the larger units by what I will call *nesting.* For example, canyons are nested within mountains; trees are nested within canyons; leaves are nested within trees; and cells are nested within leaves. There are forms within forms both up and down the scale of size. Units are nested within larger units. Things are components of other things. They would constitute a hierarchy except that this hierarchy is not categorical but full of transitions and overlaps. Hence, for the terrestrial environment, there is no special proper unit in terms of which it can be analyzed once and for all. There are no atomic units of the world considered as an environment. Instead, there are subordinate and superordinate units. The unit you choose for describing the environment depends on the level of the environment you choose to describe.

Our vision not only separates the world into potential categories, it also begins to break them down into constituent parts.

The collection of the differentiated elements of the world into conceptual categories and the arrangement of these categories into hierarchies, however, is a task assumed by cultural indoctrination and largely carried out by the culture's language. Our language names the separate elements we perceive, tells their qualities and characteristics and describes their actions and their relationships to one another. The culture into which we are born literally tells us what we are perceiving, and this indoctrination is so pervasive in structuring the way we see and the way we think that we can never be free of it.

Bruner, Goodnow, and Austin (*A Study of Thinking,* 1956) list the achievements of categorizing:

> Categorizing
> ...*reduces the complexity of* [*the*] *environment....*
> ...*is the means by which objects of the world about us are identified....*
> ...*reduces the necessity of constant learning....*
> ...*provides* [*the direction*] *for instrumental activity....*
> ...*permits* [*the*] *ordering and relating* [*of*] *classes of events....*

Before considering the uses cultures make of categories and the influence of language, let us look at the patterns involved in categorization.

PATTERNS

All categorization is accomplished by drawing inclusive/exclusive boundaries through the world, including some things and excluding others. This seems simple enough until we consider how these boundaries are drawn and understand that the drawing of a single categorical boundary usually infers three relationships to other categories.

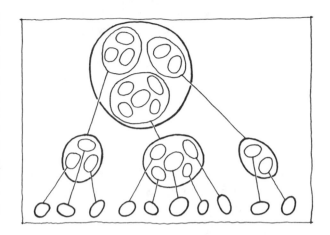

1. As a PART—most categories are parts of some larger category.

2. As a WHOLE—most categories collect and may be broken down into constituent parts.

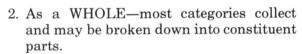

3. As a SIBLING—most categories have equal rank, with potentially competitive brother or sister categories.

Any category has these relationships, not as a *consequence* of its being a category, but as *criteria* for its becoming a category in the first place.

We are born into this categorical patterning and grow accustomed to the successive categorical boundaries which seem to surround us. As we look out at them these categorical boundaries extend the concentric shells of the *mindmodel* suggested earlier. They protectively articulate our environment into a succession of friendly circles within which we can be assured of the company of others with mutual interests and values, and above all, with a similar way of categorizing the world. Family, gender, age group, occupation, religion, political preference, nationality, and race are all protective concentric categorical rings we may draw around ourselves and many have outlived their usefulness. Obituaries often name the categorical circles which people were born into or with which they chose to surround themselves.

All categorizing can be thought of as occurring within one grand pattern, although there are several ways of diagramming that pattern. I have been diagramming it in a way which emphasizes our experience of the categorical boundaries and only implies the hierarchical relationships. The more conventional diagram for this same pattern is the branching "tree" pattern which, taken in one direction, looks like binuclear cell division, and in the other like a family tree. It is interesting that this single conceptual pattern is as ancient a part of our evolutionary heritage as the subdivision of cells, or alternately the coupling reproduction of higher organisms. This pattern is also the one recurring diagram in Darwin's notebooks.

Perhaps the most active spokesman for the pervasiveness and conceptual value of hierarchical organization is Arthur Koestler. (*JANUS, A Summing Up,* 1978).

> *...All complex structures and processes of a relatively stable character display hierarchic organization,* regardless whether we consider galactic systems, living organisms and their activities, or social organizations. The tree diagram with its series of levels can be used to represent the evolutionary branching of species into the 'tree of life'; or the stepwise differentiation of tissues and integration of functions in the development of the embryo. Anatomists use the tree diagram to demonstrate the locomotor hierarchy of limbs, joints, individual muscles, and so down to fibres, fibrils and filaments of contractile proteins. Ethologists use it to illustrate the various sub-routines and action-patterns involved in such complex instinctive activities as a bird building a nest; but it is also an indispensable tool to the new school of psycholinguistics started by Chomsky. It is equally indispensable for an understanding of the processes by which the chaotic stimuli impinging on our sense organs are filtered and classified in their ascent through the nervous system into consciousness. Lastly, the branching tree illustrates the hierarchic ordering of knowledge in the subject-index of library catalogues—and the personal memory stores inside our skulls.

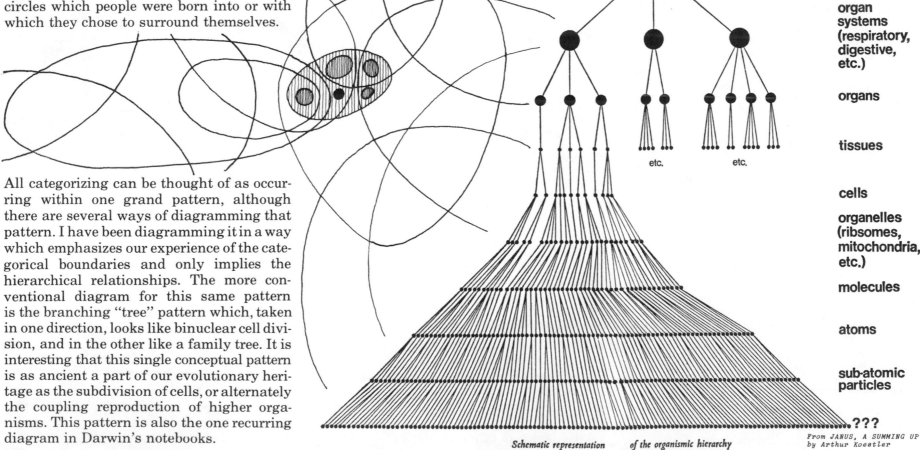

organisms

organ systems (respiratory, digestive, etc.)

organs

tissues

etc.   etc.

cells

organelles (ribosomes, mitochondria, etc.)

molecules

atoms

sub-atomic particles

???

Schematic representation   of the organismic hierarchy

From JANUS, A SUMMING UP by Arthur Koestler

The point first to be emphasized is that each member of this hierarchy, on whatever level, is a sub-whole or 'holon' in its own right—a stable, integrated structure, equipped with self-regulatory devices and enjoying a considerable degree of *autonomy* or self-government. Cells, muscles, nerves, organs, all have their intrinsic rhythms and patterns of activity, often manifested spontaneously without external stimulation; they are subordinated as *parts* to the higher centres in the hierarchy, but at the same time function as quasi-autonomous *wholes*. They are Janus-faced. The face turned upward, toward the higher levels, is that of a dependent part; the face turned downward, towards its own constituents, is that of a whole of remarkable self-sufficiency.

...I proposed, some years ago, a new term to designate those Janus-faced entities on the intermediate levels of any hierarchy, which can be described either as wholes or as parts, depending on the way you look at them from 'below' or from 'above.' The term I proposed was the 'holon,' from the Greek *holos* = whole, with the suffix *on,* which, as in proton or neutron, suggests a particle or part.

While Koestler's diagram does not model the experience of living within a set of concentric hierarchical boundaries I proposed earlier, it makes clear the linear organizational patterns on which categorizing relies: up to larger wholes, down to smaller parts and sideways to equal rank sibling rivalry. Its vertical dimension diagrams two aesthetic concepts which are often invoked in design: unity and diversity.

Unity collects diversity, while diversity articulates unity. To move in the unifying direction is to ascend toward some grand collector called the cosmos, nature or God, while to move in the direction of diversity is to descend to the bewildering articulations of our environment. Between these poles of ultimate unity and intimate diversity we have stretched a chain of conceptual categories, linked by the directional inflection of unity and diversity.

It is interesting to speculate that the interdependency relationship expressed in the complementary concepts of unity and diversity has inevitably led us to search for either end of the hierarchy. This would explain both our compulsion to investigate and classify the diversity and to postulate and deify the unity.

Koestler has also written about what the vertical dimension of the social hierarchy means in terms of human behavior (*The Ghost in the Machine,* 1967). He explains that humans exhibit two conflicting tendencies as a result of their being both an individual *whole* and an integral *part* of a biological and social hierarchy. Their "wholeness" as individuals leads them to *self-assertive* behavior, while their "partness" leads them to *integrative* behavior.

Of the two tendencies Koestler proposes, "I would like to suggest that the integrative tendencies of the individual are incomparably more dangerous than his self-assertive tendencies." And further, "Let me repeat: the crimes of violence committed for selfish personal motives are historically insignificant compared to those committed ad majorem gloriam Dei, out of a self-sacrificing devotion to a flag, a leader, a religious faith or a political conviction."

It is this integrative tendency (our apparent need to identify with self-transcendent causes and beliefs) which leads us to accept cultural indoctrination and abdicate conceptual freedom and responsibility.

The horizontal dimension of the conventional diagram of any hierarchy represents the other linear relationship which dominates our conceptual world: equally ranked, potentially competitive categories.

In its simplest form the sibling rivalry of

these brother/sister categories reduces to mutually exclusive dualities between which we must choose: mind/body, heredity/environment, republican/democrat, liberal/conservative. A more balanced view of this lateral dimension of our conceptual hierarchy is that it represents a continuum connecting polar opposites and that our choice of position may be somewhere along the continuum which accommodates both polar positions.

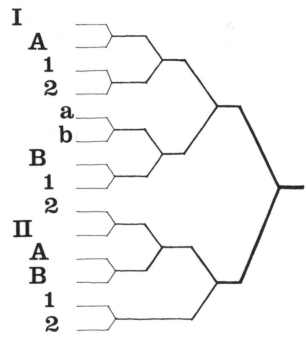

It is interesting that there seems to be only the one pattern, which with its subpatterns organizes our conceptual world. The pattern is rather clearly anthropomoric in its correspondence to the higher/lower, left/right axes of our body and is easily described by our language. The fact that it is difficult to imagine another pattern for any conceptual framework is testimony to the omnipresence of hierarchical organization. It is also evidence that patterns are more powerful conceptually than the names we write in them.

CULTURE

Categorization is never innocent. Categories separate, and in the separation provide the meaning-seeking human mind with an opportunity for assigning a meaning to the distinction, and usually a value. The reason for seeing two things as being different seems to lie in the discrimination it allows. While it is quite useful to be able to distinguish a mushroom from a toadstool, the value of being able to distinguish between a brown person, a black person and a white person is questionable. The most interesting question arising from the recent furor over Jensen's hypothesis that blacks are genetically less intelligent than whites is, *what possible value could there be in such an investigation?* Why must we compulsively continue to try to prove that the differences in skin color we perceive visually have some deeper significance? The only intelligence impugned by Jensen's findings is his own.

Cultural indoctrination begins with a categorization of the world. The differentiated world which we perceive is collected into categories, named and arranged in hierarchies and valued. Claude Levi-Strauss (*The Savage Mind,* 1962) has made clear that even the most primitive cultures have such a categorization which names and classifies the world, many more comprehensively than our own. While the variations between these "primitive" categorizations and, especially their variation with our own "scientific" world view is staggering, they all follow the same hierarchical patterns discussed previously and depend on similar "axes of reference" and mutually exclusive pairs.

The differences in the various world views with which cultures indoctrinate their members prove that the categories with which we structure the conceptual world are never objectively or necessarily "given" by

the environment. To quote Bruner, Goodnow and Austin (*A Study of Thinking,* 1965) once more:

> The categories in terms of which we group the events of the world around us are constructions or inventions. The class of prime numbers, animal species, the huge range of colors dumped into the category "blue," squares and circles—all of these are inventions and not "discoveries." They do not "exist" in the environment....

> ...Science and common-sense inquiry alike do not discover the ways in which events are grouped in the world; they invent ways of grouping. The test of the invention is the predictive benefits that result from the use of the invented categories....

> The categories in terms of which man sorts out and responds to the world around him reflect deeply the culture into which he is born. The language, the way of life, the religion and science of a people: all of these mold the way in which a man experiences the events out of which his own history is fashioned....

The conceptual framework of any culture extends to ethical and aesthetic value systems which are established by the culture's institutions and enforced by cultural sanctions. If you are a design student you are currently undergoing an indoctrination into a subculture. You should be aware of the categories in which your curriculum is divided, and their hierarchical arrangement. You should also be aware of the less obvious aesthetic categories which are currently at issue. You may be aware, if you are an architecture student, of the current foment over the birth (Caesarian in my opinion and hopefully still) of a new category called Post Modernism.

The initiation of categories in a culture, or even in the subculture of the design professions, is always difficult. This book is such an attempt. Its purpose is to establish a new category called design drawing, distinct from art or drafting. All such attempts meet with

resistance from the vested interests of the culture. Teachers of art or drafting who have spent a long time refining the traditional ways of teaching design students how to draw will understandably feel threatened. A culture's categories can only be changed very slowly and the front rank of defenders for any dogma will naturally be its teachers. They are the ones who must persuade students of the relevance of what they are teaching and change always renders a part of their lives irrelevant.

Conceptual insights for which a culture claims credit happen as much in spite of the culture's indoctrination as because of it, since the goal of all cultural indoctrination is to enforce a particular status quo, or at best a rigidly prescribed way of changing it. The resistance to change is apparent in the fanatical cultural resistance to almost every conceptual leap in our history.

Most cultural indoctrinations promote one set or another of fixed, authoritative answers, which it is heresy to look behind. These cultural conceptual sets range from the general to the specific, in matters as different as personal and group behavior, dress, eating and drinking, to notions about the origin of the world and the purpose of life.

Many of these cultural conceptual sets carry great wisdom for the good of individuals in the culture, or the culture as a whole, and can be carefully and logically explained by members of the culture. Others have long lost their logical rationale and continue mindlessly as a matter of tradition.

The danger of the conceptual categories of any culture is that they inhibit conceptual freedom by implying that there are fixed, correct answers which need only be memorized, and that the answers to all human problems are a matter of "knowing" that correct answer. Today our fixed answers don't seem to be serving us very well. What we need is the ability to make new answers, the flexibility to try them out and the attitude that this making and testing is the highest use of human intelligence.

LANGUAGE

The medium which carries the indoctrination of a culture is its language. The language names the conceptual categories into which a culture sorts the world and its syntax limits what can be said and, some linguists believe, what can be thought. What is called the Sapir-Whorf hypothesis holds that a culture's language structures the members' thought to such an extent that they are best thought of as inhabiting different worlds. Language and literacy in any culture is privileged, even today. Those who developed and used language historically were undoubtedly at the top of their cultural hierarchy. Language, like categorization, is not innocent. It retains the prejudices of the people who historically knew and used language to carry out their selfish interests.

The most striking example of our language's prejudice is its embarrassing sexism. We have no sexless singular personal pronoun. In a language which runs to nearly half a million words this is a striking oversight. Our religious language also assumes that the diety is male, and words like mankind and manmade, make it quite clear which sex was historically privileged with literacy.

THE OPEN CATEGORY

A design problem is like an open category. The designed solution will take its place, like any category, in several established hierarchies. It is as if your clients had made an opening in the hierarchy of their lives for the environment you will design for them; or like

the hillside had made a place in its hierarchy of sun, wind and view; or the neighborhood had made a place in the previously built environment for the new "category" you are designing; or like your maturation as a designer had prepared a place for this next design in the body of your work. There are several other hierarchies into which any design may be placed by a sensitive designer, and your designs will always be perceived as a part of these hierarchies, never as an isolated act or object.

Just like any conceptual category every design solution is defined by three relationships:

- *as a part.* Any building, exterior or interior space will belong to a larger whole, a natural environment, a street, a neighborhood, a city and a geographical region. Any designed environment will also become a part of people's lives and you and your profession's work.

- *as a whole.* Any built environment will also be a composition of parts. Most environments will include a spatial/circulation system, one or several environmental control systems, an illumination system, a materials system, and, if it is a building, a structural system and an enclosure system. The new category must try to integrate all these subcategories into a convincing whole.

- *as a sibling.* In the horizontal dimension each environmental design will take its place in a lateral rank of environments of similar function, budget, site, technology and along several shifting, arguable continua: modern/post-modern, natural/high-tech, site-integrated/site-dominant.

Like all categories, the open category presented by a design problem will be defined by these three relationships. The designer has the opportunity of establishing all these relationships and the choice of whether to make them clear and distinct or leave them richly ambiguous.

THE DANGERS OF CATEGORIZATION

We must have categories. Thinking is inconceivable without them, but they should always be questioned and deliberately accepted or broken and reformed. Robert H. McKim (*Experiences in Visual Thinking,* 1972) in an excellent section on the dangers of verbal categories, quotes Schachtel and then offers an example of relabeling:

. . . Schachtel, however, notes the inherent danger of labels: "The name, in giving us the illusion of knowing the object designated by it, make us quite inert and unwilling to look anew at the now supposedly familiar object from a different perspective."

Since perception is object-oriented, one way to recenter perception is to abandon object labels and to relabel the environment according to another method of classification.

8-3/rediture

Instead of labeling your perceptions according to the usual object categories, label them according to qualitative categories such as color. In place of seeing groupings of furniture in a room, for instance, see and group first all things that are red, then all things that are yellow. In other words, look for the "rediture" instead of the "furniture." Recenter again by other relabelings: look only for the "cubiture" (all things cubic), the "rounditure," the "smoothiture," and so on. Notice how a familiar room becomes new again: colors become brighter and richer; patterns, shapes, and textures suddenly emerge from the shadows of familiarity. Realize also how often you have allowed the "veil of words" to obscure and stereotype your vision.

Edward deBono (*Lateral Thinking,* 1970) has also written about the dangers of categorization:

> The major disadvantage is that a named unit which might have been very convenient at one time may no longer be convenient, indeed it may be restricting. The named assemblies of units (which are called concepts) are even more restricting because they impose a rigid way of looking at a situation. . . .
>
> The dangers of the polarizing tendency may now be summarized:
>
> • Once established the categories become permanent.
> • New information is altered so that it fits an established category. Once it has done so there is no indication that it is any different from anything else under that category.
> • At no point is it ever *essential* to create new categories. One can get by with very few categories.
> • The fewer the categories the greater the degree of shift.

If we adopt the categories of our culture, language and profession without question we severely limit our conceptual potential.

LIMITED SYNTHESES
One danger in categorization is the limitation any particular set of categories brings to any attempt at a new synthesis. The way you take anything apart completely determines the forms into which it may be reassembled. Synthesis is always prejudiced by analysis. Thus there can be no objective analysis. Because all are prejudiced no true subsequent synthesis may follow. This can be demonstrated graphically. To accept any particular categorization is to surrender part of the structuring of your intelligence to whomever sets those categories. You can't open the same limited cupboard of ingredients every day and prepare an interesting succession of meals, as any dieter knows.

OVERSIMPLIFICATION
Our cultural categories carry our values and our prejudices, and while their generalizations make it possible for us to deal with the world, they are seldom innocent or fair. Gordon Allport in *The Nature of Prejudice* (1954), proposes:

> . . . man has a propensity to prejudice. This propensity lies in his normal and natural tendency to form generalizations, concepts, categories, whose content represents an oversimplification of his world of experience. His rational categories keep close to first-hand experience, but he is able to form irrational categories just as readily. In these even a kernel of truth may be lacking, for they can be composed wholly of hearsay evidence, emotional projections, and fantasy.

AUTHORITY
The greatest danger of categorization is not its pattern or form, which seems inevitable or its content, which varies from culture to culture, but the overall authority of its structure. The seamless fabric of a culture's categories is intimidating. To look for and pick or pull vigorously at the loose threads of any hierarchy takes a lot of courage. It is much easier to sink back into the intellectual indolence that just accepts the most conventional categories available.

THE OTHER PATTERN
Even though there seems to be only one general hierarchical form which relates all our categories, there are many patterns within that form and alternative ways of diagramming them. The conventional pattern works to separate the world into closed exclusive categories by focusing analytically on the categorical boundaries. This pattern is much concerned with territorial boundaries which separate nations and with the formalities at the border crossings. The other pattern is complementary to the first and strives to comprehend the network which connects, relates or stuctures the separate categories of the first pattern. This second pattern is more concerned with essential similarities.

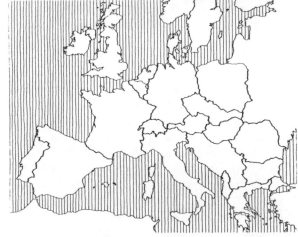

The first pattern is very much like a political map of the world consisting of the territorial boundaries of nations, while the second pattern is more like an airline's map showing the connections between the capital cities. The first pattern cuts the world into smaller and smaller pieces, measures them and names them—absolute-quantitative.

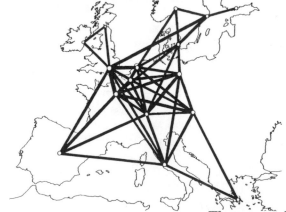

The second pattern stitches the world back together producing relational stitches and stitch patterns which it names and evaluates—relative-qualitative.

Our conceptual world seems to oscillate between these two interdependent patterns. Like the figure/field reversal demonstrations of visual perception, we tend to focus on only one pattern at a time, but a balanced oscillation is both possible and desirable. Western culture and its science-dominated intellectual world has been built on the exclusive, verbal, mathematical, linear, logical, quantifiable, left-brained pattern of definitive boundaries. We must learn to look for the other pattern in order to repair the imbalance of our cultural indoctrination. The other pattern is more often identified with Eastern cultures and is more concerned with inclusive, intuitive, qualitative, relative, right-brained unifying connections. We may understand the complementary relationship between these two patterns by turning Koestler's diagram of a hierarchy or "holarchy" on its side so that it becomes a sibling pair and listing several complementary pairs of concepts which can be seen as different forms of the same complementarity.

DIVERSITY		UNITY
EXCLUSIVE		INCLUSIVE
ANALYSIS		SYNTHESIS
DIFFERENCE		SAMENESS
ATOMISTIC		HOLISTIC
CONSCIOUS		UNCONSCIOUS
RATIONAL	OR	IRRATIONAL
VERBAL		VISUAL
QUANTITATIVE		QUALITATIVE
THOUGHT		FEELING
SCIENCE		ART
FOCUSING		COMPREHENDING

This list has a strong relationship to that assembled by Robert Ornstein (*The Psychology of Consciousness,* 1972) to demonstrate the complementary model of consciousness of the left and right sides of the brain:

THE TWO MODES OF CONSCIOUSNESS: A TENTATIVE DICHOTOMY
Who Proposed It?

Many sources	Day	Night
Blackburn	Intellectual	Sensuous
Oppenheimer	Time, History	Eternity, Timelessness
Deikman	Active	Receptive
Polanyi	Explicit	Tacit
Levy, Sperry	Analytic	Gestalt
Domhoff	Right (side of body)	Left (side of body)
Many sources	Left hemisphere	Right hemisphere
Bogen	Propositional	Appositional
Lee	Lineal	Nonlineal
Luria	Sequential	Simultaneous
Semmes	Focal	Diffuse
I Ching	The Creative: heaven masculine, Yang	The Receptive: earth feminine, Yin
I Ching	Light	Dark
I Ching	Time	Space
Many sources	Verbal	Spatial
Many sources	Intellectual	Intuitive
Vedanta	Buddhi	Manas
Jung	Causal	Acausal
Bacon	Argument	Experience

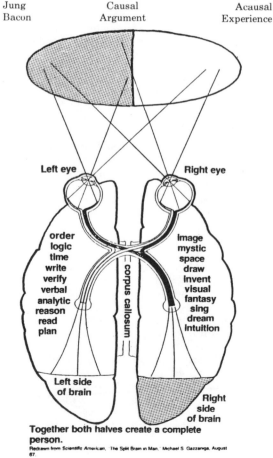

Left eye   Right eye

order
logic
time
write
verify
verbal
analytic
reason
read
plan

corpus callosum

Image
mystic
space
draw
invent
visual
fantasy
sing
dream
intuition

Left side of brain

Right side of brain

Together both halves create a complete person.

Redrawn from Scientific American, The Split Brain in Man, Michael S. Gazzanga, August 67.

CONCLUSION
We are just beginning to understand the pervasive influence of our categories, and to question the usefulness of some of our conventional categories. While such groupings have allowed the development of our minds and our language, they have also left us with our destructive compulsions for competition, discrimination, and all the abuses of privilege and power. It is clear that many of our traditional categories have outlived their usefulness, if indeed they ever had any. The continual remaking of more useful patterns and conceptual frameworks on which to organize ourselves and our world is probably the most critical task we face as designers and human beings.

51

CONCEPTUAL FUNCTION

It may seem inappropriate to make a verbal argument against *verbal* conception, and as designers you probably don't need to be convinced that words are not the primary medium of creative thought. Any book about the relationship between drawing and thinking must make the argument, however, or at least collect some of the arguments of the witnesses for non-verbal conception.

Rudolf Arnheim, in *Visual Thinking* (1969), argues that:

> ...The great virtue of vision is that it is not only a highly articulate medium, but that its universe offers inexhaustibly rich information about the objects and events of the outer world. Therefore, vision is the primary medium of thought.

Edward de Bono, in *Lateral Thinking* (1970) argues for the superiority of visual or graphic conception:

> ...The advantage of a drawing is that there is far more commitment than with a verbal explanation. Words can be very general but a line has to be put in a definite place....

> ...The advantages of a visual format are many.
> 1 There has to be a definite commitment to a way of doing something rather than a vague generalized description.
> 2 The design is expressed in a manner that is visible to everyone.
> 3 Visual expression of a complicated structure is much easier than verbal expression. It would be a pity to limit design by the ability to describe it.

Michael Polanyi, in *The Tacit Dimension* (1966), argues persuasively for another mode of knowing:

> I shall reconsider human knowledge by starting from the fact that *we can know more than we can tell.* This fact seems obvious enough; but it is not easy to say exactly what it means. Take an example. We know a person's face, and can recognize it among a thousand, indeed among a million. Yet we usually cannot tell how we recognize a face we know. So most of this knowledge cannot be put into words....

> ...The declared aim of modern science is to establish a strictly detached, objective knowledge. Any falling short of this ideal is accepted only as a temporary imperfection, which we must aim at eliminating. But suppose that tacit thought forms an indispensable part of all knowledge, then the ideal of eliminating all personal elements of knowledge would, in effect, aim at the destruction of all knowledge. The ideal of exact science would turn out to be fundamentally misleading and possibly a source of devastating fallacies.

In their beautiful book, *Seeing with the Mind's Eye* (1975), Mike and Nancy Samuels propose:

> The human mind is a slide projector with an infinite number of slides stored in its library, an instant retrieval system and an endlessly cross-referenced subject catalog....
> In a sense man has long been in conflict between the power his visual images have over him and the control he can exert over his environment through the spoken word. Both of these faculties, the visual and the verbal, are basic mental processes. Man sees; he also talks. When he talks to others, he calls it communicating; when he talks to himself, he calls it thinking. When he sees the world around him, calls it reality; when he sees in his mind's eye, what is it?
> It is only recently that this powerful, often fearful, question is beginning to be answered. What is it that goes on when we see in our mind's eye? Are we going crazy? Are demons possessing us? Are repressed terrors from the night, from our past, haunting us? These questions are so anxiety-provoking that the rise of civilization in the last 2000 years reads like a history of the social suppression of visualization and therefore a denial of one of our most basic mental processes. For visualization is the way we think. Before words, images were. Visualization is the heart of the bio-computer. The human brain programs and self-programs through its images. Riding a bicycle, driving a car, learning to read, bake a cake, play golf—all skills are acquired through the image-making process. Visualization is the ultimate consciousness tool.

EINSTEIN. One final witness for preverbal, intuitive conception may suffice. Arthur Koestler, in *The Act of Creation* (1964), documents Albert Einstein's description of the way his own mind worked:

> ...In 1945 an inquiry was organized among eminent mathematicians in America to find out their working methods. In reply to the questionnaire which was sent to him, Einstein wrote:

> "The words or the language, as they are written or spoken, do not seem to play any role in my mechanism of thought. The physical entities which seem to serve as elements in thought are certain signs and more or less clear images which can be 'voluntarily' reproduced and combined....

> ...Taken from a psychological viewpoint, this combinatory play seems to be the essential feature in productive thought—before there is any connection with logical construction in words or other kinds of signs which can be communicated to others.

> The above-mentioned elements are, in any case, of visual and some of muscular type. Conventional words or other signs have to be sought for laboriously only in a secondary stage, when the mentioned associative play is sufficiently established and can be reproduced at will.

> According to what has been said, the play with the mentioned elements is aimed to be analogous to certain logical connections one is searching for.

> In a stage when words intervene at all, they are, in my case, purely auditive, but they interfere only in a secondary stage as already mentioned."

MODELS OF CONCEPTION

Cultural indoctrination tends to explain concept formation or creativity in two different ways, obscuring the real question with another false duality. The two schools of thought or belief are extensions of the "gifted" and "science" models of the mind mentioned earlier, but which deserve further explanation since they are two more enemies of the free mind.

CULTURE'S MODELS OF CONCEPTION

REVEALED CONCEPTS. This explanation of conception is an extension of the doctrine of giftedness. The donors of conceptual "gifts" are various: Gods, ancestors, the subconscious or the environment. In all cases the conceiver is simply the passive recipient of conceptual favors. The recipient may ingratiate the various donors by certain actions and rituals, but these are always indirect. The assumption is that new concepts exist preformed in some realm remote from the average human mind and they are revealed to certain individuals in some random or predetermined (but unknowable) way. The idea of revealed concepts does not threaten the cultural status quo because by its definition creativity cannot be taught or sought directly by questioning traditional concepts.

DISCOVERED CONCEPTS also assume that preformed concepts—ultimate truths—exist but are to be discovered, not unlike an Easter egg hunt, by the analytical methods of science. Unlike revealed concepts, discovered concepts can be sought directly, but many of the assumptions we have made about that search are questionable.

Thomas S. Kuhn, in *The Structure of Scientific Revolutions* (1962), proposes:

...We may, to be more precise, have to relinquish the notion, explicit or implicit, that changes of paradigm carry scientists and those who learn from them closer and closer to the truth.

...The developmental process described in this essay has been a process of evolution *from* primitive beginnings—a process whose successive stages are characterized by an increasingly detailed and refined understanding of nature. But nothing that has been or will be said makes it a process of evolution *toward* anything. Inevitably that lacuna will have disturbed many readers. We are all deeply accustomed to seeing science as the one enterprise that draws constantly nearer to some goal set by nature in advance.

But need there be any such goal? Can we not account for both science's existence and its success in terms of evolution from the community's state of knowledge at any given time? Does it really help to imagine that there is some one full, objective, true account of nature and that the proper measure of scientific achievement is the extent to which it brings us closer to that ultimate goal? If we can learn to substitute evolution-from-what-we-do-know for evolution-toward-what-we-wish-to-know, a number of vexing problems may vanish in the process....

...The *Origin of Species* recognized no goal set either by God or nature. Instead, natural selection, operating in the given environment and with the actual organisms presently at hand, was responsible for the gradual but steady emergence of more elaborate, further articulated, and vastly more specialized organisms. Even such marvelously adapted organs as the eye and hand of man—organs whose design had previously provided powerful arguments for the existence of a supreme artificer and an advance plan—were products of a process that moved steadily *from* primitive beginnings but *toward* no goal....

Discovered concepts likewise pose no severe threat to the cultural status quo except during periods of conceptual revolution. In the relatively much longer periods of normality between revolutions, the method, direction and object of the search are all rather narrowly prescribed.

A MORE USEFUL MODEL

MADE CONCEPTS assume a free mind, and that personal human responsibility for a self-made concept is both a more true and useful way of conceiving of conception. This explanation of creativity or concept formation denies that there are any preformed or pre-existing concepts dwelling in some unknowable realm which may either be bestowed upon certain deserving recipients or discovered by dilligent searchers. It also denies that there is any particular recipe or procedure by which concepts should be made.

This notion that concepts can be, should be, and must be self-made recognizes that most creativity makes use of existing ideas and that it is only a new way of perceiving, relating or combining these existing ideas which is creative. The human potential for making new creative syntheses is, however, infinite.

The self-made model of conception also recognizes that there are many techniques which encourage creativity and that the techniques, like the conceptual realm itself, must remain infinitely open-ended.

Karl Popper's thoughts on the origin of scientific concepts are explained in Bryan Magee's *Karl Popper* (1973):

If Newton's theory is not a body of truth inherent in the world, and derived by man from the observation of reality, where did it come from? The answer is it came from Newton....

The fact that such theories are not bodies of impersonal facts about the world but are products of the human mind makes them personal achievements of an astonishing order....

MODES

We have at least three distinctly different ways of using our minds: RECALL, CONCEPT ATTAINMENT and CONCEPT FORMATION.

The first two of these dominate our educational systems, our intelligence testing and our research into cognition. Only the third mode of mental functioning can be considered free or creative and one of the unique characteristics of design education is that it asks students to function freely and creatively in this third mode. For some students this is a very confusing transition from their customary role in education, but for others it is a welcome opportunity, an isolated example of what education should be.

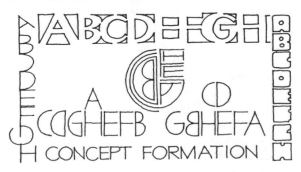

RECALL

CONCEPT ATTAINMENT

RECALL is simple rote memory and its criterion is the ability to retain and repeat information verbatum. There is no denying the continuing need for this ability and scientists tell us that the space it takes in our longterm memory is insignificant. The time it takes to adequately "address" the information so that it can be retrieved on call is what is regrettable in needless memorization. In an age of tape recorders and instant copiers it is difficult to persuade students that learning to spell, or to multiply or to develop the concentration required to retain verbal or visual information is still very important.

CONCEPT ATTAINMENT begins to be more worthy of our mental capacity, being beyond the abilities of most of our machines. The attainment of a concept requires an understanding of a set of principles or criteria which can be expressed "in your own words" and applied to varying, even novel, situations. The identification of new examples of animal life as mammals, for instance, or of a building as Gothic or Romanesque, requires the much deeper, yet more flexible, level of intelligence we call understanding.

While concept attainment is much more sophisticated than recall, its answers are still given and may be judged correct or incorrect. This "correct" categorization of ideas, actions and people is one of the devices used by indoctrinations of all kinds to assure that the members of any group will be able to tell the good guys from the bad guys and know how to react correctly in all situations.

Concept attainment, or indoctrination into an accepted paradigm is what Thomas S. Kuhn (*The Structure of Scientific Revolutions,* 1962) has called the necessary climate for normal science.

> ...Transformations like these, though usually more gradual and almost always irreversible, are common concomitants of scientific training. Looking at a contour map, the student sees lines on paper, the cartographer a picture of a terrain. Looking at a bubble-chamber photograph, the student sees confused and broken lines, the physicist a record of familiar subnuclear events. Only after a number of such transformations of vision does the student become an inhabitant of the scientist's world, seeing what the scientist sees and responding as the scientist does. The world that the student then enters is not, however, fixed once and for all by the nature of the environment, on the one hand, and of science, on the other. Rather, it is determined jointly by the environment and the particular normal-scientific tradition the student has been trained to pursue....

COMPLIANCE

The "correctness" of both recall and concept attainment make them ideally suited for the goals of conventional education because of the testing they allow.

Because of the potential for "programming" the youth of any culture with a body of information and a set of reliable reactions, recall and concept attainment comprise most of formal education. The fledgling robots can be easily tested for compliance, and sorted A, B, C, D, E on the basis of the testing. The comfortable measurability or quantification which concept attainment makes possible explains why most of education, intelligence testing and psychological research are content to stay within the limits of concept attainment.

CONCEPT FORMATION

CONCEPT FORMATION is unlike either recall or concept attainment, in that there are no fixed answers which are to be learned or discovered. The concept must be synthetically formed and evaluated by a free mind as in the previous discussion of "made" concepts vs. "revealed" or "discovered" concepts. While such concepts may provoke lively discussion or criticism, there are many different points of view and no absolute authorities. Such a use of the mind is bound to threaten the status quo and the conventional wisdom which cultural indoctrination seeks to preserve, yet this is the highest function of the human mind.

Unless we assume that humans are completely passive beings which life "happens to" or pre-programmed robots capable only of knee-jerk responses to life's stimuli, then we must assume that we are to some extent in control of and responsible for our actions. And since life is too complex to be covered by the RECALL and CONCEPT ATTAINMENT of cultural indoctrination, our dominant mental mode in day-to-day experience is CONCEPT FORMATION. We conceive and act out a day's work, a night on the town, or a two-week vacation in relative freedom and in the absence of many fixed answers. Such a view of experience makes no distinction between planning a weekend or designing a building. They are both concept formation and both are potentially creative.

The three kinds of conceptual functioning correspond roughly to a story my dad tells about a sportswriters' interview of three major league umpires on how they called balls and strikes. The first umpire recalled, "I call them like they are." (RECALL) The second answered, "I call them like I see them." (CONCEPT ATTAINMENT) Then Bill Clem, the dean of umpires at the time, allowed that, "They ain't nothin' till I call 'em." (CONCEPT FORMATION)

EXPERIENCE'S OPPORTUNITIES

The opportunities of experience offer our only chance of claiming conceptual freedom or responsibility. While evolution seems to favor freedom, cultures are generally uncomfortable with conceptual freedom and view responsibility as limited to learning, maintaining, and transmitting the culture's particular conception of the world.

In *The Ghost in the Machine* (1967), Arthur Koestler explains:

...Coghill has demonstrated that in the embryo the motor-nerve tracts become active, and movements make their appearance, before the sensory nerves become functional. And the moment it is hatched or born the creature lashes out at the environment, be it liquid or solid, with cilia, flagellae, or contractile muscle fibre; it crawls, swims, glides, pulsates; it kicks, yells, breathes, feeds on its surroundings for all it is worth. It does not merely adapt to the environment, but constantly adapts the environment to itself—it eats and drinks its environment, fights and mates with it, burrows and builds in it; it does not merely respond to the environment, but asks questions by exploring it. The 'exploratory drive' is now recognized by the younger generation of animal psychologists to be a primary biological instinct, as basic as the instincts of hunger and sex; it can on occasion be even more powerful than these....

This exploratory drive which is apparently part of our evolutionary heritage serves us well in opening cracks in our cultural indoctrination. The restlessness of youth soon discovers that many experiences which culture prohibits are at least harmless and at best very pleasant.

An important characteristic of conceivers is their experience, or lack of experience, of the self-rewards successful conception can bring. If their parents or teachers or friends valued their first efforts at "original" conceptions, by the time they reach a professional design school, "conception" has become fun, because they are confident that they are good at it.

The first attempts at this kind of conception may be making jokes or wisecracks, or providing nicknames for buddies, or suggesting how to make a Saturday afternoon interesting to a gang of friends. Children's first attempts at humor, first drawings, or first ideas about anything are usually offered very tentatively. The reception of these first conceptual offerings is more critical to their confidence in their conceptual ability, and therefore their *actual* conceptual ability, than perhaps anything else. The reception can of course be overdone, as it is when parents insist on endlessly retelling or displaying a child's creative efforts to the point of embarrassment. The trick is to accept children's first creative efforts and teach them to build on them and make them better, and most of all, to let them know that you think this kind of behavior is worthwhile, by participating with them in joking, story-telling, drawing, or just plain thinking, without trotting out any doctrine which puts down their ideas.

Ideas with which conceivers have been indoctrinated, or that they have accepted from any other source, regardless how sophisticated they might be, contribute little to experience in concept formation. Individuals may exhibit high conventional intelligence, but have little more of the conceptual ability needed in design than a filing cabinet or an encyclopedia.

This is one of the reasons that some of the best designers in professional design schools may have undistinguished academic records in high school. They may have judged, correctly, that it was much more challenging and creative to figure out how to date the prettiest girl, or become the class clown, or any number of other activities, than to become the Xerox machine or tape recorder often required to get good grades—and also a lot more fun.

Experience offers few conceptual opportunities without an initial assumption that the mind is potentially free and that concepts are made rather than given or discovered. Just as perception influences conception, so the concept of a free mind and self-made concepts will influence perception, by leading us to perceive the world and the traditional concepts of the world critically and capable of improvement. If we expect experience to be nothing more than a lifelong verification of our traditional cultural indoctrination we will probably not be disappointed.

Gibson has criticized the assumption of perceptual studies that a fixed lens on a tripod can represent our vision, and Ittleson has similarly criticized experiments involving the perception of artificially isolated objects rather than environments. Both criticisms point out that in reducing the complexity of perception for the purposes of scientific measurement the experiments lose any similarity to actual perception.

Most of the psychologists who have studied conception have done little better. They have qualified for Abraham Maslow's (*The Psychology of Science, A Reconnaissance,* 1969) comment about the behaviorists: "If the only tool you have is a hammer, you tend to treat everything as if it were a nail." Most studies of intelligence or conception are limited to tests of memory (recall) or the kind of problem solving which applies known categories and concepts (concept attainment).

The reason for avoiding the mind's most common functional mode is that the absence of fixed verifiable answers means there are no standards for quantitative measurement on which "scientific" inquiry relies. This leaves concept formation awash in the sea of value and respectable academic or scientific research prefers the solid ground of measurable certainty.

Bruner, Goodnow and Austin (*A Study of Thinking,* 1956) admit:

There is, first of all, the act of concept or category formation—the inventive act by which classes are constructed. Of this process, we have had relatively little to say here....

CONGRUENCE

This way of measuring human intelligence is as misleading as the conventional experiments in perception. In the stream of consciousness of day-to-day experience we do not normally use our minds to solve problems which have fixed answers, and we normally spend very little time in recalling verbatim information. Our minds were developed to prepare for the future, and while part of preparing for the future is certainly the remembrance and application of lessons from the past, the relationship is a link, not a chain.

Unless my consciousness is incredibly unique, the normal conceptual mode is concept formation, a continual synthesis of what I want to do with what I should do or can do. There is a continual *congruence* involved, but unlike recall or concept attainment it is not a *compliance* with some fixed standard set by science or society. I must make and take responsibility for both sides of this congruence, both the side which represents what I should do and/or can do and the side which represents what I want to do.

This is one of the great benefits of design education, and the source of a painful transition for many design students. They are suddenly criticized for *both sides* of the congruence, not just how they solved a design problem, but also their perception/conception of the problem to be solved.

Many of the great conceptual advances in human knowledge have come about because the thinkers redefined the problem side of the congruence, because they saw a different problem to solve.

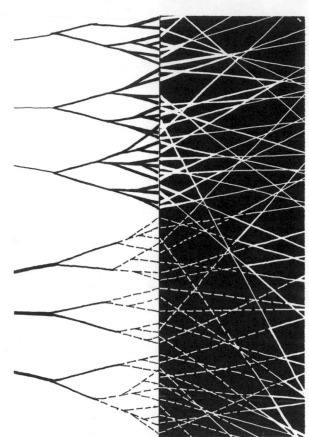

Another inhibiting habit which we carry over into free conception from our indoctrination in *concept attainment* problem-solving is the idea that the "problem" side of the congruence is antecedent to the "solution" side, and that once established should remain fixed. In normal everyday *concept formation* it doesn't work that way. Early success on the solution side of the congruence will raise my goals or aspirations on the problem side. I may begin willfully with what I want to do and change my definition of what I should do to fit it. It is only with reverse order congruences like this that I will ever raise or redefine my idea of what I can do.

The congruences involved in the normal *concept formation* mode can best be understood by considering an average day in our lives.

WEDNESDAY

Each of us in each week of our lives has a category called "Wednesday" and, unless we are content to rise every Wednesday morning like a new goose and let Wednesday happen to us, we actively PERCEIVE/CONCEIVE/ACHIEVE our Wednesdays. On Thursday morning when we awake we can never say that we "correctly" did Wednesday. We can count our money, notice in whose bed we awake, and check out bodily functions, but our Wednesday is not capable of any kind of objective measurement.

Wednesday can only be measured against what we, individually, set out to accomplish on that day. No one else can ever tell us whether we successfully perceived/conceived/achieved Wednesday or not, except within very narrow categories, like "legally" or "financially" or "physically" or "morally", and there is an obvious argument against letting others decide most of these. The fact that we can never *measure* Wednesday does not excuse our ignorance of the kind of conception involved in perceiving/conceiving/achieving Wednesday.

Wednesday, any Wednesday, is like the open category of any design problem, discussed earlier. It will be established by its relationship to the larger whole of the week, year or lifetime, and to the smaller moments that make up its 24-hour duration as well as laterally to Tuesday and Thursday, or other Wednesdays.

solution — problem
means — ends
next Wednesday — past Wednesdays
new solutions — old problems
new problems — old solutions
ACTIONS — CONSEQUENCES
RISKS — REWARDS

**line of
continual
synthesis**

Wednesdays will have certain invariables (rise, bathe, breakfast), some periodic variables (design committee luncheon meeting) and some specific variables (client meeting at 4:00 p.m.); but except in the most extremely regimented environments Wednesday will be mostly ours to conceive and, even within our regular or specific tasks, will include all sorts of opportunities for conceptual freedom (what to have for breakfast, what to discuss at the luncheon meeting, and what to think about when only our physical presence is required).

What we expect to accomplish or experience on a given Wednesday will vary according to what we can conceive based on our resources, our abilities, our experience and our environment.

I know from experience that it is difficult for a country boy to conceive of the set of experiences that can be strung together on a Wednesday in New York or London or Paris if you have the resources and the energy and some knowledge of what is available. These simple, everyday, commonsense variables still make more difference in conception than the labyrinth of methods, strategies and tactics into which some psychologists and design methodologists have led us.

Conception is only one function of the eyemind-hand triad of human intelligence and so it is interdependently related to perception and action. Experienced conceivers who are confident of their resources, their abilities and their environment perceive a much richer potential for any Wednesday; and if they are accustomed to success in matching what they want to do with what they should or can do, they anticipate Wednesdays as an opportunity for satisfying achievement. The concept of Wednesday which they form is fundamentally different from those for whom Wednesday is only another boring or threatening period of time.

Most design "problems" are as open as most Wednesdays and they are conceived by the same kind of concept formation, varying wildly with the experience, the resources and abilities of the conceiver or designer and the context of the so called "problem." To call such design opportunities "problems," in our everyday understanding of that word, or to call the activity which responds to them "problemsolving" is to make the same error of oversimplification psychologists do when they oversimplify mental functioning by removing all the complex variables in which any real world conceptual task is wrapped.

CONCEPTUAL DRAWING

The succeeding chapter on REPRESENTATION will contain a detailed discussion of drawing's relationship to the design process, including the conceptual phase. Here I would like to discuss the role of drawing in conception in a more general way by looking at the complementary kinds of synthesis it promotes, and by considering the externalizing sequence in which drawing is the catalyst.

THE ROLE OF DRAWING in conception varies widely from designer to designer, depending on their confidence and experience with drawing. There seem to be at least six different roles which drawing can play in the design process:

- drawing persuasively sells the product—

- drawing neutrally prints out the results of a mental process that occurs separately, privately and previously—

- drawing communicates the process—

- drawing participates in the process—

- drawing leads the process—

- drawing is the process—

Even prescriptions for the design process which mistrust drawing would concede its usefulness in graphically presenting certain analytical relationships as in graphs and matrices, and later in the process, the similarly neutral role of recording ultimate design decisions in plans, sections and elevations which can serve as patterns from which to estimate costs and construct the design.

These views of drawing are essentially the same as those an executive would hold of the activity of typing or key-punching—that it is some sort of automatic activity which is best delegated to some underling, demands accuracy and competence, but is not really an opportunity for creativity.

Another view of drawing's relationship to the design process is that its most useful role is that of *selling* the products of the process. In this view drawing is similarly separated from the decision-making process and may easily be farmed out to another kind of underling, a professional renderer, just as the responsibility for a firm's public relations may be given to an advertising agency.

If drawing is relegated either to the role of a neutral print-out mechanism or of persuasively selling the designed product, it is essentially excluded from any significant role in the design process. If, on the other hand, we assume that the activity of drawing is an inseparable part of designing anything that will be experienced and evaluated visually, that drawing at least *participates in the process,* then a whole range of much more useful roles for drawing emerges.

There should always be something *beyond the drawing* for which the student is responsible and for which the drawing is only a representation. Otherwise the drawing becomes an end in itself and ceases to be a design drawing.

THE DOUBLE SYNTHESIS

When we begin to draw whatever we are designing a very unique phenomenon occurs. It is as if the drawing were made with a pantograph (a device which, when one of its two drawing or writing heads is used to draw or write, produces, by a connecting armature, a remote image of variable size which is an exact copy of the original drawing or writing). The original drawing is an overt image, in the world, on the paper for all to see; but it is as if there is a simultaneous second drawing which is a covert image drawn in our consciousness, on the surface of our experience network or memory.

This double drawing manifests two kinds of syntheses, each of which is seeking a kind of congruence, and this double synthesis and the congruences it seeks deserve careful consideration.

THE OVERT SYNTHESIS is that which occurs in the world, on the paper and is open to everyone. When we begin to make representative drawings of whatever we are designing we must collect all the separate precepts, concepts, notions and hunches we have about a design problem into a committed whole. Without drawing we could continue to speculate endlessly in words about what the design should be, but the moment of truth represented by those first drawings cuts through all the verbage. For the first time the design solution must undergo a physical synthesis. For the first time it can be seen and evaluated by the designer and by others.

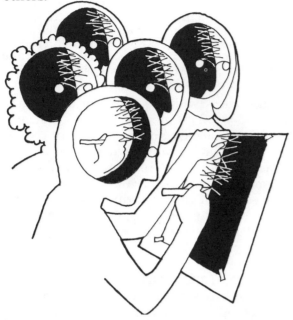

This synthesis in itself is very beneficial because of the holistic commitment it requires. The synthesis also makes possible the evaluation by the other participants in the design process; the client, the consultants, and other members of the design team, and begins to test the congruence between the physical solution proposed and its supporting rationale.

Once the design is represented by drawings it becomes a member of Karl Popper's World 3, the product of minds, and can be evaluated and tested logically. Popper, our greatest philosopher of science, makes clear the importance of objectifying ideas so that they can be openly criticized. His thoughts on the matter are summarized in Brian Magee's excellent *Karl Popper* (1973):

> Throughout his account of the evolution of life and the emergence of man and the development of civilization, Popper makes use of the notion not only of an objective world of material things (which he calls World 1) and a subjective world of minds (World 2) but of a third world, a world of objective structures which are the products, not necessarily intentional, of minds or living creatures; but which, once produced, exist independently of them....

> World 3, then, is the world of ideas, art, science, language, ethics, institutions—the whole cultural heritage, in short—insofar as this is encoded and preserved in such World 1 objects as brains, books, machines, films, computers, pictures, and records of every kind....

> ...This underlines the enormous importance of objectifying our ideas in language or behavior or works of art. While they are only in our heads they are barely criticizable. Their public formulation itself usually leads to progress. And the validity of any argument about them is again an objective matter: it is not determined by how many individuals are prepared to accept it....

THE COVERT SYNTHESIS occurs in the designer's consciousness, imprinted on the experience network, and is a very separate and private matter. When we begin to draw our ideas we integrate the third component of human intelligence, the hand, (as representative of the body) with the eye and the mind. Drawing completes the *eyemindhand* triad so that we become a perceptual/conceptual/actual whole. We no longer have the artificial detachment of the observer or the critic. We have now represented our ideas *with our hands* and that simple action commits our whole selves to an identity with the proposed solution in a way that observation and speculation never could.

This second synthesis also seeks a congruence, but not with a logical, communicable

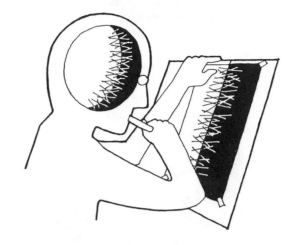

rationale like the overt synthesis. The private congruence sought by the covert synthesis in our consciousness is immediately felt, not reasoned. But it is this private inner synthesis and its congruence with our hopes, wishes and feelings for the solution that is the more important. The overt synthesis of our design can be a disaster in terms of matching the verbal or mathematic criteria of a problem's program; or in terms of being able to support it with any even remotely reasonable rationale; yet, in our gut, or in our heart, or in whatever body part you want to represent that inner synthesis that includes *all* of whatever we are, we may feel, may *know* we have the best solution. The reverse may also be the case and this is perhaps even more painful. Our solution may match the words and numbers of the problem's program flawlessly, and the rationale which supports the design may be so obvious and logical that the client grasps it immediately, but somewhere deep inside us, the inner congruence is awry and we know the design stinks.

The separateness of the double synthesis is critical. A designer must cultivate the difference between the two because the dimension which separates what satisfies clients or the general public and what satisfies the designer is in many ways the measure of the designer's ability and integrity.

When designers surrender the separate opinion of that inner synthesis and are content whenever others are content, we will have lost much of the value we have as designers.

THE SIMULTANEITY of the dual drawing is demonstrated in the immediacy of the experience of conceptual drawing. In many cases we know *as we draw* whether the particular relationship represented by a line we are drawing is congruent or incongruent with our intentions for the design. This is because our intentions for any design are represented somehow in our experience network (from the mindmodel offered earlier). When we attempt to draw the design, we are drawing *on the surface* of the experience network which holds the vague intentions, wishes, and hunches we have for the solution. We know immediately *as we draw* if the emerging physical synthesis of the design is congruent or incongruent with our intentions for the solution.

Robert H. McKim explains the simultaneity and the feedback loop involved in his excellent *Experiences in Visual Thinking* (1972):

> ...drawing and thinking are frequently so simultaneous that the graphic image appears almost an organic extension of mental processes....

> Graphic ideation utilizes seeing, imagining, and drawing in a cyclic feedback process that is fundamentally iterative. I have given this "feedback loop" the acronym *ETC* (etcetera) to dramatize the importance of repetitive cycling to the graphic development of visual ideas.

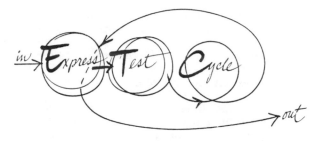

Fluent and flexible ideation, deferred judgment, and unhesitating translation of idea into sketch are important ways to open the gates that hold back ideas. However, the importance of *drawing skill* to the full expression of visual ideas must not be overlooked. Inadequate drawing ability has three negative effects on the *E*xpress phase of *ETC*: (1) a clumsy sketch usually evokes judgmental processes that restrict or stop idea-flow, (2) ideas that cannot be adequately recorded in sketch form are often lost, and (3) attention devoted to problems of drawing is attention diverted from idea-generation.

The effort at congruence also works in the opposite direction. The drawing often causes us to change the pattern of our intentions *to fit the drawing*. We may see opportunities for improving or extending our understanding of the design task as we draw tentative solutions. The act of drawing shows us, makes us see, relationships and opportunities that we would never confront verbally. This simultaneous synthesis in search of congruence also explains the spontaneous momentum we feel when drawing *becomes* design.

This is described in an unpublished Master's Thesis by William D. Martin at M.I.T. called *The Architect's Role in Participatory Planning Processes: Case Study—Boston Transportation Planning Review:*

> Sketch design manipulation of pattern relationships provides the architect with insights and information which may stimulate the recall of other patterns or may be used to modify the content of patterns currently in use. Such information may also change the architect's perception of the problem itself resulting in shifts in objective, appropriate methods and form requirements, and thereby suggesting new, more appropriate patterns and programs.

Congruences which occur from a changing perception of the design task may also be delayed. In looking over week-old or month-old drawings we may suddenly recognize a congruence or potential congruence that wasn't there before, because our perception/conception of the problem to be solved has changed in the week or month since we made that drawing—perhaps *because* we made the drawing.

EXTERNALIZATION

In considering the conceptual synthesis as happening over a period of time, I will discuss the series of activities as having an INTERNAL phase, an EXTERNALIZING phase, and an EXTERNAL phase. What follows is certainly not a method, but a collection of observations and comments on certain habits, attitudes and abilities which seem to promote or inhibit conception.

Before discussing the various phases of the externalization of design concepts I would like to propose an alternate analogy for any open category which becomes a design concept. In addition to the earlier diagrams for categories, any conceptual category may be thought of as the conjunction of many relational strings, much like the "other pattern" of connecting relationships discussed earlier.

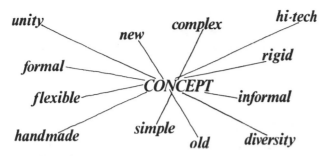

unity complex hi-tech
new
formal rigid
CONCEPT
flexible informal
handmade simple
old diversity

Each relational string represents one of the opposing pairs in an equivalent rank of any hierarchy, what was earlier called the lateral or sibling relationship. Such a set of relational strings for the concept of a particular *residence* might be communal/private, open-/secure, warm natural/cool efficient, natural handcrafted/high-tech, site dominant/site related, compact/attenuated. Any design concept may be diagrammed as one of many slip knot conjunctions which connect particular points on various relational strings. This slip knot conjunction may be thought of as only one of an infinite number in the experience network suggested earlier as a part of the metaphorical mindmodel.

THE INTERNAL PHASE of the conceptual synthesis has two parts: a conscious part, which can be discussed and a subconscious part about which little discussion is possible. The conscious part of the internal phase can be thought of as going into our *eyemind* in search of the appropriate area of our perceptual/conceptual experience network.

Newell and Simon call this our LONG TERM MEMORY. Experienced designers, dealing with a familiar conceptual problem may find a part of their perceptual/conceptual network which fits the conceptual task at hand, like a template.

The searching inside and outside the *eyemind* can be thought of as a search for a way of making relational connections from the

particular conceptual task to the existing perceptual/conceptual network. This is very much like finding or making guitar strings, attaching them, and then tuning the relational connecting strings to the proper pitch.

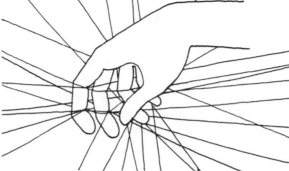

The strongest conceptual relationships are not single strings, but sets which, when tuned correctly like a guitar, strike whole chords of relationships. The relationships represented by the strings are never static. They have a direction and to move one way along a relational string is quite different from moving in the opposite direction. To see how a building is like a city is to recognize that the relationship is one of scale and complexity which changes along the string.

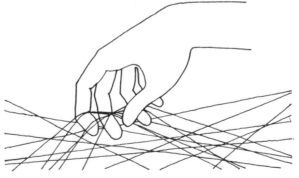

RETRIEVAL of any concept or set of concepts, to return to the language of the computer analogy, is very much like plucking one or several of the relational strings so that a portion of the perceptual/conceptual network is pulled away.

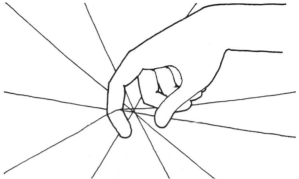

While inexperienced designers can be thought of as plucking the network with one finger tentatively, experienced designers go at it with both hands confidently. To extend the metaphor further, timid designers or thinkers are cautious in the distance they pull the conceptual subnetwork away from the larger perceptual/conceptual network.

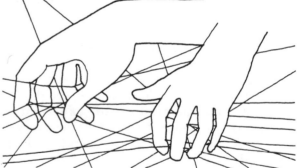

Bold designers and thinkers pull the subnetwork so far away that the tension in the relational strings at the edges becomes extreme, unafraid, and in fact, anticipating that the pull of any particular conception may shift the larger network. It is possible to think of the separation of this subnetwork from the larger network as complete, so that the subnetwork's integrity depends on naming the broken discontinuous ends. It is better, however, to look for the subnetwork's integrity in its inner relationships not its outer separations, so that the relational strings which connect it to the larger network are not broken, but alive with tension.

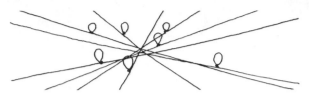

This retrieval capability is strengthened in so-called "creative" people. They store perceptions in such a way that the relational strings protrude from the network like loops or handles, in anticipation of future retrieval. Early in life they have become confident in making and using their perceptual/conceptual network and they store perceptions creatively "cocked" for anticipated conceptual retrieval.

One last extension of this metaphor is that in the better-developed of the perceptual/conceptual networks, a pull on one of the protruding relational loops pulls out a fantastically intricate and extensive piece of the network. Adel Foz, in his M.I.T. Master's Thesis (*Some Observations on Designer Behavior in the Parti*, 1972) observed that one of the distinguishing characteristics of experienced designers was that they could retrieve larger and more intricate "chunks" from their long term memory.

During the internal phase of conception, there is a great deal of searching—stretching relational strings and testing the chords they produce for a resonance which matches the designer's understanding of the conceptual task. Good designers are usually acutely aware of what has been designed by others. Any design profession shares an extensive perceptual/conceptual network in the form of books, periodicals and the existing built environment. There is also a vigorous exploration of this existing shared perceptual/conceptual network and any new perceptual/conceptual networks available. This explora-

tion may take the form of searching the library for published examples of solutions to similar problems, or the work of admired designers; or it may mean physically exploring similar built environments. The designer moves over the network like a harpist looking for chords and when promising chords are struck, there is a search for chord progressions. While inexperienced designers may have to work with individual notes and struggle to assemble them into chords, experienced designers can work almost immediately with whole complex chords and chord progressions.

Since the relational perceptual/conceptual network is multi-dimensional, there are certain manipulations which are best thought of spatially and temporally. Taking the example used before of seeing how a building is like a city, we can run all the way along the relational string in either direction. Is a room like a building in the same way a building is like a city? Is a region or country like a city in the same way a city is like a building? This might be called linear string running.

Further back are questions of what are the classes or relationships and further still, questions of evaluating the classes of relationships and then of evaluating the value systems.

Or we can step back and ask what class of relationship it is that makes a building like a city—part to whole? We have thus moved back to a more generic level of the network.

To move forward is to become more specific. Why is this particular building like this particular city? The movement in the specific direction asks for discrimination and definition, not so much relational connections as separating distinctions.

We can also move sideways and ask what things of the same scale are like a building—a ship? an airplane? Or we can jump categories radically and ask how a building is like education or civilization.

Much of this exploration and manipulation can be done internally with abstract representational images. The images may be supplemented with words, but their form is primarily visual because of their spatial/temporal relationships.

If the designer is inexperienced or if the conceptual task is unfamiliar, the designer may have to make repeated searches outside the *eyemind* network to find perceptions with which she or he can make appropriate perceptual/conceptual connections to the existing network.

William D. Martin's thesis states:

> For the "inexperienced" architect who had no appropriate conceptual framework, the orientation period was very much like learning a new language, and much time was spent building up a basic "vocabulary" of appropriate transportation—related design examples (patterns) and rules for using them (programs)....
>
> On reconnaissance trips, it was as if he had programmed his perceptual mechanisms (eyes and brain) to screen out all "irrelevant" data from the built environment and to selectively search the remaining information for the best interpretation of available data on highway form elements for addition to his expanding vocabulary of patterns.... In addition, the architect's habitual sketching and doodling helped reinforce LTM [long term memory] pattern development through simple graphic explorations of various form elements suggested by reconnaissance and research.... Most of these graphic manipulations were not at this point seeking solutions to particular problems, but were rather testing hypothetical combinations of various highway form elements.

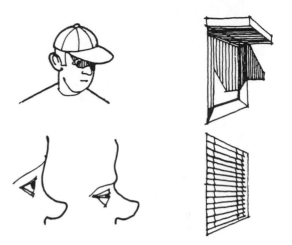

Where no appropriate sub-section of the designer's perceptual/conceptual network can be found, a conceptual task will lead us to search outside the network in order to make an appropriate perceptual/conceptual subnetwork. The search described above included and shaped perception, and used design drawing to record pieces and combinations of pieces of the new subnetwork as graphic external memories.

Externalized doodles can be used very effectively as questions or precepts to be answered or followed in subsequent conception. An excellent collection of this kind of program or precept diagramming is to be found in Tim White's *Ordering Systems* (1973), and *Introduction to Architectural Programming* (1972). This is a particularly useful way to ease into the external phase of the conceptual process since these doodles are not yet solution proposals and thus have a neutrality that brings little of the fear of failure with them. The transition from question, precept and intention doodles, to proposed solution doodles is easier than trying to hold the process internally until a fully formed solution can be externalized in a drawing.

The activity of making a new perceptual/conceptual subnetwork is an active weaving of a new conceptual category. Bruner, Goodnow and Austin, in *A Study of Thinking* (1956), write:

> ...We have found it more meaningful to regard a concept as a network of sign-significate inferences by which one goes beyond a set of *observed* criterial properties exhibited by an object or event to the class identity of the object or event in question, and thence to additional inferences about other *unobserved* properties of the object or event.... The working definition of a concept is the network of inferences that are or may be set into play by an act of categorization.

The ability to create a new category or perceptual/conceptual subnetwork for a particular conceptual task—CONCEPT FORMATION—is probably the hallmark of human intelligence. This ability is symbolic of the flexibility and adaptability that has been the key to our evolutionary success as a species. This ability demands confidence and responsibility in the use of intelligence beyond any fixed set of rules. It is beautiful to experience and to watch in other human beings.

EXTERNALIZATION, instead of representing a distinct division between the internal and external phases of conception, is better conceived as a transition or relational string. Design drawing begins to participate directly in the design process at this point and is, in fact, one of the criteria of externalization. When a design can be represented by a drawn form, pattern, or diagram, we say it has been externalized.

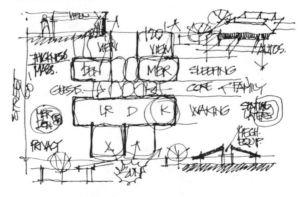

Strictly speaking externalization begins during the INTERNAL phase in the form of the graphic note-taking described in Martin's thesis and illustrated in White's books. This is a very natural way to break the blockage of giving your ideas physical form in drawing. This ability may be developed by trying to make as many of your notations to yourself as graphic as possible.

ANALOGICAL DRAWING is another way of beginning to externalize conception so that it involves the hand. "Drawing analogies" is also a rich source of conceptual relationships. Almost all prescriptions for creativity include the search for relationships between the "problem" or its parts and similar, or even dissimilar problems which have been solved. W. J. J. Gordon (*Synectics*, 1968) has identified specific analogical categories (direct, personal, fantasy and symbolic) which will be discussed later under DRAWING'S RELATIONSHIP TO THE DESIGN PROCESS.

The act of drawing an analogy usually deepens an understanding of how well or how little it is like what we are working on. If the analogy is a good one its correspondence to the problem at hand may have an unexpected richness which is extended by drawing it. It is also surprising how many facets of any design problem may be drawn analogically. The site, the function, the climatic context, the construction process, even the overall problem (not just its solution) offer analogical opportunities which will deepen a designer's understanding and provide unsuspected conceptual opportunities.

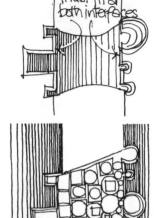

Designing a transitional space is like.
....

must fit at
both interfaces

being a go-between,
middleman or negotiator.

One final reason for drawing analogies is that they are so beautifully efficient in communicating design ideas to clients and consultants. Creative analogies synthesize the essential qualities of any design concept in a way that nothing else can and make them much more quickly accessible to anyone whose understanding and approval you need.

In the computer analogy, externalization is the "printout." This externalized printout may be graphic or verbal. I am convinced that its purest, truest form is GRAPHIC and that verbal printouts are only distorted translations in a prejudiced, if remarkable, secondary symbol system.

Language is one of the miracles on which human intelligence stands, but its inadequacies are often forgotten in the awe of the achievement. That it is a secondhand translation of thought is clearly demonstrated by the fact that so much of the language of philosophy or poetry is spatial, and spatial qualities are much more directly represented graphically than verbally.

64

Robert H. McKim, in *Experiences in Visual Thinking* (1972), argues that:

> ...The dichotomy that mistakenly links verbal thinking with abstraction and visual thinking with concretization was undoubtedly conceived by individuals who identified visual imagery with postcard realism and failed to observe visual abstraction as expressed in contemporary art and abstract graphic-language forms. Abstract graphic languages encode abstract ideas, not concrete things....

As a design teacher, I have grown increasingly frustrated with the verbal printouts of my students' conceptual processes. In creative writing or law, the appropriate conceptual printout might be verbal, but in any of the design disciplines the only meaningful printout is visual or graphic.

By permission of Johnny Hart and Field Enterprises, Inc.

The externalization of a design concept can be thought of as a rolling *eyemindhand* wheel. The stronger concepts come rolling into reality out of the externalization starting

SCREECH

By permission of Johnny Hart and Field Enterprises, Inc.

gate, rather than scooting out on one flat side soon to be stopped by inertia. The rolling of the wheel represents a chain reaction using the *eyemindhand* to conceive, present, perceive, evaluate, reconceive, represent, reperceive, and reevaluate. During this chain reaction a designer is using the three evolutionary tools which make us human and if those three tools have been carefully sharpened and we know how to use them as one confident intelligence, a real pleasure accompanies the process.

William D. Martin (*The Architect's Role in Participatory Planning Processes: Cast Study—Boston Transportation Planning Review*) witnesses:

> Sketch design in this manner might continue for only a few moments or perhaps some several hours with perceptions of form relationships between current patterns providing continuous feedback and stimulating the recall of additional patterns and pattern linking programs from LTM. The process stops when the architect reaches a desired point of design development or when he has posed questions which require informational inputs from outside his current problem space, or perhaps when he finds he has no appropriate patterns in LTM for the form relationships suggested by current problem requirements.

Drawing is often the weakest link in this cycling chain reaction and the entire purpose of this book is to bolster your drawing ability so that your *hand* can be an equal partner with your *eye* and your *mind*.

Adel Foz, in his M.I.T. Master's Thesis (*Some Observations on Designer Behavior in the Parti,* 1972) says:

> ...he continually strives to externalize his ideas and form proposals into external memory devices thereby keeping STM [short term memory] clear. By not requiring STM to hold both an object and tests of its significance simultaneously, its capacity is freed for invention and testing activities.

> ...he uses EM [external memory] devices [design drawings] to display and correlate information automatically, again freeing STM from having to perform a task and retain its results. He uses representational media as analogous as possible to the final physical product, i.e. perspective drawings and models.

Let me describe what I have observed from trying to help design students learn to get into this phase of the design process, using an *eyemindhand* wheel as a metaphor.

The design process may be triggered by any of the three components of the wheel or by indistinguishable combinations of the three components. This initial overcoming of inertia may be very difficult or very easy and most design teachers push very hard on two of the three components. They tease and provoke the mind verbally and show the *eyemind* visual examples. This "teacher push" rarely includes the *hand,* but it should, perhaps by simply asking students to draw a graphic abstraction of the problem.

Most times, teachers are more interested in talking about the direction of the rolling wheel.

Students respond to this pushing of their conceptual wheel in various ways, depending mostly on the experience and confidence they have in using the three components of the wheel. Some students begin to draw right away, but have difficulty explaining or justifying what they are drawing. Other students begin to make verbal notes or outlines or talk about their ideas. Others begin looking in libraries and at real situations.

Most of what is written about the design process or design methodology assumes that drawing is or should be delayed until there is "something to draw" in the form of an internal verbal or visual image. This view would assume that the drawing third of the *eyemindhand* wheel can never initiate the rotation. There are also writers, DeBono for instance, who advocate random verbal stimulation as a creativity technique. Random graphic stimulation is even more valuable and needn't undergo any artificial translation from words. Drawing allows the participation of our subconscious or preconscious in ways that are not fully understood. If we look at the design drawings we make carefully and expectantly in anticipation of recognizing unintended patterns and relationships, we can learn to find them. Whether such illogical, preverbal recognition is the participation of our subconscious, or is only the recognition of our subconscious participation in making the drawings is not clear, but such pattern recognition is neither verbal nor logical. There is no reason why such pattern recognition cannot be stimulated initially and directly by random drawing.

The difficulty in overcoming the inertia of the conceptual wheel may indicate a flat tire which represents the student's least confident ability and this deflated segment of their ability wheel may constitute a continuing problem to the smooth rolling of the wheel.

Teachers' responsibility is to help the design student pump up the flat areas of the wheel so the student can roll it confidently and smoothly. They may then spend most of their time in deciding the most promising direction to roll it.

Design teaching depends on the externalized printout of the conceptual process. Little communication is possible during the internal phase of conception and it is only after the printouts begin to occur that teaching can begin because until then there is no common referent for discussion. There are certain blockages to externalization which cause conceptual printouts, and particularly drawn conceptual printouts, to be withheld.

The search for a perfect full-blown concept is perhaps the most prevalent blockage to externalization. The mythology which surrounds creativity promotes this extension of the internal phase and inhibits the open, communicable process which is necessary for the participation of clients, and the learning from discussion with peers or teachers. In my experience, it is also a sign of weakness, since the really confident designers externalize a concept rather quickly and manipulate it vigorously through an extended external conceptual phase in which the initial externalized concept changes a great deal. They can draw or talk about the concept all through this external phase and they are in confident control of the changes and refinements that take place.

A second blockage to externalization is the inability, or lack of confidence in the ability, to print-out the concept in an acceptable verbal or graphic form. Design students may feel that their first attempts at verbal or graphic communication are unworthy of representing the qualities they see in the concept in their *eyemind*. Even though they feel their concept is as good as those of their fellow students, they may be intimidated by the verbal or graphic eloquence which they see in their peers' externalization of their concepts.

James L. Adams describes the difficulties he has experienced in getting his students to use drawing as a conceptual tool in *Conceptual Blockbusting* (1974):

> As I have previously mentioned, we work with an extremely verbal group of students at Stanford. A great deal of effort has been put into their verbal (and mathematical) abilities during their formal education, but little into their visual ability. When they come to Stanford many are, in Bob McKim's frustrated terminology, "visual illiterates." They often are not used to drawing, or to using visual imagery as a thinking mode. Although their drawing is generally not good, it is usually good enough (especially with a few helpful hints) to use as a thinking aid. Nonetheless, they are usually extremely reluctant to draw because their drawings compare so badly with drawings made by professionals (intended for communication with others). We try to encourage crude but informative drawings for the student's own purposes. We also try to encourage improving one's drawing skills, since we find that good drawing skill is a powerful conceptual aid....

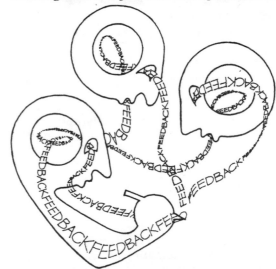

Both the first two blockages are expressions of a more basic fear of failure or ridicule by comparison, which is one of the first obstacles to design education. Unfortunately, the obstacle is increased by the pressure of deadlines and the compulsive grading and sorting of students which accompanies most design education. Students must somehow cope with externalization, however, or they will miss a great deal of the teaching and learning which they need. The early externalizers automatically get more teacher and peer attention because they have something to see and talk about.

Design drawing can be perhaps the most helpful catalyst of externalization. The internal searching of the relational perceptual/conceptual network is a search for images and patterns, but only a limited number of these can be found, held and compared, unaided by external graphics, in our *eyemind*. During this internal searching, it is natural and normal that the images and patterns with which a designer is working begin to be externalized piecemeal in the form of conceptual doodles and diagrams. The advantage of beginning externalization at this very early stage is that externalized doodles and diagrams can be evaluated for design playback, displayed and compared with alternative doodles, manipulated, revised, and kept as a record of the conceptual process.

Experienced designers, who habitually and confidently use drawn doodles and diagrams early in the conceptual process, learn to represent and see a great deal from these simple graphic images. With intelligent use, they can become a shorthand which is much superior to verbal language.

The basis of the superiority of doodles and diagrams is that they involve the *eyemindhand*—all the evolutionary tools of intelligence. The *eyemind* can perceive and evaluate more than the *mind* alone and when the *hand* has made the visual images, the *eyemindhand* is imprinted with the conceptual patterns. The drawing of the conceptual doodles or diagrams also allows a better understanding of the concept because our *eyemindhand* interactively works with it.

The *eyemindhand* wheel turns, and each rotation brings a deeper understanding of the concept's relationships, and a refinement of its best form. This process distills the concept into its most meaningful and efficient form, stripped of extraneous details. For the confident designer, the conceptual diagram becomes the concept, and the designer's *eyemind* learns to see in the externalized diagrams, qualities and relational possibilities that were impossible to discover in the concept's internal form.

THE EXTERNAL PHASE has been reached when designers experience what is called "analogue takeover": when asked about the design, they let their drawings speak for them; when instead of thinking about the design without any physical or graphic referents, they actively manipulate the representative drawings or models and spend considerable time just looking at those drawings or models. Whatever means we use to trigger the externalization of conceptual images, once externalized, and in whatever form, they can be manipulated, evaluated, and communicated to others.

Robert H. McKim (*Experiences in Visual Thinking,* 1972) explains the advantages of ideas which have been externalized as drawings:

> Drawing not only helps to bring vague inner images into focus, it also provides a record of the advancing thought stream. Further, drawing provides a function that memory cannot: the most brilliant imager cannot compare a number of images, side by side in memory, as one can compare a wall of tacked-up idea-sketches.

Adams (*Conceptual Blockbusting,* 1974) argues for the necessity of graphic externalization:

> ...In order to take full advantage of visual thinking ability, *drawing* is necessary. Drawing allows the recording, storage, manipulation, and communication of images to augment the pictures one can generate in his imagination. In the Design Division, we find it useful to divide drawing into two categories: that which is done to communicate with others, and that which is done to communicate with oneself....

These graphic manipulations should include a variety of graphic languages as they progress from conceptual doodles to realistic perspective representations. In addition to what follows under DRAWING'S RELATIONSHIP TO THE DESIGN PROCESS, my book, *Drawing as a Means to Architecture* (1968), demonstrated some of these; Paul Laseau's *Graphic Thinking for Architects and Designers* (1980), is filled with excellent examples of the flexibility and progression possible in using graphics in the design process; Kurt Hanks' and Larry Belliston's *Draw* (1970) and *Rapid Viz* (1980), are excellent stimulating collections of externalized conception; and one of the most handsome demonstrations, ranging over several design disciplines, is collected in Robert H. McKim's *Experiences in Visual Thinking* (1972), in which he proposes:

> ...Indeed, ability to move from one graphic language to another, along the dimension of abstract-to-concrete, is probably the most useful kind of graphic-language flexibility....

In McKim's chapter, "Out of the Language Rut," he makes very clear, with beautiful examples from the personal graphic languages of a great variety of designers, the fantastic ranges of conceptual graphic languages:

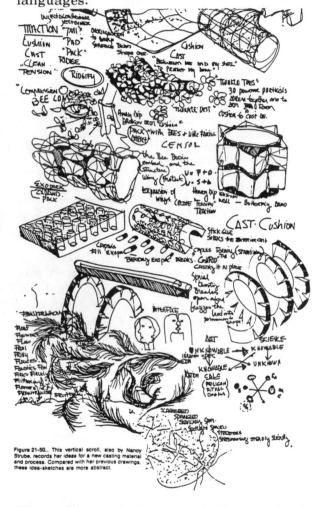

Figure 21-50.. This vertical scroll, also by Nancy Strube, records her ideas for a new casting material and process. Compared with her previous drawings, these idea-sketches are more abstract.

The rolling of the *eyemindhand* wheel through these design drawing manipulations will soon need to begin to leave a track of words, by which the design can be explained verbally. The verbal questions of teachers, bosses, and clients, outside your personal conceptual process, will need to be answered.

As the designers roll the wheel toward more realistic representational design drawings, they look back over the ground it is covering for a supporting rationale. If they perceive a track of verbal rationale, the wheel settles into and deepens that track. If no track of rationale is perceived, the designer must change the direction of the rolling wheel in search of more impressive ground. Some design methods imply that the design process proceeds on the basis of verbal or mathematical logic, although none can explain the "magic leap" from words to three-dimensional form. I believe it is much more honest to admit that the words are literally an afterthought. Words can describe a conceptual design task and, after the conceptual design solution is established, they can frame its rationale; but in the white heat at the core of the conceptual synthesis, words are only in the way, and are replaced entirely by groans, whistles, sighs, expletives, and the scratch of pen or pencil. Words may also mislead by the many glowing, honorific adjectives which carry our hopes for the design solution. The eye is little persuaded by verbal eloquence, however, and may not see these qualities in the drawings. Verbal descriptions may also be spatially impossible. You may think you are going to organize the house around an atrium, but until you draw it

you won't know if you have enough rooms or budget to go around. As long as design concepts remain in designers' minds or words they may be impossible or irrational. It is only when they are synthesized in drawings that they become subject to open objective rational argument.

Drawing can make at least these contributions to the conceptual sequence we call EXTERNALIZATION:

- Drawing can make graphic notes which efficiently record spatial or temporal relationships and clear our SHORT TERM MEMORY for more important tasks.

- Drawing can record and extend the analogies for various aspects of the design task which deepen understanding and are the source of unexpected creative relationships.

- Drawing is a catalyst which can trigger, provoke, symbolize and record formative images, some of which may change the designer's perception of the conceptual task.

- Drawing as an activity completes the integration of the *eyemindhand* triad of human intelligence.

- Drawing allows the participation of the subconscious in the forms and patterns it offers for recognition and inclusion in the design synthesis.

- Drawing synthesizes the various precepts, concepts, wishes and hunches about the design task in concrete physical form which can then be openly evaluated and manipulated by the designer and others during the external phase of the design process.

REPRESENTATION

This section of the book is concerned with the various drawings we make as representations of whatever we are designing, from concept to finished product. These drawings are very important because they represent the design to our eyeminds, and we must be very careful to understand their limitations and the prejudices they carry. Of all the strongholds of traditional dogma in design education, the conventional drawings and the order in which they are undertaken is the most strongly defended, if indeed it is ever questioned at all. It is time we inquired critically into the traditional representational drawings, their relationship to experience and to the design process, as well as alternative techniques for making them. The ways of thinking about these drawings and the methods advocated here for making them are not presented as the most technically accurate or artistically admired, but because I have found they can be understood and applied by design students with little previous background in drawing—they work. My aim is to help any student of design learn to use drawing as a design tool, not to teach students who already know how to draw to make masterpiece renderings, nor to demonstrate how well I can draw.

In order to see drawings in a more useful way it is necessary to rethink the conventional categories which we normally employ in describing and thinking about drawings. Traditionally we categorize drawings by their media and form, and we believe when we have described a drawing as a *pen and ink plan* or a *pencil perspective* we have said something very significant about the drawing. These two traditional categories, media and form, are a hybrid inheritance from art and drafting. From art we have adopted the notion that the chemical composition of the drawing (ink, graphite, charcoal, etc.) is of great importance. In schools of art the curriculum is normally categorized, at least in part, in terms of the media used, with courses called Beginning Watercolor or Advanced Oil Painting. From drafting we have accepted the formal naming of a drawing (plan, section, elevation, etc.) as being as significant as naming the medium. This traditional categorization is almost useless for design drawings. The *medium* in which a design drawing is made is of no significance whatsoever, even secondarily, and unless the designer is aware of and deliberately chooses a particular drawing for its relationship to experience or to the problem or the solution, the *form* of the drawing may also be meaningless.

I believe there is a much more relevant way to categorize design drawings, and to structure this chapter on REPRESENTATION.

• *the drawing's relationship to experience*

• *the drawing's relationship to the design process*

In the light of these two relationships the conventional ways of thinking about design drawings in the categories of form and media seem trivial.

These two relationships are the best way I have found for a designer to think about representational drawings, but it is much more important that you, as a designer, make and continually remake your own best way of thinking about them, so that you can make intelligent choices. Never mindlessly accept and use any kind of drawing without questioning its value and never assume that the drawings you are making have any particular or necessary relationship to experience or to the design process. The choices and relationships are your responsibility as a designer, and you should keep them alive and well. To always make the same drawings in the same way and in the same order is to continue unquestioningly using the same method, when we know that choice of method may be the most potent variable in anything we do.

DRAWING'S RELATIONSHIP TO EXPERIENCE

The word "design" or "designing" implies an activity which is separated from "making." Sculptors, painters or poets can enjoy a direct interaction with their creations through the clay, the paint, or the language which forms their means of expression. They do not *design* their sculptures, paintings or poems so much as they *make* them. In contrast to this immediate experience of making, we environmental designers are always separated from the reality of what we are designing. The making of our designs is normally carried out by other people and increasingly by machines, separated from our designing of them by time and space.

This separation requires us to work with *representations* of reality to propose, see, evaluate, change and communicate our designs; and we must be very clear in our understanding of the relationships these graphic representations have to the experience of the built environment. It is important to remember that design drawing is *always* representational. A design drawing repre-

sents a thought or a synthesis of several thoughts, which is one of a set or series of possible alternatives to be evaluated in a design process. Design drawings must communicate honestly, openly and with essential accuracy. This also means that design drawing should be as quick and free as your thought process. Like the verbalization of an idea, a design drawing is a statement, more or less congruent to a thought, whose truth and eloquence can only be evaluated visually.

TRANSCENDENCE. The goal of all representational drawing should be to make the environment being designed *real* to the designer's eyemind. Representational drawings must be more than just an assemblage of lines and tones on paper. They must take on a separate reality of their own in space or as space, and in relationship to their context and their users. They must transcend all the trivia of technique and their physical form *as drawings* and become a believable presence in the consciousness of the designer.

TRANSPARENCY. The best way of achieving the desired transcendence is to learn to accept your drawing ability, wherever it is at the moment, and look *through* your drawings to the potential reality of whatever you are designing. This transparency is promoted by drawing very credibly, so that the accuracy of the representation is unquestioned, and by drawing very simply, in a way that calls little or no attention to the drawing, *as a drawing*.

This neutral transparency can be illustrated by an analogy using our written language. In reading these words you are probably unaware of the form or style of the typeface. The letters are *transparent* as letters, and you look right through them to the meaning of the words they form. It is possible, however, to begin a series of *CHANGES which will make the* LETTERING PROGRESSIVELY CALL MORE & MORE ATTENTION TO ITSELF, lose its transparency and become almost opaque TO ANY MEANING BEYOND the style of the lettering.

71

DESIGN DRAWINGS must retain their transparency so that the attention of the designer is always focused *beyond* the drawing, on the reality of what is being designed, not at the level of the drawing itself. To be separated from what we are designing by time and space is difficult enough; we mustn't allow the form or technique of our representative drawings to separate us even further from reality.

THE RELATIVE REALISM OF THE DRAWINGS

When the forms of the various drawings used in design are arranged in a descending hierarchy based on their relationship to experience, such a hierarchy reverses the traditional order in which drawings are discussed, taught or even named. In the design professions, "Plan, Section and Elevation" enjoys the same dogmatic invocation as "Father, Son and Holy Ghost" in the Christian religions. The test for the depth of the hangup is to find the three words written in any other order—in our literature—in our schools—anywhere. This conventional order is a *construction* order which we have mindlessly adopted as the best or only way of thinking about the drawings.

Architects, and perhaps other designers, have for too long tended to conceive and represent their buildings as objects, viewed from outside, and to concentrate their efforts on the perception of their designs as built objects. This has always seemed to me (*Drawing As a Means to Architecture*, 1968) a strange way to design and evaluate buildings, since the entire reason for building the building is to enclose space. The quality of the enclosed space would seem to be much more important than the exterior of the enclosure.

This way of looking at what we are designing, as an object, is indispensable in the design process, in conceiving and working out the integrity of any design as an object. The sense of reality I am concerned with here, however, is the perception and representation of the building, interior or exterior space, as an *environment*. Environment perception is fundamentally different from object perception. The reality we experience every day is perceived as an environment which surrounds us, and in which we actively participate. Any representation of the built environment which artificially separates the experiencers and makes them merely observers of a separate object denies reality.

PERSPECTIVES

When we take the drawing's relationship to experience as the ordering criterion, perspectives immediately surface as the most realistic drawings. Their closeness to experience depends on the skill with which they are drawn, but even the crudest perspectives show more of the experiential qualities of an environment than elaborate plans, sections or elevations. In the representational phase of any design process, they offer the best possible prediction of what the environment will be for several reasons:

PERSPECTIVES are more qualitative than quantitative. The experiential qualities of an environment can be perceived directly from a perspective. Light and texture, which are the main qualities of surfaces, are much better shown in perspective as they are in reality. The qualities of the spacetimelight continuum are much better represented and understood in perspective.

PERSPECTIVES represent the third dimension realistically. The depth or thickness of objects or spaces contributes more than anything else to their achieving a real presence in the designer's eyemind. This three-dimensional quality helps the drawn environment transcend the flatland of lines on paper and become a believable reality.

The third dimension which the perspective reveals allows the perception and study of inside and outside corners both vertically, as at a wall corner, and horizontally, as at intersections of wall and floor or wall and ceiling. These three-dimensional corners are the key to the making of environments and they can only be seen and studied in perspective.

PERSPECTIVES represent, more than any other drawing, the human kinesthetic experience of an environment. Correctly drawn, perspectives can predict much of the interest that will be available in moving through a space or around an object.

While multiple perspectives are needed to show extended spatial sequences, a clear sense of the spatial experience promised by movement through an environment can be shown in a single perspective. This anticipated kinesthetic experience is what gives environments much of their experiential interest and it can be sensed from the entrance to a space or from a single viewpoint as in a perspective.

PERSPECTIVES include the viewer by presenting the environment from a particular viewpoint. The perspective's viewpoint is a place made especially for the viewer by the drawing, into which he or she steps in a way not possible in any other drawing. This inclusion of the viewer is uniquely like experience which always includes us. Unlike the other drawings, in which reality is a separate object which we look AT, we are always included in experience, and of all the design drawings, only perspectives accomplish this inclusion.

PERSPECTIVES need no artificial supporting dogma about their relationship to experience. The qualities of the environments they represent can be judged directly in an instant. They are subject to less misinterpretation, because the qualities are either there or they are not, and their presence or absence is sensed directly in almost exactly the same way we perceive environments in reality. This direct communication allows us to use the lifelong development of our senses, not just the pseudosenses developed to overcome the obscure communication of the orthographic abstractions.

The drawing of perspectives was first mastered during the Renaissance and developed, according to Bronowski, from the insights of the Moorish mathematician Alhazen. Brunelleschi, Alberti, Ghiberti, da Vinci, and Michelangelo all knew and eagerly used perspective in representing their designs. Albrecht Durer traveled to Italy to learn the method and wrote a treatise on it upon his return to Germany. Bronowski credits the development of the rules of perspective as having been one of several significant discoveries of the underlying structure of reality. In *On the Rationalization of Sight* (1938), William M. Ivins, Jr. proposes that perspective construction allowed all the successive

From GIOVANNI BATTISTA PIRANESI. DRAWINGS AND ETCHINGS AT COLUMBIA UNIVERSITY

From CANALETTO: GIOVANNI ANTONIO CANAL, 1697-1768 by W. G. Constable

discoveries of science by accounting for the changes in the external appearances of the world, so that objects might retain the internal integrity which science assumes.

The remarkable ability of perspectives to represent the experience of any existing environment has been largely forgotten with the subsequent invention and development of photography. There is no longer any reason to *draw* an existing environment, and the ease with which any environment may be photographed makes us forget the relatively brief period during which the cityscapes of Canaletto or the vast interiors of Piranesi demonstrated the excitement of being able to reproduce the visual experience of an environment by perspective drawing.

Although we no longer need to draw the existing world, the *only* way those who propose alternative environmental futures can accurately represent those environments to themselves and to others (short of the photography of very large and meticulous models) is by drawing perspectives.

FIG. 18. THE COSTRUZIONE LEGITTIMA AS IT WAS DRAWN BY LEONARDO

THE OTHER 3-DIMENSION DRAWINGS

Next in the hierarchy of realism come the other three-dimensional drawings. These drawings are called AXONOMETRIC or PARALINE and while they are much easier to draw than perspectives, because all their parallel lines remain parallel in the drawing, and all their orthogonal lines are directly measurable, these advantages eliminate the convergence and foreshortening we perceive in reality.

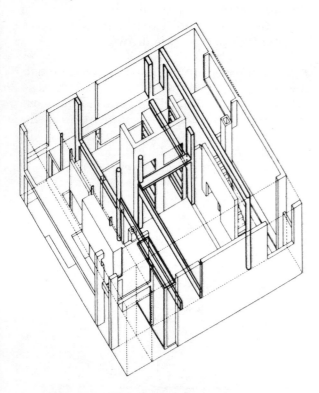

When considered in the hierarchy of realistic drawings AXONOMETRIC drawings are clearly a regression from experience toward quantification; their lack of convergence and foreshortening distort reality, and their man-

datory aerial viewpoint and exclusion of the viewer further sacrifice the experiential quality which perspectives offer. Axonometric drawings (ISOMETRIC, OBLIQUE, etc.) are currently enjoying a renewed popularity because, in addition to their requiring less skill in the delineator, they make a very nice *set* of drawings when formally published with plans and sections. Their visual consistency with the orthographic projections

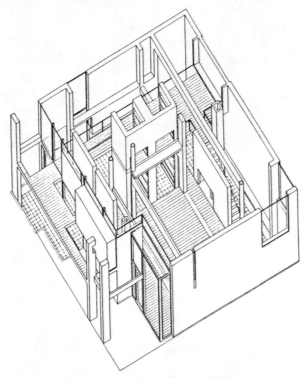

From FIVE ARCHITECTS: EISENMAN, GRAVES, GWATHMEY, HEDJUK, MEIER
by Peter Eisenman, Philip Johnson, Colin Rowe & Kenneth Frampton

(plan, section and elevation) is precisely because they have retreated a similar distance from experience. They, like plans, sections and elevations, are drawings of objects, not environments.

PLAN, SECTION AND ELEVATION

The conventional drawings which we use in designing any environment are the traditional orthographic abstractions which are necessary as working drawings. In any hierarchy based on the drawing's relationship to experience, however, they run dead last, and no amount of tradition can raise them any higher. These drawings are valuable for taking off quantities of materials and for ordering certain structural and mechanical systems and for studying certain functional relationships. However, they were developed as patterns from which to build a space or object, and have a very limited relationship to experience. They are inadequate and misleading as representative design drawings for the following reasons:

PLANS, SECTIONS AND ELEVATIONS are entirely quantitative, not qualitative. The qualities of a designed environment cannot be read directly from the conventional drawings. We talk endlessly about these qualities and supposedly value them above anything else, but in the conventional drawings which we use to represent our designs, they are completely invisible. The orthographic abstractions do not directly indicate functional pattern or anything about the qualities of privacy, light, sound or tactility. The plan shows an object or space here—this shape—this orientation—this wide—this long—with these openings. The section shows, in addition, this volume—these thicknesses—this high and with this relationship to the ground. The elevation shows an object or space this long—this high—with these openings. These are very clear instructions for building something, and that's about all they are.

The ability to see qualities in a quantitative drawing can supposedly be acquired, but I seriously question the extent to which they can ever be seen, and surely the idea of deliberately using an obscure form of communication and its rationalization is perverse.

PLANS, SECTIONS AND ELEVATIONS are two-dimensional and give no indication of the third dimension. Plan, section and elevation are often explained in reference to a fold-out box. This is an excellent way to explain the drawings and their limitations as design drawings. They present a flat face to the observer that is an abstraction, since the space or object can never be viewed in a similar way. Because of this two-dimensional flatness, they tend to just lie there on the paper, incapable of becoming a real three-dimensional presence in the designer's *eye-mind*. Further, the evaluation of these two-dimensional drawings tends to degenerate into sheet borders, line weight, north arrows, and the many trivia connected with the abstract formality of such drawings—trivia related to the paper, the graphite or ink, and the formal rules for making the drawing.

PLANS, SECTIONS AND ELEVATIONS offer fragmented views of what will be experienced as a three-dimensional whole. An indication of the obscurity of such fragmentation is that drafting teachers often assign drafting "puzzles" in which their students are given two of the three orthographic views of an object, and then asked to *discover* the correct form of the object and draft the third and missing orthographic view. Such exercises would seem more appropriate for cryptographers than for environmental designers.

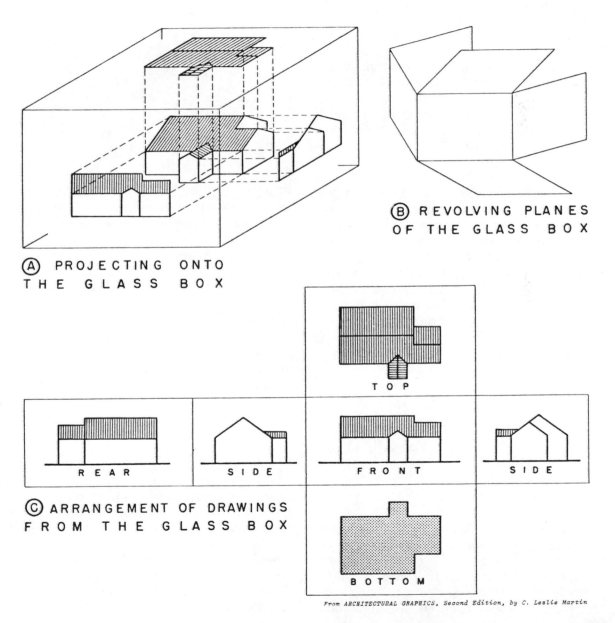

(A) PROJECTING ONTO THE GLASS BOX

(B) REVOLVING PLANES OF THE GLASS BOX

TOP

REAR

SIDE

FRONT

SIDE

(C) ARRANGEMENT OF DRAWINGS FROM THE GLASS BOX

BOTTOM

From ARCHITECTURAL GRAPHICS, Second Edition, by C. Leslie Martin

75

PLANS, SECTIONS AND ELEVATIONS, unlike perspectives, whose space *envelops* and *includes* the viewer, *exclude* the viewer and are therefore preceived as separate objects in space. Our perceptual prejudice for seeing wholes and for perceiving a dominant *figure* on a recessive *field* results in our manipulating such drawings as separate, formal, visual images. This perception of the conventional drawings results in configurations that are *of the drawing* and that make little sense in reality. T, H, and I-shaped buildings and all symmetrically-designed arrangements probably result from this preoccupation with overall form as seen in the plan abstraction.

PLANS, SECTIONS AND ELEVATIONS have little to do with human experience. Perhaps the most damning of all the inadequacies of plan, section and elevation is that they are almost impossible to evaluate experientially, expecially by the layman. Yet we say that we are designing environments primarily for our fellow human beings and we hope they will participate in the design process and we wonder why they have difficulty relating to the environments we design.

By drawing human figures in elevation, you can tell the viewer how high a window sill is, but there is no way to tell him if it is deep enough to sit in. A light line in plan might indicate a floor-material change, a step, or a 36" high counter. There is no indication whether a human will trip over it or lean against it. The entire future experience of the environment must be imagined with very little qualitative help from the drawings.

PLANS, SECTIONS AND ELEVATIONS are particularly weak in conveying any sense of time or movement—the kinesthetic experience of space or objects. Some vague notion of the experience of movement can be perceived in looking at the plan, but a section or elevation tells us absolutely nothing about the experience of moving toward, through, or around the spaces they represent.

If the ultimate evaluation of designed spaces and objects is to be the experience of the human senses, then it is perverse to limit the predictive representative drawings to those which have such a tenuous relationship to experience.

PLANS, SECTIONS AND ELEVATIONS are supported by centuries of unquestioned dogma which misleads us in thinking about them. This dogma implies that they are the best, most proper, easiest and often *only* representative drawings for the design of an environment. I will concede that they are the easiest, but the unquestioned propriety of tradition and convention does not persuade my intelligence that they are the best.

The traditional dogma with which we support the exclusive use of plans, sections and elevations stands on a very strange foundation.

THE USE OF CONSTRUCTION DRAWINGS AS DESIGN DRAWINGS. Initially, the design professions were not separated from the construction or craft professions. The functions for which spaces or products were designed were uncomplicated, the forms and ways of making environments were traditional, and the range of innovation very limited. In addition, the people involved in any decision-making process were fewer— the owner or patron and his chosen builder or craftsman. In such a context there was perhaps no need for an extensive investigation of alternatives, and the conventional drawings which were used to make the space or object could adequately predict and communicate whatever slight modifications were proposed from some previous design.

Most important of all, the practice of using the orthographic construction drawings to represent designed spaces or objects was firmly established centuries before the drawing of perspectives was developed during the Renaissance.

INCOMPETENCE IN DRAWING PERSPECTIVES. Our incompetence in drawing perspectives is also understandable, if inexcusable. Perspective drawing has been taught as a complicated procedure that can only be initiated after the design's appearance has already been determined in plan, section and elevation. It has generally been badly taught in the drawing courses for designers, because these are usually large classes with not enough time allowed to give individual attention and correction to perspective drawing. Subsequently, design teachers often allow the skill to atrophy by seldom demanding that students draw perspectives or certainly never more than one. All this amounts to a tacit agreement that the drawing of perspectives is too difficult and time-consuming to teach and, probably, is beyond the ability of most students. This attitude leads to the mistaken notion that to require students to present their work in perspectives is to give those who happen to be able to draw perspectives an unfair advantage and, therefore, is discriminatory. We have now completed one of those elaborate excuse systems with which we manage to rationalize incompetent teaching as being morally mandatory.

The ambivalence of our attitude toward perspectives often shows up in exhibitions of students' design projects. The projects selected for exhibition usually display a reasonable balance in the presentation drawings. Even in the best projects, however, the lonely perspective which actually shows the experiential qualities of the design is often the weakest drawing, has had the least design and drawing attention, and was drawn last.

In the projects which receive mediocre or low grades and are never displayed, this weakness in perspective is even more exaggerated, and very clearly shows an inept design. I think this says several things about design teachers and design students. It indicates that those students who understand perspectives well enough to use them as representational drawings in their design process produce the best designs. It also indicates that design teachers appreciate perspectives as well as the other drawings, even though they spend little time teaching the skill of drawing perspectives and require only one or two to communicate the design.

THE EMBELLISHMENT OF THE ORTHOGRAPHIC ABSTRACTIONS. The embellishment of the orthographic abstractions is often promoted to extend or improve their lack of experiential quality. This embellishment takes two forms: an elaborate, tedious rendering of materials and shadows, or an applied, supposedly qualitative, notation system.

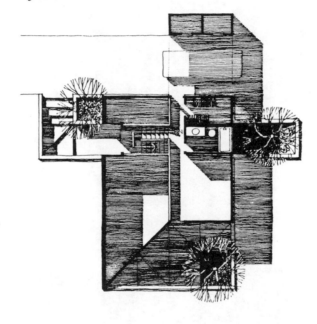

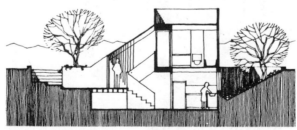

The tedious, pseudo-realistic rendering of plan, section or elevation in order to add experiential qualities is a waste of time. These drawings are basically abstractions and valuable as such, but to try to make them into drawings which represent reality is nonsense when you can draw perspectives.

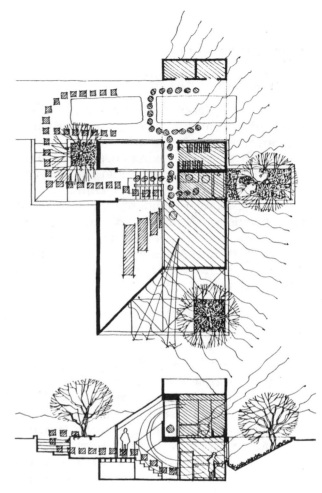

Notation systems applied to plan, section and elevation are also valuable at the conceptual level to symbolize the designer's intentions, but during the representation phase their appearance on the orthographic abstractions signifies nothing as to whether they could actually be experienced in the built space or product. I have wasted hours in architectural design reviews listening to students' glowing descriptions of experiential qualities that supposedly existed in their floor plans, and neither they nor I will ever know whether they were there or not.

77

DRAWING TECHNIQUES

Having considered the relationship of the forms of the various drawings to experience, we can now turn to the different techniques by which design drawings are made, *their* relationship to experience and the possible criteria for choosing one technique over another. Before we evaluate the realism of the various ways of drawing, however, we need a way of categorizing the techniques, and even at this secondary level, I would not recommend the traditional categorization based on medium.

BASED ON PERCEPTION
SURFACES AND EDGES

Since design drawings must represent a proposed environmental reality, and since we gain most of the information about our environment through visual perception, it would seem more meaningful to classify drawing techniques as to how they represent the most important cues by which we perceive space rather than by the media in which they are drawn. As Gibson points out, our perception of space is dependent on our perception of continuous spacebounding SURFACES, and as a corollary of our perception of surfaces, our perception of the discontinuities between surfaces—their EDGES. Looked at in this way, drawing divides into two complementary ways of representing the environment: edge drawing and surface drawing, which I have called LINE DRAWING and TONE DRAWING (*Drawing As a Means to Architecture,* 1968). This way of categorizing drawing is thus based on the environment and the way we perceive it, rather than on the tools with which we draw it.

From THE TECHNIQUE OF DRAWING BUILDINGS by Richard Welling.

LINE DRAWING delineates the *edges* and not the *surfaces*. The drawing effort is concentrated in representing all the edges in the environment directly with a line, indicating the relative depth of edges by variations in line weight. In contrast, surfaces are not directly rendered, although their overall shape is indicated by their edge lines.

From ARCHITECTURAL ILLUSTRATION: THE VALUE DELINEATION PROCESS BY Paul Stevenson Oles

TONE DRAWING delineates the *surfaces* and not the *edges*. The drawing effort is concentrated in rendering the texture and relative illumination of the various surfaces. In contrast, edges are not directly delineated with an edge line, but remain simply a discontinuity between two surfaces.

LINE DRAWING and TONE DRAWING thus take opposite approaches in representing our perception of reality, and the astounding thing is that line drawings can even come close to tone drawings as representations of the real world. Tone drawings *look* most like reality, their ideal being a black and white photograph. Line drawings can compete because they are condensed abstractions of most of the important cues to our *experience* of space.

The success of line drawing stands on the number of perspective cues that can be carried by lines, the fact that as perceivers we are perpetually moving systems, and the attention we have paid to edges through our millions of years of evolution and in our daily experience of the world.

Using the thirteen kinds of perspective abstracted from Gibson in Edward T. Hall's *The Hidden Dimension* (1966), and quoted earlier in the chapter on perception, we find that:

• Five of the thirteen perspective cues to the perception of space are never directly available in drawings:

    4. binocular perspective
    5. motion perspective
    7. the perspective of blur
    11. shift in the amount of double
        imagery
    12. shift in the rate of motion

• This leaves eight of the cues which can be directly represented in drawings. Three of these eight can only be directly represented in TONE drawings:

    1. texture perspective
    6. aerial perspective
    13. transitions between light and shade

• The remaining five cues which can be represented in drawings can all be directly represented in LINE drawings:

    2. size perspective
    3. linear perspective
    8. relative upward location in the
        visual field
    9. shift of texture or linear spacing
    10. completeness or continuity of outline

These five cues are all carried by planar corners and spatial edges, which are represented directly by the lines of a line drawing No. 3—linear perspective—also assures that surfaces, though not directly rendered in LINE drawings, are represented rather well by their edge lines, whose shape in linear perspective tells us the surface location, orientation and relative depth.

• In addition to the direct representation of these five cues, LINE drawings can *indirectly* represent two cues from the initial list of five which can never be represented *directly* in any drawing, and these two cues cannot be represented effectively in TONE drawings, even *indirectly*:

    4. binocular perspective
    12. shift in the rate of motion

While these perspective cues are only directly perceived by moving through an environment they occur at the spatial edges of any environment and if a line drawing is spatially profiled, as I will recommend, it can represent these cues indirectly by emphasizing the edges at which they will occur. Such an emphasis is impossible in TONE drawings.

• LINE drawings can *indirectly* represent a third perspective cue which can only be *directly* represented in TONE drawings:

    13. transitions between light and shade

Since such light/shade transitions must always occur at planar corners or spatial edges, however, they are always represented *indirectly* by lines in any LINE drawing.

Of Gibson's thirteen perspective cues, LINE drawings can directly represent five and indirectly represent three others (two of which involve movement and are not available to a similar emphasis in TONE drawings). TONE drawings can directly represent eight of the thirteen perspective cues, but their inability to emphasize the *kinesthetic* perspective cues makes them surprisingly little better than LINE drawings as representations of the experience of space.

The ideal photographic representation of the TONE drawing is a *still* photograph, and by contrast human perceivers are almost never still. We make micromovements of the pupils of our eyes out of consciousness; we constantly change the focus and direction of our eyes; we move our heads; and we move our entire bodies through our environment in a variety of ways. In those movements which actually change the position of our eyes (head and body movements, or when we walk or are carried through our environment) there is a violent slipping or sliding at all the edges within our visual field. All the surfaces and some of the objects in our visual field undergo either progressive hiding or revealing by the edges of nearer surfaces or objects. Our perception of any environment just during our brief movement *into* it has informed us of all the edges which hide space. We *never* perceive our environment as a still photograph. Our initial movement into any environment tells us more than hours of subsequent staring will reveal.

The last reason line drawings can represent reality so well is the most interesting to me, and it also has to do with edges. *Everything* that the human race has ever seen throughout the millions of years of our evolution has invariably appeared from behind an edge.

The edges in any environment carry the kinesthetic experience of the space, and a LINE drawing which uses line weight to indicate a spatial hierarchy at these edges can abstractly represent the experience of the space.

The edge may be the moving edge of our peripheral vision, or an edge around which we move or around which some other mover moves. It is over edges we have fallen; it is from behind edges that our enemies have surprised us; and beyond edges that our loved ones have disappeared. The future has always marched out at us from behind the edges of our visual world. One of the first games babies learn and love to play is peek-a-boo. Our evolutionary survival has depended on our close attention to edges, and even if such a valuable perceptual habit is not yet transmitted genetically, we can count on our experience to imprint it at an early level of our learned responses to the environment. If some 85% of our information about the world comes to us through visual perception, and all of that 85% appears to us from behind the edges in our visual world, we learn to attend to edges very early in our lives.

LINE DRAWING succeeds because it condenses and emphasizes the cues on which our perception of space most depends. LINE drawings are like an *outline* of our experience of the visual world.

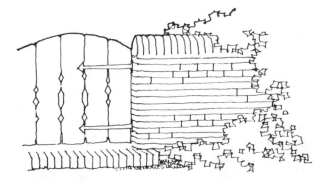

From THE TED KAUTZKY PENCIL BOOK by Ted Kautzky

TONE DRAWINGS can add the three spatial cues which are impossible to communicate in line drawings:

> 1. *texture perspective*
> 6. *aerial perspective*
> 13. *transitions between light and shade*

In addition, tone drawings can bring all the realistic richness of the visual world offered by what Gibson in *The Senses Considered as Perceptual Systems* (1966), calls, "The Structuring of Ambient Light." Gibson points out three conditions which structure ambient light:

DIFFERENTIAL FACING. The main reason for the existence of borders in an ambient array is the faces of reflecting surfaces—that is, the differing inclinations of their planes to the prevailing illumination.... At a fine level the array may be said to have *texture;* at a coarse level it has *form;* but there is no clear separation between them.

SURFACE COMPOSITION. A second reason for borders in the array is the differing reflectances of adjoining substances in the world caused by their differing chemical compositions. *Reflectance* is defined as the proportion of the incident light that is reflected (or transmitted) back into the air instead of being absorbed.... In commonsense terminology, it is the *whiteness* of a substance, the variable from white to black....

ATTACHED SHADOWS. The relative inclinations of terrestrial surfaces facing the main source of illumination cause differences in the structure of light, as noted above, and so do the relative inclinations of surfaces facing *away* from the illumination, but the latter gets much less light to reflect and are said to have *attached shadows*. The plane angle, or dihedral angle, between a surface facing toward and a surface facing away from the illumination therefore yields an especially strong border....

All these conditions which structure light can be represented in TONE drawings; this is their main contribution to the representation of reality and not possible in LINE drawings.

All other drawing techniques are variations or combinations of LINE drawing and TONE drawing, and rather than repeat a detailed verbal description of the various techniques (see *Drawing As a Means to Architecture,* 1968), I will complete this brief discussion of the variations and combinations using examples of various buildings drawn by other architectural delineators.

*From ARCHITECTURAL DELINEATION
by Ernest Burden*

TONE OF LINES drawing is an alternative way of making a TONE drawing by replacing the smooth flat tones with tones built up of individual lines. The line weight is constant, with the relative lightness or darkness of any tone depending on the spaces between the lines.

*From NEW ARCHITECTURAL DRAWINGS
by Helmut Jacoby*

LINE AND TONE drawing is a combination of the two basic techniques which exploits the strengths of each and offers more flexibility and manageability than any other drawing technique. This technique will be discussed at length in the next section, BASED ON UTILITY—CRITERIA FOR EVALUATION and again under DRAWING AS AN INVESTMENT HIERARCHY.

*From MORE THAN STREETS (forthcoming)
by William Kirby Lockard*

BLACK AND WHITE ON MIDDLETONE is a variation which may be applied to all three tone techniques: TONE, TONE OF LINES and LINE AND TONE. It begins with a middletone paper and goes in both directions at once—toward white and toward black. Its apparent efficiency is always impressive, and it is a great technique to use whenever you think you might not get finished, because you somehow get credit for all that middletone paper. Unfinished drawings are much more acceptable on middletone paper than on white.

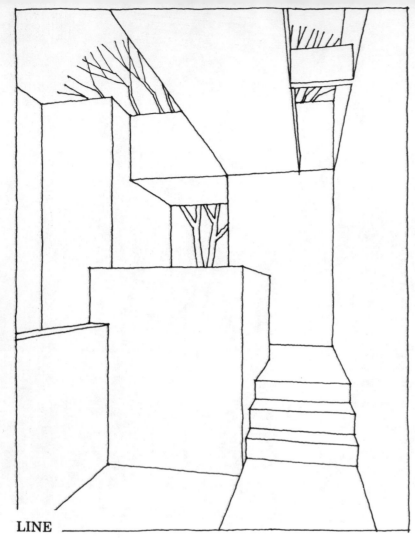

LINE ───────────────

- *spatial edges and planar corners defined with lines.*
- *surfaces unrendered.*

time factor: 1
skill factor: 1

The series of drawings which follows demonstrates the most useful way I have found of categorizing the various drawing techniques. Any thorough understanding of representational drawing needs some deeper way of thinking about drawing than in terms of medium. The basis for the present categorization is the way each technique represents the visual cues by which we perceive space.

LINE·SPATIALLY PROFILED ───────────

- *spatial edges and planar corners defined with lines.*
- *spatial edges profiled — the farther an edge lies in front of its background the heavier the line should be, except that its heaviness should be lightened in proportion to the distance it is away from the viewer.*
- *surfaces unrendered.*

time factor: 1½
skill factor: 1

If you will learn to look at drawings in some such structured way, you will find an infinite number of variations and combinations all around you and your understanding of the range of alternative ways of drawing will become much clearer.

TONE

- *surfaces toned evenly in relation to their differential reflectance of light.*
- *spatial edges and planar corners defined by a change in tone — no lines.*
- *stroking direction should respond to vertical or horizontal orientation of the surfaces, with the horizontal stroking always going toward the farthest vanishing point.*
- *surface tones may be graduated within the surface to heighten contrasts with other tones at the surface's edges.*

time factor: 10
skill factor: 10

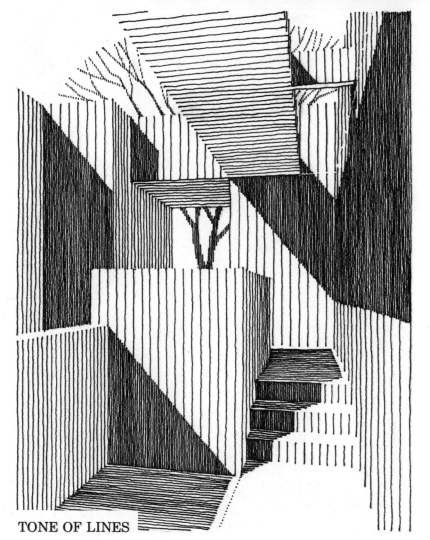

TONE OF LINES

- *surfaces toned in relation to their differential reflectance of light.*
- *tones made up of evenly spaced lines.*
- *spatial edges and planar corners defined by a change in line spacing — no spatial edge lines.*
- *direction of lines should respond to vertical or horizontal orientation of the surfaces, with horizontal lines always going toward the farthest vanishing point.*

time factor: 12
skill factor: 8

LINE AND TONE

- *spatial edges and planar corners defined with lines.*
- *spatial edges profiled — the farther an edge lies in front of its background the heavier the line should be, except that its heaviness should be lightened in proportion to the distance it is away from the viewer.*
- *surfaces toned evenly in relation to their differential reflectance of light.*
- *stroking direction should respond to vertical or horizontal orientation of the surfaces, with the horizontal stroking always going toward the farthest vanishing point.*

time factor: 8 and variable
skill factor: 4 and variable

84

LINE AND TONE
BLACK AND WHITE ON MIDDLETONE

- *spatial edges and planar corners defined with lines.*
- *spatial edges profiled — the farther an edge lies in front of its background the heavier the line should be, except that its heaviness should be lightened in proportion to the distance it is away from the viewer.*
- *surfaces toned evenly in relation to their differential reflectance of light — black for shadow, white for sunlight, unrendered middletone paper for shade.*
- *stroking direction should respond to vertical or horizontal orientation of the surfaces, with the horizontal stroking always going toward the farthest vanishing point.*

time factor: 7 and variable
skill factor: 4 and variable

TONE OF LINES
BLACK AND WHITE ON MIDDLETONE

- *surfaces toned in relation to their differential reflectance of light.*
- *tones made up of evenly spaced lines — black for shadow, white for sunlight, unrendered middletone paper for shade.*
- *spatial edges and planar corners defined by a change in line spacing — no spatial edge lines.*
- *direction of lines should respond to vertical or horizontal orientation of the surfaces, with horizontal lines always going toward the farthest vanishing point.*

time factor: 11
skill factor: 8

TONE
BLACK AND WHITE ON MIDDLETONE

- *surfaces toned in relation to their differential reflectance of light — black for shadow, white for sunlight, unrendered middletone paper for shade.*
- *spatial edges and planar corners defined by a change in tone — no lines.*
- *stroking direction should respond to vertical or horizontal orientation of the surfaces, with horizontal stroking always going toward the farthest vanishing point.*

time factor: 9
skill factor: 10

Before leaving this classification of drawing techniques I would like to emphasize two drawing disciplines which I think are critical for learning and using drawing, and add a few comments on drawing tools and the time and skill required for the various techniques.

SPATIAL PROFILING. The spatial profiling which I recommend in line drawings has two purposes. I believe the profiling actually helps any viewer perceive the space of the drawing by emphasizing the moving edges which carry our kinesthetic experience of space (discussed later under PERSPECTIVE); but there is another reason which, especially for beginning students of drawing, may be much more important. Requiring students to spatially profile their drawings is the strongest way I have found to assure that they perceive their drawings as spatial representations. Getting involved in graduated spatial profiling requires seeing and thinking about any drawing as a real environment. The drawing can never again be a flat collection of lines on a two-dimensional surface, and this establishment of the drawing as a transparent, transcendent means of seeing a real environment is the primary purpose of design drawing.

SURFACE STROKING. The discipline of stroking surfaces in a direction consistent with their orientation has several purposes beyond the consistency it brings to any drawing. The requirements of stroking horizontal surfaces to the farther VP avoids two pitfalls—one perceptual, the other technical. If horizontal surfaces are stroked toward a near VP within the perspective, too much perceptual attention is focused toward that point and, technically, too much graphite or ink will be accumulated in the convergence. The stroking discipline also has a much more important purpose for beginning drawing students. Like spatial profiling, disciplined

surface stroking forces delineators to get spatially involved with the drawing in such a way that to understand the relative orientation of the various surfaces they *must* perceive the drawing as a real environment.

DRAWING TOOLS. The conventional drawing tools are pens or pencils and, recently, the great variety of felt or bamboo-tipped pens or markers. These tools are often categorized according to the chemical composition of the mark they make: ink, graphite or marking fluid. There is a way of thinking about drawing tools that is more basic to drawing: *the visual quality of the line the tool makes,* regardless of its chemical composition.

There seem to be two basic kinds of lines and some variations within those:

LINES OF CONSISTENT OPACITY:
ink or vertically applied pencil or marker; within this category there are:
    lines of constant width
    lines of variable width.

LINES OF VARIABLE OPACITY:
pencils and some markers applied at an angle and/or with variable pressure.

Line drawings are best controlled by a line of consistent opacity and constant width within any individual line. The feathered line and lines which vary in width are more appropriate for making tone drawings.

TIME AND SKILL REQUIRED. One of the most dramatic differences in drawing techniques is the time and skill they require. Although this can be somewhat anticipated in looking at examples of the techniques, actual drawing in each of the techniques is the only way to really experience these differences. As an indication of the time and skill I think each technique requires, I have numbered the preceding drawings with a time factor and a skill factor, with the lower numbers indicating the quickest and easiest techniques and the higher numbers the most time-consuming and difficult. Since drawing is such an integral part of design and encourages or inhibits design in so many ways, designers should experience all the ways of drawing. Only from such experiences can they make intelligent choices of drawing techniques which correspond to the time available, the subject matter, and their drawing ability.

BASED ON UTILITY—
CRITERIA FOR EVALUATION

The most useful reason for developing and classifying various drawing techniques is to have alternative choices of ways to draw, and the ultimate question is always: *Which technique is the best and why?* Answering such a question, however, depends on first answering another question: *What should be the criteria for evaluating a design drawing technique?*

The value system for *design drawing* techniques will differ from those of art or drafting. *Art* would probably choose a technique which obviously required great skill or was innovative—a showcase for the technique of the artist. *Drafting* would offer little choice of technique—no real alternative and no flexibility in the making of drawings.

In contrast, *art's* requirement for great skill or innovation in the drawing technique would seem uniquely unimportant for *design drawing*. Designers should consider the pursuit of virtuoso skill or innovation a case of misplaced creativity and aim rather for a neutrally transparent drawing of a very skillful or innovative design. The rigid formality of *drafting* would be equally undesirable since the time available and the purpose of the drawing—its relationship to the design process—vary greatly in *design drawing* so that the most flexible technique would be the most useful.

Another criteria, especially in initially learning to draw and to use drawing in the design process, is that the technique should require as *little* skill as possible and be dependable and manageable. This is very necessary in learning to draw because the first hurdle is getting student designers to accept their own drawings and be able to see *through* them to whatever is being designed, so that the making of each drawing ceases to be a traumatic experience.

One of the most useful tools of the kind of dependable management we are seeking in drawing is suboptimization—the breaking down of a complicated task into subroutines which may be perceived and dealt with more or less independently. Suboptimization is especially useful in teaching and learning drawing. Like practicing the hands separately in beginning piano lessons, it allows students and teachers to concentrate on and master the subroutines independently as well as promoting a structured perception of drawings so that the constituent parts of the technique may be balanced.

If the preceding arguments are convincing, then design drawing techniques should be:

NEUTRALLY TRANSPARENT, calling as little attention to the drawing technique as possible;

FLEXIBLE, allowing great choice as to the time spent and degree of skill and finish required;

MANAGEABLE AND LEARNABLE, requiring as little skill as possible and capable of being broken down into subroutines.

Of the previous categorization of drawing techniques, LINE AND TONE uniquely meets these criteria. Because it is a mixed media technique, it has largely been ignored by artists who tend to draw in the more demanding pure media techniques: pencil or charcoal TONE or pen and ink TONE OF LINES. These techniques tend to be the traditional showcases for virtuoso drawing technique. By contrast, LINE AND TONE drawings have a modest transparent neutrality and never look like "works of art" at the level of drawing.

LINE AND TONE is also the most flexible of the tone techniques since its basic line framework will represent space very well by itself and any tones that can be added are bonuses. A LINE AND TONE drawing never looks incomplete once it has become a line drawing since the completeness of the application of the tones has no particular optimum and is, therefore, very flexible. An unfinished drawing in the pure tone techniques (TONE or TONE OF LINES), on the other hand, is always conspicuously incomplete.

LINE AND TONE is also the only technique which can be broken down into subroutines. This is possible because of the composite nature of the technique and probably could be done in several different ways. The most useful subdivision I have been able to make is

a breakdown into categories of interest in the environment.

The manageability which such suboptimization allows will be demonstrated at length later in this chapter under DRAWING AS AN INVESTMENT HIERARCHY. The drawings which follow are intended only to introduce the basis for the interest categories. I have found them to be very useful in sophisticating students' perceptions of drawings, in concentrating on one or two of the categories, in understanding the categories' interrelationships and in balancing the synthesis of the categories.

SPATIAL INTEREST is the most basic of all the categories of environmental interest since it structures or forms the framework for all the other categories. The three categories which follow all occur *on* or *within* a spatial framework and they are therefore all closely related, and to a great extent limited or enhanced by this initial interest category.

Spatial interest in any environment is promised kinesthetic interest—the anticipated experience of objects, spaces and vistas which are only partly seen, but which will be revealed by our movement through the environment. The sources of spatial interest are the hiding places created by placing objects in front of surfaces and other objects—follow the bouncing ball and the paper airplane. The sum of these partially revealed spaces is the sum of the spatial interest and literally can be counted.

In a drawing, the hidden spaces which constitute spatial interest will all be partially hidden/revealed by a profiled spatial edge, and these spatial laps may also be counted. Spatially interesting drawings may have stacks of these spatial laps which are ten or twelve deep.

ADDITIONAL INTEREST is that interest we find in all the additions we, and nature, make to any built environment. I have previously called this collection of stuff "humanizing elements" (*Drawing As A Means to Architecture,* 1968) and "figural interest" (*Drawing As A Means to Architecture,* revised edition 1977 and *Design Drawing,* 1974); but I believe *additional* is a much better name for the category. I like the double meaning that is inherent in the word *additional* because this interest category is not only made up of all the additions to any environment, it is also a separate, additional category—in contrast to the inherently integral categories of spatial, tonal and textural interest.

In the environment, additional interest comes from trees, plants, furniture, automobiles,etc., and other human beings—the additive trappings with which we furnish any human environment.

In drawing, this interest category is perhaps even more clearly additive, but remains indispensable in specifying the scales, indicating the use and demonstrating the space of any environment. Although many of our additions to the environment are frankly ornamental we must be careful not to reduce them to mere decorations in our drawings. Objects which provide additional interest must be carefully placed into a drawing so that they do not cover the planar intersections by which we perceive spatial volumes; and they should generally be textureless in contrast to the background space-defining surfaces. While it is detached and separate from the other three interest categories, additional interest must be tightly integrated with them in design drawings.

TONAL INTEREST in any environment is the result of light reflecting differently off the various surfaces which make up the environment. Visually, tonal interest is the most basic of the interest categories—the last to be squinted out, diluted by distance—or lost as we cross the threshold into blindness.

In the environment, tonal interest depends primarily on a rich collection of surfaces which have various orientations to light, and secondarily on material selections and color schemes. The composition of variously oriented surfaces which will provide strong tonal interest is in turn directly dependent on the previous category of spatial interest.

In drawings, tonal interest depends on using the full range of grays—from pure white to solid black—over broad areas of the drawing. The main sources for this tonal range are the light conditions on the various surfaces: sun, shade and shadow. Color and material variations are much less important since many drawings must remain black and white and the textural interest of materials is generally more important than their tone.

TEXTURAL INTEREST is tactile interest—the interest we find in touching various materials and surfaces. While we may be directly experiencing this interest category by contact with the surfaces on which we are standing or sitting or touching, most textural interest is the promised or potential interest of distant surfaces which we perceive *visually.*

Drawings can promise this same potential textural interest that we perceive visually. The main source, virtually the only source of textural interest in the environment, is the collection of materials of which it is made. Textural interest should always be added to a drawing beginning with the space-bounding surfaces. These surfaces establish our perception of space and are also the critical and permanent material choices in any environment.

PERSPECTIVE

STRUCTURING AND LIGHTING EXPERIENTIAL SPACE

The two most basic categories of environmental interest discussed earlier, SPATIAL interest and TONAL interest, both depend on perspectives for realistic representation in design drawings. It should be apparent from the preceding section on the relative realism of the drawings that spatial interest is best represented in perspectives, but tonal interest's relationship to perspective is not that obvious. Tonal interest consists primarily of what is normally taught as *shade and shadow* or *shadow-casting* and is traditionally introduced in a fragmentary way on plans and elevations. I believe any understanding of the lighting of the environment is an extension of perspective and is much better learned whole, in three-dimensions, so that shadows on plans and elevations are correctly reduced to secondary derivatives of that holistic understanding.

WHY. Because the built environment is designed primarily for human experience, and because perspectives are the best drawings for representing experience, and because we have understood how to draw perspectives since the Renaissance, it might be anticipated that perspectives would be the dominant drawings used in the design process and in design education. However, this is not the case. Perspectives are little used in design processes except as occasional presentation devices and, although the individuals who learn to use perspectives in their design processes tend to be the designers in specialized architectural practice (rather than the spec writers or field supervisors), perspectives are used much less than might be expected in general architectural practice.

WHY NOT. Some of the reasons for not using perspectives are obvious, but I have tried to speculatively extend the list into some unsuspected areas. The most obvious reasons perspectives are disused as design drawings stem from the way perspective is traditionally introduced to designers—*from the way it is taught.* In *art,* perspective is often sloppily taught and distortions are actually valued. In *drafting,* perspective is taught as a difficult, mechanically tedious way of drawing given objects. Neither discipline teaches perspective as the best representational drawing for predicting the experience of alternative designs in the design decision-making process.

TAUGHT AS A TERTIARY NON-DESIGN DRAWING. Perhaps the primary reason for avoiding perspectives in the design process is because the conventional methods of drawing perspectives relegate them to the position of being tertiary drawings. Traditionally, you can't even draw a perspective until the plan, section or elevation are established, because perspectives are taught as projections from plan, section or elevation. This fact is extremely important when we remember we are dealing with a decision-making process in time. If you as a designer conceive a plan first and show such a plan or any particular single drawing to a client or critic, or even look at it yourself, your evaluative and creative mind and that of your client or critic will begin to change and refine whatever is shown. Show a design teacher, a client, a boss, or yourself a plan, and they or you will begin to change it.

As a teacher of architectural design, I have seen and been responsible for the results of this in design problems, which had beautifully refined plans, and crude, clumsy perspectives promising a dismal three-dimensionl reality. The first reason, then that we

don't use perspectives, is that because of the traditional method of drawing them, they come third or fourth in the series of representational drawings we make and we never get to them, because we get caught up in revising the first drawings we make.

REPRESENTATION OF DESIGN PRODUCTS AS OBJECTS rather than environments. This has been mentioned earlier as favoring plans, sections, elevations and axonometric drawings which adequately depict objects, but which misrepresent our dominant perceptual experience, which is of an environment which surrounds and includes us.

DIFFICULTY AND INEFFICIENCY OF METHOD. Another reason we avoid drawing perspectives is because the traditional methods for drawing them are rather difficult, tedious, drafted procedures. And, what is worse, only long experience with the method can guarantee that your selection of station point and position of picture plane will result in the view you want or even be the size you want.

Designers need drawing or modeling techniques which will keep up, as nearly as possible, with their design minds; a quick predictive way of drawing perspectives which will tell them what the environment is like and which will invite change or refinement. The difficulty and inefficiency of conventional perspective methods encourages procrastination in drawing the three-dimensional reality and, once drawn, so much time and effort is invested in the construction of the perspective that any change or redrawing is out of the question.

FALLACIOUS RATIONALE. Because of the preceding reasons for avoiding perspective, a rationale has even been developed to defend the avoidance of drawing perspectives. The rationale proposes that designers can and should "think" the three-dimensional reality of the objects or spaces they are designing while drawing the traditional orthographic abstractions—plan, section and elevation. This rationale is comparable to the "think method" of music instruction advocated by Professor Harold Hill in *The Music Man*. If it is really possible and desirable to draw one reality and think another, why don't we just draw a picture of Aunt Maude and also "think" the plan, section and elevation.

MISNAMED LIKE THE OTHER ORTHOGRAPHIC ABSTRACTIONS.

The word PERSPECTIVE is, unfortunately, also a hindrance. The fact that it has such a name implies that this particular view is another one of the abstract drawings like plan, section, elevation, and isometric. It would be more fair if they were called plan abstraction, section abstraction, elevation abstraction, and then perspective were simply EXPERIENCE or AS IT REALLY IS.

This is what the word perspective is supposed to mean, if we accept Webster:
    1. the art of picturing objects or a scene in such a way as to show them as they appear to the eye with reference to relative distance or depth. 2.a) the appearance of objects or scenes as determined by their relative distance and position. 3. the relationship or proportion of the parts of a whole, regarded from a particular standpoint or point in time. 4. a proper evaluation with proportional importance given to the component parts . . . .

SHADOW-CASTING TAUGHT ONLY ON PLANS AND ELEVATIONS.

Traditionally, shadow-casting has been taught only on the orthographic projections. Shadows add most of the tonal interest to any drawing and greatly enhance its realism. The production of heavily rendered, shadow-cast plans and elevations is understood by design students and often required in design schools, since the skill is taught in basic drawing courses.

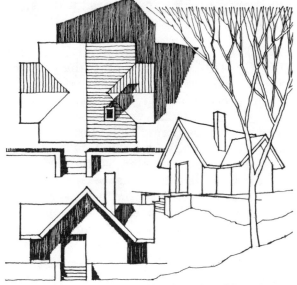

Perspectives, on the other hand, seldom have shadows cast on them because students seldom master the skill. This practice results in pale, valueless perspectives which have little realism or visual interest and which have difficulty competing with shadowed plans and elevations in any composite presentation. This is one more reason students come to the opinion that perspectives are valueless as design or presentation drawings or beyond their drawing ability. It is one more of the subtle subsidies design drawing tradition has bestowed on the orthographic abstractions.

PERSPECTIVES UNNECESSARY AS WORKING DRAWINGS.

Normally, perspectives are not a part of any set of working drawings or mechanical drawings the design professions make to take off the materials or use as a pattern in the construction of the spaces we design. Actually, perspectives would make the details of corners, intersections and connections much more clear, but because of the previous five reasons, the drawing of perspectives is assumed to be beyond the ability of the ordinary working-drawing draftsperson.

The fact that, traditionally, perspectives are not necessary to production drawings leads some bosses and head draftspersons to look upon them as superfluous, "eye-wash" drawings, and any time spent making then as completely wasted, except as necessary to the "selling" of the job. Compared to plans and elevations, which can be readily translated into production drawings by any draftsperson, those concerned with the financial end of any design firm often find it difficult to justify time spent drawing perspectives.

There is even a tendency to use the production drawings themselves as the only drawings to communicate the design, leaving the very difficult task of imagining what the design will really look like to the untrained perception of the client or user. In such a firm, the recent design graduate may soon discover that the highest paid people in the drafting room are production draftspersons, none of whom can draw perspectives. This practice is really the clincher, since the recent design graduate is persuaded that in the "real world" perspectives are useless—*nothing could be further from the truth.*

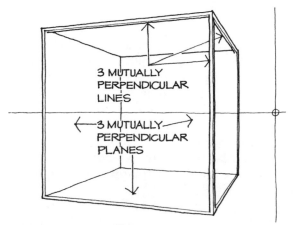

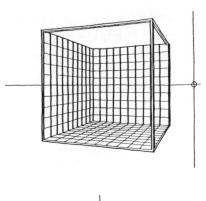

THE STRUCTURE OF RECTANGULAR SPACE

All the relationships of rectangular space can be represented in an open cube which consists of three contiguous, mutually perpendicular planes and three contiguous, mutually perpendicular lines.

Notice that in such a cube one plane is horizontal and two planes are vertical, and complimentarily two lines are horizontal and one line is vertical.

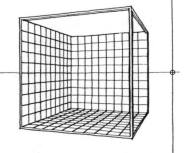

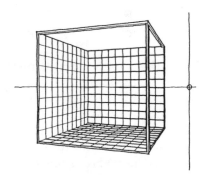

SPATIAL INTEREST AND STRUCTURE

Perspectives are the best representations of spatial interest and especially of the kinesthetic or experiential interest of environments. The various ways of drawing perspectives all reduce to methods of structuring a two-dimensional piece of paper so that it becomes a measurable three-dimension space. Perspectives structure the two-dimension space of the paper so that the third dimension is added and all three dimensions are made measurable.

Whether we like it or not, western civilization inhabits a rectangular world. Our language (front, back, top, bottom, right, left), our bodies (head, foot, front, back, right, left), our orientation (up, down, north, south, east, west), the Cartesian coordinates (X,Y,Z), the measurement and subdivision of land reflected in our street grids and the dominant rectilinearity of our spaces and objects all conspire to base our understanding of the environment, and perspective, on the three axes of rectangular space.

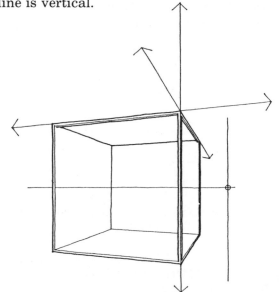

Also notice that the three lines represent the three axes of any rectangular environment.

Also notice that each of the three planes may be thought of as consisting of parallel sets of two of the three possible sets of linear orientations and that any two contiguous planes share one such set of parallel lines.

It is a good idea to build such an open cube and draft the grid of constituent lines on each of the three planes. We will be using this same cube to understand shadow-casting in the next section.

THE PRINCIPLES OF PERSPECTIVE

The first principle of perspective can best be understood by considering the eyelevel line and the way it relates us to the horizontal surface of the earth.

The eyelevel line should be perceived as the edge of a horizontal plane, about 5 feet high, stretching to infinity. This can be established by drawing figures of different sizes with a common eyelevel.

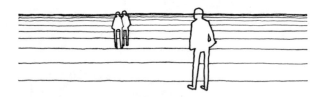

Next, the ground plane needs to be represented by drawing one of the sets of parallel lines of which it can be thought to consist. Above, the set of horizontal lines which are parallel to the eyelevel line recedes toward and disappears into the eyelevel line. This is the basic perceptual background of the millions of years of evolution of our species. We live and move on a horizontal plane which recedes to the horizon; we judge both the size and distance of objects in relation to that receding plane; and its recession gives us the most basic understanding of perspective:

*PLANES RECEDE INTO LINES
AT VISUAL INFINITY.*

We will call the lines into which planes recede *vanishing lines*, abbreviated as VLs.

The eyelevel line is really the coincidence, at visual infinity, of two planes: the level plane of our vision and the horizontal surface on which we stand and move. This is the key to the eyelevel line's uniqueness. It is the infinite slot into which the two most important planes of our existence coincide. This understanding is the key to extending our understanding of planes vanishing into lines.

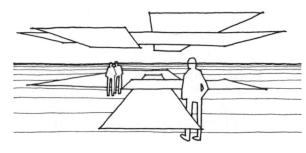

The eyelevel line is the VL not only for the ground plane, but for *all* horizontal planes—for the set of planes to which it is parallel. All horizontal planes recede toward and disappear into the eyelevel like letters into a mail slot.

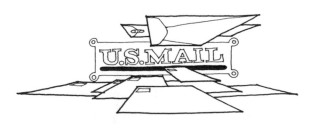

This brings us to a more general restatement of the first principle:

*SETS OF PARALLEL PLANES RECEDE
INTO A COMMON VL AT
VISUAL INFINITY.*

Sets of parallel vertical planes will also recede into a vertical VL at visual infinity.

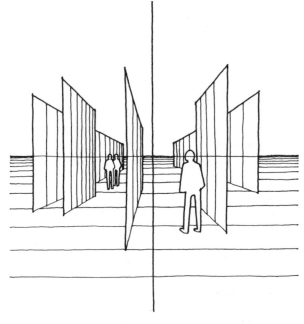

Like the ground plane, these converging planes may be drawn and conceived as consisting of a set of parallel vertical lines receding to infinity.

To illustrate the perceptual dominance of the ground plane in our evolutionary history, look at the drawing below and ask yourself if the vertical plane on the right has reached infinity—and I think you'll find that there seems to be a lot of space beyond it.

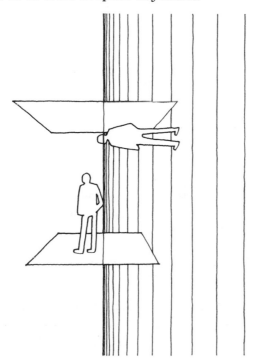

Now turn the page 90° clockwise so that you perceive the plane as the horizontal ground plane, and I think you'll find that you can easily perceive the plane as extending to the horizon. This is because, unlike the horizontal plane of the earth or sea, we, nor any of our ancestors have ever seen a wall stretch to visual infinity.

Unlike the sea or ground plane, however, (which beachcombers and Kansans have seen extend to the horizon) it is much more difficult to perceive the vertical planes which are perpendicular to the eyelevel line as extending to a vertical VL at infinity—because no one has ever seen one that long.

By permission of Johnny Hart and Field Enterprises, Inc.

The second principle of perspective has to do with the rules for the convergence of lines which lie in the plane of any rectangular environment. Understanding the rules for the convergence of lines begins with perceiving any plane as containing an infinite number of sets of parallel lines.

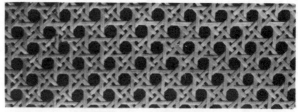

It may be helpful to make an analogy to the threads in a piece of cloth or the individual pieces of cane in a woven chair bottom, in which the plane *consists* of individual lines. It is always necessary to understand in which plane a particular line lies in order to understand where it converges.

Returning to the ground plane we can see that the set of parallel lines which is precisely perpendicular to the eyelevel line, unlike the set which is parallel to it drawn earlier, will converge to a point on the eyelevel line which is exactly in the center of the visual field.

This illustrates the simplest form of the second principle of perspective:

SETS OF PARALLEL LINES CONVERGE TO POINTS AT VISUAL INFINITY.

These points to which lines converge are traditionally called *vanishing points*, abbreviated as VPs.

93

The principles governing convergence also apply to sets of parallel lines lying in vertical planes.

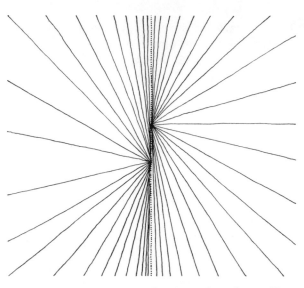

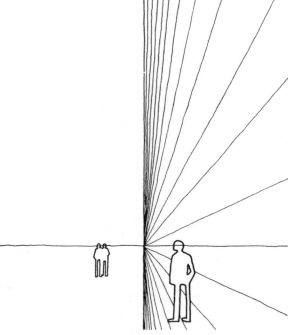

This convergence of sets of parallel horizontal lines toward a single point on the eyelevel line is not only true for the set which is perpendicular to the eyelevel line, but for all sets of parallel lines *EXCEPT* the single set which is coincidentally parallel to the eyelevel line.

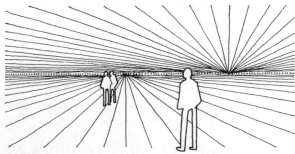

This leads us to a deeper understanding of vanishing lines. Any VL may be thought of as the collection of VPs (vanishing points) for the infinite sets of parallel lines which lie in the set of parallel planes receding into it.

That set of horizontal lines which lies in vertical planes and is perpendicular to the vertical VL will converge toward a single point, on the vertical VL, which is exactly in the center of the visual field.

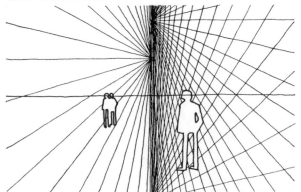

All sets of parallel lines lying in vertical planes *EXCEPT* that single set which is coincidentally parallel to the vertical VL will converge to a single point on the vertical VL.

Vertical VLs may also be thought of as collections of VP's for the infinite sets of parallel lines which lie in the set of parallel planes receding into them.

We can now state the second general principle of perspective:

ALL SETS OF PARALLEL LINES CONVERGE TO VPs ON THE VL FOR THE PLANES IN WHICH THEY LIE.

The third general principle of perspective is concerned with the relationship between the first two principles when applied to the structure of rectangular space discussed earlier.

If we draw the eyelevel VL and the set of parallel lines which are perpendicular to it, we will find they converge to a VP in the exact center of the visual field.

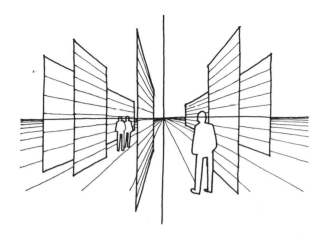

Any vertical plane which grows out of one line of the parallel set of converging horizontal lines will also contain horizontal lines which converge to the same VP.

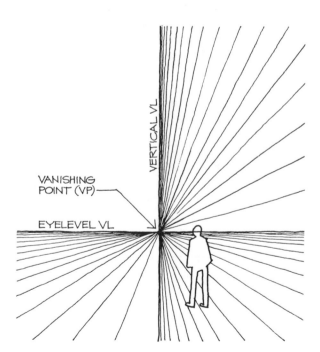

VERTICAL VL

VANISHING POINT (VP)

EYELEVEL VL

If we could extend any such vertical plane to visual infinity it would recede into a vertical VL passing through the VP we have established.

The VP is then better understood as the intersection of two VLs and we can now state the third priciple of perspective:

THE VPs FOR ANY RECTANGULAR COMPOSITION ARE THE INTERSECTIONS OF THE VLs FOR TWO (of the three) SETS OF MUTUALLY PERPENDICULAR PLANES, AND ARE THE POINTS TO WHICH THE SET OF PARALLEL LINES COMMON TO BOTH PLANES CONVERGES.

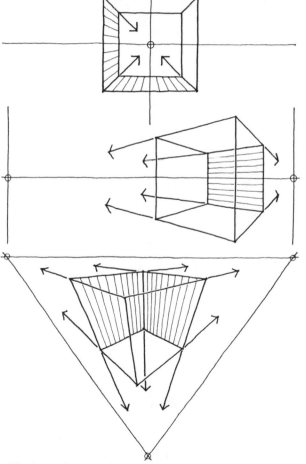

The number and arrangement of the VLs and VPs varies according to the particular perspective framework used, which is the subject of the next section.

PERSPECTIVE FRAMEWORKS

All perspective frameworks are made up of arrangements of *vanishing lines* and *vanishing points*. The VLs are those for the three sets of mutually perpendicular planes of any rectangular environment and the VPs are those for the three sets of mutually perpendicular lines in any rectangular environment.

The variations of the different perspective frameworks are based on differing relationships between the viewer and the environment. These variations in the viewer's relationship to the environment result in the advantages and disadvantages each has as representations of the experience of the environment.

In building an understanding of the frameworks it is best to begin with the simplest framework and progress to the most complex.

TWO-LINE/ONE-POINT PERSPECTIVE

Most of the walls of the built environment, as mentioned earlier, are either parallel or perpendicular to one another, so that they have an axial geometry like our own body, for which the words top, bottom, front, back, left and right are meaningful. In perspectives, the viewer may or may not be aligned with the walls of the environment, but the simplest of the perspective frameworks assumes that the viewer is axially aligned with the environment.

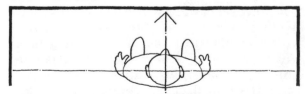

This axial alignment with the environment means that in the simplest perspective framework the walls of the environment will either be parallel or perpendicular to the eyelevel line.

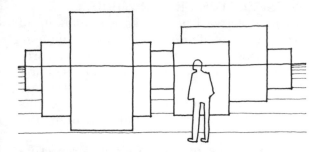

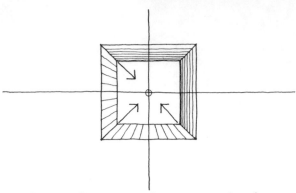

This simplest perspective framework is traditionally called ONE-POINT perspective, but is better understood as *TWO-LINE/*ONE-POINT perspective because that slightly longer name fully describes the framework and emphasizes the more basic understanding of perspective as a system of VLs.

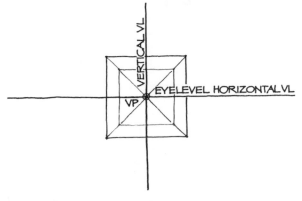

The set of walls which is parallel to the eyelevel will arise out of the set of parallel lines which are parallel to the eyelevel VL as *transverse planes*. These walls will not recede to any VL because they are, coincidentally, precisely perpendicular to our line of vision and will appear as simple rectangles with their edges parallel to the edges of the paper or the drawing board.

Although *two-line/*one-point perspectives usually assume that the viewer's head is erect and that the eyelevel VL is horizontal, it is also possible to draw them looking straight down, as into buildings or rooms with their roofs removed.

In the *two-line/*one-point perspective framework two of the three sets of mutually perpendicular planes recede into VLs and one of the three sets of mutually perpendicular lines converges to a VP.

The views of the environment which are possible on the *two-line/*one-point perspective framework have two serious limitations as well as two distinct advantages. Both the limitation and the advantages derive from the forced relationship between the viewer and the environment.

Disadvantages of the *two-line/*one-point perspective framework:

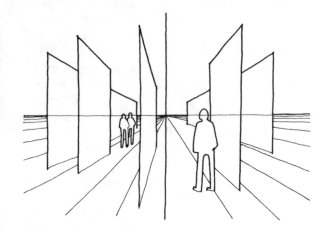

The other set of walls will be perpendicular to the first set as well as to the eyelevel VL and will arise out of the set of converging lines which are perpendicular to the eyelevel line. This set of *converging planes* will recede in a vertical VL in the exact center of the visual field, and the intersection of this vertical VL with the eyelevel VL will be the VP for the set of parallel converging horizontal lines which are common to the two sets of planes whose VLs intersect at that point.

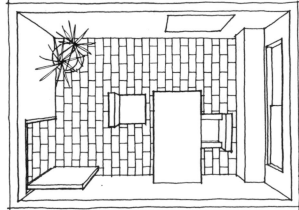

This kind of perspective is easy to draw, rather impressive in relation to the effort required and sometimes helpful in communicating with a client who has difficulty understanding floor plans.

- *two-line/*one-point perspectives offer only static, coincidental views of the environment.

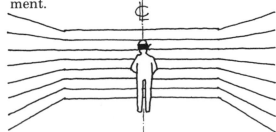

Because they lock the viewer into axial alignment with the environment, *two-line/*one-point perspectives offer only brides', bowlers' or firing squads' views of space. Such a fixed, static view of space is least characteristic of the constant movement we depend on as perceptual systems.

- *two-line*/one-point perspectives are generally dull as exterior perspectives.

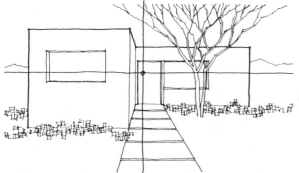

Because they can never show either end of a building, *two-line*/one-point perspectives result in very uninteresting exterior perspectives. If there are projections or recesses in the facade, or if the building is an open pavilion, enough converging planes (walls and ceilings) may be visible to make an interesting drawing, but perspectives of simple block buildings offer little more than flat elevation drawings.

Advantages of the *two-line*/one-point perspective framework:

- *two-line*/one-point perspectives are acceptable as interior perspectives.

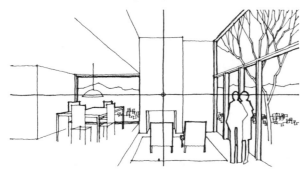

Because they show three walls and one horizontal dimension of any interior space, *two-line*/one-point perspectives offer a clear, if static, understanding of the shape and extent of interior space.

- *two-line*/one-point perspectives are easy to draw.

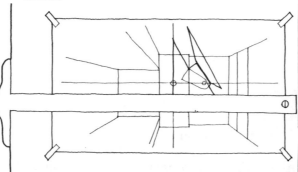

Since one set of horizontal lines and one set of vertical planes are dead parallel to the eyelevel VL, they may be drafted with a T-square or parallel edge; and since the single VP in the center of the visual field is easily reachable, *two-line*/one-point perspectives are the easiest of perspective frameworks to draft.

THREE-LINE/TWO-POINT PERSPECTIVE

The next, more complex, perspective framework unlocks the axial relation between the viewer's body and the environment, and allows an infinite number of angular views along one of the axes of rectangular space.

While the axis which is freed for turning by this perspective framework is usually the horizontal axis, the framework can also be turned vertically so that the body remains aligned with the environment and only the head tips vertically.

The more common horizontal rotation gives us the most representative human views of space and the angular relation to the environment suggests the freedom and dominance of horizontal movement of our eyes, heads and bodies so necessary for surveillance and survival on the African savannahs on which we evolved.

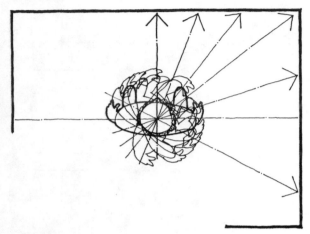

Because of the dominance of horizontal movements, our ability and habit of swiveling our eyes and heads horizontally and turning our whole bodies horizontally, the horizontal rotation of view offered by the *three-line*/two-point perspective framework is most characteristic of the human experience of the environment.

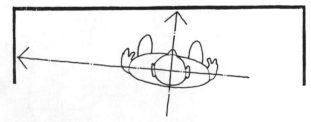

At the slightest deviation between the geometry of our orientation and the building's orientation we will see the horizontal lines which were dead parallel to the eyelevel line begin to converge to a very distant (initially infinitely distant) VP.

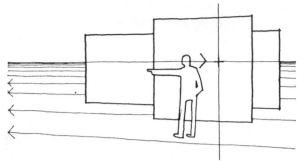

The set of vertical planes or transverse walls arising out of that parallel set of horizontal lines will also no longer be dead parallel to the eyelevel VL, but will recede into a new, very distant (initially infinitely distant) vertical VL.

Simultaneously the original vertical VL and VP will begin to shift away from the exact center of the visual field, *away* from the new distant VL and VP.

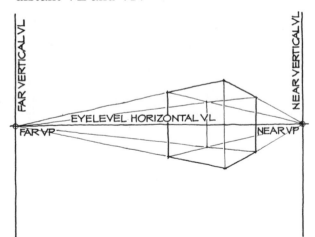

Perspectives drawn on the *three-line*/two-point framework are traditionally called two-point perspectives, again ignoring the number and arrangement of VLs basic to any perspective framework. *Three-line*/two-point perspective more completely describes this framework which adds a second vertical VL and a second VP to the previous *two-line*/one-point framework.

Except where we draw the coincidental view when the relationship of our line of sight is precisely 45° to the geometry of the building, one of these two VLs will be farther from and one nearer to our line of sight.

Calling the VLs and VPs *far* or *near* is much more sophisticated than referring to them as the right VP or the left VP—just as strong side/weak side says a lot more about a football or basketball offense than right/left.

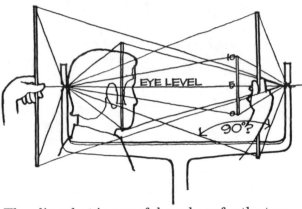

The slingshot is a useful analogy for the two-point perspective framework, having the horizontal construction lines connected to two fixed points but allowing you to place the perspective anywhere you wish within the framework.

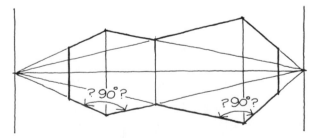

The *three-line*/two-point perspective framework introduces the complication of having to establish the two VPs along the eyelevel VL. The only real criterion for the location of these two VPs is the viewer's acceptance of the horizontal angles produced as being 90°.

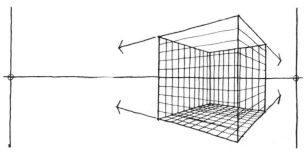

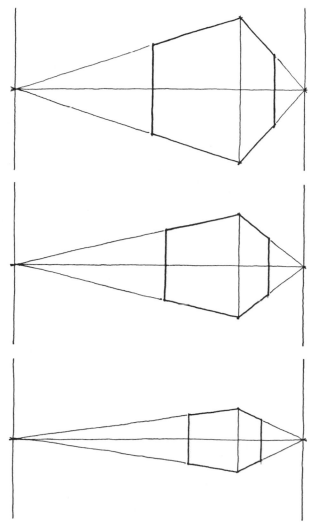

We have great tolerance in the perception of these angles, however, as can be demonstrated by our acceptance of various photographs of an object or an environment shot from the same point with lenses of different focal lengths.

Our eye will accept any of these as a 10′ cube, either nearer or farther away from us. We simply need to be reasonable in our positioning of the VPs and then apply the other rules we have discovered previously.

In the *three-line*/two-point perspective framework all three of the parallel sets of mutually perpendicular planes recede into VLs and two of the three parallel sets of mutually perpendicular lines converge to VPs. Only the vertical lines remain dead parallel.

The range of views of the environment which are possible on the *three-line*/two-point perspective framework has one disadvantage and three advantages.

The disadvantage of the *three-line*/two-point perspective framework:

- *three-line*/two-point perspectives may be more difficult to draw because of the establishment of, and projection from, the second (far) VL and VP.

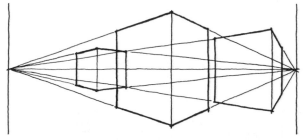

In the *two-line*/one-point perspective framework there is only one VP and there is no question of correctly estimating 90° plan angles, or difficulty in reaching a distant VL and VP. The addition of a second (far) VL and VP means the VLs must be

reasonably located so that the viewer's perception will accept all the horizontal (plan) angles as 90° and reaching the far VP and the even more distant VPs for diagonals and perpendicular shadows (discussed later under LIGHT) along the far VL may be difficult.

Advantages of the *three-line*/two-point perspective framework:

- *three-line*/two-point perspectives offer the full range of dynamic relationships between the viewer and the environment.

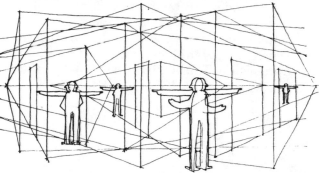

The horizontal rotation allowed by the second VL and VP offers all the most characteristic human views of the environment.

- *three-line*/two-point perspectives are excellent for exteriors.

Since the horizontal rotation allowed by the second VL and VP allows the viewer to walk around a building, viewing it from all sides, this perspective framework is excellent for representing the exterior of a building as an object.

• *three-line*/two-point perspectives, employed freely and directly, are excellent for interiors. The conventional plan-projected perspective methods inhibit the most dynamic and typical views of interior space, but by employing the framework directly these views are available on this perspective framework. This will be discussed in the next section on PERSPECTIVE METHODS.

The series of perspective frameworks at right illustrates the views offered for exterior and interior perspectives by the various orientations to the geometry of the space. Notice that the converging walls continue to go to the original vertical VL which must now be distinguished by calling it the *near* vertical VL. Notice also that the coincidental view of the one-point perspective is acceptable for interiors, but worthless for exterior perspectives, and as the orientation approaches 45°, where the VPs will become equidistant, both the exterior and interior perspectives become less interesting.

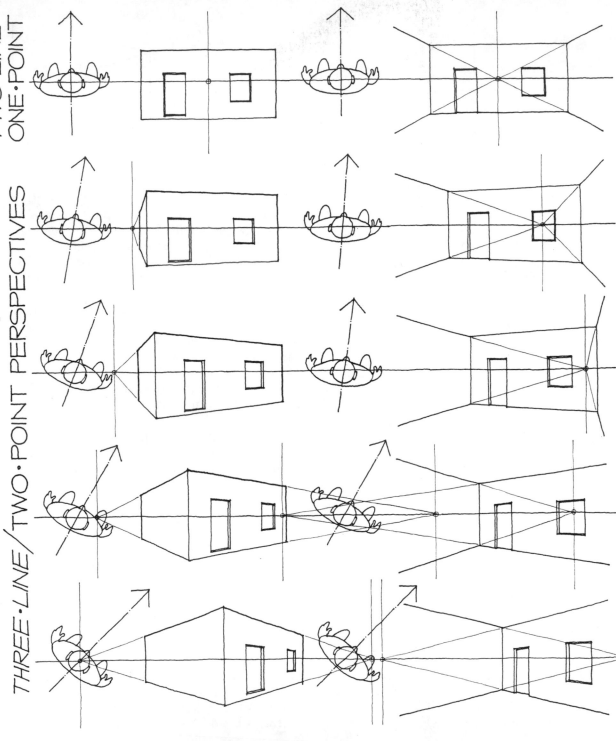

TWO·LINE ONE·POINT

THREE·LINE / TWO·POINT PERSPECTIVES

THREE-LINE/THREE-POINT PERSPECTIVE

Unlike the previous *two-line*/one-point and *three-line*/two-point perspective frameworks, which were content to hold the head level, the *three-line*/three-point perspective framework tips the head vertically. This most complex perspective framework is the least used of the three frameworks because the benefits derived from tipping the head are generally not worth the complications involved.

The moment the head is tipped vertically the two vertical VLs of the *three-line*/two-point perspective framework rotate and intersect in a third VP which affects what we see. The rotation may occur above or below the eye-level VL, depending on whether the head is tipped upward or downward.

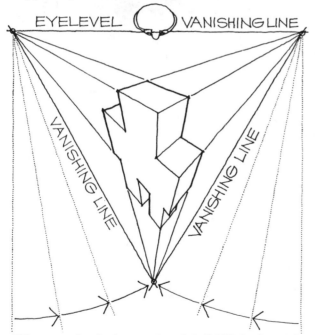

When we look down, the third VP is formed below the eyelevel line by the rotation of the two vertical VLs toward each other until they intersect. The point of their intersection is the third VP.

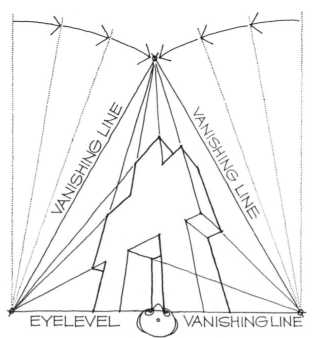

When we look up, the third VP is formed similarly above the eyelevel line by the rotation and intersection of the vertical VLs.

In the two previous, simpler frameworks, which hold the head level, the vertical lines did not converge and could be conveniently drawn dead vertical by using a triangle sitting on the T-square or parallel edge. The vertical planes, while they did recede into VLs at least remained upright and dead parallel.

The major complication of the *three-line*/three-point perspective framework is that the last remaining element of orthogonal environments, the vertical lines, now converge to a vertical VP. In the *three-line*/three-point perspective framework all three sets of mutually perpendicular planes recede into VLs and all three sets of mutually perpendicular lines converge to VPs.

The *three-line*/three-point perspective framework has three disadvantages and one advantage.

Disadvantages of the *three-line*/three-point perspective framework:

- *three-line*/three-point perspectives are misleading as representations of environmental experience.
  While the dramatic views of space provided by this perspective framework are typical of the gawking of urban sightseers, they have little to do with the ordinary human experience of the environment. I have noticed that the inhabitants of downtown Manhattan spend little time looking up at the World Trade Center's twin towers, in *three-line*/ three-point perspective, lest they be trampled or run over in *three-line*/two-point perspective.

- *three-line*/three-point perspectives are relatively useless for interiors.
  The vast vertical interiors of Gothic cathedrals would have been appropriate for the *three-line*/three-point perspective framework, but today the only spaces for which such vertical interior views would be needed would be John Portman's Hyatt-Regency lobbies or the rocket assembly buildings at Cape Kennedy.

- *three-line*/three-point perspectives are complicated and awkward to draw.
  The third VP and the necessity of reaching it in order to draw vertical lines seriously complicates the use of this perspective framework.

The advantage of the *three-line*/three-point perspective framework:

- *three-line*/three-point perspectives of exteriors can correctly show the effects of tipping the head vertically to look down or up at tall buildings.

SUMMARY
The three perspective frameworks may be thought of in terms of three analogies:

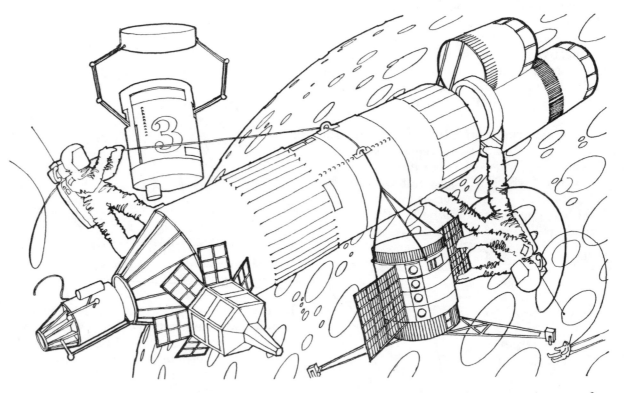

- *two-line/*one-point perspectives are like class pictures taken by a still camera on a fixed tripod.

- *three-line/*three-point perspectives are free of the earth's surface and its gravity—the free-floating views of space from 2001.

- *three-line/*two-point perspectives are most like the earthbound human experience of the

environment, held by gravity between the surface of the earth and the level of our vi-

sion, but able to move, to turn, to swivel and to scan that wide-angle, horizontal realm.

102

PERSPECTIVE METHODS

I have devoted quite a bit of time and space to a discussion of the structure of orthogonal space, the general principles of perspective, and the various perspective frameworks and their advantages and disadvantages. Books on perspective too often rush into the nomenclature and procedure for one or two specific *METHODS* of drawing perspectives without any general explanation of the principles or alternatives involved in choosing a particular way of drawing the environment in perspective. An understanding of perspective does not *begin* with perspective method; it should rather *end* with the alternative choices of method only after a thorough understanding of what is involved in the choice.

1 PRINCIPLES

2 FRAMEWORKS

3 METHODS

The various perspective methods are usually named by the perspective framework they use (*one-point, two-point* or *three-point*) but the frameworks, discussed earlier, actually stop short of the most basic methodological choice. The most basic methodological choice in perspective drawing is between the conventional *projected* perspective methods and what I will call *direct* perspective. The conventional classification of perspective method based on the framework they use masks this most important methodological distinction and favors the continued prejudice for the projected methods as the supposedly superior or *only* way of drawing perspectives. The continued dominance of this prejudice for projected perspective methods is the most damaging of the misconceptions surrounding the teaching of perspective to environmental designers.

The supposed superiority of projected perspective methods is based on their claim to optical and dimensional accuracy, and the prejudice which favors them is largely the result of the attitudes of drawing teachers. Perspective is usually introduced in "technical" drawing courses in the first year of professional design education or in similar community college or high school courses. These courses are usually taught by "technical" drawing teachers and consist mostly of traditional drafting procedures. The pervasive emphasis, value system and mind set of such courses and their teachers, understandably, holds dimensional accuracy very high—higher than any questions about what effect such an attitude might have on the actual use of perspective in the design process. Such courses produce competent technical draftspersons who can accurately *draw* a built or predetermined environment, but the perspective methods taught in such courses are inadequate and inappropriate for the *design* of the environment.

The concern for optical and dimensional accuracy and the way we have allowed it to prejudice the teaching of perspective has become the greatest inhibiting factor in the use of perspectives in the design process. Environmental design students who are introduced to perspective in the form of the conventional projected procedures come to associate perspective with drafted projection and technical accuracy. Because students are seldom taught the basic principles and structure of perspective frameworks, or any direct way of drawing accurate perspectives, they have only two choices: they can "eyeball" or "fake" inaccurate, distorted perspectives, or they can wait until they have completed plans and sections and then project perspectives (as after-the-fact presentation drawings) by the traditional methods. Environmental design students, or graduates, often have no choices between these two extremes because of the way perspective is taught. What is needed is a deeper understanding of perspectives so that freehand perspectives can be directly drawn, correctly structured and made relatively measurable and usable as design drawings.

PLAN: Assume picture plane (P.P.) and locate plan of object as desired. Assume point of view, or station point, S_1. To minimize apparent distortion, this point is commonly taken about opposite the center of the drawing, and far enough away to keep the field of view within about 60° latitude.

ELEVATION: Locate ground line where convenient. Place elevation as indicated, or measure heights directly on any vertical "Line of Heights". Locate S' on vertical through S_1 and at assumed height above ground line.

PERSPECTIVE: Through S' draw horizon. Draw parallel to principal horizontal lines of object through S_1 (in plan), and project intersections with P.P. down to the horizon, giving principal vanishing points V_L and V_R.

NOTE: To find VPs for inclined lines, swing S_1 about 0 into P.P. and project to horizon at M_L. Draw through M_L parallel to actual slopes (angles 1 and 2) to intersection with vertically projected line through V_L. Vanishing points for inclined lines are not absolutely essential, but are frequently found very useful as is shown in the determination of the inclined lines of the gambrel roof in this perspective. Follow arrows and numbered lines. See figures 4 and 1 on following page.

ABBREVIATIONS FOR PERSPECTIVES

S S_1	Station point (in plan)
S' S"	Station point (in elev)
VP	Vanishing point
V_L V_R V_v	Left, right & vertical vanishing points
P.P.	Picture plane
G.L.	Ground line
HOR.	Horizon
M_R	Point for plotting distance to right
M_L	Point for plotting distance to left
M_v	Point for plotting hts.
$V_{45°}$	45° vanishing point

PROCEDURE (ONE POINT)

Draw A.B.C.D., section which is cut by P.P., at any desired scale, and locate S' (point of view in elevation) on line of sight from S_1. Locate the 45° vanishing points V_L and V_R on either side of S' and as distant as S_1 is from the picture plane. All lines parallel to P.P. will remain parallel and all plane figures parallel to P.P. will show their true shape. Vertical lines will be vertical in perspective. Horizontal lines parallel to P.P. will be horizontal. Horizontal lines perpendicular to P.P. will vanish at S'. Horizontal lines at 45° to F.P. (used to measure distances ⊥ to P.P.) will vanish at 45°VPs.

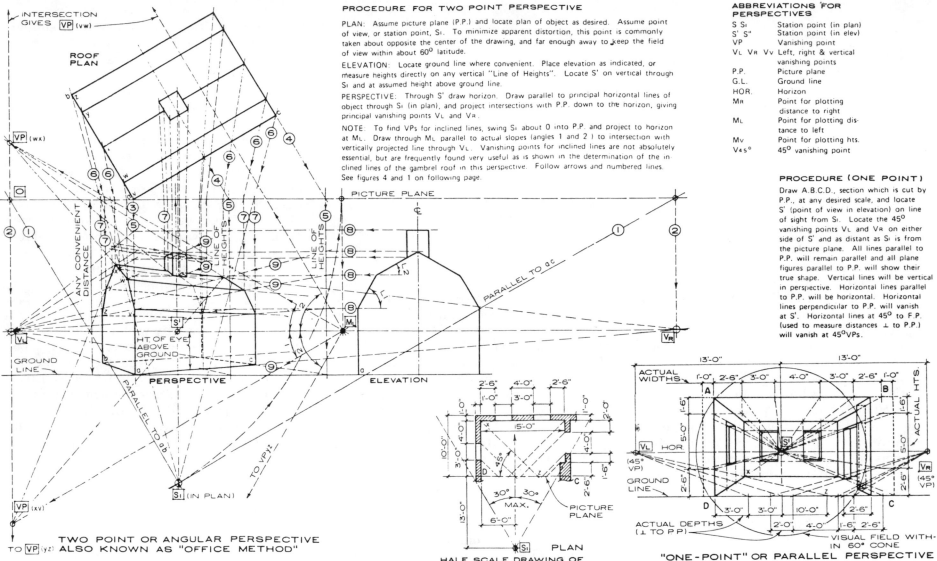

TWO POINT OR ANGULAR PERSPECTIVE ALSO KNOWN AS "OFFICE METHOD"

From ARCHITECTURAL GRAPHIC STANDARDS, 6th Ed., by Charles G. Ramsey & Harold R. Sleeper

HALF SCALE DRAWING OF ASSUMED CONDITIONS

"ONE-POINT" OR PARALLEL PERSPECTIVE

PROJECTED PERSPECTIVE METHODS
based on projected, dimensional measurability

The most common "one-point" and "two-point" perspective methods are reproduced here as examples of the projected methods. I will not explain the methods as they are well-known, appear with slight variations in many books on drawing, and actually have the procedures drawn or described in the reproductions. These and other projected methods have great value and are worth knowing and mastering but, I believe, have no place in the introductory courses for environmental designers because they are of little use in the design process. The projected methods can be learned easily by anyone who first understands the methods I will advocate here and the optical and dimensional accuracy they offer are often worth the effort involved, and should be a part of any designer's range of drawing choices. The projected methods are reproduced here as examples of the complexity involved in the procedures which aim at optical and dimensional certainty in establishing measurability, and also as examples of supposedly superior procedures which I intend to question.

Most projected perspective methods:
- establish a "station point" from which the view is taken;
- establish a "picture plane" through which "vision rays" are projected;
- locate "vanishing points" by projected procedures based on the location of the "station point" and the "picture plane";
- transfer scaled dimensions by various means of projection from completed plans, sections and elevations to the perspective.

A critical analysis of the projected perspective methods reveals some very questionable logic and some serious disadvantages in ever using them as design tools.

1. The need to establish a precise point from which the perspective view is taken is not necessary because:
- We seldom know precisely, dimensionally where we are. At this moment, as you read this, you are probably unaware of the exact dimensions of your position in relation to any referent point in your environment.
- Treating the eye as a fixed camera on a tripod is the least characteristic of what we are as perceptual systems.
- We use our visual perception to predict future experience so that our vision is anticipatory of our movement through space.
- Our visual perception will accept photographs shot with lenses of various focal lengths, indicating that while the *line* of vision is inevitably given by any photograph or perspective, the exact location of the viewer along that line is relatively unimportant.
- Unless the perspective drawing is also viewed at precisely the same distance from the object as the station point was distant in the plans from which the perspective was projected, the whole system of dimensional and optical certainty collapses.

2. The traditional "two-point" projected perspective methods prohibit or ignore what are both the most common and dramatic views of rectangular space.

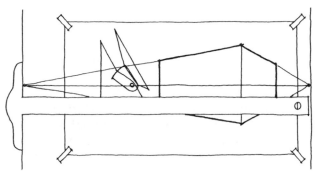

- Because the VPs for conventional *three-line*/two-point perspective methods must be reached for projection, the available views of space are limited by the necessity of having both VPs on the drawing board. This usually eliminates those views of space where the viewer is at a 1°-30° angle to the environment.

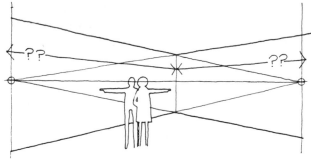

- Most conventional *three-line*/two-point methods limit views of space, at least by implication or recommendation, to those which can be drawn *between* the two VPs, making interior perspectives showing three walls of any space impossible.
- The dynamic views from the sides of spaces like that from an urban sidewalk or from the side aisle of a church or auditorium are impossible to draw.

3. If perspective drawing is to be of any use in the actual design of the environment, then perspectives must have the same independence as the other drawings, not be in the dependent position of being the third or fourth drawing made because they must wait for the plans, sections and elevations to be completed.

- If we know the dimensions of a piece of furniture to be designed, or an existing room to be remodeled, or a patio to be landscaped, we can draw its plan or section directly and independently. In order to draw a perspective of any of these by the projected perspective methods, however, we must first draw the plan and section of the piece of furniture, or room, or patio, even though we know all their dimensions, and then *project* those plan and section dimensions onto the perspective.

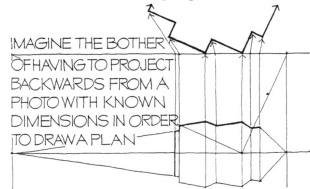

IMAGINE THE BOTHER OF HAVING TO PROJECT BACKWARDS FROM A PHOTO WITH KNOWN DIMENSIONS IN ORDER TO DRAW A PLAN

- Another example may make the absurdity of such dependence clear. Suppose we had a photograph of the piece of furniture, room, or patio, and knew their dimensions but our drawing conventions or traditions held that we must not draw their plan or section directly but must project backwards somehow from the photograph (use the projected perspective procedures in reverse) in order to draw the plan and section. Could such a tradition be said to inhibit the use of plans and sections in the design process?

THE DIRECT PERSPECTIVE METHOD
based on relative, proportional measurability

The direct method of drawing perspectives which follows is based on the use of the diagonal to proportionally subdivide and extend rectangular space. The principles involved are best understood in two-dimensional geometry.

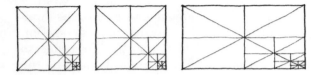

PROPORTIONAL SUBDIVISION
The diagonals of any rectangle subdivide it into quarters, and quarters again, and quarters again, infinitely—limited only by the sharpness of your drawing instrument and your eyesight.

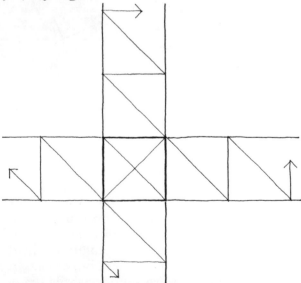

PROPORTIONAL EXTENSION
Successive diagonals will mark off successive identical rectangles along an extension, in either direction, of either pair of an original rectangle's boundary lines.

THE INITIAL SPATIAL UNIT
This subdivision and extension of rectangular space by diagonals can be applied directly to perspectives. First, however, we must learn to draw an initial spatial unit, and that takes a little practice.

Jay Doblin (*Perspective: A New System for Designers,* 1956) first proposed the ability to draw an acceptable cube in various perspective views as basic to the ability to draw perspectives. Even more basic than drawing a cube is the ability to draw acceptable squares in all three mutually perpendicular planes, in each of the perspective frameworks, and understand to which VLs the squares recede and how to establish the VPs for the square's diagonals.

The ability to draw such squares, identify the VLs to which they recede, and locate the VPs for their diagonals, gives us the ability to extend three-dimensional space with a structured accuracy.

Notice that, as in the two-dimensional examples used to introduce extension by diagonal, any square in perspective may be extended in the square's two axial directions by using either diagonal. A VP for successive parallel diagonals in any plane may be located by extending either diagonal till it intersects with the VL for the plane in which it lies. This procedure is an application of the second general principle of perspective:

ALL SETS OF PARALLEL LINES CONVERGE TO VPs ON THE VL FOR THE PLANES IN WHICH THEY LIE.

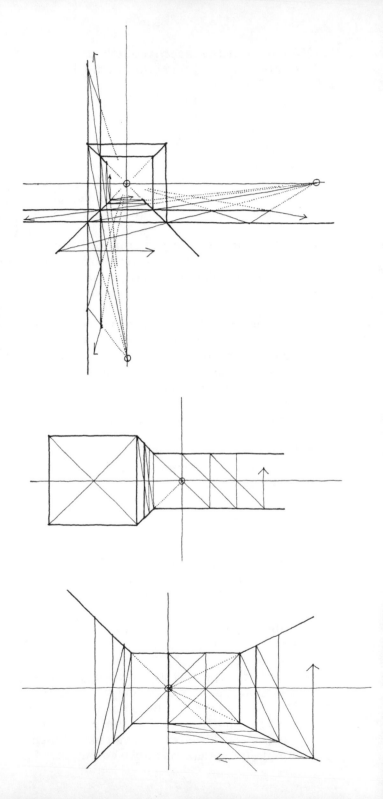

106

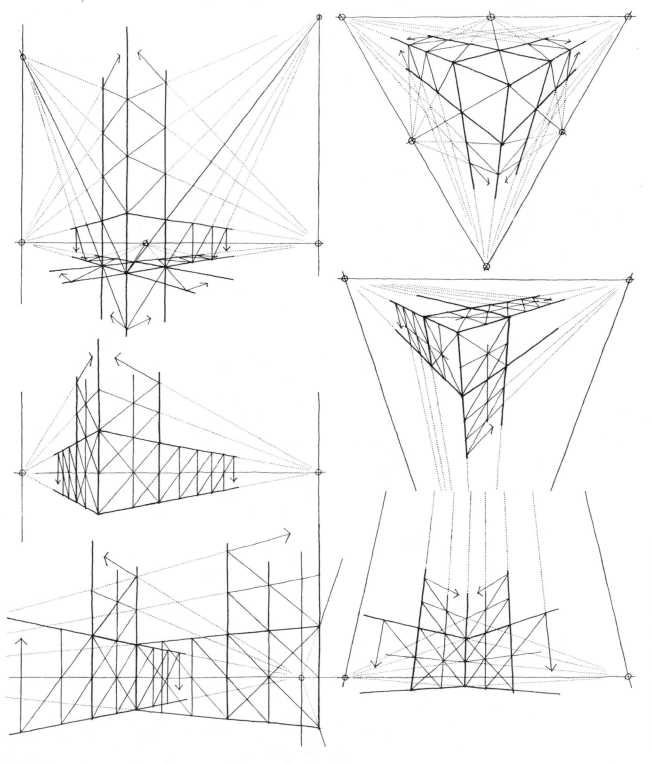

Either pair of boundary lines of any square in perspective may be extended toward or away from their appropriate VP and successive duplications of the initial square may be marked off in either direction by extending successive diagonals from the VP for diagonals. This principle of extension by diagonal works for any square in any of the three mutually perpendicular planes in any of the perspective frameworks (*except* in the transverse vertical plane of *two-line*/one-point perspectives which are dead flat and two-dimensional so that the diagonals do not converge but may be drafted with a 45° triangle). The one limitation of such extension is that it is difficult to extend the space more than one square into the foreground. Subsequent foreground squares usually result in unacceptable distortion.

SHORTCUT
It is necessary to understand the principle involved in the location of the VP for diagonals on the VL for the plane in which they lie, because in the shadow-casting procedures in the next section, LIGHT, you will need to bring shadows from a similar VP. There is, however, a way to shortcut the diagonal extension procedure, when diagonal VPs are distant and difficult to reach.

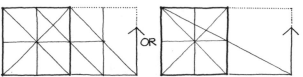

The principle is best illustrated in two-dimensional geometry and is called the "diagonal through the bisector." The bottom row of perspective frameworks at left shows how an initial spatial unit may be extended using the shortcut. If the drafting is accurate, the results will be identical to projections from a VP for diagonals.

107

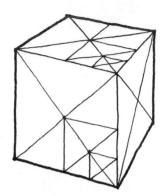

The subdivision of squares into quarters and quarters again in perspective by using diagonals is much simpler than extension, since no VP need be found. Drawing the diagonals is a simple matter of connecting the diagonal corners of any square in perspective.

Once the ability to dependably draw acceptable squares in perspective has been mastered, drawing cubes becomes merely a matter of assembling the squares. We can now assemble such cubes, as well as our understanding of the proportional extension and subdivision of space in each of the perspective frameworks.

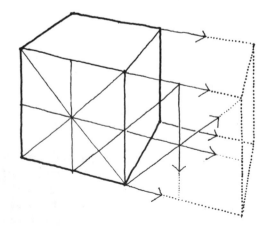

It is easy to see how the extension of any face of an initial cube may be extended to become an identical cube.

108

We now have all the procedures to draw, extend and subdivide rectangular space in *direct* perspective, without being dependent on plans or sections. We no longer need to stoop to plan projection, but may draw three-dimensional space straight up, erect, in the perceptual posture that is uniquely human.

The only arbitrary step in the direct perspective method is the judgment involved in estimating the depth of the initial squares, and the 90° plan angles involved in locating multiple VPs and assembling the squares into cubes. Instead of these judgments needing any kind of defense or apology I regard them as one of the most valuable steps in the direct perspective method. These judgments insure that the delineator's perception is responsible for the accuracy of the perspective, not some set of rules or procedures, and the delineator's perceptual ability will actually be improved with the drawing of each perspective.

Some students, especially those who have already been introduced to the dimensional certainty of plan-projected perspective methods, find the need to guess, estimate or judge the initial unit of depth in direct perspective uncomfortable or unacceptable. I try to persuade these students that they should develop a little more confidence in their own perception; that in the construction supervision phase of architectural practice, they can't walk through the job with a level and a plumb-bob; that they will have to learn to trust their eye to tell them what is straight and level and plumb; and that if they are going to expect clients to trust their judgment in spending millions of dollars in constructing additions to the environment, they should learn to trust their own perception in judging what a square would look like in perspective.

The best story I have ever heard to illustrate the extremes to which this particular men-

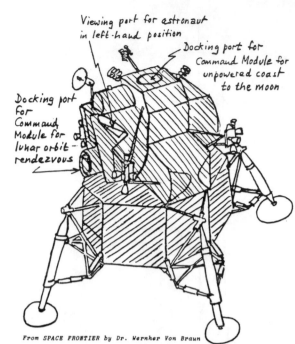

From SPACE FRONTIER by Dr. Wernher Von Braun

tality can go concerns the designing of the lunar landing module of the Gemini Moon-landing Mission. The team which was designing the guidance system of the lunar lander was so caught up in the quantification and instrumentation of this kind of mind set that they were going to have the two astronauts inside the lander looking at dials and gauges which monitored the lander's precise elevation and orientation in relation to the moon's surface. The astronauts would then maneuver the lander by manipulating the appropriate controls in response to what they read on the dials. After experiencing difficulties with the complexities of controlling such an instrument landing, one member of the design team pointed out that if they simply cut a window in the lander, the two highly skilled pilots could fly the module to a safe lunar landing by using their own hands and eyes, *directly*. There are few feedback loops as sensitive, responsive and intelligent as the human *eyemindhand*, especially if we are willing to develop a justified confidence in its use.

RELATIVE MEASURABILITY

Notice that the subdivision and extension of space just explained is dimensionless and still only proportional to the initial spatial unit. Making direct perspectives measurable is usually one of the first steps in the procedure, but I have deliberately separated it here so that the constituent parts of the method can be seen independently.

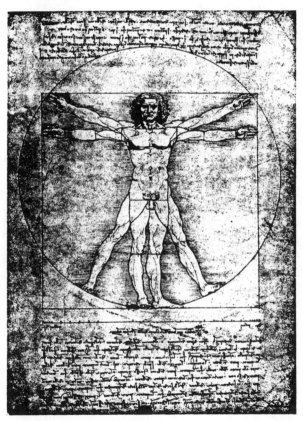

All meaningful measurement is anthropometric. Leonardo's "Man is the measure," though sexist in expression, is still true. The critical scale involved in environmental design is human scale, not metric scale, nor English scale, nor any other *dimensional* scale.

One of the interesting observations you may make in surveying the books on projected perspective methods is that they seldom include the human figure in their perspective examples. This is perhaps because their emphasis is on *dimensional* precision, not *human* scale.

Just as we understand our orientation in space and give directions in terms of our own bodies, our bodies are the most natural *direct* way of measuring space. The best way to make perspectives measurable is to draw them at the level of the human eye. Direct vertical measurability is possible anywhere in the space of an eyelevel perspective by placing a figure wherever you need a measurement. You may assume human eyelevel to be 5'6", 1.5m, 5' or (seated) about 4'. I use 5', even though it is lower than my own eyelevel because of the convenience of the 5' module.

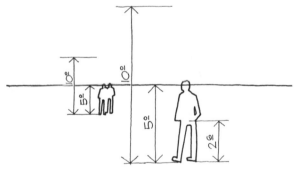

Twice 5' is 10' which comfortably conforms to our base 10 mathematics. Half of 5' is 2'6" or 30" which is an excellent module for furniture: 30" is the height of desks and dining tables; a 30" cube contains a club chair or card table; two 30" cubes make a standard desk or loveseat, and half the 30" height is lounge chair or coffee table height.

Using the 5' assumed height from the eyelevel to the feet of the figure you may directly duplicate or subdivide that distance to reach any needed dimension.

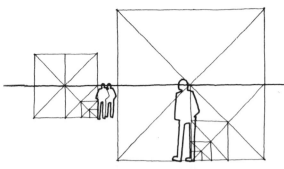

Direct horizontal measurability in the transverse direction is similarly possible anywhere in the perspective by using a 45° triangle (in *two-line*/one-point perspectives) or by establishing a 5' square receding toward the far VL (in *three-line*/two-point perspectives) and using its diagonals to extend or subdivide 5' squares.

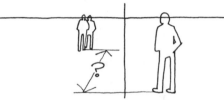

Horizontal measurements in the converging direction (toward the only or near VP) are more difficult and most of the complexities of the various projected perspective methods are devoted to gaining some kind of certainty in these depth measurements.

The method advocated here for drawing perspectives directly, without resorting to plan projection, is based on your willingness to estimate—to guess—to *judge*—an initial unit of depth. Like all skills worth mastering this requires practice and self-confidence built on experience, but once mastered allows perspectives to be drawn freely and directly.

The initial depth judgment is more apt to be accurate if it is made on a vertical plane as far as possible from the near VL. You simply estimate what a 5' square would look like lying in such a converging plane.

109

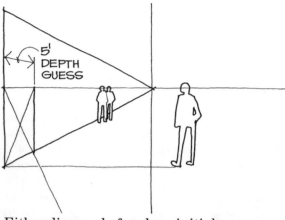

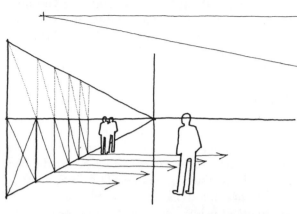

Either diagonal of such an initial square may then be extended to find the VP for the parallel set of such diagonals on the vertical VL. This is simply following the procedure for spatial extension by diagonals explained earlier. The only difference is that now we have assumed the relative size of the initial unit and its extensions.

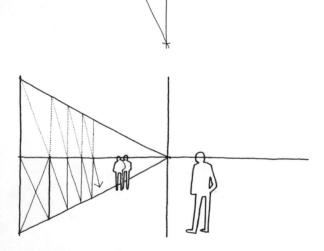

We may also use the shortcut of a diagonal through the bisector explained earlier, if the VP for vertical diagonals is distant or difficult to reach.

110

The depth measurements thus determined may then be projected across the floor to wherever they are needed. This horizontal projection is dead horizontal in *two-line*/one-point perspectives, from the far VP in *three-line*/two-point perspectives.

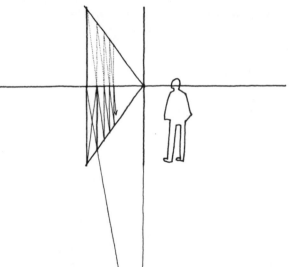

In very small perspective sketches the depth judgment may be made on a vertical plane quite near the near VL and without danger of too much distortion;

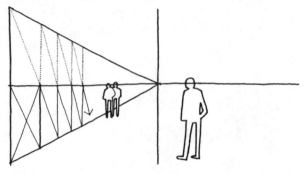

or even on the horizontal ground plane, in which case the VP for the set of diagonals will be on the eyelevel VL;

but for deeper, more extensive perspectives the initial depth judgment and extension should be made on a plane as far from the near VL as possible.

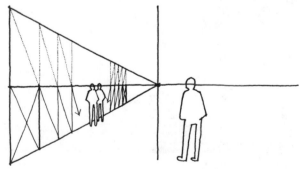

The initial depth judgment should also be made as far forward as possible and the diagonals extended toward the near VL, rather than making the initial depth judgment deep in the space and extending the diagonals forward. Extension of the diagonals more than 10 or 15 feet in front of the initial depth judgment will usually result in distortion.

VARIATIONS

There are several variations in the procedure for drawing direct perspectives and the choice of which variation to use should be based on the size or extent of the perspective you wish to draw.

In drawing exterior perspectives or objects it is usually best to use a three-dimensional cube as the initial spatial unit.

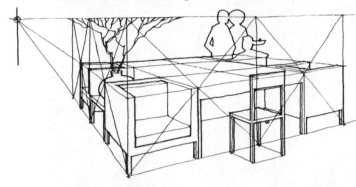

In drawing a single piece of furniture or a furniture arrangement the initial spatial unit may be a 30″ cube. Such a cube may then be extended or subdivided by diagonals as necessary.

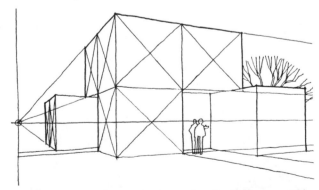

In drawing the exterior of a building a 10′ cube may be the best initial spatial unit, if the building is relatively small and only one story.

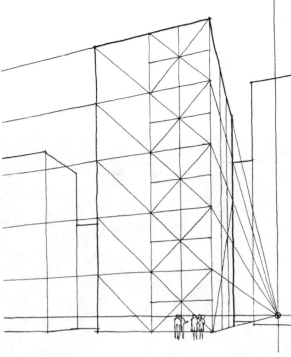

If the building is large and has multiple stories it may be best to begin with a 20′, 30′, 50′ or even 100′ cube.

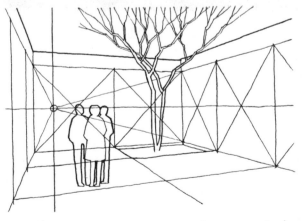

In drawing interior perspectives or exterior spaces which have architectural boundaries, it is probably better to use only two perpendicular vertical planes, one transverse or receding toward the far VL and one converging or receding toward the near VL.

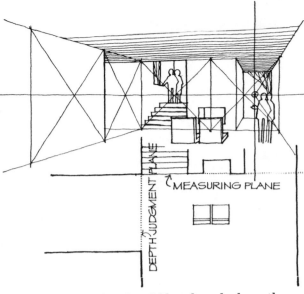

These two planes should be placed where they may most conveniently measure the space to be drawn. The planes may be any convenient height.

In drawing small or moderate sized spaces, 5′ or 10′ high planes using 5′ or 10′ squares as measuring units work well.

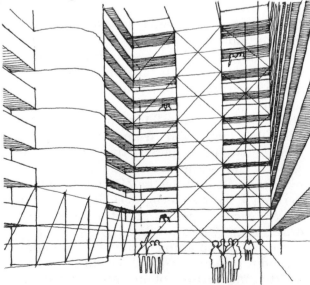

In larger or taller spaces it may be better to use 20′, 30′ or 50′ high planes and squares.

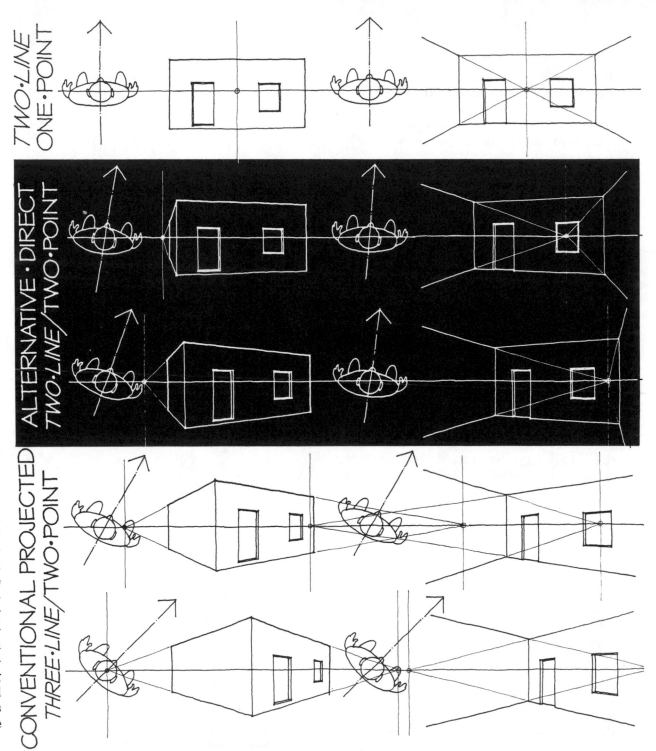

TWO·LINE ONE·POINT

ALTERNATIVE · DIRECT
TWO·LINE/TWO·POINT

CONVENTIONAL PROJECTED
THREE·LINE/TWO·POINT

The colored pages which follow summarize this section on perspective and show a detailed framework for one specific application of the direct perspective method. This particular framework and procedure was developed to fill the gap between the conventional "one-point" and "two-point" plan-projected methods. This particular framework is called *two-line*/two-point perspective because the slightly converging transverse plane recognizes the influence of a far VP without having to reach it; but also recognizes the impossibility of reaching points along a far VL and draws sets of parallel lines lying in transverse, "far-vanishing" planes (including extending diagonals) dead parallel. The grid of the measuring plane also introduces dimensional measurability anywhere in the perspective.

112

AN ALTERNATIVE METHOD

TWO-LINE/TWO-POINT PERSPECTIVE

The perspective method which follows, and which I strongly advocate for design drawing, is a further simplification of the conventional methods. It is not original with me, having been used in similar forms for a long time by professional designers and delineators. I claim only the particular form, nomenclature and rationale which follow. I take some pride in them, however, because the disuse of perspectives as design drawings has resulted, as much as anything, from the lack of an exposition and argument for a particular simplified form capable of persuading teachers to venture beyond the exclusive dogma of plan-projected methods.

I do not recommend the abandonment of the conventional methods. They are still very worthwhile to know about. The fact that they are so little used in the design process, however, seems reason enough to consider quicker, more useful methods, leaving the traditional methods for final presentation perspectives after all design decisions have been made.

As an alternative to the traditional perspective methods described above, the two-line-two-point method which follows offers these advantages:

- It avoids static, coincidental views of space.
- It overcomes the limitation of drawing board size.
- It may be drawn directly without a predetermined plan or section.

The simplification of the *two-line*/two-point perspective method and the reason for its name is that it uses both VPs of the conventional "two-point" method without having to reach the farther one for projection. It always has a near VP located within the drawing on the wide side of the perspective framework, and a far VP out of reach to one side or the other.

In the *two-line*/two-point method we will assign names to the three sets of planes which make up any orthogonal composition:

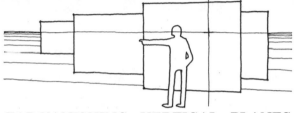

FAR-VANISHING VERTICAL PLANES which vanish very subtly to a vertical VL which is too far away to reach;

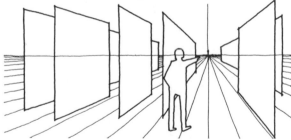

NEAR-VANISHING VERTICAL PLANES which vanish sharply to the vertical VL which is always included at the wide side of the perspective framework; and

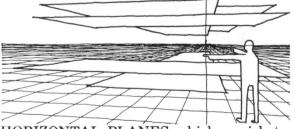

HORIZONTAL PLANES which vanish to the horizontal eyelevel VL.

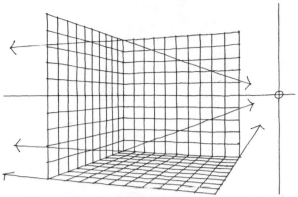

It is useful to conceive the three sets of parallel planes as each being made up of two sets of parallel lines which are parallel/perpendicular to the edges of the planes. There are only three sets of parallel lines altogether because each set occurs in two adjacent planes. For simplification the influence of the far VP is recognized but the far VL and other VPs on it are not. Diagonals on far vanishing planes are drawn dead parallel.

The *two-line*/two point perspective method consists entirely of two vertical planes at right angles to one another which are imposed on three-dimensional space in order to measure it and draw it. In this way it joins a large family of artificial measuring systems which we impose on various aspects of the world in order to quantify them in some relative way. Lines of longitude and latitude, the Cartesian coordinates, or in a broader sense, the months, days and minutes, and the notes of the musical scale are all arbitrary measuring systems which we impose on space, time and sound in order to make them more manageable and communicable.

The method is just another of these measuring systems, perhaps more useful than the traditional methods, because during the design process it allows us to measure and draw three-dimensional space directly, straight up, viewed from the erect stance which is uniquely human, without bowing our heads to the tedium of plan projection.

113

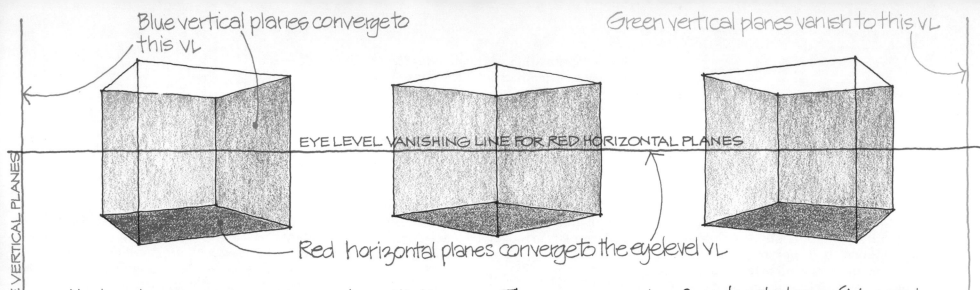

Green vertical planes vanish to this VL

EYE LEVEL VANISHING LINE FOR RED HORIZONTAL PLANES

VANISHING LINE FOR BLUE VERTICAL PLANES

Red horizontal planes converge to the eyelevel VL

Understanding perspective begins with the comprehension that all rectangular compositions consist of 3 sets of mutually perpendicular planes (blue, green and red above.)

There are 2 sets of vertical planes (blue and green) and one horizontal set (red) Each set of planes converges to its own vanishing line—slipping into it at infinity like letters into a slot.

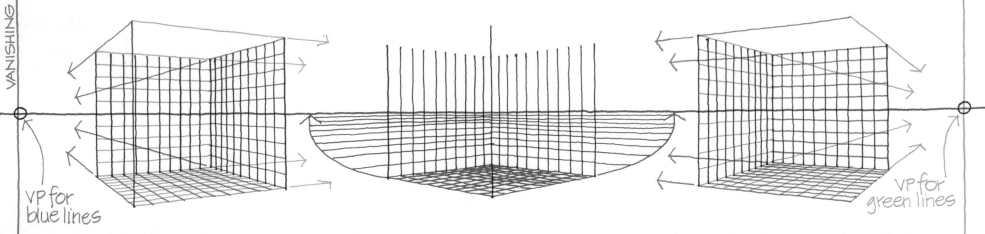

VP for blue lines

VP for green lines

The 3 sets of planes may be thought of as consisting of perpendicular pairings of 3 sets of parallel lines. 2 of the pairs are horizontal lines (blue and green) and vanish toward a VP where the eye level VL intersects the blue or green VL.

The 3rd set of parallel lines is vertical and does not converge. The 2 sets of lines which make up the horizontal planes (red) may also be conceived of as rotating like the ribs of a woman's fan and collapsing into the eye level VL at infinity since their VPs are on that VL.

114

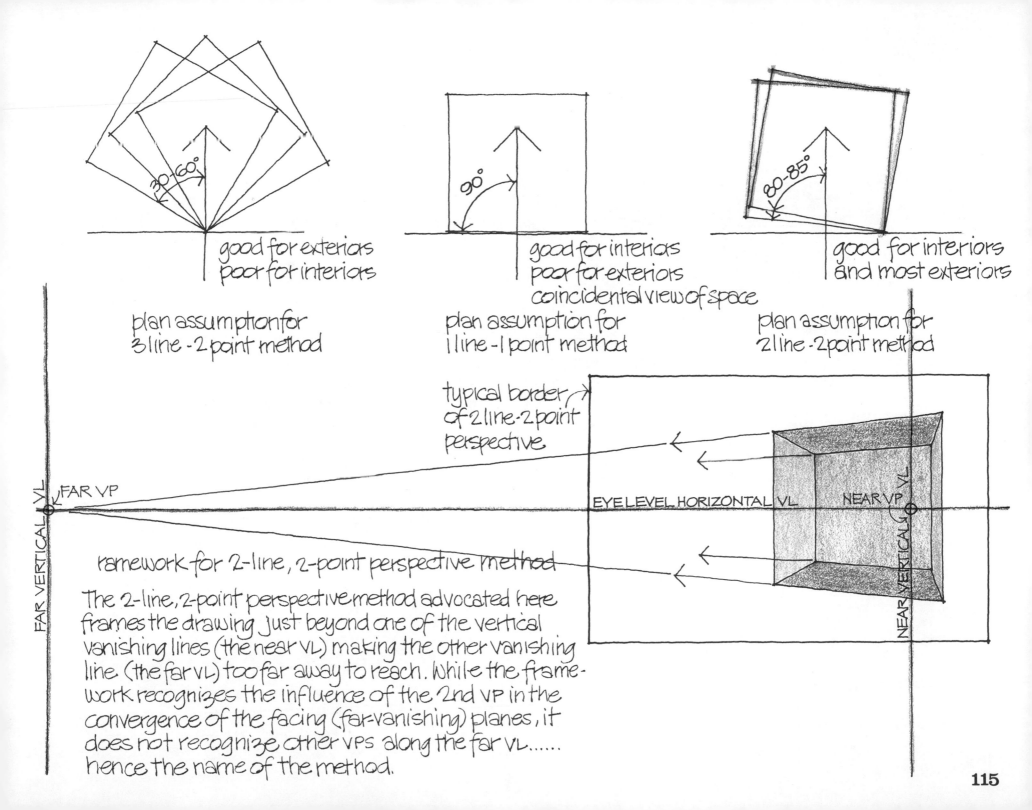

good for exteriors
poor for interiors

plan assumption for
3 line - 2 point method

good for interiors
poor for exteriors
coincidental view of space

plan assumption for
1 line - 1 point method

good for interiors
and most exteriors

plan assumption for
2 line - 2 point method

typical border
of 2 line - 2 point
perspective

FAR VERTICAL VL

FAR VP

EYE LEVEL HORIZONTAL VL

NEAR VP

NEAR VERTICAL VL

framework for 2-line, 2-point perspective method

The 2-line, 2-point perspective method advocated here frames the drawing just beyond one of the vertical vanishing lines (the near VL) making the other vanishing line (the far VL) too far away to reach. While the framework recognizes the influence of the 2nd VP in the convergence of the facing (far-vanishing) planes, it does not recognize other VPs along the far VL...... hence the name of the method.

115

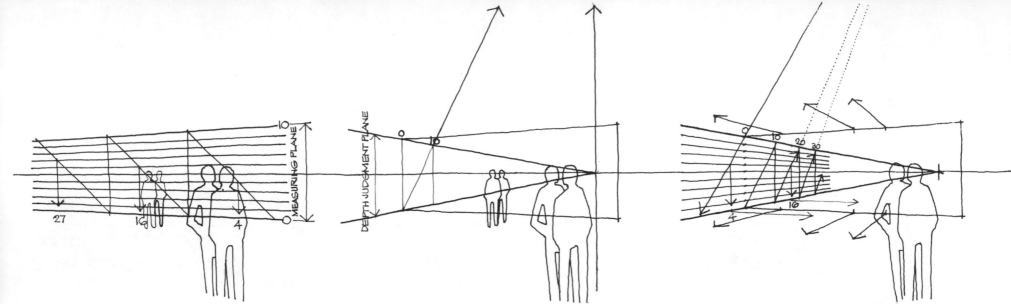

- MARK OFF VERTICAL & LATERAL MEASUREMENTS BY INTERSECTING THE GRID OF THE MEASURING PLANE WITH A 45° DIAGONAL.

PERSPECTIVE METHOD

- PLACE A NEAR-VANISHING DEPTH-JUDGMENT PLANE AS FAR AWAY FROM THE NEAR VP AS POSSIBLE.
- JUDGE A 10' DEPTH AND ESTABLISH THE VP FOR DIAGONALS IN NEAR-VANISHING VERTICAL PLANES.

- MARK OFF DEPTH MEASUREMENTS BY INTERSECTING THE CORNERED GRID WITH DIAGONALS FROM THE VP FOR VERTICAL DIAGONALS.
- EXTEND THE VERTICAL, LATERAL AND DEPTH MEASUREMENTS TO COMPLETE THE PERSPECTIVE.

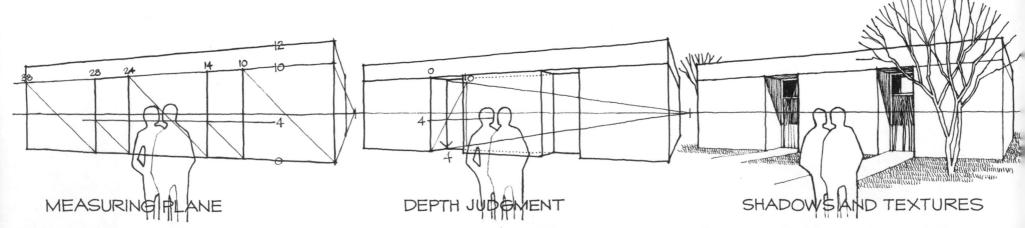

MEASURING PLANE   DEPTH JUDGMENT   SHADOWS AND TEXTURES

DRAWING A MODULAR BUILDING MADE UP OF 3 10' CUBES CONNECTED BY 2 4' WIDE ENTRY LINKS CONSISTING OF A 3' DOOR AND SIDELIGHT RECESSED 4' UNDER A 2' DEEP ROOF STRUCTURE

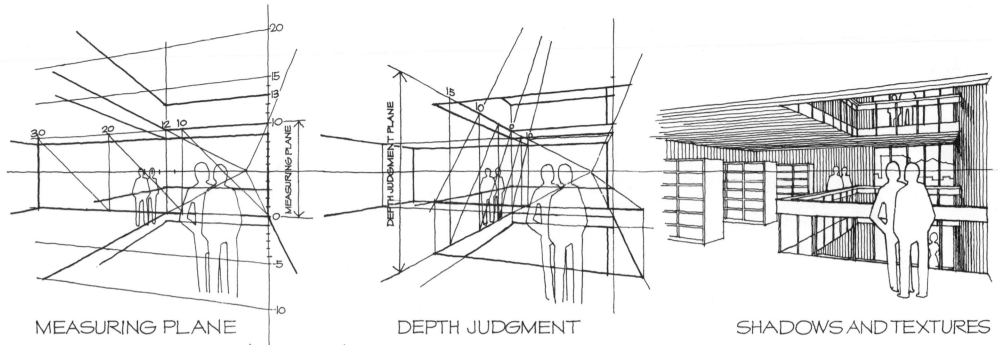

MEASURING PLANE   DEPTH JUDGMENT   SHADOWS AND TEXTURES

DRAWING A SPACE 30¹ WIDE & 9¹ HIGH CONNECTING VERTICALLY TO SIMILAR SPACES ABOVE & BELOW
BY A 12¹ WIDE X 17¹ DEEP OPEN WELL SURROUNDED BY A 3¹ RAILING. WELL AT RIGHT SIDE OF THE SPACE

17

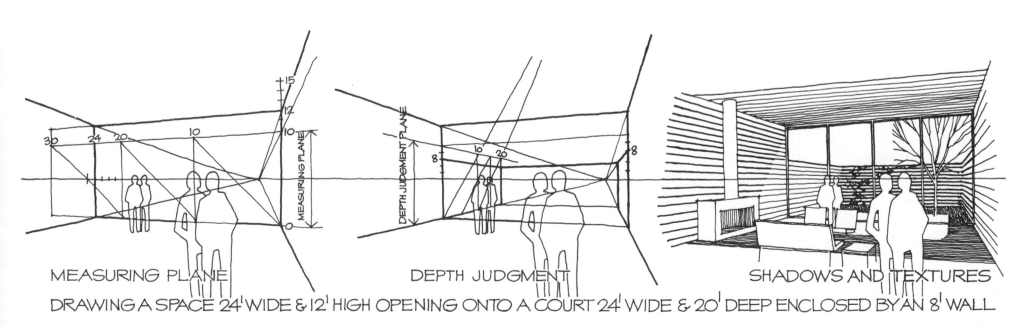

MEASURING PLANE   DEPTH JUDGMENT   SHADOWS AND TEXTURES

DRAWING A SPACE 24¹ WIDE & 12¹ HIGH OPENING ONTO A COURT 24¹ WIDE & 20¹ DEEP ENCLOSED BY AN 8¹ WALL

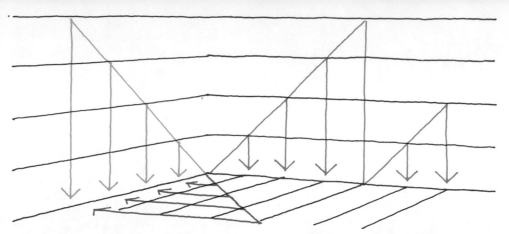

A measured grid on any plane may be transferred
to any other plane by intersecting it with a diagonal.

Spatial Subdivision By Diagonal

A rectangle in any plane may be subdivided
into half and half again by intersecting diagonals.

Spatial Extension By Diagonal

diagonals in near-vanishing vertical (green) planes
will emanate from a VP on the near vertical VL and
will strike off successive 10' squares either vertically
(as shown) or in depth.

diagonals in far-vanishing vertical (blue) planes
are drawn dead parallel because their VP is
too far to reach. these diagonals will mark off
successive 10' squares sideways (as shown) or vertically

diagonals in horizontal (red) planes will
emanate from a VP on the eye level line and
will strike off successive 10' squares either
in depth (as shown) or sideways.

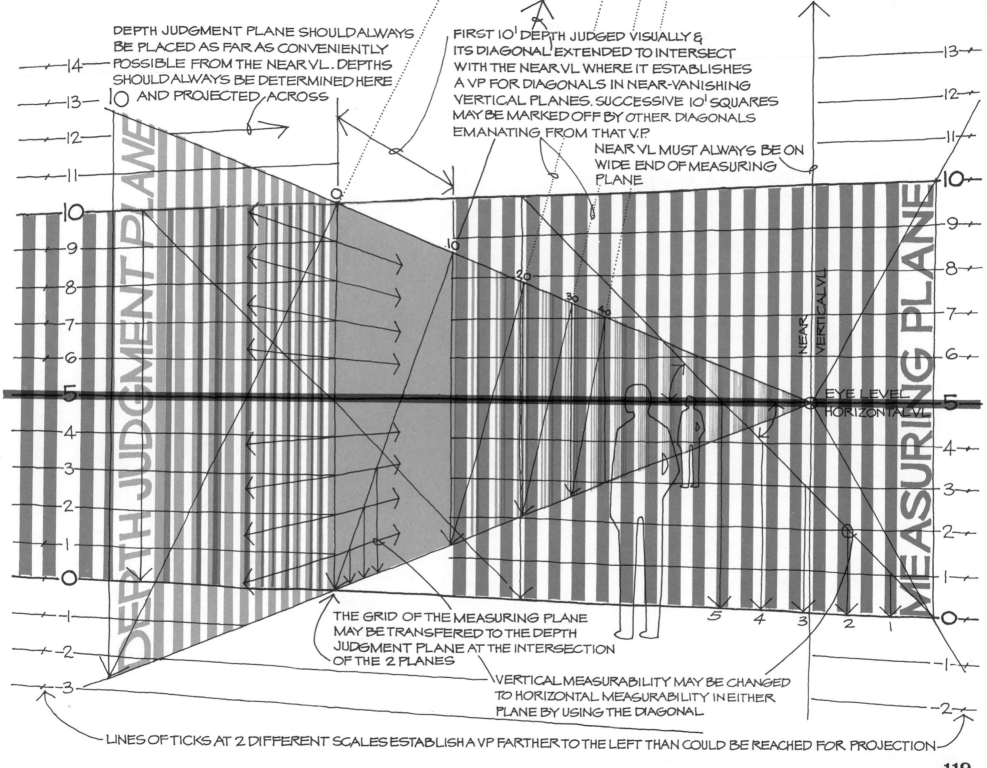

DEPTH JUDGMENT PLANE SHOULD ALWAYS BE PLACED AS FAR AS CONVENIENTLY POSSIBLE FROM THE NEAR VL. DEPTHS SHOULD ALWAYS BE DETERMINED HERE AND PROJECTED ACROSS

FIRST 10' DEPTH JUDGED VISUALLY & ITS DIAGONAL EXTENDED TO INTERSECT WITH THE NEAR VL WHERE IT ESTABLISHES A VP FOR DIAGONALS IN NEAR-VANISHING VERTICAL PLANES. SUCCESSIVE 10' SQUARES MAY BE MARKED OFF BY OTHER DIAGONALS EMANATING FROM THAT V.P.

NEAR VL MUST ALWAYS BE ON WIDE END OF MEASURING PLANE

DEPTH JUDGMENT PLANE

MEASURING PLANE

NEAR VERTICAL VL

EYE LEVEL
HORIZONTAL VL

THE GRID OF THE MEASURING PLANE MAY BE TRANSFERED TO THE DEPTH JUDGMENT PLANE AT THE INTERSECTION OF THE 2 PLANES

VERTICAL MEASURABILITY MAY BE CHANGED TO HORIZONTAL MEASURABILITY IN EITHER PLANE BY USING THE DIAGONAL

LINES OF TICKS AT 2 DIFFERENT SCALES ESTABLISH A VP FARTHER TO THE LEFT THAN COULD BE REACHED FOR PROJECTION

119

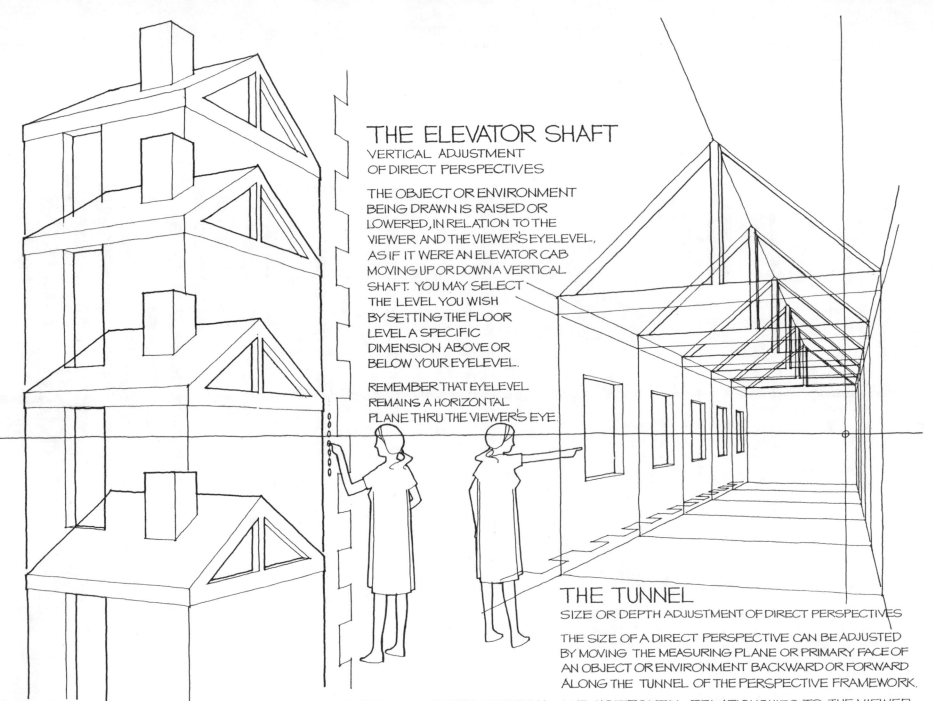

THE ELEVATOR SHAFT
VERTICAL ADJUSTMENT
OF DIRECT PERSPECTIVES

THE OBJECT OR ENVIRONMENT
BEING DRAWN IS RAISED OR
LOWERED, IN RELATION TO THE
VIEWER AND THE VIEWER'S EYE LEVEL,
AS IF IT WERE AN ELEVATOR CAB
MOVING UP OR DOWN A VERTICAL
SHAFT. YOU MAY SELECT
THE LEVEL YOU WISH
BY SETTING THE FLOOR
LEVEL A SPECIFIC
DIMENSION ABOVE OR
BELOW YOUR EYE LEVEL.

REMEMBER THAT EYE LEVEL
REMAINS A HORIZONTAL
PLANE THRU THE VIEWER'S EYE.

THE TUNNEL
SIZE OR DEPTH ADJUSTMENT OF DIRECT PERSPECTIVES

THE SIZE OF A DIRECT PERSPECTIVE CAN BE ADJUSTED
BY MOVING THE MEASURING PLANE OR PRIMARY FACE OF
AN OBJECT OR ENVIRONMENT BACKWARD OR FORWARD
ALONG THE TUNNEL OF THE PERSPECTIVE FRAMEWORK.

ONE OF THE ADVANTAGES OF DIRECT PERSPECTIVES IS THAT THE VERTICAL AND HORIZONTAL RELATIONSHIPS TO THE VIEWER
ARE DIRECTLY ADJUSTABLE AS THE DRAWING DEVELOPS – WITHOUT THE REPOSITIONING AND REPROJECTION NECESSARY WITH
THE PROJECTED METHODS. THIS FLEXIBILITY ALLOWS BOTH THE VERTICAL POSITION AND SIZE OF DRAWINGS TO BE EASILY ADJUSTED.

CHOOSING THE VIEW

While the wisdom required to choose the best perspective view of any space or object is largely the product of experience, there is some initial advice which may be worthwhile. First of all, the idea that you are only ALLOWED a single perspective view of any space or object is questionable. The attempt to try to show all the aspects and qualities of any designed environment in any single view is obviously futile. At least two perspectives are needed to show any rectangular space or object, and complex environments require many more.

THE DIRECTION OF THE VIEW.

Choosing the direction of the perspective view is much like choosing the best section and should always be taken toward the most interesting or characteristic profile of the space.

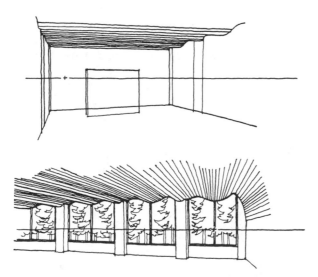

A space which has an undulating ceiling, like Alvar Aalto's Viipuri Library, for example, should not be shown head on. A straight ahead view will obscure half of the undulating profile and not show the real shape of the space.

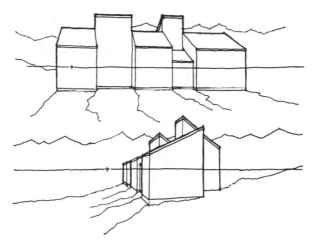

The same criterion also applies to objects. A building which is a collection of shed roofs will be very dull and uncharacteristic drawn head on—up the slopes, and should rather be drawn from the side—across the slopes.

THE LEVEL OF THE VIEW

offers other opportunities or pitfalls in multi-level space. Generally it is always wiser to take all perspectives of multi-level environments from the lowest level. This is because stairs and level changes are much easier to draw from the lowest position since the faces of the stair risers or level changes will appear directly. On the other hand it is almost impossible to show any part of a descending stair in an eyelevel perspective.

For those times when it is necessary to show a multi-level environment from the top or from a mid-level balcony I offer the following advice. The temptation is to try to draw balcony views head-on looking over the railing. It requires only a few frustrating attempts to reveal that if the view is taken standing at the railing, the railing will not show in the drawing so there will be no sense of standing anywhere. And if you move the head-on balcony view back so the balcony railing shows, it will obscure the view down into the space below. The better alternative is to take the view sideways ALONG the balcony so that both the viewer's position on the balcony and the view into the space below are revealed.

SPATIAL EXTENSIONS.

One last piece of advice is to always choose the perspective view which reveals the most interesting spatial extensions. This would seem rather obvious, but we often forget that the most powerful category of interest in a perspective is spatial interest and that spatial interest is potential kinesthetic interest. This means that perspectives must never be considered as flat, two-dimensional wall decorations that you stand and look AT. You should rather look/walk into them with your *eyemindbody*. Never miss the opportunity to show successive layers of space in a perspective, and remember that the promise of the kinesthetic experience of space by the most careful rendering may be severly limited by an initially stupid choice of view.

121

KINESTHETIC SPACE

Spatial interest in the environment is potential kinesthetic interest—the anticipated experience of objects, spaces and vistas which are only partly seen, but which will be revealed by our movement through the environment. This kind of interest was discussed earlier in the chapter on PERCEPTION and redefined as a category of drawing interest under the preceding section on DRAWING TECHNIQUES. Now we need to consider how spatial interest is best represented in drawing. Perspectives represent the promise of the potential kinesthetic experience of space because we normally use vision to predict experience in advance. On entering a room, we can sense, from the doorway, whether further exploration will be rewarding or dull. There are several details in drawing perspectives, however, to which we must attend if our perspectives are to reach their full potential as representations of kinesthetic space.

SURFACES. As Gibson has pointed out, the evolution of our visual perceptual system has always included the perception of the earth's surface and the textural gradient of that surface from coarse to fine as it recedes into the distance. The perception of this surface and all similar continuous surfaces is essential to our perception of three-dimensional space. For design drawing this means that the bounding surfaces of spaces should be indicated with a graduated texture, in response to their distance from us. The spotty rendering of continuous surfaces can destroy the spatial reality of drawing. This also means that, given the choice of where to place texture in a perspective, *always* place it on the continuous *surfaces* (paving, carpet, masonry, paneling, grass or gravel) rather than the *objects,* which may be on or in front of the surfaces (furniture, people, etc.) At the spatial edges where a surface texture disappears,

make sure the texture actually touches the edge. Beginning students often stop textures short and create a "halo effect" all around any object which sits on or in front of a textured surface. Such "halo effects" completely destroy the spatial quality of the drawing and it begins to degenerate into a collection of lines on paper.

VOLUMES. The perception of the spatial volumes with which environmental designers compose environments is dependent on the perception of the intersections of their bounding surface—their *corners*. In placing objects (people, furniture or plants) in

a perspective, and especially on or in front of one of the textured, space-defining surfaces, be careful not to obscure edges or corners which define the space. To hide the resolution of a corner, or the end of a carpet and the beginning of floor tile behind a table, for instance, is to destroy the definitions on which the perception of spatial volumes depend.

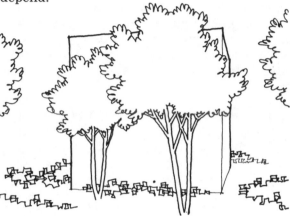

This can be illustrated by demonstrating how much of a cube can be removed between the corners without destroying the perception of a cube;

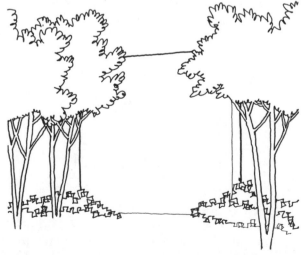

and how the same cube is quickly destroyed by removing only the corners.

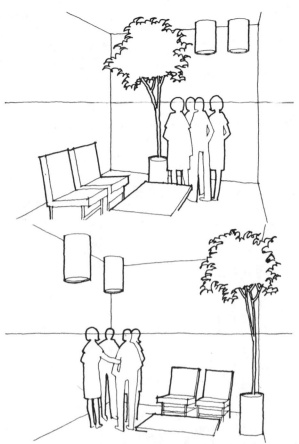

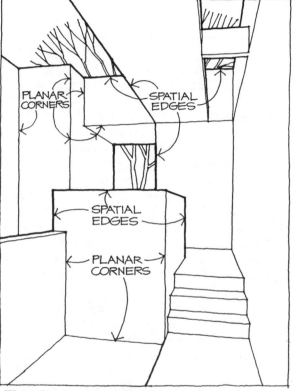

ceiver is positioned, while planar corners are only a physical fact. An outside planar corner *physically* also may be a spatial edge, but only if one of the planes which form it is hidden from the viewpoint of a perceiver, so that *perceptually* it becomes an edge and not a corner.

This distinction is critical because in a line drawing the only means of expression is the relative visual weight of the lines, and if we draw all the lines the same weight we forfeit the opportunity of saying that *spatially,* and particularly *kinesthetically,* those lines represent two categorically different things. In no way are they the same, for as we move through any environment one just lies there passively (planar corners) while the other slides dynamically against its background either progressively revealing or hiding more of whatever surface lies behind it.

EDGES. When we represent space with a line drawing, the lines we draw represent two quite different constituents of the environment: *planar corners* and *spatial edges.* Planar corners are the intersections of planes where both, or all three intersecting planes are seen. These corners define spatial volumes and are essential to the perception of space in a drawing. The careful rendering of both *surfaces* and *volumes* is essential to the drawn representation of kinesthetic space because they form the definite backgrounds against which the real action of kinesthetic perception occurs. The action in the perceptual experience of kinesthetic space is always concentrated at the *spatial edges* of any environment. Spatial edges are a *perceptual phenomena,* dependent on where the per-

So there is no misunderstanding about what constitutes a spatial edge, let me detail the definition. By edge I mean the masking outline of any form or surface that is perceptually separated from its background. In geometric forms this edge will always be one of the form's planar corners, but in curved or irregular forms, like the human figure or a tree, this outline of the form's silhouette will shift freely over the form in relationship to the perceiver's position. The best analogy is perhaps the children's cardboard scenes in which various figures and objects are punched out and have tabs inserted into a base so that they stand up as flat silhouettes. Looked at from the front each silhouette hides or masks part of other silhouettes and whatever else is in the background. A line drawing of the spatial edges of an environment is essentially like a line drawing of one of these cardboard scenes.

123

Since we are a constantly moving perceptual system, the edges which carry the most information about the environment are the spatial edges. They are the hemlines of kinesthetic perception. The movement of spatial edges against their backgrounds which accompanies the movement of a perceiver through space varies in three ways, and in the variance carries or confirms three kinds of spatial information:

- *the edge's relationship to our line of movement*
- *the edge's distance in front of the surfaces it partially hides*
- *the edge's distance from us*

Any hierarchy of line weights in a line drawing which attempts to represent the kinesthetic experience of space would seem to need a basis in these three variables. The first one, however—*the edge's relationship to our line of movement*—although extremely meaningful in the real experience of moving through an environment is only confusing when used as a basis for profiling a drawing. In the moving perception of space the slipping, sliding movement which occurs at all spatial edges is accelerated in direct proportion to the edge's lateral displacement from the target point of our direction of movement. The spatial edges move faster and faster against their background as they approach our peripheral vision, like the acceleration of telephone poles viewed from a moving train. The reason this perceptual phenomena doesn't seem to work as a basis for profiling a perspective is that the direction of movement into a drawing does not necessarily follow from the framework of a perspective. Since we swivel our heads and our eyes, there is no particular relationship between our view of a space and our potential direction of movement into it.

I have found that a hierarchy of line weights based on a combination of the last two variables seems to be very effective in representing the kinesthetic experience of an environment in a perspective, and in assuring that students do perceive their perspective drawings as space.

In representing the kinesthetic experience of an environment I would recommend that planar corners be drawn with the lightest line weight and that all spatial edges be profiled with a darker line. This is the basic step, to simply indicate that these two weights of line represent two completely different kinds of things. A more sophisticated representation of kinesthetic space would then establish a hierarchy of line weights with the heaviness of the line indicating the relative depth of the spatial separation or the distance any spatial edge lies in front of its background. This hierarchy indicating *the edge's distance in front of the surfaces it partially hides* must be overlaid, and thereby diluted by another hierarchy based on *the edge's distance from us*. That is, if two edges were each separated by twenty feet from their backgrounds, but one was immediately in the foreground and the other across the street, the nearer one would be profiled heavier. To put the relationship between the two hierarchies another way, the spatial separation between a distant range of mountains and its infinitely deep spatial background is *infinite* and under the *depth* hierarchy would seem to be the darkest line in the drawing, but its dilution under the *distance* hierarchy by being far away from us would reduce the line weight to being just a little darker than a planar corner.

Experience, and the available time, will govern when the point of diminishing returns is reached in applying such a hierarchy of line weights to a drawing. Even the beginnings of such a hierarchy, however, will make an ordinary line drawing begin to represent the kinesthetic experience of space which is the basis of all spatial interest in a drawing, or in the environment.

CONTEXT
The peripheral space which surrounds any designed environment offers opportunities for design and drawing which should never be ignored. The responses which any designed space or object can make to its context constitute perhaps the richest collection of determinants with which a designer can work. The quality of our collective environment depends on sensitive contextual responses.

In drawing, the context gives us the means to make a drawing believable as three-dimensional space by appealing to the perceptual cues by which we have perceived space all down our evolution. We can use the context to make a drawing be perceived as space by:

- *establishing the ground plane*
- *layering the background*
- *articulating the distance*

ESTABLISHING THE GROUND PLANE.
As Gibson points out, our perception of space depends on a continuous "ground" beginning at our feet and receding to the horizon. In *The Perception of the Visual World* (1950), he explains:

> The world with a ground under it—the visual world of surfaces and edges—is...the prototype of the world in which we all live....

> An out-of-doors world is one in which the lower portion of the visual field (corresponding to the upper portion of each retinal image) is invariably filled by a projection of the terrain. The upper portion of the visual field is usually filled with a projection of the sky. Between the upper and lower portions is the skyline, high or low as

the observer looks down or up, but always cutting the normal visual field in a horizontal section. This is the kind of world in which our primitive ancestors lived. It was also the environment in which took place the evolution of visual perception in *their* ancestors. During the millions of years in which some unknown animal species evolved into our human species, land and sky were the constant visual stimuli to which the eyes and brain responded....

We perceive this horizontal surface on which we have evolved as a series of horizontal receding spatial contours, each of which occludes some hidden space behind it. The nearer horizontal contour lines will simply be minor ripples in the earth's surface, or curbs, steps and walks in an urban environment. Depending on the terrain, these will generally appear closer together as the distance between them is foreshortened as they recede. Any simple stack of horizontal lines in which the lines get progressively closer together as they go up will be perceived as a horizontal plane, because it will abstractly represent the context in which our vision evolved.

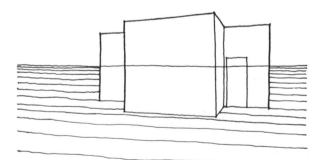

This means that the representation of three-dimensional space begins with establishing the ground plane, and that this can be done in drawing by applying a receding texture emphasizing, or consisting solely of, horizontal lines which *cross* our visual field. The horizontal spatial contour lines may be paving textures, joints in a sidewalk, low hedges, or lines of grass blades, and they may be molded

to describe slopes or deformations of the ground plane. If the ground plane is to appear to lie down horizontally and form the necessary base for the spatial perception of the drawing, however, the dominant lines which render the ground surface must cross the visual field horizontally and must appear closer together as they recede.

LAYERING THE BACKGROUND. In traditional pictorial composition the contextual space of any painting is conceived as a foreground and background providing a setting for the dominant interest of the middleground. If we set any object, such as a building on the ground plane we have established, it immediately divides the remaining space into a foreground and background. Notice how the horizontal spatial contours with which we established the ground plane disappear and reappear behind the building. This interrupted continuousness is the key to layering the background of any perspective.

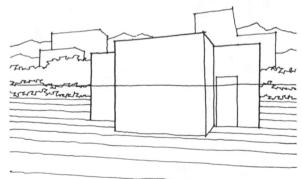

Unless the building is sited in the Australian outback or on one of our endless midwestern planes, there will be something behind the building. In an urban context this background would consist of layers of other buildings. In other contexts the background might be layers of hedgerows, trees or mountains. Whatever happens to be back there is best and most efficiently rendered as receding lay-

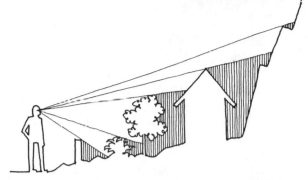

ers of space indicated by simple overlapping outlines. The one criterion is *continuity*. Always render the same background layers disappearing behind one side of a building and reappearing beyond the other side. It is very disconcerting to see a row of trees disappear behind one side of a building and, say, a freight train emerge from behind the other.

ARTICULATING THE DISTANCE. The last perceptual cue to be included in using the context to make a drawing look like three-dimensional space is the placing of other objects on the ground plane, especially in the foreground, to articulate the distance into various spatial units. Just as the initial placement of the building on the ground plane divided the continuous space into a foreground and background, so the placement of additional vertical objects will subdivide the space further and promote the perception of the flat drawing as three-dimensional space.

Trees, figures, tall shrubs, light standards, and various structures are all potential spatial articulators. Although their placement to the side of a perspective may help frame the building, the most dramatic position in which to place these objects is directly in front of the building. Such placements must be carefully studied so as not to obscure the building, especially its volume-defining corners, but the risk is worth taking because they have the great benefit of directly subdividing the space in front of the building. The effect of these vertical objects can be further enhanced by extending horizontal bands (hedges, contours, low walls etc.) *between* the vertical objects and the building.

INTERIOR PERSPECTIVES also need an indication of their context in order to be accurate predictive representations of designed environments. As in exterior perspectives the building or enclosure is the middleground. What was the background in an exterior perspective, however, is now the distant exterior space seen through the doors and windows of the interior and what was the foreground of the exterior perspective becomes the figures and furnishings of the interior.

In drawing the exterior space it is important to indicate continuous bands of trees, mountains or buildings which disappear and reappear through the various doors and windows, causing the exterior space to be perceived as continuous and surrounding, as in the backgrounds of exterior perspectives. The figures and furnishings which make up the additional interest of the interior space should be very carefully placed so as few of the corners and space-defining planar intersections are obscured as possible. Vertical elements like lamps, columns, figures and plants will help articulate the space, however, by extending upward from the floor or downward from the

ceiling to intermittently break the horizontal intersections of wall/floor and wall/ceiling. The figures and furnishings should be collected into groups or layers insofar as possible so that their individuality is not emphasized.

Both the continuous layers of exterior space and interior groups of figures and furnishings should be drawn very simply so that the effort and emphasis of the drawing remains on the interior walls of the enclosure.

SIMPLIFIED CONTEXTUAL INDICATIONS which are reduced to simple but carefully descriptive outlines are best because:

- *they keep the emphasis on the middleground*
- *they correspond to our focal vision*
- *they take less time to draw*

and they still allow the context to contribute the believable three-dimensional setting which only it can accomplish.

SPECIFIC SLIDE-PROJECTED CONTEXTS. Perspectives used to study anything intended to relate to its context should accurately represent that context. There is no point in spending the time making drawings of the context if you have a camera available. Photographic slides of any context can be easily projected and traced. If you have a projector with a zoom lens available, it is worthwhile to make a permanent framework for the projector over your drawing board. Such a slide-projected setup will allow you to trace people, cars, trees—anything you have on slides—into your representational drawings.

TONAL INTEREST AND LIGHT

Tonal interest in the environment is entirely the result of light reflecting differently off the environment's various surfaces. Although this reflected light carries *all* the visually perceivable information about the world, this particular interest category is only concerned with that visual array—ranging from white through all the shades of gray (and other colors) to black—that is reflected by the various surface orientations in an environment. Tonal interest is the most powerful interest category in the environment and the last category to be lost as we cross the threshold into blindness.

The articulation of reflected light into patterns of dark and light happens in two general ways:
- *relative whiteness of the reflective surface*
- *relative orientation of the reflective surface to the source of light*

We will be concerned exclusively with the second kind of reflected light, since relative surface whiteness is a matter of the physical properties or inherent color and texture; and, as such, only an inevitable additive to the surface's relationship to light.

The relative orientation of a reflected surface to the source of light also occurs in two ways, or under two different conditions: *direct* light and *indirect* light. These two conditions under which surface reflectance occurs are presented here as an extension of perspective method, because the environment is best represented whole, in perspective; and the understanding of how to render the alternatives for illuminating the environment must be built on the foundation of perspective method.

We perceive our environment immediately and confidently from the patterned reflectance of lights and darks because it is one of the first sets of sensory signals we master. We can understand a complex three-dimensional environment from the shadow patterns of a black and white photograph by using an ability developed long ago below the level of consciousness. If we are to learn the ability to draw light falling on the objects and in the environments we design, however, we must learn the ability consciously, with considerable effort. We must belatedly learn to write or *draw* a language which we read effortlessly.

TRADITION. Books on drawing traditionally call the sections devoted to light "Shades and Shadows" or "Shadow-casting." This has always seemed backward to me, since it is the light which is the actor—the positive force, while shade and shadow are simply special negative conditions of the absence of light. One reason for this traditional approach may be the fact that we normally draw with a dark-making tool on white paper so we cannot draw the light, but are limited to drawing the absence of light—the shades and shadows. In order to break with tradition and perhaps see light more correctly, this chapter is deliberately printed on a gray background.

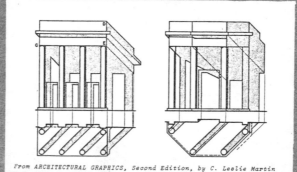

From ARCHITECTURAL GRAPHICS, Second Edition, by C. Leslie Martin

Further, the sun angle is normally assumed to be 45° over the viewer's left shoulder, arbitrarily freezing the movement of the sun and

virtually reducing shadow-casting to another graphic convention like the north arrow. Such a rigid convention simplifies the grading of shadow-casting exercises, but inhibits any understanding of the freedom necessary to intelligent sun placement.

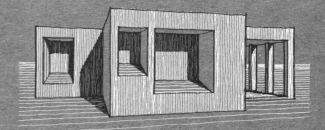

Shadow-casting is also taught almost exclusively on objects, never within spaces.

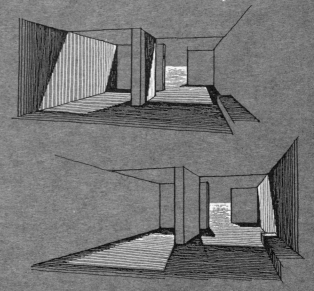

I think it is much more useful to learn shadow-casting three-dimensionally, in perspective, so that the whole shade/shadow system is seen at once, and further, to practice moving the sun and drawing several optional shadow patterns based on alternative sun angles. It is also mandatory to learn shadow-casting from within spaces on *interiors* instead of exclusively on the *exteriors* of objects.

127

DIRECT LIGHT

The most dramatic kind of illumination and the one which offers the most descriptive information about the environment is direct light. The bright whites of sunlit surfaces and the contrasting pattern of dark shadows form at once the clearest and most forceful description of space.

The shadow-casting necessary to render the tonal patterns of direct light has traditionally been taught using plans, sections and elevations, presuming that the object is a known object and chasing back and forth between plan and elevation to learn exactly where the shadows would be at one coincidental moment in time. While this way of learning shadow-casting is very helpful in analyzing the geometric relationships and the resultant shadows on the separate drawings, it tends to be remembered as a fragmented set of rules for manipulating points, lines and angles with little or no holistic understanding of the overall three-dimensional *system* of shadows in the environment.

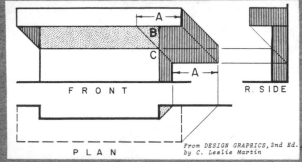

From DESIGN GRAPHICS, 2nd Ed. by C. Leslie Martin

The traditional practice favors the use of plans and elevations as design drawings, since designers understand how to cast shadows on them. Perspectives, on the other hand, are avoided because students are seldom taught how to cast shadows on them, and they remain bland, unilluminated representations compared to the strongly shadowed plans and elevations.

THE SHADOWS OF LINES ON PLANES

In building an understanding of the way light illuminates the built environment it is best to start, as we did in perspective, with the ground plane and the shadows cast on it. We will also begin with the most basic shadow-casting relationships—the shadows of lines on planes; the simplest geometry—rectangular compositions; and the simplest views of space—one-point perspectives. These limitations leave us with only two possible relationships between any line and any plane on which its shadow falls. The line will either be perpendicular or parallel to the plane on which its shadow falls. We will symbolize these two relationships as ⊥ (perpendicular) and ∥ (parallel).

PERPENDICULAR SHADOWS

Shadows cast by a line which is ⊥ to the plane on which the shadow falls will be considered first because this is the relationship that can occur alone (unlike ∥ shadows) and it also is the relationship which initiates all shadow systems.

ON HORIZONTAL PLANES— GROUND OR FLOOR

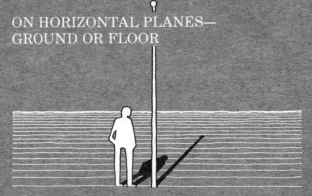

Anytime we stand in the sunlight we cast a shadow on the ground, except in that coincidental position when the sun is precisely⊥ to the point on the earth's surface where we are standing. Because we stand vertically, ⊥ to the horizontal ground plane, our own shadow gives us the basic ⊥ shadow-casting relationship: *the shadow of a vertical line on a horizontal plane.* Another familiar example of this kind of shadow is the shadow cast by a flagpole on the ground.

6am 8am 10am 2pm 4pm 6pm

We can discover by observation that both the angle and length of any ⊥ shadow on the ground will vary dramatically during the day as the sun traverses its arc in the sky. Another basic characteristic of ⊥ shadows is that when they occur alone they are always attached at one end to the line which casts them.

We can better represent and study the characteristics of this kind of shadow if we simply drive a series of vertical stakes into the horizontal ground plane and then study their shadows.

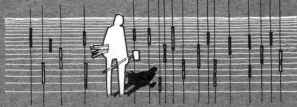

We will find that the shadows of the stakes, like the stakes themselves, will be ∥ to one another, which for the stakes means that they stand as a vertical dead ∥, non-converging set of lines; but for their shadows, since they are horizontal lines lying in the ground plane, being ∥ means that they will all

converge to a common point on the VL for the plane in which they lie, the eyelevel VL. We will call this VP the "flag-pole" shadow VP since it would be the VP for shadows cast by a flagpole on the ground.

This relationship to a VP on the eyelevel VL occurs whether the sun is behind the viewer (so that the shadows converge *toward* the VP), or in front of the viewer (so that the shadows emanate *from* the VP).

The other characteristic we will notice is that at any moment the lengths of all ⊥ shadows will have the same proportion to the length of the line that casts them. In perspective this means that they will foreshorten according to the rules of perspective, and therefore not be measurably the same as they would if you went out in the sun and checked them with a tape measure.

ON VERTICAL PLANES— TRANSVERSE WALLS

If we take our handful of stakes and drive them horizontally into a transverse vertical plane, we will have a second ⊥ relationship: *the shadow of a converging horizontal line on a transverse vertical plane.*

In this case the set of ‖ horizontal lines which cast the shadows will converge to a VP on the eyelevel VL, but their shadows will be dead ‖ (nonconverging) because they lie in a plane which is exactly ‖ to the eyelevel VL and precisely ⊥ to the axis of our vision. As in the previous example each shadow's length will have the same proportions to the length of the line (stake) which casts it.

ON VERTICAL PLANES— CONVERGING WALLS

The third and final ⊥ relationship between a line that casts a shadow and the plane on which the shadow falls is: *the shadow of a transverse horizontal line on a converging vertical plane.*

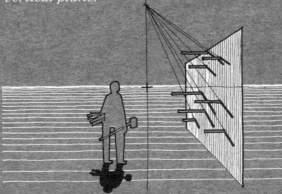

In this case the set of ‖ horizontal lines which casts the shadows is dead ‖ (does not converge). Their shadows are also ‖ to one another but they *do* converge to a VP on the VL for the plane in which they lie.

Here we need to consider the difference made by whether the sun is in front of or behind the viewer. If the sun is in front of the viewer, as shown above, the ⊥ shadows will *emanate* from a VP on the vertical VL somewhere *above* the eyelevel VL. If, on the other hand, the sun is behind the viewer as shown below, the ⊥ shadows will *converge* toward a VP on the vertical VL somewhere *below* the eyelevel VL.

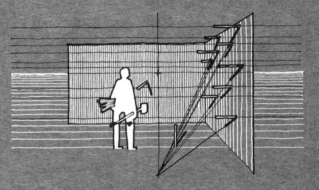

PERPENDICULAR RELATIONSHIPS— SUMMARY

There are only three possible perpendicular shadow-casting relationships between a line and the plane on which the line's shadow falls:

- *the shadow of a vertical line on a horizontal plane*
- *the shadow of a converging horizontal line on a transverse vertical plane*
- *the shadow of a transverse horizontal line on a converging vertical plane.*

We now understand the characteristics of ⊥ shadow-casting relationships. Shadows cast by the set of lines which are ⊥ to the plane on which the shadows fall:

129

- *vary dramatically in angle and length during the day, but remain attached at one end to the line which casts them*
- *at any moment will all be ∥ to one another*
- *will have lengths of the some proportion to the lengths of the lines which cast them.*

A further general characteristic of ⊥ shadows is:

- *they always cut diagonally across any built environment, adding a dynamic element to any sunlit space.*

PARALLEL SHADOWS

Parallel shadows differ from ⊥ shadows in several ways. The most basic difference is that they are always physically separated from the surface on which their shadows fall. This means that, unlike ⊥ shadows, ∥ shadows can never occur alone. They always must rely on ⊥ shadows to spring them free from the surface to which they are ∥, and may only occur as a member of a shadow system.

ON HORIZONTAL PLANES—
GROUND OR FLOOR

In order to build an understanding of ∥ shadows, let us begin with ∥ shadows on the ground plane and use what we have learned about ⊥ shadows.

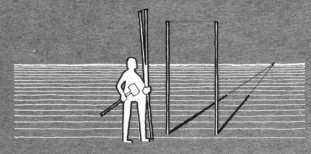

If we drive two tall stakes into the ground so that their tops are level and the same distance from us, the lines which would connect their tops and their bottoms would be ∥ to the

eyelevel VL. Because the length of ⊥ shadows always has the same proportion to the length of the lines which cast them, the line which would connect the ends of the two shadows of the stakes would also be ∥ to the eyelevel VL and to the two previous horizontal connecting lines.

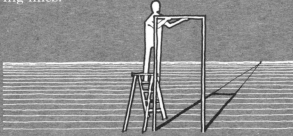

If we lay a crossbar across the tops of the two vertical stakes we will immediately get a corresponding ∥ shadow where we had anticipated. We now have a shadow system made up of the simplest possible combination of ⊥ and ∥ shadows. The crossbar and its shadow demonstrate the first relationship: *the shadow of a transverse horizontal line on a horizontal plane.*

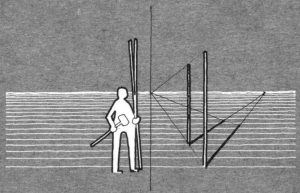

The same principles apply to two stakes of equal height driven into the ground plane so that the pair is on a line ⊥ to the eyelevel VL. The shadow of their crossbar will be ∥ to the crossbar and therefore converge to the same VP. This is the second ∥ relationship: *the shadow of a converging horizontal line on a horizontal plane.*

Notice that in both cases the length of the shadow of the crossbar must be exactly the same length as the crossbar itself. This is because the two shadows which it connects are ∥ to one another and any connector will span the same distance. This will be true for all ∥ shadows.

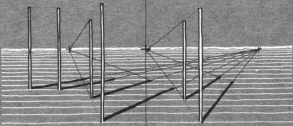

Although we are only considering rectangular compositions, you should understand that this characteristic of ∥ shadows applies to any pair of vertical stakes of the same height, at any angle to the eyelevel VL.

The alignment of each pair of stakes will have its own VP on the eyelevel VL and both the crossbar and its shadow will converge to that VP.

ON VERTICAL PLANES—
TRANSVERSE WALLS

When we drive our pairs of stakes horizontally into a transverse wall, the crossbars will each cast a ∥ shadow on the wall. In this case being ∥ means the crossbar and its shadow will be dead ∥ (non-converging) in the drawing because they lie in planes which are exactly ∥ to the eyelevel VL and precisely ⊥ to our axis of vision.

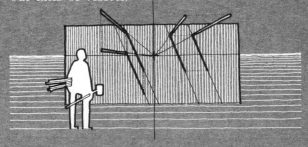

The horizontal crossbar represents the third ⊥ relationship: *the shadow of a transverse horizontal line on a transverse vertical plane.* And the vertical crossbar represents a fourth ⊥ relationship: *the shadow of a vertical line on a transverse vertical plane.*

ON VERTICAL PLANES—
CONVERGING WALLS

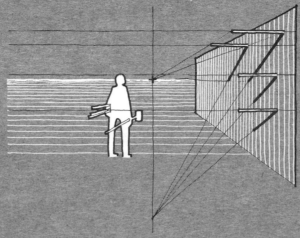

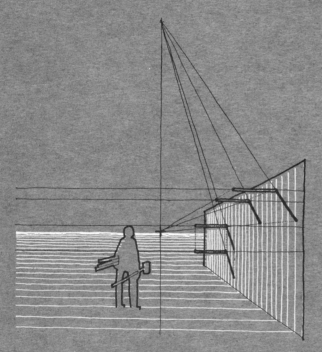

The final pair of ‖ shadow-casting relationships appear when we drive pairs of stakes horizontally in to a converging vertical plane. Their crossbars, as in the preceding four relationships, will cast ‖ shadows on the wall. The vertical crossbar will be dead ‖ to its shadow while the horizontal crossbar will express its ‖ relationship to its shadow by converging to the same VP.

These relationships hold whether the sun is ahead or or behind the viewer.

In this case the horizontal crossbar represents the fifth ‖ relationship: *the shadow of a transverse horizontal line on a converging vertical plane.* And the vertical crossbar gives us the sixth and final ‖ relationship: *the shadow of a vertical line on a converging vertical plane.*

PARALLEL RELATIONSHIPS—
SUMMARY

We can now summarize what we have discovered about ‖ shadows beginning with the six ‖ relationships which are possible between a line and the plane on which the line's shadow falls:

- *the shadow of a transverse horizontal line on a horizontal plane*
- *the shadow of a converging horizontal line on a horizontal plane*
- *the shadow of a transverse horizontal line on a transverse vertical plane*
- *the shadow of a vertical line on a transverse vertical plane*
- *the shadow of a converging horizontal line on a converging vertical plane*
- *the shadow of a vertical line on a converging vertical plane*

The characteristics of the ‖ shadow-casting relationships are that shadows cast by lines which are ‖ to the plane on which they fall:

- *are always ‖ to the line which casts them*
- *are always the same length as the line which casts them*
- *are never attached to the line which casts them*

A further general characteristic of ‖ shadows is:

- *they are always quietly ‖ to the lines, planes, edges and joints of any built environment.*

In applying the rules for ⊥ and ‖ shadows to any shadow-casting situation in perspective we need to be clear about the applied differences between the construction of ⊥ and ‖ shadows.

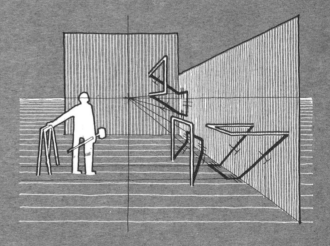

Parallel shadows always converge to the same VP as the line which casts them. That is what being ‖ *means* in perspective. The VPs for ‖ shadows are thus already a permanently established part of any perspective framework.

131

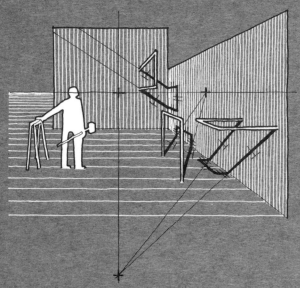

The VPs for ⊥ shadows, on the other hand, vary with the movement of the sun and must be established for each sun position. Troublesome as this responsibility may seem, as with most responsibilities, it is also the source of all freedom and opportunity in shadow-casting.

HOW HIGH THE SUN

We discovered earlier that both the angle and the length of ⊥ shadows varies dramatically during the day. The angle of ⊥ shadows on the ground plane depends on the horizontal angle or orientation of the sun—manifested in the location of the "flagpole" VP (the VP for ⊥ shadows cast by a vertical line on the horizontal ground plane).

The length of ⊥ shadows, however, depends on the vertical angle or height of the sun. The sun's rays fall in a set of ‖ vertical planes arising from the set of ⊥ flagpole shadows.

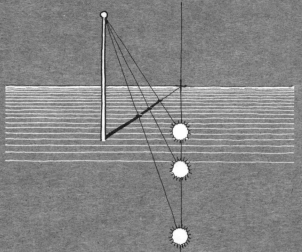

This is a special set of planes. They are not a part of the environment like the walls and floors we have been working with. Instead, they cut across the spaces of any rectangular composition at the flagpole shadow angle, and they have their own special VL, which crosses the eyelevel VL at the flagpole VP. The sun's rays always cut diagonally through space in these planes, and their vertical angle is adjustable up or down their vertical VL, depending on how high or low you want to place the sun.

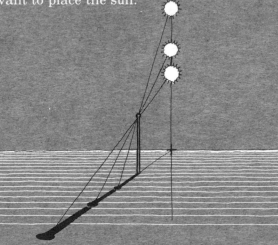

Notice that when the sun is behind us, the VP for sun's rays is below the eyelevel VL; and when the sun is in front of us, the VP for the sun's rays is above the eyelevel VL.

CONVERSIONS

When the sun is low enough, the shadows of vertical lines which begin as ⊥ shadows on the horizontal ground plane will reach the vertical planes of the built environment.

When these elongated ⊥ shadows extend onto transverse vertical planes, they become ‖ shadows, because the relationship between the line that is casting the shadow and the plane on which the shadow is falling changes from ⊥ to ‖. Following the rules we established for shadows, the continuing shadow will start straight up the transverse wall, ‖ to the line that is casting it.

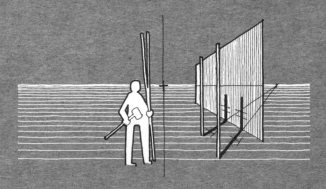

This same change in the casting relationship, and therefore the shadow, also occurs when such elongated ⊥ shadows reach converging vertical planes.

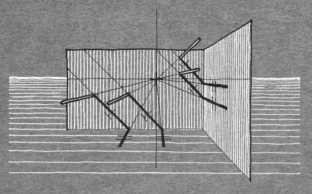

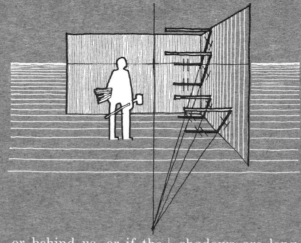

You should actually build one of these cubes out of illustration board and balsa, and color-code the three⊥ relationships (coloring each balsa rib and the plane to which it is ⊥ a distinct color). Then take the cube out into the sun and move it around to see directly the various shadow-casting relationships in rectangular environments. In order to cast the shadows on the built environment, you must thoroughly understand those relationships.

A similar conversion from ⊥ shadows to ‖ shadows happens when ‖ shadows on the transverse walls are long enough to reach the ground or a converging wall.

or behind us, or if the ⊥ shadows are long enough to extend onto a transverse wall.

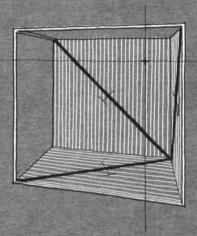

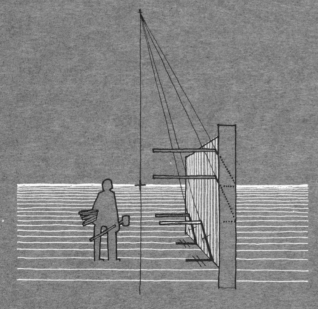

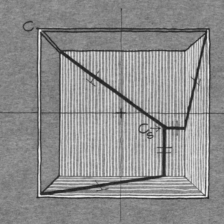

THE SHADOW-ANALYSIS CUBE

We may now combine all we have learned about the three ⊥ shadow-casting relationships, the three pairs of ‖ shadow-casting relationships, and the sun's rays on one model. The three planar orientations and three linear orientations which are possible in rectangular compositions can be accurately represented in the open cube above.

Perpendicular shadows on converging walls also convert to ‖ if they are long enough to reach the floor, whether the sun is in front of us,

If you take the shadow analysis cube out into the sunlight, you can easily manipulate it to get all the relationships we have just been through. You can get the shadow of point C to fall precisely in the corner of the three intersecting planes at point 1, and you can then move it out onto each of the three planes and watch the ‖ shadows appear in pairs. When you tire of ‖ shadows you can magically make them disappear by returning the shadow of point C to its coincidental corner.

133

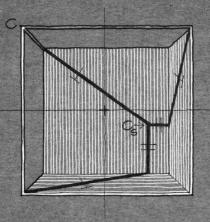

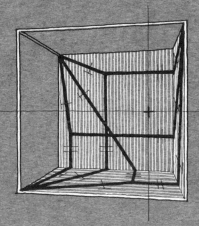

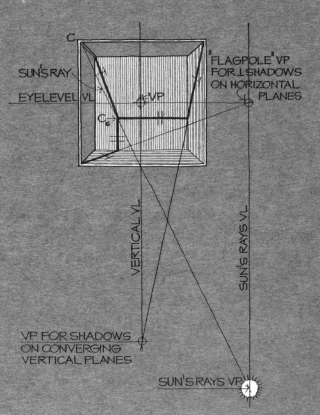

While you are making these manipulations, be aware that all the shadow-casting relationships we have been discussing (the three ⊥ shadow-casting relationships and the three pairs of ∥ shadow-casting relationships) are directly visible as shadows on the surfaces of the three ⊥ planes of the shadow-analysis cube. These are the visible effects of the one *invisible* relationship, *the sun's rays*, which never (except in extreme coincidence) lie on any of the cube's surfaces but always cut diagonally and invisibly through space.

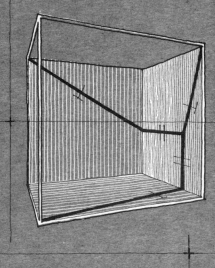

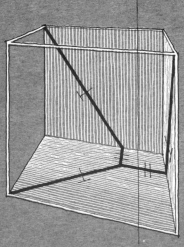

Also notice the differences in behavior between the ⊥ shadows and the ∥ shadows. Notice that while you can make the three ⊥ shadows vary wildly, both in their angle and their length, you can never get the pairs of ∥ shadows to forsake their ∥ relationships with the edges of the cube. Notice also that no matter how you manipulate the cube, the three ⊥ shadows remain steadfastly anchored to points V, N and F and that they are also confined to the respective planes to which their casting lines are ⊥. The ∥ shadows from each of the casting lines, however, may be placed on each of the two planes to which they are ∥.

SHADOW-CASTING IN ONE-POINT PERSPECTIVES

In one-point perspective, only two of the ⊥ shadows have VPs. The ⊥ shadows on horizontal planes converge to what we have called the flagpole VP on the VL for the plane in which it lies—the eyelevel VL; and the ⊥ shadows on converging vertical planes converge to a VP on the VL for the planes in which they lie—the vertical VL. The ⊥ shadows of the third ⊥ relationship—those on transverse vertical planes do not converge, but are drawn dead ∥ because the planes in which they lie do not converge toward any VL. This is because they are dead ∥ to the eyelevel VL and precisely ⊥ to the axis of our vision.

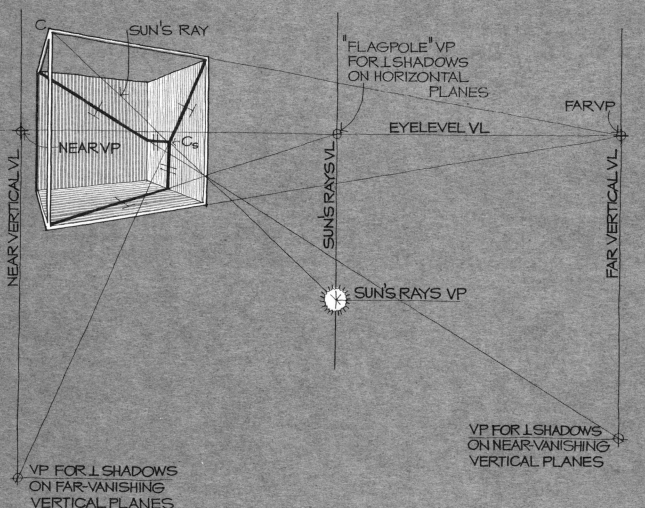

C
SUN'S RAY
"FLAGPOLE" VP
FOR ⊥ SHADOWS
ON HORIZONTAL
PLANES
FAR VP
EYELEVEL VL
NEAR VP
C$_s$
NEAR VERTICAL VL
SUN'S RAYS VL
FAR VERTICAL VL
SUN'S RAYS VP
VP FOR ⊥ SHADOWS
ON NEAR-VANISHING
VERTICAL PLANES
VP FOR ⊥ SHADOWS
ON FAR-VANISHING
VERTICAL PLANES

FREEDOM IN SHADOW-CASTING

Now that we understand the complete framework for casting shadows in perspective, it is important to understand how such shadow-casting ability may be used deductively or inductively.

Shadow-casting in perspective, when it is taught, is traditionally taught by specifying the sun angle and then asking students to cast the shadows based on this predetermined sun angle. This makes the student work easier to grade because there is one single answer against which each shadow pattern may be compared. While this may be understandably expedient for grading great stacks of student drawings, it is very misleading in that sun angles are never *given* in reality. Designers are always able to choose the best sun angle and they may choose it in a variety of ways.

DEDUCTIVE SHADOW-CASTING.

The traditional deductive shadow-casting method, in which the sun's angle is determined by establishing the shadow of a particular point in space, has the disadvantage of determining the most critical shadows, the ⊥ shadow angles, as secondary resultants of the initial choice of sun angle. This may result in weak or awkward shadow patterns and in unreachable VPs.

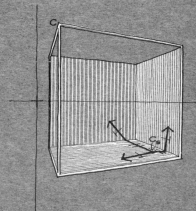

SHADOW-CASTING IN TWO-POINT PERSPECTIVES

Since most views of space are the more complicated and interesting two-point variety, we need to extend our understanding of shadow-casting to two-point perspectives.

When we rotate the shadow-analysis cube so that a second VP and VL (*far* VP and *far* VL) appear, we also get a VP for the third ⊥ shadow-casting relationship (on far vanishing vertical planes) on the VL for the planes in which they lie—the far VL.

The sun's rays will still lie in planes which recede into a third vertical VL through the flagpole VP.

We can now assemble the entire framework for shadow-casting in perspective, including the sub-system for sun's true rays, and all its nomenclature. If you can remember this set of relationships you will have the foundation of the holistic understanding needed to cast shadows in drawings of the environment.

INDUCTIVE SHADOW-CASTING. In contrast, the inductive method of shadow-casting allows you to choose any two of the three shadow angles *directly* so that they may initiate the strongest and most dynamic shadow pattern possible and have reachable VPs. This freedom of choice of any two of the ⊥ shadow angles is extremely helpful because the ⊥ shadows are always the most dynamic members of any shade/shadow system and offer the greatest opportunities in the choice of their length and angle.

The ⊥ shadows are infinitely flexible in angle and length, always cut diagonally across all the other lines and edges of rectangular compositions, and shade/shadow systems always begin and end with ⊥ shadow-casting relationships. For all these reasons it is usually most beneficial to establish the sun angle by choosing any two of the three ⊥ shadow-casting relationships. The two may be chosen independently to produce two particularly desirable ⊥ shadow angles. The only relationship between the two angles you choose for two of the three ⊥ shadow-casting relationships is that those two choices will fix the sun's angle and together determine the third ⊥ shadow-casting relationship.

The reason using the ⊥ shadow-casting relationships to initiate a shadow pattern may be more useful is that you often want the shadows on your building or inside your space to fall at a particular angle, or two particular angles. You may not care much what the precise location of the sun is, being content to let it simply be the resultant of the two angle choices.

Taking this method of initiating a shadow pattern step by step, we may choose any angle we want for two of the ⊥ shadow-casting relationships (in this case the shadows of lines CN and CV). We simply make

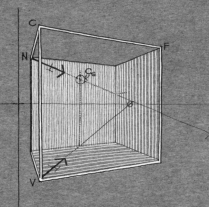

two choices and then extend them, following the rules for the two shadow-casting relationships until they intersect. Their intersection will be the shadow of point C (Cs), because that is the point of intersection of the two lines which are casting the shadow.

If we extend the shadow of each line until it changes planes (and the shadow-casting relationship changes to ∥) we can see that the two shadow routes intersect high on the back, far-vanishing wall.

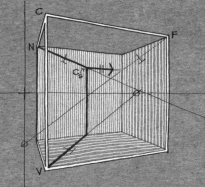

Having found point Cs by first determining two of the three ⊥ shadow angles we can complete the pattern by extending the shadow of line CF from point Cs as previously.

We could just as easily have chosen either of the other two possible combinations of ⊥ shadow angles to determine the sun's position.

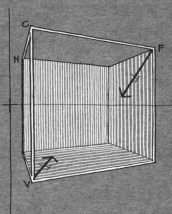

We could have first chosen the ⊥ shadow angles of far-vanishing line CF on the near-vanishing vertical plane and of the non-vanishing vertical line CV on the eyelevel-vanishing horizontal plane;

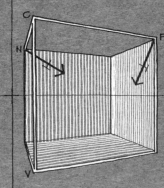

or we could have first chosen the ⊥ shadow angles of far-vanishing line CF on the near-vanishing vertical plane and of the near-vanishing horizontal line CN on the far-vanishing vertical plane.

Try to complete these last two shadow patterns to test your understanding of completing shadow patterns initiated by choosing two ⊥ shadow angles.

You may perceive, correctly, that in simple shadow systems the distinctions between the two approaches are trivial because the entire shadow pattern can be conceived almost simultaneously. The distinction I would argue for, however, is that to introduce design students to shadow-casting as a free and flexible way of lighting the environments they design is in every way more useful than to introduce shadow-casting as another inevitable convention, which leaves students with a rigid set of procedures rather than with the freedom that comes from a deeper understanding.

MANIPULATION OF A SHADOW SYSTEM

Another negative implication of learning shadow-casting from *given* or *fixed* sun angles is that students may never question, evaluate or consider *changing* a shadow pattern once it is determined. This is a great shame because once a shadow system is established and understood, it is very easy to manipulate the entire system to a more flattering or dynamic pattern. This is done entirely by changing the angles and lengths of the ⊥ shadows.

Just as you would never consider a design process valid which didn't consider a single alternative solution, so should you never just accept your first sun placement as an act of fate. You are free to place the sun wherever you like, and the responsibility which is the other side of all freedom coins may be a little uncomfortable, but surely it's better than a world eternally lit from over your left shoulder at 45°.

SHADE

So far we have been working with only two light conditions: *direct sunlight* and *shadow*. This was possible because we have been considering the lines which have been casting our shadows as abstractions having only one dimension. When we begin to fill in our stick figures and make planes, however, we must add the third light condition, *shade*, and carefully consider the characteristics of each of the light conditions.

If we visualize the crossbar which connected our pair of vertical stakes as being a rolled up window shade, we can simply pull down the shade to form an opaque plane. The filling in of the open rectangle by the opaque shade will result in the similar filling in of the parallelogram of the ground shadow pattern. We now have the shadow of one plane on another and a new light condition on the back of the shade which is called "shade".

Although we can't see the back of the vertical plane we have just created, we know that the back surface can't be in sunlight because the sun is behind us and is striking the front of the vertical plane, and therefore cannot be striking the back since that surface is *turned away* from the sun. We know from our experience that this is true of all planes—one side will be sunlit but the other side will be impossible for the sun to light because of its orientation.

We can now define the three light conditions involved in casting shadows in the built environment:

- sun—*the light condition on a surface turned toward and lit by the sun*
- shadow—*the light condition on a surface turned toward the sun but unlit because of an intervening object*
- shade—*a surface turned away from and unlit by the sun.*

By permission of Johnny Hart and Field Enterprises, Inc.

From their definitions we can also see that:
- *sun and shadow are the only two conditions that can occur side by side on the same surface, and that*
- *shade always occurs alone.*

If we rotate the sun 180° so that the sun is in front of us, we find that we are now looking at the surface of the window shade which is in shade and we are in position to comprehend one of the characteristics of all shade/shadow systems.

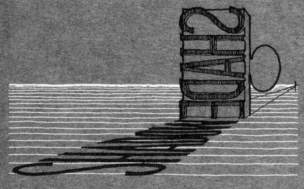

Shade and shadow always occur together in what I will call a shade/shadow system, and a useful analogy for understanding such systems is to think of any surface which is turned away from the sun, in shade, as being the bottom of an ink pad stamp smeared with the ink of *shade* that must make a *shadow* stamp somewhere, and that together the two form a shade/shadow system.

If we suspend the shadow-analysis cube in mid-air, we can analyze the light conditions on the six surface orientations of which any rectangular environment consists. Direct sunlight will always light three contiguous surfaces (in this case the three surfaces we

see), but the other three surfaces, also contiguous, will be in shade because they are the *backs* of the three sunlit surfaces.

Since each of the three light conditions (sun, shadow and shade) occurs on three different surface orientations (sun and shadow on the same three), and because each surface's relative lightness or darkness will vary with the sun's angular relationship to the surface, we need a way of analyzing the relative lightness or darkness of each surface. This analysis can also be done on the shadow-analysis cube.

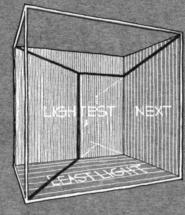

The plane on which the shadow of the corner Cs falls will be lightest because it is struck most perpendicularly by the sun's rays. This is true because the corner is equidistant from the three planes and its shadow being on a particular plane indicates that the sun travels the least distance to cast that shadow, and is therefore more perpendicular to that surface on which the corner's shadow falls than to the other two. The second lightest surface will be the one which the sun's ray would strike next if the sun's ray and the plane were extended until they intersected. The third lightest, or darkest, sunlit surface would be the remaining surface which would be reached last by the sun's ray because of its acute angle to the surface.

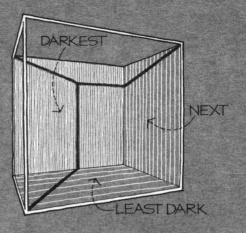

The order of darkness or lightness of the three surfaces which are in shade, however, is the exact reverse of the sunlit surfaces. The back of the lightest sunlit surface will be the darkest shade surface because it will be most difficult for reflected light to reach that surface. The darkest of the three sunlit surfaces will have the lightest shade surface as its back, and the medium sunlit surface will be backed by the medium shade surface.

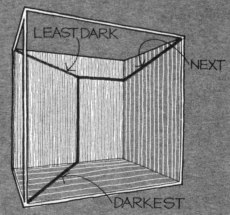

The relative darkness or lightness of shadows is influenced by the related lightness of the sunlit surfaces on which they occur. The lightest shadows will occur on the lightest sunlit surface, the darkest shadows on the darkest sunlit surface and the medium shadows on the medium sunlit surface.

The shadow-analysis cube below explains the relationships between the nine light conditions on the six surfaces. If we take 1 as the lightest sunlit surface and 9 as the darkest shadow, the relative order of the nine light conditions from light to dark is as follows:

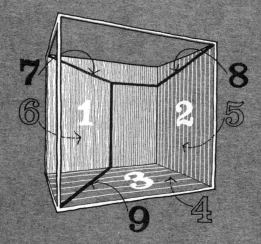

1. lightest sunlit surface
2. medium sunlit surface
3. darkest sunlit surface

4. lightest shade surface
5. medium shade surface
6. darkest shade surface

7. lightest shadow
8. medium shadow
9. darkest shadow

Notice that the sums of the sunlit number and the shade number will total 7 on each plane, and the difference between the sunlit number and the shade number is always 6 on any surface. This kind of detailed analysis is necessary in tone drawings, where the distinction between planes of various orientations to light must be made by a difference in tone alone, without the benefit of a separating line.

THE THIRD DIMENSION—THICKNESS

We are now ready to leave the relative simplicity of lines and planes and extend our knowledge of shadow casting into the third dimension—filling in all the sides of the open shadow-analysis cube to make it a three-dimensional solid. When we illuminate any rectangular composition with sunlight, the three sets of mutually perpendicular planes which make up any rectangular environment actually offer six different orientations to the light since each plane has two sides. The six faces offered to the light are represented in our language by the words top/bottom, front/back, and right side/left side; and only one member of each pair can be lighted at any one time. The opposite side will always be turned away from the light, in shade. The six different orientations to light are represented in any rectangular solid.

THE CASTING EDGE

When we cast the shadow of a vertical plane on the ground by pulling down the imaginary window shade and filling in the plane, the configuration of the boundary of the shadow will be cast by the edge lines of the plane. In three dimensions the edge which casts the boundary of any shadow becomes more complicated, for it is always the edge which separates a surface which is sunlit from one which is in shade. In rectangular environments this casting edge will always be an outside corner at the intersection of two planes, and you must learn to visualize this edge which separates sun from shade even when it is hidden.

Another way of understanding the concept of the casting edge, which builds on an earlier understanding, is that if you were the sun, looking down on the built environment, the casting edge and what we earlier called *spatial edges* would be the same, because every surface the sun "sees" is sunlit. Casting edges are the sun's spatial edges, and it will help you understand shadow-casting if you can visualize the spatial edges which the sun would see, for these are the edges which will cast the boundaries of the shadows.

Notice the configuration of the edge which separates the three sunlit surfaces of the cubes from the three shade surfaces as the sun rotates through the four alternate quadrants. This is the casting edge which will cast the boundary of the object's shadow. Notice how it jumps from outside corner to outside corner as the rotation of the sun progressively illuminates or shades the various vertical faces of the cubes.

In order to represent the complete shade/shadow systems of the built environment we must set the cube down on a plane, providing a surface on which the cube's shadow may fall. Notice that the bottom of the formerly suspended cube has now been eliminated and the cube may be thought of as an integral projection from the base plane.

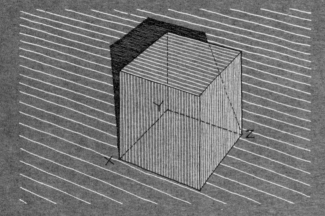

Notice also that the shadow is attached to the two remaining shade faces along line XYZ. This demonstrates a characteristic of all isolated shade/shadow systems: *shade/shadow systems resolve*. Unlike the continuous casting edges on the suspended cubes, complete shade/shadow systems begin and end with "dead-end" ⊥ shadows, as at points X and Z.

Notice also that the planes of the cube are really only fillers, that the configuration of the shadow boundary is cast by lines of identical orientation to the struts of the earlier, open shadow analysis cube.

This can be demonstrated by first stripping away the sunlit faces of the cube, so that we are back to the open shadow-analysis cube;

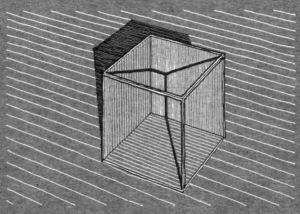

and then stripping away the shade faces so that only the edges of the cube remain as struts.

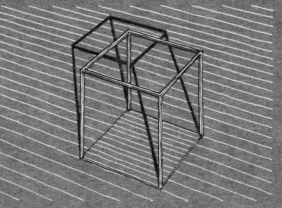

All through this process of removing the planes the shadow's boundaries and finally the open linear shadow pattern cast by the strut framework remain consistent with the ⊥ and ∥ shadow-casting relationships and their VPs established earlier with the shadow-analysis cube.

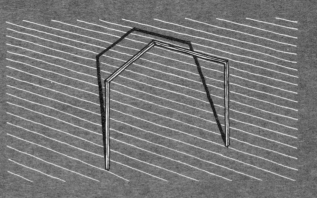

A final understanding is that if all the planes were stripped away from the casting edge, so that it stood alone, like some sort of mutated croquet wicket, it would cast a shadow identical to the boundary of the solid cube's shadow.

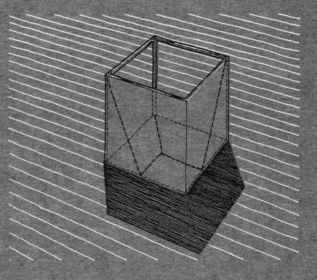

The sun's position and/or the viewer's position may change, but you need to be able to reassemble the cube in such a way that wherever the sun is you can replace the 3 panels so that their convex shadow-catching pocket faces the sun and the shadow pattern of the open struts may be understood and drawn on the sunlit faces, even when they are turned away from you, and would actually be hidden from your sight.

140

SHADE/SHADOW SYSTEMS

Let us now study the simplest kinds of shade/shadow systems. Complex shadow patterns may be thought of as assemblages of these simple systems, and one of the most useful abilities in shadow-casting is that of being able to simplify the shadow-casting situation by breaking down complex compositions into their constituent parts.

PROJECTED SYSTEMS

The first system to be understood is what will be called a projected system, as if a rectangular object had been pushed up through a plane. Notice that the system is initiated the instant the rectangular solid breaks through the ground plane, and immediately has all the characteristics of taller blocks. The casting edge in this system is made up of two vertical and two horizontal lines and the shadow pattern they cast on the ground plane is made up of two ⊥ and two ∥ shadows. The two ∥ shadows will remain ∥ to and the same length as the lines which cast them. The two ⊥ shadows which initiate the system may vary wildly in angle and length but at any moment they will always be the same length and parallel to one another.

It is most critical to understand that *all* the shadow-casting relationships in the rectangular environment are represented in the shadow-analysis cube, and to be able to see how every casting edge in the environment is oriented exactly like one of the struts of the cube and how every shadow-catching plane is oriented exactly like one of the shadow catching planes of the cube.

INDENTED SYSTEMS

The opposite kind of shade/shadow system is one involving a rectangular void pushed into a plane. Such a system has the same number of sun and shade surfaces as the previous projected system, but here they occur in a reversed configuration.

Notice that indented systems only have two casting edges (both parallel) because the other edges which separate the sunlit vertical sides from the shaded vertical sides are *inside* corners and cannot cast shadows. And while there are only two casting edges, the shadow pattern again has two ⊥ and two ∥ shadows because the casting relationship of each ⊥ shadow changes to ∥ on the bottom of the indention. In indented systems the ∥ shadows will always be ∥ to the lines that cast them, but the ⊥ shadows will vary wildly in angle and length.

This is perhaps an appropriate place to remember that shade/shadow systems are not something *over there* that we look *at*. We rather *occupy* shade/shadow systems, like we inhabit any other characteristics of the environments which surround us. The interiors of buildings, in their simplest form, are INDENTED shade/shadow systems, and when we are inside the building we are inside the shade/shadow system as well.

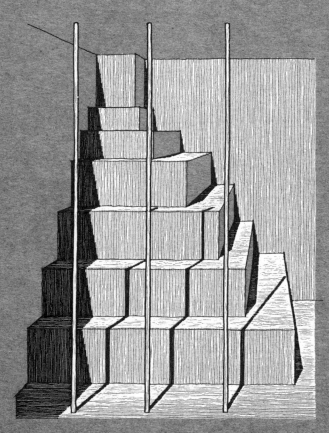

STEP SYSTEMS

The third kind of shade/shadow system is different from either the projected or indented systems in that the shadow falls across a series of alternating planes which causes the shadow-casting relationships to alternate from ⊥ to ∥. This alternation will occur because the planes on which the shadow is falling are ⊥ to one another so that the relationship of the casting edge to the planes must alternate.

In all shade/shadow systems it is important to see clearly the shadows of corners. Always lengthen shadows if you can reveal the shadow of another corner, and never draw the coincidence where the shadow of a corner falls in a corner or on an edge.

SHADOW CASTING METHOD

Now that we have established all the relationships in any shade/shadow system we can consider a general shadow-casting procedure which uses those relationships. The first step in the general shadow-casting method should be:

1. Assume the general direction of the sun and make a sun/shade analysis, to determine which three contiguous surfaces of the six-faced rectangular world will be sunlit, and which three will be turned away from the sun, in shade.

This is always the most basic step in any rendering of light in the environment. The analysis must be made for every surface, including hidden surfaces, based on the surface's orientation to the sun, ignoring for the moment the fact that some surfaces will be in the shadow of intervening objects. You may complete this first step by actually applying a gray tone to the surfaces in shade, because these surfaces cannot have either sun or shadow, because they are turned away from the sun. You may begin by applying a gray tone to all *under* surfaces (soffits, ceilings etc.) because they will always be in shade. The only problematic surfaces are the vertical surfaces and these can be analyzed from your general sun assumption.

Upon completion of the sun/shade analysis, the next step is to:

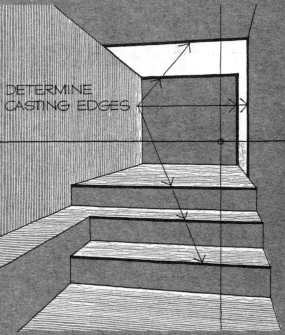

2. determine the casting edge—the line that will cast the boundary of the shadow.

The casting edge will always be that line which separates sunlit surfaces and shaded surfaces, *except* at inside corners. The edge which separates sunlit surfaces from shaded surfaces will always run along the corner of two intersecting planes, but it is only the *outside* corners that cast the boundary of the shadow pattern. We will find that the sunlit surface at *inside* corners will eventually receive a shadow cast by the shaded surface with which it intersects.

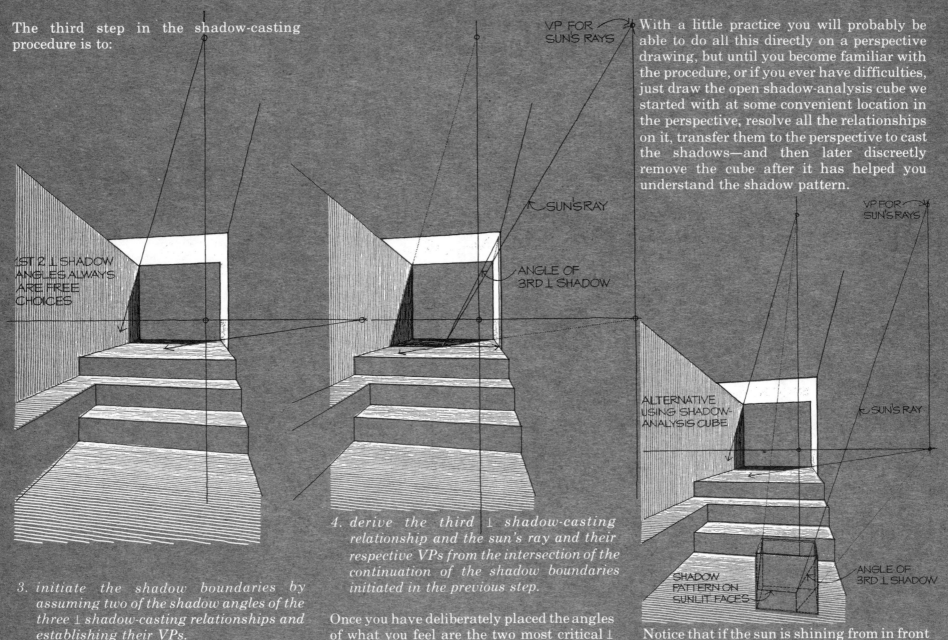

The third step in the shadow-casting procedure is to:

With a little practice you will probably be able to do all this directly on a perspective drawing, but until you become familiar with the procedure, or if you ever have difficulties, just draw the open shadow-analysis cube we started with at some convenient location in the perspective, resolve all the relationships on it, transfer them to the perspective to cast the shadows—and then later discreetly remove the cube after it has helped you understand the shadow pattern.

3. initiate the shadow boundaries by assuming two of the shadow angles of the three ⊥ shadow-casting relationships and establishing their VPs.

Remember that you are free to choose any shadow angles you wish for the first two ⊥ shadow-casting relationships, but once you have chosen any two of the three, the next step is predetermined:

4. derive the third ⊥ shadow-casting relationship and the sun's ray and their respective VPs from the intersection of the continuation of the shadow boundaries initiated in the previous step.

Once you have deliberately placed the angles of what you feel are the two most critical ⊥ shadow-casting relationships and found their VPs, you can quickly find the third ⊥ shadow-casting relationship and its VP and the sun's ray and its VP by extending lines until they intersect with the VLs for the planes they lie in.

Notice that if the sun is shining from in front of the viewer so that the fronts of all the far-vanishing vertical planes are in shade, the sunlit backs of all those far-vanishing planes and the shadows on them will never be seen. In such cases you won't need the third ⊥ shadow-casting relationship or its VP.

144

After you have established the angles and VPs for the three ⊥ shadows and the sun's rays the next step is to:

After all ⊥ shadows have been extended across their planes you should:

Once a shade/shadow system is initiated it may be continued by simply alternating the shadow-casting relationship from ⊥ to ∥ to ⊥ as it moves across the alternating, mutually perpendicular planes of any rectangular environment. The shade/shadow systems initiated by the various ⊥ shadows will eventually close and complete themselves by intersecting at the shadow of some corner of the casting edge.

This is the simplest and most direct way to cast shadows, staying on the architectural surfaces and simply "running with the rules" of the ⊥ shadow angles you have assumed and the inevitable ∥ shadows. The sun's ray seldom needs to be used as it is in most traditional shadow-casting methods.

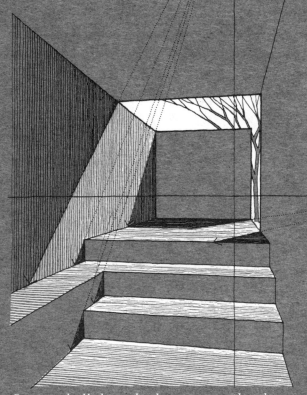

5. extend all the ⊥ shadows across the planes on which they lie.

Perpendicular shadows will extend from every point where the casting edge intersects a sunlit plane. All these ⊥ shadows may now be extended toward their VP, (on the VL for the planes in which they lie) across the plane on which they lie to the next intersecting plane.

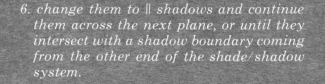

6. change them to ∥ shadows and continue them across the next plane, or until they intersect with a shadow boundary coming from the other end of the shade/shadow system.

Shadow-casting can't be learned by reading a book. Like drawing ability in general, it must be learned by actually trying to cast shadows; and the explanation of shadow-casting has probably already been given more space than it deserves in a book of this scope. The hope is that the approach here might lead to a better holistic understanding of light, shade, and shadow as a three-dimensional system, rather than simply a procedure involving the manipulation of points, lines and measurements.

Consistent with the above approach there are a few more analogical mechanisms and rules of thumb that you may find helpful as you cast shadows.

DEFORMATIONS IN THE SHADOW-CATCHING PLANE

In initiating the casting of any shadow pattern it is always easy to extend the ⊥ shadow emanating from the dead end of any casting line by simply applying the relational rules of shadow-casting. The ⊥ shadow just keeps going until the shadow-catching plane intersects with another plane. The shadow-casting relationship will always change at any such intersection. This is because the line that is casting the shadow is ⊥ to the first plane and can't possibly also be ⊥ to a plane which intersects the first plane. And since there are only two possibilities for casting relationships between the lines and planes of rectangular compositions, the new relationship must be the other one— ‖. At the next planar intersection the relationship must change back to ⊥ and this alternating pattern will continue until the end of the casting line is reached.

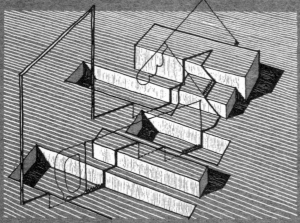

If the shadow boundary which falls across a deformation is a ⊥ shadow, it cuts through the deformation like a great cleaver falling ⊥ to the shadow-catching plane. If the shadow boundary is a ‖ shadow, it cuts through the deformation at an angle, as if the cutting edge slid down an inclined plane from the edge which is casting the shadow.

DEFORMATIONS OF THE SHADOW-CASTING EDGE

The casting of the shadows of continuous edges is generally easy, even when they fall over planar intersections or deformations. It is the locations of the corners, where the casting line changes direction, that are difficult to establish and critical to the reading of any shade/shadow system.

In principle there is only one way to establish such corners. You must get one of the ⊥ relationships started from a dead end of the casting edge, as above, and then intersect it with one of the other three relationships, (one of the other two ⊥ shadows or a sun's ray). (This technique will be discussed in detail in the next section.) Once the shadow of such a corner is reached, a new series of shadow-casting relationships will begin and continue until the shadow of the next corner.

The shadows of corners in the shadow-casting edge will be one of two types:

- if the two casting edges which form the corner are both ‖ to the plane on which their shadows fall, the angle of the shadow of the corner will be 90°.

- if one of the two casting edges which form the corner is ‖ and the other is ⊥ to the plane on which their shadows fall, the angle of the shadow of the corner will always be more than 90° or obtuse. (This presumes that all shadow casting elements will have *thickness* and that the thickness itself will cast a shadow.)

These are the only two possibilities in orthogonal compositions since both lines which form a corner can never be ⊥ to any plane on which their shadows fall.

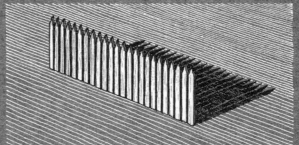

THE PICKET FENCE ANALOGY is a manipulation which adds auxiliary lines in order to find the shadow of a ‖ shadow which is irregular. We can imagine that such a wall is actually made up of many vertical pickets.

146

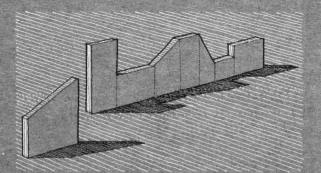

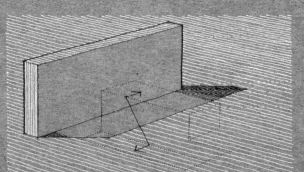

This analogy means that whenever it is convenient, we can dissolve a wall into individual lines and use those lines to cast its shadow. Given a sloping wall, we can cast the shadow of the top of the wall by using two auxiliary vertical lines or "pickets" and their shadows. The shadow of a wall with several different heights can be found by adding auxiliary lines or "pickets" and their shadows, at the points of change.

SIMPLIFYING THE SITUATION

Perhaps the most useful ability to develop in shadow-casting is the simplifying of complex shadow-casting situations by temporarily **removing** parts of the composition or substituting simpler parts in order to clarify the underlying relationships. Casting shadows on complex objects or in complex spaces need not be intimidating if you learn how to reduce each shadow-casting situation to its simplest form. Sometimes the simplification actually involves adding or extending lines or planes, but the effect of these changes is to represent the shadow-casting relationships at their most basic level.

To completely catalogue the various situations where these techniques could be used would require another book, but a brief categorization of representative examples may suffice to suggest the range of possibilities.

FILLING POCKETS AND REMOVING BUMPS. The simplest of the simplification techniques is to temporarily remove or smooth out minor deformations, either of the object which is casting the shadows or of the surfaces on which the shadows are falling. This allows the shadow-caster to deal with a simpler shadow-casting form and simpler shadow-catching surfaces in order to establish the overall shape and extent of the shadow pattern.

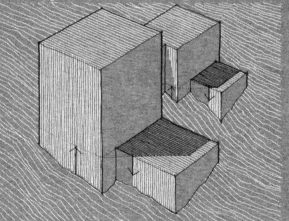

RAISING OR LOWERING A SURFACE. Another effective simplification technique is to temporarily raise or lower the level of the ground or any surface on which shadows are being cast. If you bring in sand and fill the whole ground surface to a higher level, or sandblast a surface down to a lower level, certain shadow-casting relationships will be reduced to their most basic form.

DISASSEMBLY AND REASSEMBLY.

Most complex objects will cast shadows on themselves as well as on the floor or ground plane and, at first, this collection of multiple overlapping shadows may seem impossibly complex and confusing.

The best approach to simplifying such a complex shadow-casting situation is to disassemble the shadow-casting object into simple pieces, beginning with those nearest the ground plane or shadow-casting surface and progressing upwards or outwards, casting the shadows from each successive piece as you reassemble the object.

This technique may seem inefficient because some of the lower shadows will be covered and cancelled out by subsequent shadows as you reassemble the object, but I know of no shortcuts which avoid a complete analysis and understanding of all the shadow-casting relationships.

147

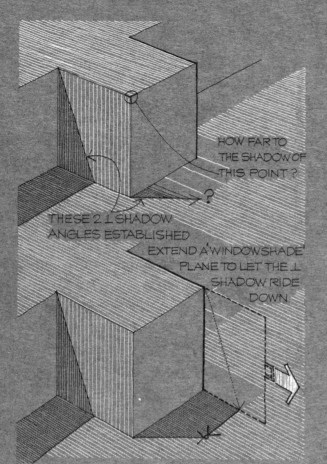

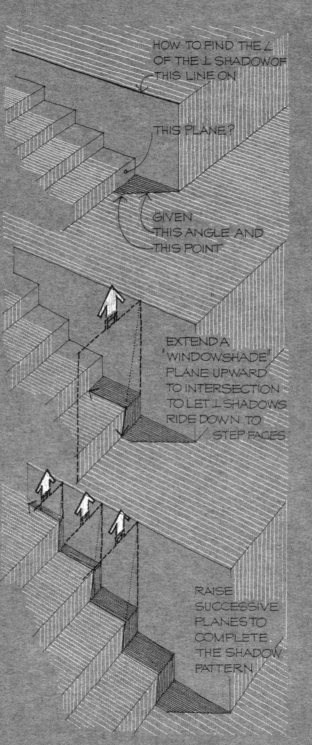

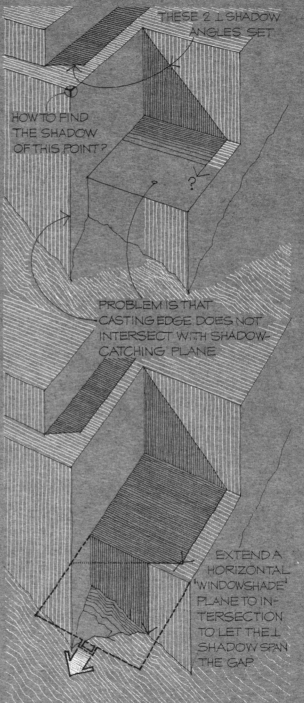

HOW FAR TO THE SHADOW OF THIS POINT?

THESE 2 ⊥ SHADOW ANGLES ESTABLISHED

EXTEND A "WINDOWSHADE" PLANE TO LET THE ⊥ SHADOW RIDE DOWN

HOW TO FIND THE ∠ OF THE ⊥ SHADOW OF THIS LINE ON THIS PLANE?

GIVEN THIS ANGLE AND THIS POINT

EXTEND A "WINDOWSHADE" PLANE UPWARD TO INTERSECTION TO LET ⊥ SHADOWS RIDE DOWN TO STEP FACES

RAISE SUCCESSIVE PLANES TO COMPLETE THE SHADOW PATTERN

THESE 2 ⊥ SHADOW ANGLES SET

HOW TO FIND THE SHADOW OF THIS POINT?

PROBLEM IS THAT CASTING EDGE DOES NOT INTERSECT WITH SHADOW-CATCHING PLANE

EXTEND A HORIZONTAL "WINDOWSHADE" PLANE TO INTERSECTION TO LET THE ⊥ SHADOW SPAN THE GAP

THE WINDOW SHADE ANALOGY— EXTENSION TO INTERSECTION

One of the most troublesome conditions is where the edge which is casting a ⊥ shadow is separated from the plane on which the shadow is falling in such a way that they never actually intersect. The most effective technique for solving this problem is to imagine attaching a handle to the plane and extending it, pulling it up, in, out or sideways until it intersects with the casting edge. This point is always the dead end of the shadow and we can extend the shadow from that point of intersection to the VP for that ⊥ relationship and draw in as much as we need of the shadow, where we need it.

148

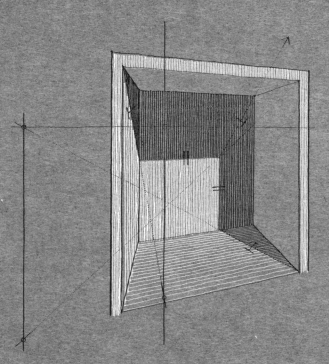

FINDING THE SHADOW OF ANY POINT

The method of finding the shadow of any point by establishing the four shadow-casting relationships (three ⊥ plus the sun's ray) and their VPs, and then continuing any two of the four relationships until they intersect, is demonstrated in the matrix above. Traditional shadow-casting relies on intersecting extensions of relationships No. 3 and No. 4 by adding an auxiliary vertical line and then intersecting it with a sun's ray. You should understand, however, that this same technique may be applied in the five other ways demonstrated in the matrix.

This demonstration matrix assumes that the VLs and VPs for all four shadow-casting relationships have been established by the methods discussed previously. Finding the shadow of any point is then simply intersecting any two of them that may be most convenient. Freedom always means having more than one option.

ANGLE OF ⊥ SHADOWS ON TRANSVERSE VERTICAL PLANES

ANGLE OF ⊥ SHADOWS ON CONVERGING VERTICAL PLANES

ANGLE OF ⊥ SHADOWS ON HORIZONTAL PLANES

ANGLE OF ⊥ SUN'S RAYS

THE SHADOWS OF CORNERS are especially critical in shadow casting, because a thorough understanding of them can help you place the sun more beneficially, avoid common errors—both of accuracy and judgment—and make the shade/shadow systems in your drawings read much more clearly. The shadows of the corner of the casting edge are where the casting relationships change from ⊥ to ‖ to ⊥, and unless you know where the shadows of the corners fall, you won't know what the casting relationship is and when it changes. You should be able to simultaneously follow the casting edge and its shadow from corner to corner in any shade/shadow system.

- Check all corners of the shadow-catching surface to make sure the shadow changes correctly at each corner.

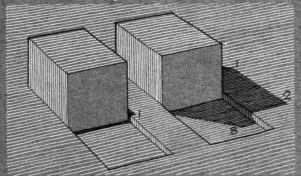

- Wherever possible, the shadows of the corners of the casting edge should be placed prominently where they can be seen.

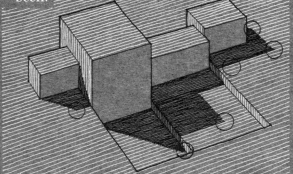

- Check all corners of the casting edge to make sure the shadow changes correctly at each corner.

- Check the entire composition for consistency at the corners; that is, carefully go over all similar spatial conditions to assure that the shadows of each are cast similarly.

COMMON ERRORS, which everyone seems to make in learning to cast shadows, may be avoided by observing the following rules:

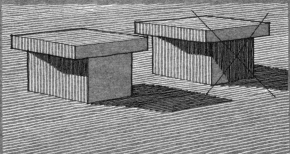

- Shade and shadow can't occur on the same surface.

- Shade and shadow always exist together, though never on the same surface. There can never be a shadow unless there is shade and the casting edge which separates sun from shade. Wherever there is shade there will be a casting edge and somewhere there will be a shadow.

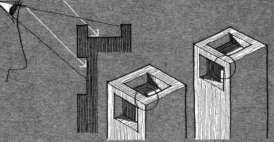

- Since sight lines are slightly divergent, or at least never convergent, and the sun's rays are assumed to be ‖, if you see certain shadows, you definitely *won't* see others.

150

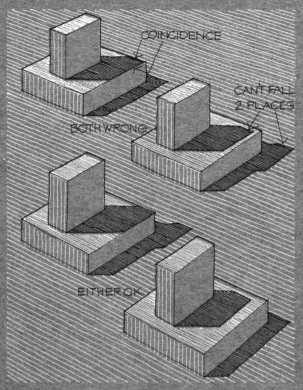

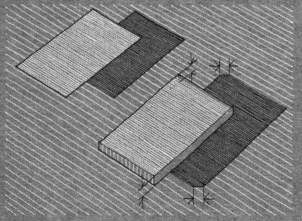

- The shadow of any point can only fall one place, but it will always fall *someplace*.

- Most planes that cast shadows have thickness, which means there will be small ⊥ shadows at the corners where the casting edge changes from the top of the thickness to the bottom.

CHOOSING THE BEST SUN POSITION

can have a most beneficial affect on your shade/shadow systems. Any spatial composition reads better when the shadows fall across the most broken up or changing surfaces. Never miss an opportunity to cast a shadow across a flight of steps or any level change, or to cast a roof shadow across openings in the wall below.

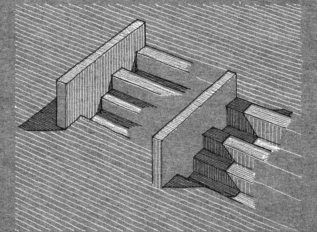

Sun positions which offer a balance between sun, shade and shadow are generally more interesting.

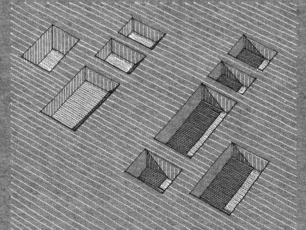

Sun positions which offer the greatest number of dramatically angled ⊥ shadows are also more interesting.

Any environment you are designing will have a definite orientation, and you shouldn't draw the sun coming from a place it will never, or hardly ever be. The design problem itself may dictate the sun angles to be used in design drawings—a breakfast patio or a ramada intended to shade the west side of a house. Simply stated, the best sun angles are those which tell the most about the environment you are designing.

151

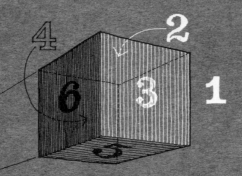

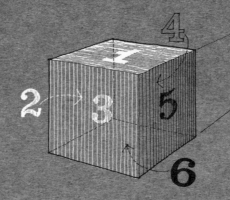

Upon identification or assumption of such a source of indirect light, and taking a suspended cube as a referent, there are six possible variations in the intensity of indirect light. The first, or brightest intensity, will occur on the face of the cube which faces the source of indirect light. The sixth, or darkest condition, will occur on that surface which is turned away from the source of indirect light.

INDIRECT LIGHT

There are lighting conditions which completely exclude direct sunlight, such as the interiors of rooms facing north, or exterior porches which are totally in shade and shadow. The surfaces in such areas are more difficult to delineate and demand a consistent set of light assumptions. Since there is no direct light and, therefore, no shadows, the surface modeling of any perspective drawing using tonal interest rests entirely on the differential facing of the surfaces which reflect light toward the viewer.

The assumptions for indirect or diffused light begin with the identification or assumption of the direction of incoming indirect light. This source of indirect light might be a large window, in which case the light enters laterally, or an overhead skylight, in which case the light comes down vertically from above.

The other four surfaces of the cube (top, bottom, and sides) are lateral to the source of indirect light and will be the middle tones. Of these lateral surfaces, the top will generally always be lighter because sunlight is diffused and multi-reflected by the earth's atmosphere and may be thought of as "falling" in such a way that it lights the tops of objects much more brightly than their bottoms. The two remaining sides will be illuminated 3 and 4 (third and fourth brightest) depending on the plan angle of the entering light.

If the principal source of light is an overhead skylight, the top surfaces will be brightest and the bottom surfaces darkest, with the sides being the laterally-lighted middle tones. A similar analysis of indirect light must be made in rendering the shade/shadow realm beyond the reaches of incoming sunlight or on the various surfaces of the underside of a roof.

The important thing in differentiating between surfaces in indirect light is to make the preceding assumptions and then stick with them consistently for all surfaces. By being consistent I mean that all surfaces having a similar orientation should have the same relative lightness or darkness. All the bottoms should be the same and darker than all the tops. All right sides should be the same and darker than all the left sides, etc. This consistency will do more than anything else to differentiate surfaces lighted by indirect or diffused light.

INTERIORS. Since architectural interiors are often lighted by indirect light, this is perhaps the best place to say a little about the correct tonal rendering of interiors.

Most drawings of interiors include at least a peek of the outdoors and many emphasize the spatial connection or ambiguity between interior and exterior. The most important characteristic of an interior perspective which includes a view of the exterior, is that in the daytime any interior will be much darker than any exterior. This is true no mat-

ter how many windows there are in the room, or their orientation, or no matter how brightly the room is lighted by artificial illumination. There is no way to illuminate the interior as brightly as the exterior. The experience will always be that of being within a very dark volume looking out on a much brighter exterior space. This contrast will be most pronounced where a dark interior ceiling is seen against the bright sky beyond or where the frame around any opening is silhouetted against the bright sky beyond.

153

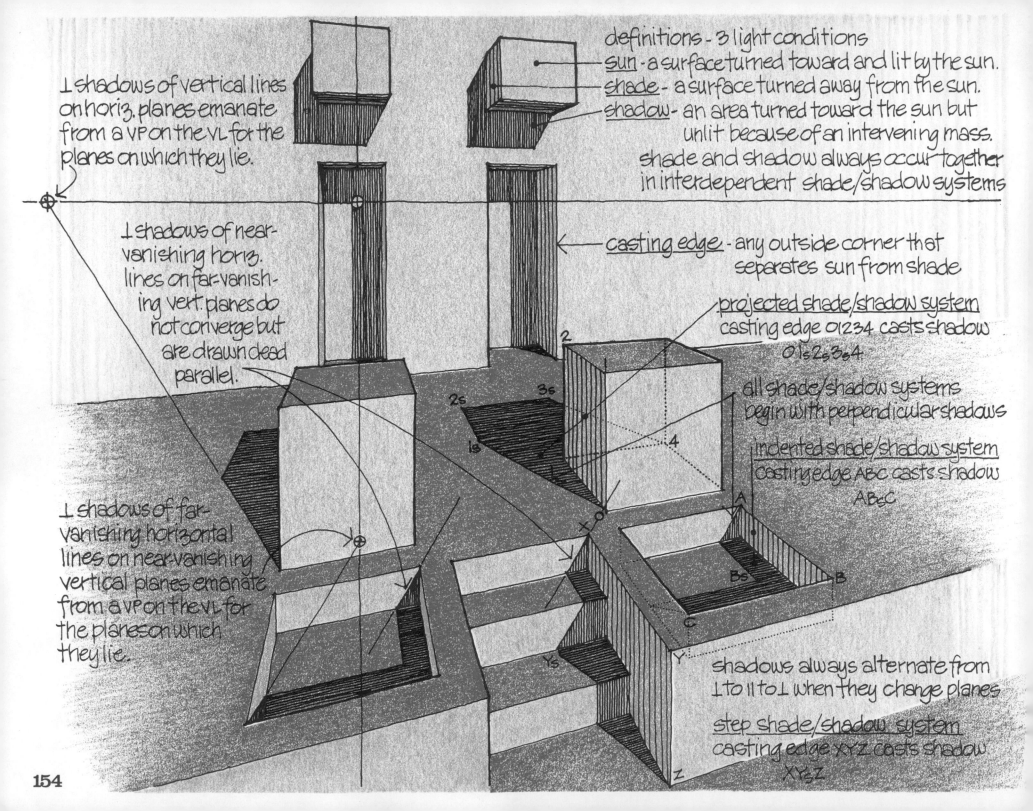

⊥ shadows of vertical lines on horiz. planes emanate from a VP on the VL for the planes on which they lie.

definitions - 3 light conditions
sun - a surface turned toward and lit by the sun.
shade - a surface turned away from the sun.
shadow - an area turned toward the sun but unlit because of an intervening mass.
shade and shadow always occur together in interdependent shade/shadow systems

⊥ shadows of near-vanishing horiz. lines on far-vanishing vert. planes do not converge but are drawn dead parallel.

casting edge - any outside corner that separates sun from shade

projected shade/shadow system
casting edge 01234 casts shadow 0 1s 2s 3s 4

all shade/shadow systems begin with perpendicular shadows

indented shade/shadow system
casting edge ABC casts shadow A Bs C

⊥ shadows of far-vanishing horizontal lines on near-vanishing vertical planes emanate from a VP on the VL for the planes on which they lie.

shadows always alternate from ⊥ to ∥ to ⊥ when they change planes

step shade/shadow system
casting edge XYZ casts shadow XYsZ

Each set of perpendicular shadows has its own VP on the VL for the planes on which the shadows lie.

Perpendicular Relationship
(horiz. pole to blue surfaces) perpendicular shadows vary dramatically in both length and angle but at any moment are parallel to one another.

Parallel Relationship
(horiz. pole to red surfaces) parallel shadows are always parallel to the line which casts them.

Parallel shadows always converge to the appropriate VP of the perspective or remain vertical if cast by vertical lines.

Shadows always begin with a ⊥ shadow and then alternate between ⊥ and ∥ as they change planes because the 2nd plane will always be ⊥ to the first.

In rectangular compositions there are only 2 possible relationships between any line which casts a shadow and the plane on which the line's shadow falls: perpendicular ⊥ or parallel ∥.

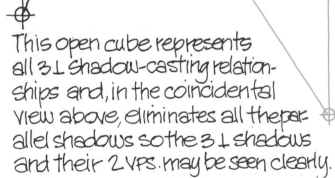

This open cube represents all 3 ⊥ shadow-casting relationships and, in the coincidental view above, eliminates all the parallel shadows so the 3 ⊥ shadows and their 2 VPs may be seen clearly.

Free shadow-casting begins with choosing the angles of 2 of the 3 ⊥ shadows.

You will learn a great deal about shadow-casting by building a cube like the one above and taking it out in the sunlight.

- Free shadow-casting begins with choosing the general direction of the sun (in this example in front of and to the right of the viewer).

- Next make a sun/shade analysis to determine which surfaces will be in sun and which in shade.

- Render the surfaces in shade and identify the casting edges (outside corners which separate sun and shade) including those which are hidden.

- Notice that with the sun assumption in this example all the far-vanishing planes (blue) are in shade. This means that there will only be 2 ⊥ shadows to deal with and both may be chosen freely, and independently of one another, because the remaining ⊥ shadows will fall on the sunlit backs of the far-vanishing (blue) vertical planes which can't be seen in this view.

- The shade/shadow systems will all begin at points where a casting edge intersects a sunlit plane.

- The shadows which emanate from such points will all be perpendicular shadows and the choice of their angles will determine the over-all shadow pattern.

- There are 7 such points in this example.

- Identify the most prominent or most frequently occuring ⊥ shadow angle (in this example it is the shadows of far-vanishing horizontal lines on near-vanishing (green) vertical planes - 4 of 7).

- Assume the most beneficial angle for this set of ⊥ shadows and establish its VP on the VL for the planes on which the shadows lie.

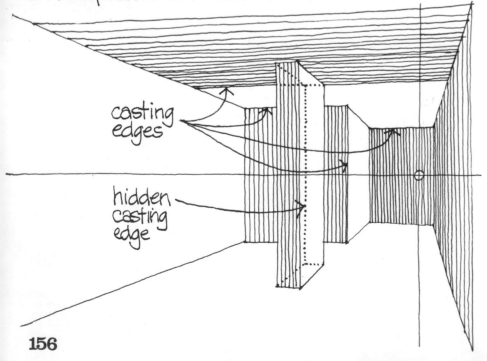

casting edges

hidden casting edge

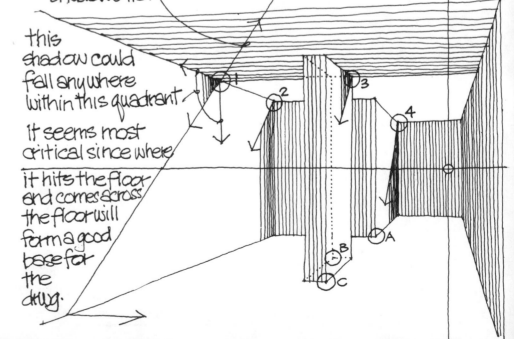

this shadow could fall anywhere within this quadrant

it seems most critical since where

it hits the floor and comes across the floor will form a good base for the drug.

- Extend this set of ⊥ shadows from its VP at all 4 of the initial points of the shade/shadow systems, following the rules for alternating ⊥ and ‖ shadows on perpendicular planes (page 67) until the shadows reach a surface in shade.

- This is the maximum length of these shadows. They will be intersected by the extension of ⊥ shadows coming from the other end of each shade/shadow system.

- They could be intersected before they even get off of the green planes by ‖ shadows extending up the walls (see the alternate shown in the next step).

Finally we choose an angle for the other set of ⊥ shadows (the shadows of vertical lines on horizontal [red] planes.) We may choose this angle anywhere within the quadrant shown - independent of the preceding ⊥ shadow angle. The greatest opportunity in this choice seems to be the placement of the shadow of point A where it shows.

With the angle chosen the VP for the entire set may be found on the VL for the planes on which the shadows lie. The other ⊥ shadows of the set may then be extended from the VP to close the shade/shadow systems initiated in the previous steps.

Once the shadow pattern is completed and all the relationships established it is easy to vary the pattern to integrate it with the placement of figures, trees and furniture.

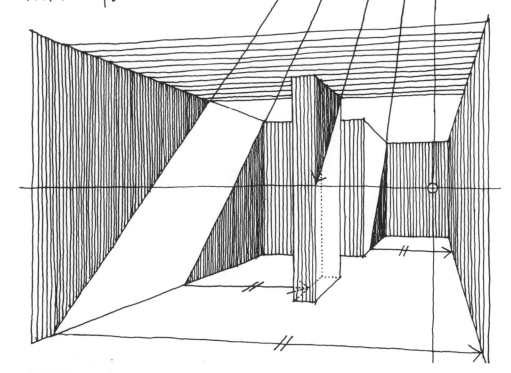

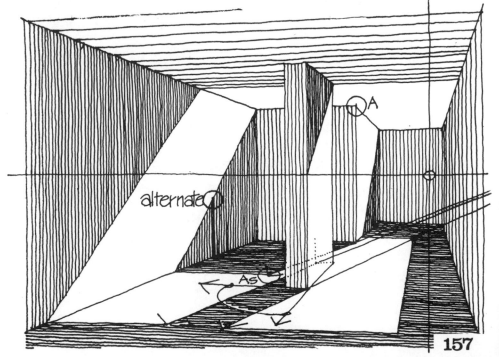

alternate

A

As

157

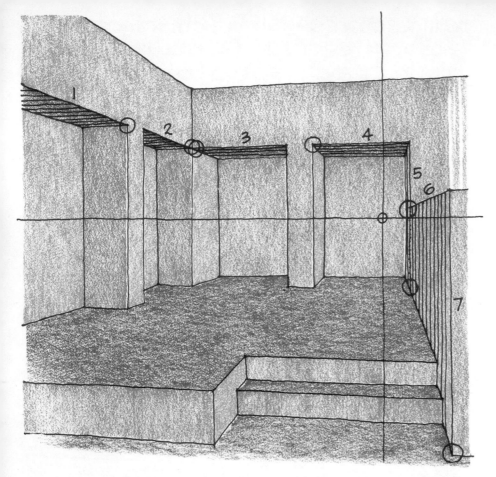

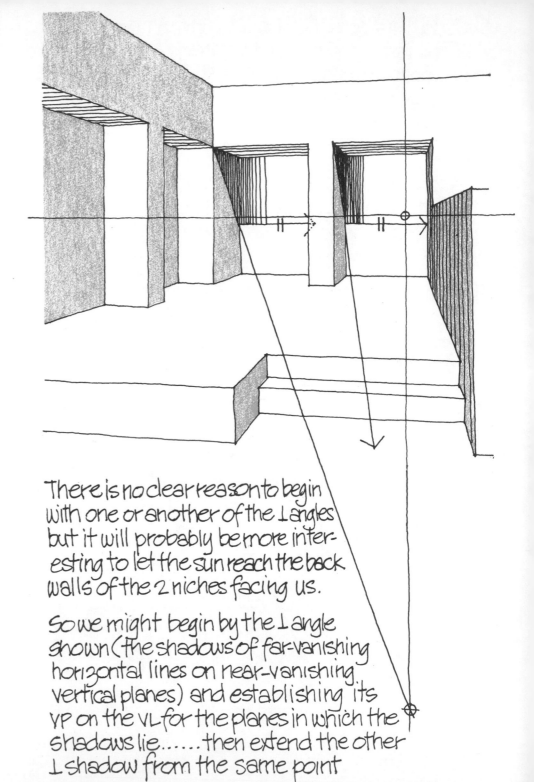

In this example the sun is assumed to be behind and to the right of the viewer, so that we will see all 3 sets of sunlit planes and the perpendicular shadows on them.

A sun/shade analysis reveals 7 casting edges, 2 of which (5 and 6) must be extended to reach a perpendicular sunlit plane on which to initiate a shade/shadow system. With the establishment of those 2 points we also have a total of 7 points from which ⊥ shadows will begin shade/shadow systems.

There is no clear reason to begin with one or another of the ⊥ angles but it will probably be more interesting to let the sun reach the back walls of the 2 niches facing us.

So we might begin by the ⊥ angle shown (the shadows of far-vanishing horizontal lines on near-vanishing vertical planes) and establishing its VP on the VL for the planes in which the shadows lie......then extend the other ⊥ shadow from the same point

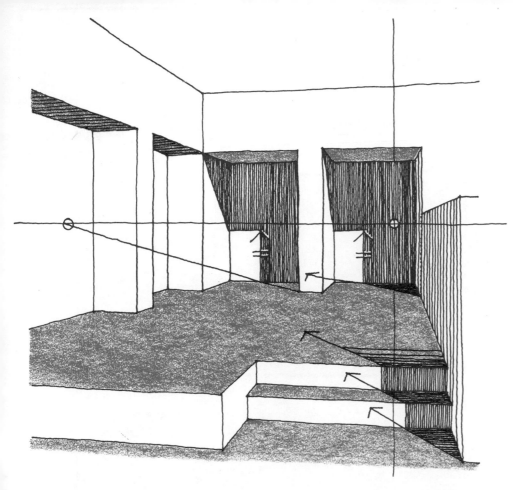

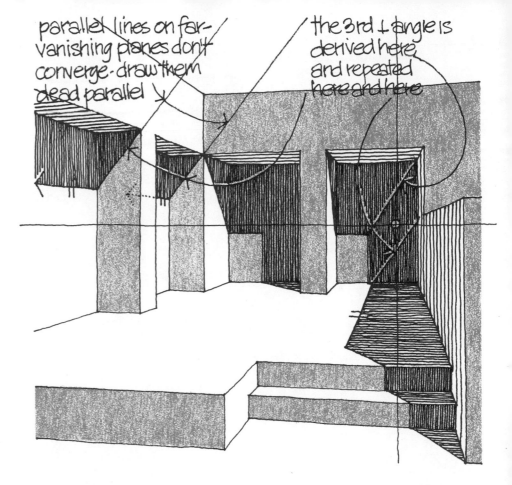

parallel lines on far-vanishing planes don't converge-draw them dead parallel

the 3rd ⊥ angle is derived here, and repeated here and here

A second ⊥ shadow angle may be chosen freely, and independently from the previous choice, and here it seems that we need a strong floor shadow without completely filling up the facing niches with shadows.

So, we choose one in the left hand niche, extend the choice to establish a VP on the VL for horizontal planes, and then cast the floor shadow in the other niche and initiate the shade/shadow system up the stairs.

Having freely chosen 2 of the 3 ⊥ shadow angles we must now derive the 3rd angle, since it is not a matter of choice but was determined by the 2 previous choices.

In this example this 3rd ⊥ angle is the shadow of near-vanishing horizontal lines on far-vanishing vertical planes. This angle is special in that its VP would be too far away to reach for projection so these shadows are drawn dead parallel.

159

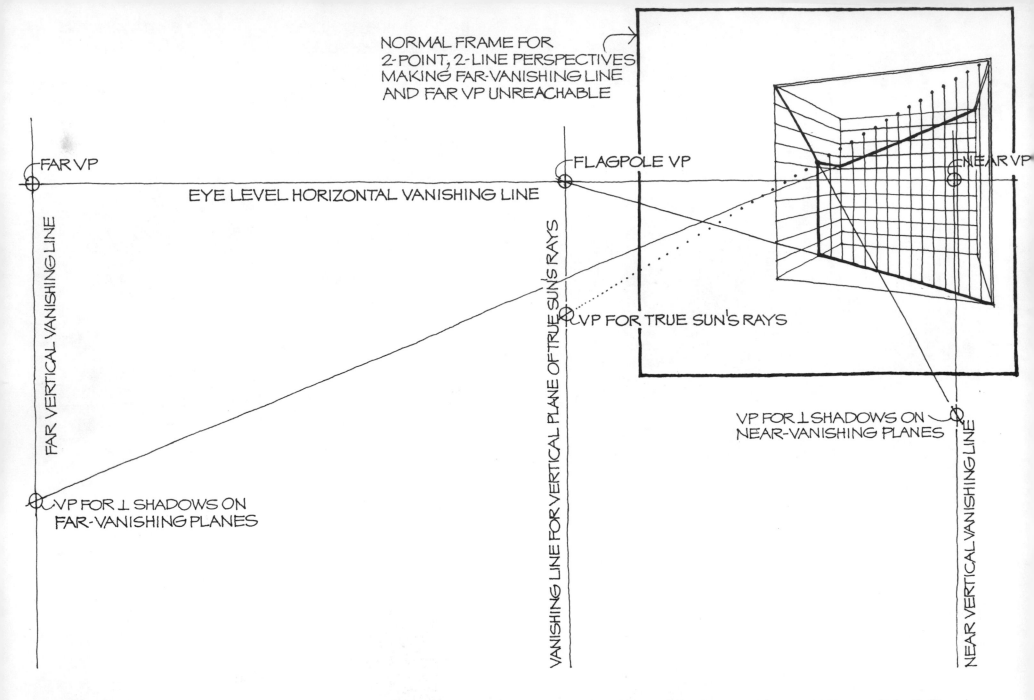

NORMAL FRAME FOR
2-POINT, 2-LINE PERSPECTIVES
MAKING FAR-VANISHING LINE
AND FAR VP UNREACHABLE

FAR VP

FLAGPOLE VP

NEAR VP

EYE LEVEL HORIZONTAL VANISHING LINE

FAR VERTICAL VANISHING LINE

VANISHING LINE FOR VERTICAL PLANE OF TRUE SUN'S RAYS

VP FOR TRUE SUN'S RAYS

VP FOR ⊥ SHADOWS ON
NEAR-VANISHING PLANES

VP FOR ⊥ SHADOWS ON
FAR-VANISHING PLANES

NEAR VERTICAL VANISHING LINE

PERSPECTIVE STRUCTURE AND NOMENCLATURE FOR ORTHOGONAL SHADOW-CASTING RELATIONSHIPS

TEMPLATES AND TAPES
DEVELOPING A RETRIEVABLE GRAPHIC VOCABULARY

Perspectives provide a structure for measuring and lighting experiential space and for representing the most basic environmental interest categories. ADDITIONAL interest and TEXTURAL interest, however, are provided by selectively retrieving certain graphic "templates" which the designer has acquired and carefully adding them to the drawing. Just as every draftsperson comes to own a set of plastic cut-out templates for drawing circles, ellipses and bathroom fixtures, so do designers acquire a set of perceptual templates which allows them to add figures, trees, furniture, cars, material indications and landscape textures to a drawing.

Learning to draw the trappings and textures which add additional and textural interest to a drawing can be thought of as the prerecording of videotapes which are stored and indexed for convenient retrieval. While *template* serves as a very familiar introductory metaphor, *videotape* is really a much more accurate analogy for the learned, stored and retrievable ability to draw the objects and patterns with which this section of the book is concerned. *Videotape* is better, because the ablity involves mastering a controlled procedure occurring in a particular sequence. If you will develop the habit of looking at design drawings as the graphic records of a series of acts and try to discover what was done first, second and third, and then practice duplicating the process and discovering and applying the controls, you will begin to build a memory bank of such videotapes.

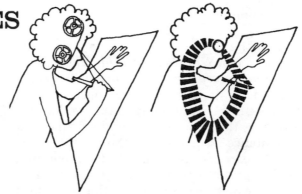

All such videotapes include a feedback loop which links the eye and hand, and allows a continual monitoring and control of the developing drawing. This kind of continuously adjusted control is called "cybernetics" and in drawing is dependent on having a perceptual videotape of the process of drawing the tree, figure, chair or leaf texture stored in your experience. Learning to draw is much more correctly thought of as the training of your *perception* rather than your hand, for only your trained perception has any hope of controlling your hand.

What appears to be incredible drawing ability is simply the replaying of such perceptual tapes pre-recorded long ago and stored for convenient retrieval. The tapes or templates need to be learned and indexed in several scales—just like the familiar green toilet templates distributed by American Standard. The "scale" of the templates should be graduated in three generally parallel ways: their distance from the viewer, their amount of detail and the time they take to draw. As an example of this scale-detail-time graduation, your tree-template collection should include a thirty-second tree, a five-minute tree and a thirty-minute tree; and these should roughly correspond to your 500 yard (away) tree, your thirty-yard tree and your twenty-foot tree; and you shouldn't just have one set of these tree templates, but eventually your stored templates should extend laterally through all the various drawing techniques and include a growing number of specific kinds of trees.

The most valuable templates are those which are time-flexible so that they become visually acceptable very quickly, but can accept and continue to benefit from further attention if the time becomes available. I have tried to illustrate this incremental detailing in all the examples of templates which follow. It is important that you learn to conceive of any drawing or part of a drawing as offering an extensive range of alternatives: alternatives of drawing technique, alternatives of what to include and what to exclude in the drawing, and alternatives of level of detail in what you have decided to include in the drawing. Such a flexible conception of any drawing and the ability to execute any of the alternatives is the primary source of freedom in drawing.

Speed in drawing is the most impressive manifestation of the freedom and confidence which comes from having a bulging memory bank of perceptual videotapes. The ability to make quick sketches comes from the confident selection from and management of this memory bank and is a perfect illustration of the apparent paradox of disciplined freedom.

An experienced design-delineator can begin a representational design drawing within a very limited time frame, and hold an incredible number of alternatives open for an incredible length of time and still finish the drawing. And all this is done without gnashing of teeth or frenetic hand speed. To watch it is very intimidating for the beginning design student who finds it hard to believe that she or he is really only witnessing the synchronized meshing of an interdependent network of decisions involving the selection, coordination and application of perhaps only a few pre-recorded perceptual videotapes: say two foreground trees, a figure group, a ground texture and a background of other trees, other buildings and mountains. Each individual pre-recorded videotape in this very small set may have, however, a nearly infinite variety in its specific conformation and in its level of detail. If they are all time-flexible templates, then most of the drawing time may be spent in studying the coordination of their placement in the drawing, allowing only whatever time remains to fill in their detail.

To illustrate how this disciplined freedom works in practice, let's say that I have decided that the building of which I am making a very early conceptual sketch needs a tree in front of it. The decision to draw the tree is initially no more than that—*tree here*. What kind of tree, its exact placement in a raised planter or growing out of paving with the help of a grating, whether or not to draw a figure group under the tree, whether or not to draw the entire tree or just up to its leaf canopy and whether or not to cast its shadow are all decisions that can be held in confident procrastination, knowing that there are several alternatives from which an appropriate selection can be made at a later time when the decision can be better related to all the other decisions about the drawing. The tree's importance in the overall drawing and its appropriate level of detail should be continually re-evaluated as the drawing develops, and this can be done with cool confidence *if* you have the template collection with which to draw all those alternatives. If you don't have the templates the whole situation deteriorates into, "Oh wow, how will I ever draw a decent tree right out there in front of the building? It's got to have one but I'll screw up

the whole drawing sure as anything. I saw a neat, easy-to-draw tree the other day—let's see, I think the trunk started out like this—oops, Charlie, did you bring your electric eraser tonight?"

One of the best collections of tapes or templates is Tim White's *A Graphic Vocabulary for Architectural Presentation* (1972). *Vocabulary* is a particularly appropriate word because, if we use language as an analogy for drawing, then perspective is the framework or sentence structure and the figures, trees, furniture, cars, material indications and landscape textures are the *words* of the language which we hang on the structural framework. And, as in using language, whatever you manage to say with a drawing is absolutely limited by the extent of your graphic vocabulary.

Fortunately environmental designers only need to master the drawing of a very limited slice of the visual world, and almost all of what they need to draw can be reduced to pre-recorded perceptual videotapes. I have been making architectural design drawings for a long time, but my memory bank of perceptual videotapes is embarrassingly meager compared to that of a cartoonist or commercial artist. If you asked me to draw an elephant or a helicopter I'd have to say, "I'm sorry, I don't have that tape."

Designers must develop a very critical, but forgiving, visual appraisal of their own designs and drawings. Through such a cold-eyed evaluation you will probably soon discover that there is an imbalance in your drawing skill—you will draw some things better than other things—and the continual balancing act required to make your drawings transparently consistent should become one of your endless tasks. Some delineators, even professional cartoonists, don't really

draw *anything* with great skill, but they have learned to draw *everything* with a consistency in which nothing stands out as being poorly drawn. The development of a parity in everything you draw, and especially in those things which contribute additional interest, will contribute more than anything else to the sought-for *transparency* of your design drawings.

Until you have achieved an acceptable balance in your ability to draw the necessary contents and context for your designs, I would suggest that you collect well-drawn examples of figures, trees, furniture, and cars and trace them directly into your drawings whenever it is necessary to make slick persuasive drawings. Meanwhile, however, you should strive to build the balance of all your template/tape categories, and this is little advanced by tracing. You should rather use your same file of collected figures, etc., and try to copy them freehand. If you approach the pre-recording of the necessary perceptual videotapes by searching for a structure and set of controls for the drawing procedures, they will become much more quickly learnable and retrievable. Remember that you need to make the ability to draw them repeatedly, not just once, and that ability demands the pre-recording of a perceptually controlled process.

The suggestion that learning to draw can or should be reduced to template-making may seem to remove all the creativity from drawing; but creativity in design drawing does not consist in continually inventing new ways of drawing the designed environment. Your creativity should perhaps be expended on the *design* of the environment *not its delineation*. If your reason for making a design drawing is primarily to show off your creativity *as a renderer* you misunderstand and are misusing design drawing.

TEXTURAL INTEREST

Textural interest is tactile interest—the interest we find in touching various materials or surfaces. While this is the most intimate of the interest categories, demanding direct physical contact for its full experience, the anticipation of potential tactile interest is cued *visually* like all other interest categories. We *remember* what a brick floor feels like barefoot or what a teak table top feels like, and the sight of such surfaces prompts that remembered tactile interest.

Drawings can represent tactile interest by prompting our perception in much the same way as distant vision. Textures can be made in the various drawing techniques which represent, with varying degrees of realism or abstraction, the various textures of the natural and built environment. All drawn textures are learned and applied as the perceptual videotapes just discussed and require the practiced coordination of eye and hand. Knowing where to place the textures in a drawing, however, is equally important and takes only the time required to understand the principles of spatial perception.

The main source, virtually the only integral source of textural interest in an environment is the collection of materials of which the environment is made. The increased cost of handmade and hand-installed unit materials and the concurrent development of modern technology have drastically changed the palette of materials which are realistically available to an environmental designer. There aren't nearly as many textures to enjoy or to draw in today's buildings as there once were.

This change can be seen in two of Ted Kautzky's drawings. Kautzky was a master of pencil tone drawing and his "broadstroke" technique was ideally suited to the architectural materials of his day (rubblestone, cedar shakes, brick, shutters) which were all rich in the textural interest we are talking about. Near the end of his career, however, Kautzky was asked to draw modern buildings, and with his drawing technique he found nothing to draw. He drew everything *but* the building itself, for how can you render white stucco, steel, aluminum, formica or glass with a *surface rendering* tool like a pencil? This is one reason for the change to line drawings or line and tone drawings: our modern materials have very little textural interest and are better represented by *edge-drawing* techniques.

Above drawings from THE TED KAUTZKY PENCIL BOOK by Ted Kautzky

163

MATERIALS

The materials of which any designed object or space is constructed are an integral part of the design. The choice of materials should be appropriate to the form and function of the environment, for materials contribute greatly to the sensory experience of any design.

Designers must represent materials realistically in the design drawings they make so that material choices will be an early and continuing consideration in the design process. The inability to draw a particular material may mean that we seldom consider using it—simply because we can't represent it to ourselves or our clients adequately.

TONE OR COLOR. In drawing materials it is usually better to represent their texture and configuration and let their relative lightness or darkness be entirely dependent on light (sun, shade or shadow) instead of trying to represent the material's integral tone or color.

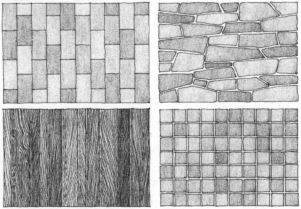

UNIT MATERIALS. Forms or surfaces which are made up of individual pieces (masonry, panelling, shingles) should be drawn so that the individual unit is defined and by toning some of the units slightly darker or lighter.

EDGE CONFIGURATION. The best place to show a material's texture is at a corner or edge where it can be seen in profile. The joint indentation of a masonry wall, the projecting seam of a standing seam roof or the overlapping profile of horizontal wood siding tell more about the texture of those materials than any amount of rendering on their surfaces.

INSTALLATION DETAILS. Careful attention to a material's realistic application can also help in its drawn representation. The drawing of chamfered edges at the top of a concrete retaining wall, the mitering of a wood door frame or the jointing of a terrazzo floor are examples of installation details which offer efficient and unmistakable clues to the identity of the materials being represented.

164

The drawings which follow render a combination of materials in the various drawing techniques introduced earlier. The drawings of the same set of materials in the various techniques is intended to demonstrate the ease or difficulty of drawing a particular material in a particular technique. The drawing is a sampler of materials such as would never be combined in a single design and was contrived to show as many different materials as possible.

LINE

TONE

TONE OF
LINES

LINE AND
TONE

LINE AND
TONE

167

TONE

TONE OF LINES

168

REFLECTIONS

While reflective surfaces have no texture of their own, they reflect all the textures and tonal values around them. Glass and water are the most common reflective materials and they are also the most misrepresented of materials. This misrepresentation is unfortunate, and especially so for glass since it is one of modern architecture's favorite materials. To represent water or glass viewed from the outside as being either transparent or opaque is to seriously misunderstand them as materials.

Many other materials (stainless steel, aluminum, polished marble or terrazzo and some plastics) are also reflective, but their reflectivity is limited and need only be suggested in drawing compared to the mirror-like reflectivity of glass or water. Glass viewed from the outside or water viewed from above reflect their surroundings because they are smooth surface membranes separating a relatively dark interior (or underwater) volume from a relatively bright exterior space.

Reflections in glass or water, or on any reflective surface, are easily drawn with the understanding of one simple analogy. You are probably familiar with sterile, or highly controlled environments which demand that scientists stand behind a vision panel and insert their hands into rubber gloves which are hermetically sealed to the vision panel. In drawing reflections, just imagine that you are the scientist and you reach from behind the glass, or from beneath the water, or from *within* any reflective surface, and you grab *everything* that is out there, or up there, and pull it back through, under or inside the reflective surface. You then draw it in its new position just as if you have removed your hands from the gloves by pulling them *inside* the reflective surface and they now stood out, wrong side out, inside the reflective surface.

This is the way you draw the world that is reflected in any reflective surface: as if it existed the same distance *inside* the reflective surface as it actually exists outside. The reflection always pulls the reflected world through the glass *perpendiculary* at 90° to the reflective surface, and it always foreshortens in perspective as if it actually existed behind the reflective surface.

GLASS

The perception of a vertical glass wall, window or door is always a variable combination of reflectivity and transparency, with the reflections usually being dominant. The variables which affect this mixture of reflectivity and transparency are four:

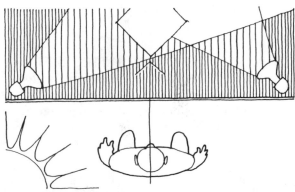

THE ILLUMINATION OF THE INTERIOR. If the interior is brightly illuminated by direct sunlight shining through the glass or even by extremely bright artificial lighting, the reflectivity will be decreased and the transparency increased;

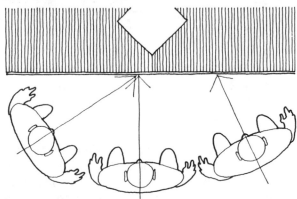

THE ANGLE OF THE VIEWER TO THE GLASS. The glass will be most transparent when viewed perpendicularly. As the viewer's angle to the glass becomes less and less the glass will become more and more reflective;

169

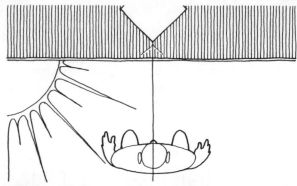

THE ILLUMINATION OF THE REFLECTED EXTERIOR.
If the world which is reflected in the glass is brightly illuminated by direct sunlight giving it the full tonal range from bright sunlight to dark shadows its reflection will be stronger on the glass, decreasing the glass's transparency;

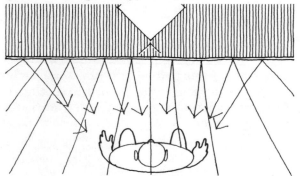

THE INHERENT REFLECTIVITY OF THE PARTICULAR GLASS.
Artificially darkened and mirrored glass will all be much more reflective and thereby less transparent than ordinary clear glass.

Since glass is normally a vertical plane, this vertical orientation of the reflective surface is best represented by rendering all the reflections in vertical tones of lines—even in a line and tone drawing. In pencil tone drawings the reflections should all be stroked vertically to represent the orientation of the reflective surface. Whatever is seen through the glass should be drawn in first, and then the reflections rendered directly on top of it.

Vertical glass reflects two different realms. The first realm is that between the viewer and the glass and includes everything that appears in front of the glass in perspective. This realm should be reflected as having the same tonal values (darks and lights) as it actually has in the drawing. The second realm is everything that lies behind the viewer and does not appear in the perspective *except* as reflections in the glass. This second realm is best delineated as receding, progressively lighter layers of space—distant buildings, trees, mountains—rendered as vertical tones of lines. Above the reflections of this second realm, beginning a little above eye-level, the sky behind the viewer will be reflected, and this sky reflection will normally be the brightest part of the reflections in the glass. In black and white drawings this sky reflection should be left white; in colored drawings it should be tinted a light blue.

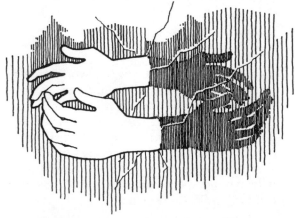

GLASS
- Pull everything which is in front of the glass through the glass in a direction perpendicular to the glass, toward the VP.
- Draw these reflections as if they were the same distance (foreshortened) behind the glass as they are actually in front of the glass.
- Indicate all reflections on the glass with vertical tones of lines since the reflecting glass surface is vertical.
- Tone reflections of objects between the viewer and the glass the same relative darkness or lightness as they are in the drawing.
- Tone reflections of everything behind the viewer as progressively lighter layers of receding space.

WATER

Since water is normally a horizontal surface, water reflections are best delineated by horizontal lines representing the orientation of the reflective surface. I recommend rendering water reflections as horizontal tones of lines in all the drawing techniques except tone, where the stroking direction of the reflected tones should still be horizontal.

The horizontality of water as a reflective surface eliminates many of the complications encountered in drawing reflections in glass. In normal perspectives there is no vertical convergence to a VP and therefore no fore-shortening of the reflections, allowing the reflections to be measured directly. Neither is there any problem with variable reflectivity/transparency since the normal viewer's angle to the surface of the water is so flat that the surface remains steadfastly reflective. Nor are there two realms reflected in water. The relationship of the viewer to any reflective water surface is such that nothing *behind* the viewer will ever be reflected. Only that portion of the world seen directly in the perspective will ever be reflected in the water.

There is, however, one slight complication with reflections in water that is not often encountered with glass. There will normally be objects reflected in the water which do not actually touch the surface of the water—like buildings or trees slightly inland from the water's edge. For these you must imaginarily, or mechanically, extend the plane of the water's surface to a point directly below them, and then measure the reflection downward from that point, *not from where they hit the ground.* Imagine that you simply took the land away, leaving the tree or building suspended in mid-air and then ran the water level back under it. If you measure the reflections in this way they will be correct.

The reflecting relationship is between the object and the plane of the reflecting water surface. The land has nothing to do with it.

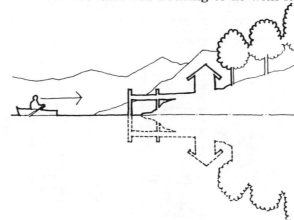

Reflections are the most characteristic and exciting contributions of glass and water as exterior materials in the environment. The reflections in glass double the perception of wall thickness by reflecting the reveal of the opening. Both glass and water can reflect a beautiful natural environment or a respected built environment in a way no other materials can, and your designs and the drawings with which you represent them should reflect this understanding.

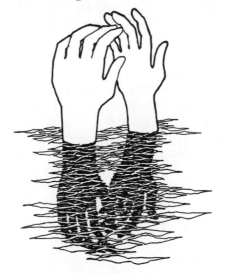

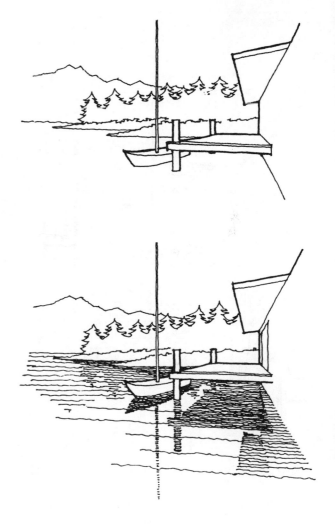

WATER

- Pull everything which is above the surface of the water down through the water in a vertical direction.
- Draw these reflections as if they were the same distance below the water as they actually are above the water.
- Indicate all reflections on the water with transverse horizontal tones of lines since the reflecting water surface is horizontal.
- Tone reflections the same relative darkness or lightness as they are in the drawing.

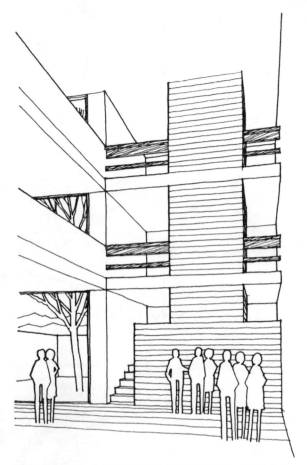

PLACEMENT TO DEEPEN THE SPACE

The determinants which affect the placement of textures in an environment and in a drawing are somewhat different. In any environment the most critical determinants are functional. Imperviousness to wear, ease of cleaning, comfort or pleasure in physical contact, acoustic absorption, reflectance or non-slip floor surfaces are examples of some of these functional determinants. In a drawing there is really only one determinant for the placement of textures and that is to place them where they will help the viewer perceive the space, and that means they should always be placed on the farthest space-bounding surfaces.

The placement of textures on the farthest space-bounding surfaces will deepen any drawing in two ways:

1. The gradation of the texture from coarse to fine on the surfaces as they recede from us will make us perceive them as existing in three-dimensions (Gibson's 1. TEXTURE PERSPECTIVE).
2. The disappearance and reappearance of the background surface textures behind untextured foreground objects will make us perceive continuous underlying background *space* (Gibson's 9. SHIFT OF TEXTURE OR LINEAR SPACING and 12. COMPLETENESS OR CONTINUITY OF OUTLINE).

The difference the placement of textures can make in a drawing can be demonstrated in a two-dimensional plan. If you choose to texture the table and chairs in drawing a dining room, that effort will accomplish nothing in helping a viewer perceive the drawing as having depth; but if the same textural effort is applied to the floor, so that the textural pattern disappears and reappears beneath the furniture we *must* perceive a continuous background surface *under* the table and chairs and therefore a mandatory depth in the drawing.

ADDITIONAL INTEREST

Additional interest in drawing or in the environment is that interest we find in all the *additions* we, and nature, make to any built environment. The category consists of trees, plants, other human beings and all the human artifacts we bring with us into any place we inhabit: furnishings of all kinds, signs, automobiles, etc.

Much of this interest category is frankly ornamental and past generations of environmental designers unblushingly designed it into their buildings as integral ornament. Early in this century, however, architects condemned all ornament as decadent and superficial, and the lack of ornament became one of modern architecture's hallmarks. We are only recently beginning to ornament our buildings once again. The morality we claimed in stripping all the ornament from the built environment proved to be as superficial as the decorations we condemned, however, for all through the purge we carried this kind of interest back into our environments in the form of scheffleras, bentwood rockers and Marimekko prints.

The collection of things which provide *additional* interest can also enrich the perception of any environment or drawing in three ways which need to be considered separately. Items of *additional* interest can:

- *specify the scale*
- *indicate the use*
- *demonstrate the space*

SPECIFYING THE SCALE. Because the class of objects which provide *additional* interest has an established relationship to, and in fact includes, the human figure, it is our primary source of mensurate scale in the environment. The scale of any designed environment is one of the designer's traditional means of expression. A space may be designed to look larger or smaller than its actual dimensions and a deliberate ambiguity in the scale of an environment can make the experience of it more interesting. Whatever the designer's intentions regarding the scale of the space, the actual scale is always specified as a direct result of the items of *additional* interest, especially the human figure.

INDICATING THE USE. The second kind of information carried by the items of *additional* interest which we add to an environment or a drawing of an environment is some indication of the use of the space. The equipment, furnishing, signs, and the activity of the people in the space should communicate the functions for which the space is designed. A shopping center should have signs for the various shops and lots of shoppers looking and pointing at window displays and carrying packages. A perspective of a bank should show the tellers' counter with depositors being served, a prominent clock and calendar and, if possible, the vault door.

173

In addition to all the good things that the inclusion of elements of additional interest can add to a drawing they can also:

- *obscure the perception of the space*
- *preempt the design emphasis*
- *make the drawing "opaquely" self-conscious*

show how the same number of elements of additional interest can be placed in the same drawing of an environment, one in a way which covers the space-defining corners and makes the space difficult to understand, and the other in a way which lets all the space-defining corners show, so that the space can be clearly perceived. Great lengths of planar intersections can be covered as long as they reappear near the corners where the enclosure is resolved. We sort of trust them to stay straight behind sofas and bushes if we can see their resolution at either end.

DEMONSTRATING THE SPACE. Perhaps the most important opportunity items of *additional* interest offer is that their placement can demonstrate the space of a perspective. By simply occupying upper and lower levels, or distant courtyards, or by disappearing and reappearing behind other elements in the environment they can demonstrate that certain spaces exist, or that they have a particular height, depth or configuration. This demonstration of space is so important and must be so carefully integrated with the spatial interest of a drawing that I will return to it at the end of this section.

OBSCURING THE PERCEPTION OF THE SPACE. Elements of *additional* interest must be added to a drawing very carefully so that they promote the perception of the space rather than obscuring it. Because our perception of space depends on the perception of the space-bounding surfaces of any environment, and the perception of the configuration of any surface-bounded space depends on seeing the surfaces' edge or intersections, figures, trees, furniture or automobiles should never be placed so that they completely hide planar intersections at corners. This can be demonstrated in the drawings above which

TRANSPARENCY. Earlier I used the metaphor of transparency to describe the goal of drawing in such a way that the drawing is completely transparent so the viewer looks *through* the drawing to the environment it represents. The most critical need for such transparency lies in the present category of *additional* interest. Because human figures, trees, plants, furniture, and automobiles are so familiar to us and normally command so much of our attention and compulsive discrimination they can very easily dominate a drawing by:

- *preempting the design emphasis*
- *making the drawing self-conscious*

As an example of both preempting the design and making the drawing self-conscious, let me draw a few figures the way we did when I was an undergraduate at Illinois. The figures are hardly recognizable to the uninitiated because they are both a redesign and an oh-so-self-conscious way of drawing the human figure.

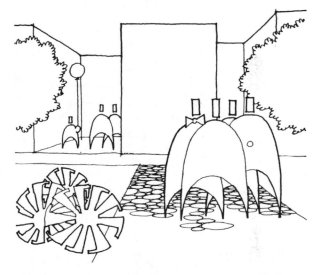

There were very definite rules for drawing these figures. The heads were always rectangular and disconnected from the body. Some were distinguished by a small circle drawn in the center of the figure which could be interpreted, I suppose, as either a Dagwood button or a navel. They were unisex except that some might have bow ties, and further detail could be added in the form of a circular hand holding a ballon or leading a dog (which I never mastered). We drew great groups of these androids standing around our drawings, as proud evidence that we had mastered the reigning graphic cliche. Later I discovered such figures never failed to elicit comments from clients, which is always a sure sign that they are preempting the design and making the drawings self-consciously opaque as drawings.

PREEMPTING THE DESIGN EMPHASIS is easily done be attempting to *design* all, or any, of the elements of additional interest. Since furniture and automobiles, for instance, are familiar items on which great design attention is lavished, and we are all familiar with the state of the art in terms of designs, styles or models, any attempt to design an original automobile or piece of furniture will be immediately apparent and can easily preempt the design emphasis of the drawing.

MAKING THE DRAWING SELF-CONSCIOUS is similarly accomplished by drawing any of the elements of additional interest in an overly self-conscious way that calls too much attention to itself. Unfortunately some of the first "templates" or "perceptual tapes" acquired by beginning designers are of this variety. They are so-o-o-o clever and cute and their placement at center stage in the drawing makes it very clear that the delineator is more proud of her or his ability to draw a particular tree or automobile or figure than to design an environment.

There are two approaches to drawing the elements of additional interest in such a way that they specify the scale, indicate the use and demonstrate the space, but remain *transparent* so that they neither preempt the design or make the drawing *opaque* as a drawing.

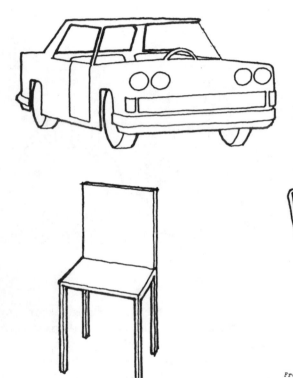

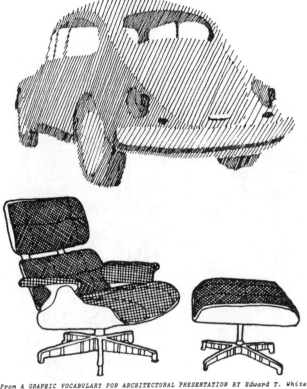

From A GRAPHIC VOCABULARY FOR ARCHITECTURAL PRESENTATION BY Edward T. White

PLATO'S CHAIR. The first approach is to draw elements of additional interest that are so simple and essential that they make no design statement whatever. With this approach each chair becomes Plato's chair, with the seat, back and four legs necessary to all chairs but *nothing* else, nothing particular to this chair that would in any way distinguish it from the quintessential chair of chairs. In addition to keeping the elements of additional interest transparent this approach is always the most efficient way to draw.

EAMES' CHAIR. The second approach is to choose particular well-known, well-designed elements and draw them with great accuracy and realism like a Charles Eames chair or a Volkswagen. This approach requires having a photograph or drawing of the item for reference and always takes a little more time, unless you can trace the items, but in the end it has the same effect. It takes the elements of additional interest out of the realm of self-conscious design or self-conscious drawing so that they do not compete for the viewer's attention.

CREDIBILITY. The second approach has one further advantage which is very important. If you include one or more well-known elements of additional interest in your representational drawings they will do more than anything else to establish the credibility of the drawings. This is particularly true if the selected elements are essential to the environment being represented. If you are designing a gymnasium, for instance, the very meticulous drawing of a side horse, a set of parallel bars or a basketball goal and its braces will do more to establish the drawing's credibility as a representation of that environment than anything you could do. And strangely, perhaps, your credibility as a designer is always somehow related, for good or ill, to the credibility of your drawings.

If you are the designer of the gymnasium and your drawings indicate that you don't know what equipment is normally found in that environment or that you are so unfamiliar with it that you can't draw it accurately, what can the client assume about your ability to design the space?

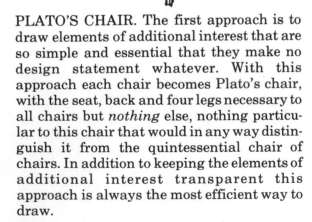

FIGURES

Unlike the other elements of additional interest, the inclusion of human figures in the drawings which represent a designed environment has a more basic purpose, than those discussed earlier. In addition to specifying the scale, indicating the use, and demonstrating the space, human figures remind the designers that their ultimate clients are the people who will inhabit the spaces they design, and unless the space is designed to accept the human figure it may deserve to be uninhabited.

When we stripped the ornamental detail from our buildings early in this century, we also stripped much of the ability of a human being to relate to buildings physically. Older buildings offer moldings, belt courses, chair rails, bay windows and all kinds of other details and elements which you could sit on, lean against, put your feet or elbows on and generally handle and become physically involved with. Many modern buildings, both in their material choice and their detailing are, literally and perhaps intentionally, untouchable.

The inclusion of human figures in your design drawings, from the earliest sketches, will perhaps remind you that there should be places on which to sit, lean, rest your elbow or foot or to just touch with your hands. And if there aren't, if all the humans can do in the space is stand uncomfortably, perhaps you are designing a very inhuman space.

Most designers will never, and need never, become virtuoso delineators of the human figure. Designers need to draw figures competently, so that the figures never detract from a design drawing, but they should never be drawn better or in greater detail than the product or space which is being designed. Neither should the designer attempt to *rede-*

sign the human figure; it is a reasonably workable design, or evolutionary result, and if you give the figures in your drawing design content by trying to redesign them, they may preempt the room, patio, or building which you were asked to design and which is more entitled to your design attention. Designers are much wiser if they confine their efforts to learning to draw the human figure competently, placing it carefully, and designing *for* it, instead of trying to redesign it.

As in drawing furniture and automobiles, there are two approaches to figure drawing which give beginning designers much needed flexibility in adding figures to their drawings.

TRACING FIGURES is the safest approach and it is comforting to be able simply to select appropriate figures from a well-drawn advertisement and trace them directly into a drawing. You may need to dismember and reassemble some of them to make them fit the

context of your drawing, but if your perspective is taken at eyelevel, standing figures of any scale can simply be hung on that eyelevel. Although this tracing of figures adds only a little to your ability to draw figures from scratch, it gives you much needed experience in placing figures in perspective and until your homemade figures are as good as your other drawing skills, it is only intelligent to build a collection of well-drawn figures for tracing.

MAKING YOUR OWN FIGURES is the only other way of drawing figures and should be pursued concurrently. While you are collecting a "morgue" of well-drawn figures for tracing, you should also be building a similar collection of the pre-recorded perceptual "tapes" which will allow you to draw figures of your own. The building of this second collection is much slower but much more worthwhile because of the freedom it will eventually give you.

The advice which follows is not from some-one who is very good at drawing figures per se, but from a designer who has struggled to learn to draw, and teach others to draw, competent figures for inclusion in design drawings.

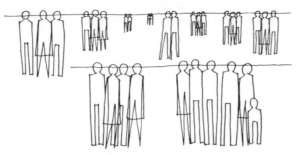

The best way I have found to draw home-made figures is to begin with your first crude design doodles and refine them as you refine the design. This means that you never attempt to draw a finished figure the first time out, but each drawing of a figure or group of figures is rather a progression of tracing paper overlays capable of consider-able refinement which will correspond to the refinements of the design drawing for which the figures are drawn. I am still not capable, and probably will never be capable, of draw-ing the slick detailed figures some presenta-tion drawings require, without referring to or tracing figures drawn by figure delineators more skilled than I.

In prerecording a retrievable perceptual tape for drawing figures, or anything else, it is best to develop a flexible hierarchical tape composed of progressive stages or levels of detail or refinement. The hierarchy of such a tape has a double meaning. It arranges ways of drawing figures in an ascending order of detail, refinement, or skill and time required, from the crudest, quickest sketch figure to the most meticulously drawn figure; and this same hierarchy also represents the overlay stages necessary to reach the highest, most time-consuming level of detail in figure draw-ing. I will try to present the drawing of all the perceptual tapes of additional interest (fig-ures, trees and growies, furniture and auto-mobiles) as this kind of flexible hierarchy.

A standing figure in an eyelevel perspective is best begun by drawing a balloon head hung on the eyelevel line, and below that a rectangular body split into two legs by a deep crotch notch. Male and female figures can be distinguished by the shape of the ends of the legs—rectangular for male, resulting in squared-off pant cuffs vs. triangular for women, resulting in pointed feet. With the modest addition of a straight shift dress to the female figures such crude figures can suf-ficiently represent human beings in rough sketches.

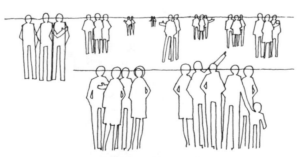

The next level of detail adds indications of arms, either as asymmetrical elbow bulges or extended in talking or pointing gestures. Fig-ures should always be collected into groups and the addition of a gesturing arm on one figure and the addition of chins and slight head inclinations can indicate who is talking and who is listening. Such indications of typi-cal social relationships between individual figures can help greatly in indicating the use of a space.

Next come a few indications of clothing details such as collars, necklines, cuffs and belts which begin to make the male/female distinctions more sophisticated as well as some difference in head outlines which begin to indicate the differences in male and female coiffures.

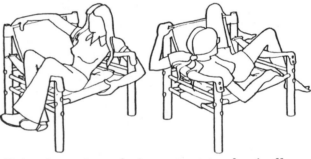

It is also extremely important to physically relate figures to their environment by show-ing them touching, holding, sitting or lean-ing against their environment in various postures. This requires another level of refinement which includes the hands, knee/seat bends and elbow locks. Except when inhibited by very formal contexts, humans generally get really physically involved with their environment. We sit all over a chair, throw our legs over the arms and our arms over the back, put our elbows on tables, hang our heels on chair rungs, etc. Figures sitting or standing in primly symmetrical postures are not only more difficult to draw, they never look like they belong in the environment. I have found that figures drawn in a variety of postures, all in the most direct physical contact with their environment are much easier to draw and look as though they belong there.

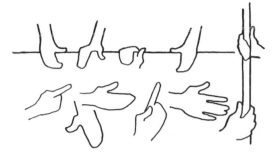

At this level it is best to draw the hands as mittens, indicating only the opposing thumb which distinguishes us from the rest of the animal kingdom. The thumb, in drawings as in reality, allows us to grasp handrails, chairbacks or door pulls and thus convincingly attach ourselves to our environment.

The knee/seat bend is necessary in drawing a seated figure and the curves of the knee caps and the buttocks are extremely important in showing various seated leg postures. The elbow lock is a good way of relating a seated figure to a chair back or a standing figure to a bar height surface or a guard rail. I think you find that if you will learn to draw a grasping hand, knee caps for various seated postures and various elbow lock relationships, your figures will look convincing and related to their context even though some of their details are crudely drawn.

The relationship of figures to their context involves the bending of the torso and the arms and legs so that the figure occupies space or depth. This is a very important advance over the stick figure which exists in a decal-flat plane facing the viewer and whose body and limbs are always seen full-length like one of the rivet-jointed cardboard skeletons we hang up at Halloween. In order to occupy space, one part of the limb or torso must be foreshortened so that it comes at the viewer in space while the other part of the arm, leg or body is still seen full length. This ability to draw figures which occupy space is a major step up the hierarchy of detail and makes any figure much more convincing.

Some details of figure drawing may be worth a little more explanation and these are best understood as hierarchical refinements in the figure drawing process. Because we perceive most about our fellow human beings by looking at their faces, the further detailing of a drawn figure should begin with the head and I would recommend adding the following details in the following order:

chin and nose—
tells where the person's attention is directed;
hair outline—
can specify sex and age;
glasses—
suggests eyes and reinforces direction of attention;
hair texture—
best place to add textural interest to a figure.

I would always recommend stopping short of drawing the eyes and mouth because they are very difficult to draw and they take the figure into facial expression which is the realm of the cartoonist. Cartoonists usually vary only the mouth and eyes and eyebrows to indicate the full range of human emotions. If you draw eyes and mouths you risk having your figures turn your drawing into a soap opera with the range of emotions their faces express.

179

For hands and arms the ascending order of detail I would recommend is:

mitten hand—
allows grasping of railings, handles, and edges;
cuff or short sleeve—
suggests clothing;
foreshortening of upper or lower arm—
makes figure occupy space;
separate fingers—
for closeup hands;
muscle placement on bare arms—
biceps attached to inside of upper arm.
NEVER DRAW THE ARMS SYMMETRICALLY.

For feet and legs the progressive detailing is similar:

feet—
shows facing direction and gives figure stability;
pant cuff and shoe heel—
suggests attire;
foreshortening of upper or lower leg—
makes figure occupy space;
shoetop, sole or strap details—
indicates shoe style;
muscle placement on bare legs—
calf muscle attached to *inside* of leg.
NEVER DRAW THE LEGS SYMMETRICALLY.

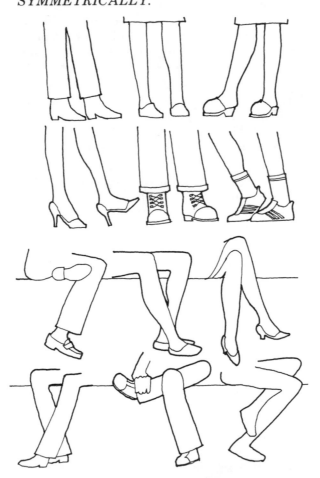

CLOTHING. Certain standard articles of clothing are easier to draw than others and this simpler attire avoids getting bogged down in the details of a fashion designer. Certain garments can also reinforce the sexual identity or age of a figure. In general, garments which overhang the waist eliminate the drawing of belts, and the shoulder straps of jumpers and vests are helpful in adding easily drawn detail. The basic garments shown below may not be the latest styles but they allow some variety of easily drawn attire without ever being mistaken for a fashion ad.

PROPS. Accessory elements can also be added to figures which will further clarify age and sex distinctions and indicate occupations or functional activities. Canes, balloons, purses, packages, stethoscopes, briefcases may be a little stereotypical but can be helpful in clarifying a human situation or indicating the use of a space.

GROUPS. Figures should be collected into groups of various sizes. People are gregarious and, except in the most hostile environment, will stand or sit in conversational groups. Solitary figures will seldom enhance a drawing. Unless you want the drawing to express the alienation of 20th Century man or to look like a Freshman Mixer before the introductions, you should always collect your figures into groups. Groups are easily accepted by the viewer, because they are obviously talking to one another, having come together or arranged to meet here. On the other hand, the lurking about of lone figures is suspect.

PLACEMENT. The placement of figures in a design drawing is extremely important and demands great care. In addition to the criteria for the placement of any element of *additional* interest, which have been covered earlier, the placement of figures has a few extra pitfalls and opportunities. Beyond the criteria for never preempting or obscuring the design, figures should be spaced rather evenly throughout the drawing, but always avoiding any regimentation in the spacing or the numbers of figures in the groups. They mustn't be planted 15' on center as you would plant an orchard. There should be figures in the foreground, background and middle ground, to either side and on all levels of the space, generally avoiding dead center. Figures can also be placed to demonstrate spaces, particularly sunken spaces like conversation pits which are almost impossible to show otherwise.

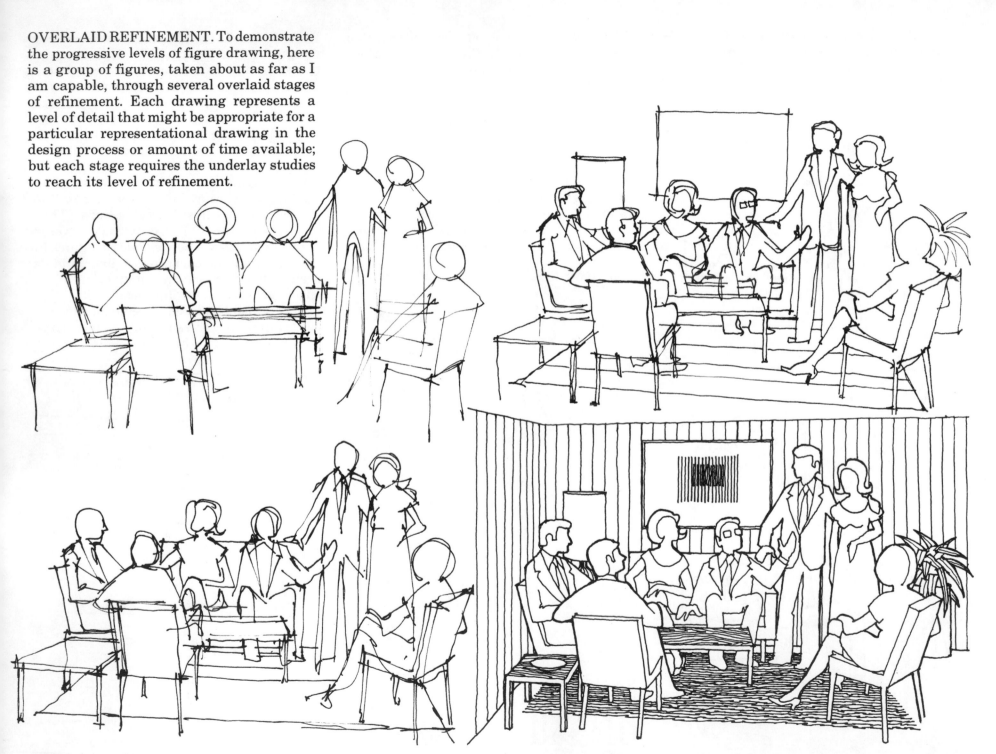

OVERLAID REFINEMENT. To demonstrate
the progressive levels of figure drawing, here
is a group of figures, taken about as far as I
am capable, through several overlaid stages
of refinement. Each drawing represents a
level of detail that might be appropriate for a
particular representational drawing in the
design process or amount of time available;
but each stage requires the underlay studies
to reach its level of refinement.

HUMANIZING ELEMENTS. Making a space human requires more than just sprinkling a few figures around a representational drawing of the space. There are architectural elements, landscape elements, and pieces of furniture that have special significance for human beings because of familiar, intimate human use. Furniture will be covered separately in a later section, but I would like to demonstrate the potential for physical interaction with certain elements of the environment.

Landscape humanizing elements would include fountains, benches, planters, seat-high walls, steps, and trees—and the more human of these allows and invites human participation.

Architectural humanizing elements would include doors, windows, and fireplaces—and the more human of these includes or accommodates the human figure: window seats, recessed doorways, or fireplaces with hearth seats.

Designing environments for the human figure and drawing human figures in the environment are inseparably related. They promote one another. Figures are much easier to draw in environments which have been designed for them and the habitual inclusion of figures in design drawings will inevitably result in a more human design.

183

TREES AND GROWIES

Trees and "growies" (as they are called by architecture students at the University of Arizona) constitute an important category of *additional* interest. Trees have a special relationship to humans in the shade they give, the fruit they bear, and because our ancestors probably lived in them.

Trees embellish any drawing because they include all the interest categories: spatial, tonal, textural, and additional, and they enhance any environment in precisely the same ways. They even hold interest for the other senses in that you can hear a tree when it rustles in the wind and smell a tree when it blooms.

Trees can create a space as a leafy roof or articulate it as a row of columns. They contribute tonal interest in the pool of shadow they cast and their leaf mass adds both tonal and textural interest. Their branch structure is highly figural, especially the bare branches of deciduous trees in winter.

Drawn trees can be abstracted into simple graphic conventions, which should be mastered first; but the realistic rendering of specific trees depends on knowing the characteristic branch structure, overall form, and the leaf detail of each species. Trees are probably the most demanding single thing a designer needs to know how to draw.

The accompanying drawings begin with simple abstract "tree" trees and progress to some of my limited vocabulary of specific trees.

The simplest tree indications are open circles with stick trunks which are sufficient for the roughest small scale sketches.

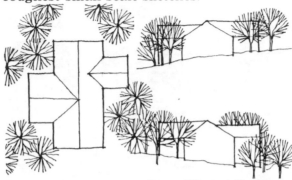

The simplest structured tree fills out the basic "lollipop" outline of the previous tree indication with a single line branch structure growing from the initial stick trunk. This skeletal branch structure is usually leafless, but may have various configurations, as demonstrated in the series of trees which follow.

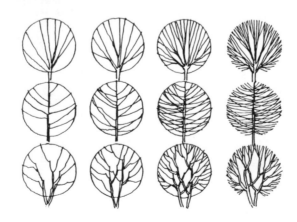

The branch structures all end at a circular or oval perimeter guideline, which is later erased, and the more graceful of them begin low on the trunk so that their length is maximized.

So far, the developing tree templates are flat, two-dimensional "decals" which do not yet demonstrate that they have depth.

Depth in the branch structure is only accomplished with a double-line trunk and branch indication which communicates thickness. Such a double-line indication begins with the trunk and can be continued into the secondary branches.

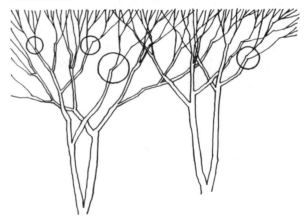

At some point the two lines which have been indicating the two sides of a trunk or branch must become single-line indications of minor peripheral branches. This transition becomes almost imperceptible and maintains the delicacy of the outer branches while offering the spatial capability of the double-line branch indication in the lower parts of the branch structure.

The potential of the double-line branch indication lies in the ability to cross double-line branches over one another so that they must be perceived as occupying space in depth. This crossing of branches requires a little planning of the branch arrangement but this is easily accomplished in even the briefest series of overlays.

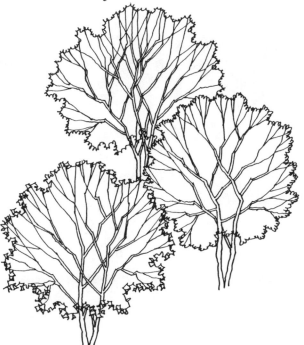

The next level of detail is the return to some more sophisticated delineation of the outline of the tree mass. Instead of just a simple smooth circle or oval, but without getting into the tedium of drawing individual leaves, we can suggest the shape of the individual leaves with the configuration of the boundary line we draw around the tree's mass of leaves. A leaf-boundary line can have at least three kinds of configuration. It can be made by a line whose deformations are always concave, always convex, or neutral. The concave configuration is appropriate for oak, maple or holly; the convex for olives, ash or eucalyptus and the neutral for non-specific trees.

In addition to suggesting the conformation of the tree's individual leaves, the boundary line of any tree's leaf mass allows the tree's foliage to be toned or colored while remaining transparent. Buildings and other elements of the environment can be shown right through such transparent trees while still rendering a light tone or green tint within the boundary line of the leaf mass.

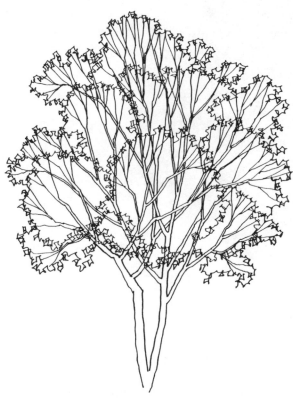

The next step shown in the developing tree template is the subdivision of the entire leaf mass into smaller clumps of leaves carried by the major branch structures. This is done by simply extending lines of the same configuration as the leaf-boundary line across the leaf mass to give the appearance of some clumps of leaves in front of others. This step in the ascending hierarchy of detail is relatively

worthless unless you follow it up by toning or coloring the various leaf subdivisions differently.

Now comes what is in some ways a regression. In the next step the tree template loses its transparency and becomes an opaque object with all attention called to the configuration and subdivision of the leaf outline and no suggestion of the inner branch structure.

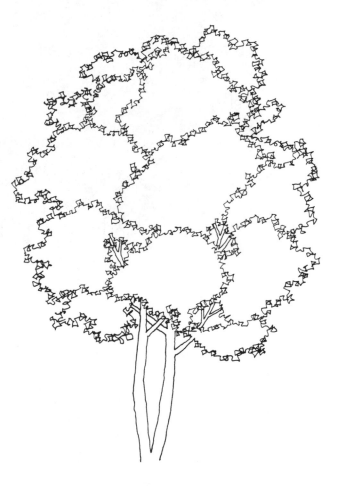

185

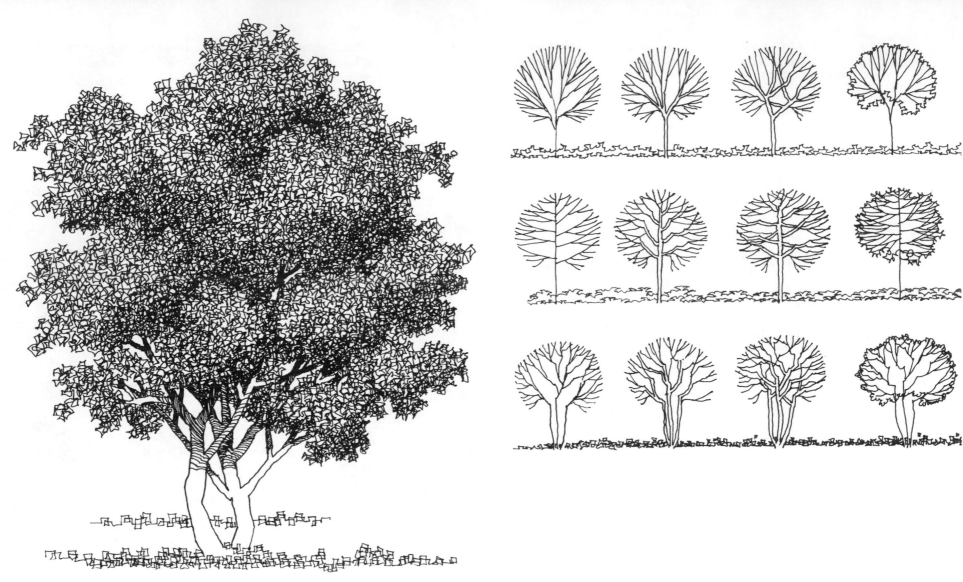

The final step in any progressive detailing of a drawn tree is to draw or suggest the definition of all the individual leaves. This can be accomplished rather efficiently with any of several repetitive hand motions much like those with which the leaf-boundaries were drawn. Such repetitive hand motions must be mastered and prerecorded as perceptual tapes to be retrieved and played on demand.

In building up the individual leaf indication the entire mass of leaves should still be subdivided by the shading or relative density of the built up texture. This should be done by shading each clump of leaves individually—from dark at the bottom and one side (depending on the light direction) to light at the top and other side. The light edges of the nearer clump of leaves will then stand out in sharp contrast to the dark side and bottom of the clump behind.

In this progression of tree templates, as in any prerecorded perceptual tape which allows you to draw any item of additional interest, the most valuable templates to master are those which have a time-flexible form. By time-flexible I mean that they can be drawn to an acceptable level very quickly but that, if more time becomes available, they can be returned to and further detailed in a way that adds richness to the drawing.

186

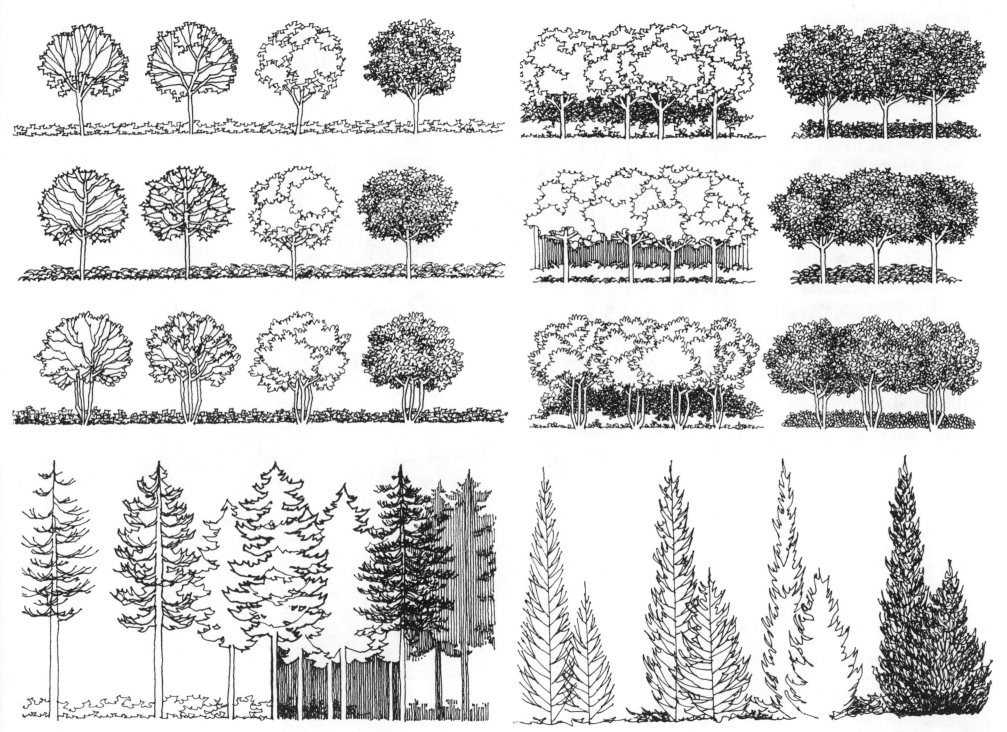

187

SHRUBS AND HEDGES are like trees except that branch structure is of little or no importance in drawing them. Overall form and leaf detail must be mastered, and like trees, drawn shrubs range from simple abstraction to complex realism.

Drawing shrubs and hedges is mostly a matter of building up a texture which represents the leaves of the plant. This may be done laboriously, leaf by leaf, but it is much more efficiently accomplished by developing a continuous hand motion which produces the texture. As with the leaf-boundary lines mentioned earlier, there are, generally, three possible kinds of repetitive hand motions:

CONCAVE

CONVEX

NEUTRAL

VINES AND GROUND COVERS are even simpler in that they require only the textural indication of the leaf detail. Vines do have a certain form, but it is relatively easy to master.

Drawing vines and ground covers is similarly a textural build up. The concave and convex textures are better for ground covers because they give the appearance of foreshortening, which helps the ground covers look flat.

In quick sketching, these textural scribble strokes are the fastest way to add a little textural interest to a drawing. They represent the textural interest provided by landscaping and yet are appropriately non-committal in the early stages of the design synthesis— before you know which specific plants to recommend.

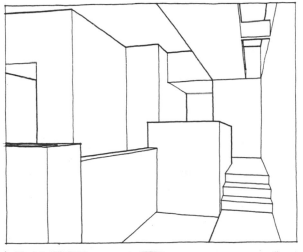

THE PLACEMENT of trees, shrubs, hedges, vines, and ground covers is extremely important in drawing and in design. They can add greatly to all the drawing and environmental interest categories. They can demonstrate space by disappearing and reappearing behind architectural elements; they can add the textural interest needed in a stark environment; and they can provide the *additional* interest needed in a stiff orthogonal environment by spilling over edges and delighting the eye with their structure.

189

DRAWING FURNITURE IN SCALE is sometimes difficult, especially in the foreground of eyelevel perspectives. There seems to be a tendency to draw foreground tables and chairs much lower than they would actually be. I can only guess at the reasons for this depression of the foreground. It may be caused by a compulsion to return to plan view, the drawing board's horizontal position (compared to the vertical position of the drawing surface in easel painting or of a blackboard) or a desire to stretch out the foreground furniture so that it doesn't obscure other furniture or figures already drawn. The best way I have found to keep the furniture in scale is to draw a figure standing directly beside the piece of furniture, with the figure's head on the eyelevel line and its feet next to the chair or table. The scale of the piece of furniture will be immediately apparent.

THE 30" CUBE MODULE is another help in drawing correctly scaled furniture. The 10' cube which we used to structure and measure space can easily be subdivided into 5' cubes and again into 2'6" cubes by using intersecting diagonals. When we reach the 30" cubes we have arrived at a module of uniquely useful dimensions for drawing furniture, since 30" is approximately desk or table height, desk top depth and the depth and back height of most sofas; and half the 30" height (15") is also the approximate height of coffee tables and sofa and lounge chair seats.

FURNISHINGS

Human beings have always surrounded themselves with whatever useful and symbolic objects they could acquire. Of all the world's and history's cultures, the affluent societies of the 20th century are perhaps the most self-indulgent collectors of this material clutter which gives us comfort and pleasure. While environmental designers are often not responsible for the design or even the selection of such furnishings, we must include them in the drawings of any spaces we design in order to represent the spaces accurately. In many cases the design of the spaces must be integrally related to the furnishings they will hold and cannot possibly be evaluated without an indication of that integration.

The most important advice to remember in adding furnishings to a drawing is that offered earlier as a general approach for all elements of additional interest: *don't attempt to design the furnishings yourself; be content either to choose existing well-designed items (Eames' chair) or draw completely characterless prototypes (Plato's chair).* Beyond this warning there are several secondary tips which may help you add furnishings to your drawings efficiently, accurately and without preempting the design of the space.

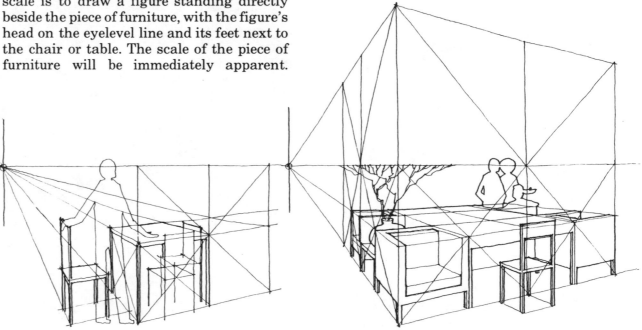

Since all furniture is designed to accommodate the human figure, it is virtually impossible to draw it out of scale when a figure is drawn standing right next to it. You may eliminate the figure in the final drawing since it will have served its purpose in helping you draw the furniture in scale.

It is very easy to establish a 30" cube anywhere in an eyelevel perspective since 30" is half the 5' eyelevel anywhere in the perspective. And once the initial 30" cube is established it can be multiplied in any direction by the use of diagonals as explained earlier under the section on perspective.

PLAN CIRCLES present another problem which is most often encountered in drawing cylindrical lamps, circular tables and other furnishings generated by horizontal circles.

In any perspective, all horizontal circles should be drawn flat, not tipped or responding overtly to any projected perspective lines. This is best understood and experienced by drawing a vertical stack of plan circles at various distances from eyelevel.

At eyelevel, a circle or any two-dimensional horizontal shape will simply appear as a line. As the horizontal circle is moved up or down away from eyelevel, the shape will begin to reveal its true shape, first as a narrow ellipse and successively as a fatter and fatter ellipse approaching a circle.

There is a phenomenon long noted by psychologists and other students of perception called "constancy," which is a tendency to perceive foreshortened geometric shapes in their plan shape. This tendency can be verified by most drawing teachers because students carry it into their first perspectives.

The tendency is to draw all horizontal surfaces tipped up toward the viewer and it takes quite awhile to persuade students that they should draw the perspective as a camera would photograph it—with all the horizontal surfaces foreshortened and lying down—that our perception of the drawing will perform the constancy phenomenon without needing additional help from the delineator.

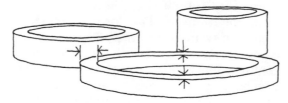

Concentric plan circles can be a particular problem and they are also an excellent vehicle for understanding foreshortening in perspective. The distance between two concentric circles will appear to be quite different when foreshortened in perspective; the front and back of the ring between the circles will foreshorten and become quite thin, while the sides of the circle will appear their true size.

PLAN ANGLES of pieces of furniture can present the same difficulties encountered in drawing circular forms. As with plan circles the problem is usually created by allowing the furniture, as it turns in plan, to occupy too much space in depth, which results in the furniture appearing as if it were tilted forward. Rectangular pieces of furniture, when they are turned at an angle to the spatial framework of the room, will have their own special pair of VPs on the eyelevel line, and it is important to keep those VPs far enough apart so that the furniture is limited in plan to its true depth in space. This necessary limitation can be further understood by realizing that any square piece of furniture, as it pivots through the 360° of possible plan angles, will always remain within the foreshortened ellipse of its plan circle.

VISUAL FURNISHINGS have few scale or perspective problems, but do present some other pitfalls and opportunities. So far, the discussion has been limited to furniture—what might be called *haptic* furnishings which we relate to *physically* by sitting, eating or writing on them. There is a separate set of furnishings which we experience primarily or exclusively *visually*. This group would include pictures, wall hangings, ornamental plants and pottery, sculpture and what used to be called knick-knacks.

This class of additive objects should be used for the purpose of enriching or ornamenting a drawing exactly as they are used in any human environment. They can add textural interest as well as that *figural* interest which may otherwise be lacking in the drawing or the environment.

In real human environments, such objects will always have deep personal meaning for the people who select and place them in their environment. Portraits, souvenirs and prized objects of art all obviously have personal associations related to their specific content. Because of this any representation of content in these objects when they are included in a design drawing risks being both distracting and objectionable and will inevitably call unwanted attention to itself. For this reason any indication of this class of furnishings should be of the most abstract characterless kind.

VEHICLES

Another class of technological trappings which inevitably clutters or ornaments our environment, depending on your point of view, is that of the various vehicles we ride. In *Drawing As a Means to Architecture* (1968), I limited any discussion about drawing such vehicles to automobiles, and even included some remarks favoring automobiles as symbolic of our personal freedom. While that may still be true, our continued use of automobiles as our almost exclusive means of transportation seems much more self-indulgent and irresponsible than it did then, and my mind has changed to the point where I think we must include bicycles and buses in our discussion, even in a book on drawing.

This means you should have a brochure or advertisement picturing a specific model, and trace or copy that particular automobile into your drawing, or you should learn to draw completely innocuous "car" cars which simply have four wheels and a body Ghia would never claim.

There are a few tips for drawing the characterless kind of automobile which may be worth mentioning. The form of most passenger cars can be abstracted to a small box sitting on a longer box. Sloping the sides of the upper box begins to make it look like the passenger compartment, and headlights, bumpers, wheelwells and license plates begin to make the lower box look like the chassis.

In adding cars to a perspective, and especially in tracing a photograph or advertising brochure, be very careful that the VPs for the car are on the eyelevel line of the perspective. They often are not because the car was photographed from below or above eyelevel in an attempt to make it appear beneficially lower or longer or wider and if the VPs for the car are on some other level than the eyelevel of the perspective, the car will look like it is propped up or is in some kind of skid. The usual mistake in drawing your own cars is to allow those sitting at some plan angle to the axes of the building to occupy too much depth or have their VPs too close together. (See the previous discussion on PLAN ANGLES under FURNISHINGS.)

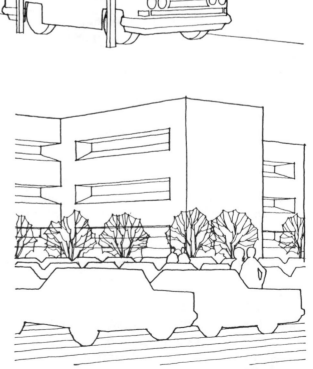

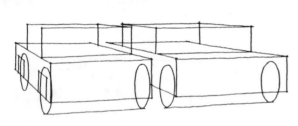

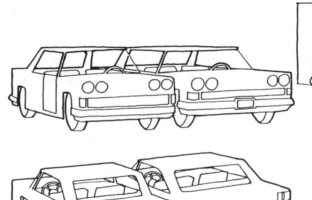

Once again, the two recommended approaches are either to draw a specific model or a completely characterless prototype. Either approach will allow the inclusion of vehicles in the drawing to indicate means of arrival or departure and the area designed for parking, without preempting the drawing by calling too much attention to themselves. The mistake is to attempt to design the vehicle yourself. Although bicycles and buses are generally not that different in their visual design, automobiles are extremely self-conscious in their "styling" and the various models and years are so well known that any new design you might offer is more than likely to attract the viewer's attention.

Remember that the tops of all modern passenger cars are well below eyelevel so that in any eyelevel perspective an individual automobile or an entire parking lot full of them will lie well below the eyelevel line. Great masses of parking may be usefully simplified by drawing only a descriptive collective outline of their tops, and this simplified delineation may also be applied to individual automobiles so that they never call too much attention to themselves.

Buses are probably easier to draw than automobiles and are easily made credible by drawing the route sign on their front, the special way their doors open, a bus stop sign and benches and shelters for waiting riders. I strongly encourage the inclusion of public transportation vehicles in design drawings because I am convinced that we will never seriously consider those alternative modes of transportation we so desperately need or propose their accommodation in the design proposals we offer our clients until we learn to draw them.

Bicycles are more difficult to draw, and I haven't yet discovered how to simplify their delineation in any very successful way. I think the effort to find ways to draw bicycles and to design their necessary parking racks is seriously worth pursuing, however, so that they become as acceptable near the entrances to our buildings as the obligatory planters and trees or the late model limousine pulled up at the curb.

INTEGRATION WITH SPATIAL INTEREST

I recommended earlier that *additional* interest be closely integrated with *spatial* interest, but here I would like to extend the discussion and demonstrate some of the advantages of such an integration. While figures, trees, furniture and automobiles will add a certain interest by just being mindlessly sprinkled around the drawing like cake decorations, that practice does nothing to enhance the drawing as a design communication. I believe items of additional interest should never be added in order to *decorate* a drawing, but only when they can be beneficially and tightly integrated with the spatial interest of the drawing.

Some of the best illustrations of spatial integration involve the use of trees to demonstrate continuous background space. A perspective of an interior courtyard may be difficult to make read as unroofed and open to the sky. The minute you draw a tree standing in the courtyard, however, with its branches disappearing above the ceiling of the enclosed foreground space, it becomes apparent that the tree is occupying an exterior space which extends upward above the roof.

An even more dramatic demonstration of this principle can be shown in a space with several windows of different sizes and positions, including high clerestory windows. If you draw individual trees or plants in each window they will look like individual landscape paintings, but if you draw continuous hedges and large trees appearing and reappearing in several windows the viewer must perceive a continuous space outside the building.

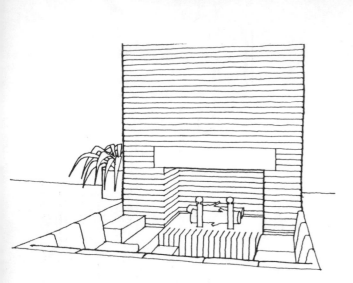

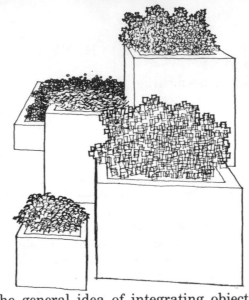

Figures may be integrated with spatial interest in a similar way. A sunken conversation pit may be very difficult to indicate in an eyelevel perspective of a living room, but a pair of figures sitting in such a pit will make the existence of the sunken space immediately apparent.

The general idea of integrating objects of additional interest into any drawing so that they make its space manifest can be illustrated in drawing a single plant in a container, or in the basic principles of flower arranging. The foliage should be drawn spilling over the container's edge in such a way that it demonstrates the space in front of, to either side, behind and above the container.

In the lapping that indicates spatial layers the nearer object must always be drawn as having thickness; that is, it must be drawn with a double line indication so that more distant lines and textures can be perceived as disappearing and reappearing behind it. For the same reason, the nearer object should never be textured since the rendering of the texture will focus attention on that spatial layer and not the deeper layer beyond. Textures should always be applied to the deepest spaces so that they can disappear and reappear behind the nearer objects.

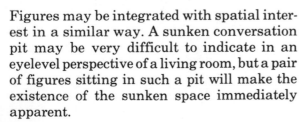

194

DRAWING'S RELATIONSHIP TO THE DESIGN PROCESS

The entire subject matter of this book would seem to fall under such a heading. The other chapters present a separate and more general discussion of the context in which the design process occurs, while in this chapter I will concentrate on the activity of designing and the specific relationships it can have to drawing.

All drawing may be seen as communication, and in the previous section I discussed the various ways design drawings can communicate the experience of the environment. This section will look at drawing in the various relationships it can have to the design process, from simply selling or recording the products of the process to leading or even becoming the process.

The relationships which are possible between drawing and the design process arise from a number of variables which differ for every designer and every design process. The extent of this list of variables makes clear the folly of always using the same drawings in the same fixed order. The variables may be thought of in five categories:

DESIGNER'S PERSONAL MODEL OF THE PROCESS—variations in the model held by the designer for what does or should happen during the activity of designing anything;

ASSUMED ROLE OF DRAWING—variations in the designer's beliefs and expectations regarding the general relationship drawing has to the design process;

COMMUNICATIVE PURPOSE—variations based on the purpose of the drawing in the design dialogue, asking questions as well as making statements;

KIND OF PROBLEM OR SOLUTION—variations in the tailoring of analytical, exploratory drawings to a particular problem, or of synthetic study and refinement drawings to a particular solution;

CHOICE OF DRAWING—variations based on the kind of drawing and its relationship to its predecessors and successors in the process, as well as the level or finish of the drawing.

Some understanding of the range and complexity of these variables would seem to be mandatory for anyone who uses drawing in the design process at all because of the kind of *eyeminds* we have. What we show ourselves and the order in which it is shown is extremely important since the dominant sense in the perception, conception, and decision involved in environmental design is vision. And if we intend to be clear and persuasive, the choices of which drawings and in what order they are shown is also critical in our communication with those for whom we are designing.

The preceding list of variables which affect the relationships between drawing and the design process deserve discussion and elaboration because, as I hope to show, the range of each variable may be wider than we realize.

PERSONAL MODEL OF THE PROCESS
The continuing proliferation of descriptions and prescriptions for what does or should happen during the design process shows no sign of diminishing the healthy variety in what designers actually do during the time in which they design anything. Although architects, landscape architects and interior designers seem prepared to let all kinds of people from other disciplines try to tell them how they should design, and eagerly try various suggested vocabularies and analytical techniques, the methodological paradigm (like scientific method in the sciences) which seems to be the goal of much of this interest in the design process seems as remote as ever. What we have forgotten is that the resistance to any particular method and the abandonment of the futile search for certainty, of which methodological certainty is only the latest version, *is* the paradigm we seek, and we have had it all along.

The design process combines two distinctly different, but complementary kinds of behavior, and these behaviors each have a tradition and a value system, and probably originate in the patterns of the left and right cerebral hemispheres which make us human. These two approaches are very similar to the traditional attitudes and values of art and science, intuition and logic, or the subjective and objective views of the world. They are also much like deBono's *lateral* and *vertical* thinking, Guilford's *convergent* and *divergent* thinking, Jones's *black box* and *glass box* designers, or the right brain and left brain functioning described by Ornstein and others.

Objective, analytical, logical behavior needs little advocacy or defense in the design professions or in society in general. Subjective, synthetic, intuitive behavior, however, has few advocates in the recent writing about design, partly because it has nothing to do with language, and one of my purposes here is to argue for its essential and equal partnership in the design process.

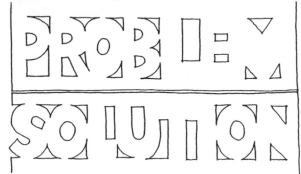

To illustrate the differences between the two behaviors I would like to propose the so-called design process as being analogous to the joining of two pieces of cloth, one called the "problem" and the other the "solution," with the activities of joining being analogous to two completely different kinds of techniques for joining pieces of fabric.

ZIPPERS AND STITCHES

Today's faith in method and our culture's demand for rational explanation give us the prevailing model of the design process: the *zipper*. The *zipper* closes the gap which separates the problem from the solution by connecting separately-solved piecemeal congruences in a predetermined linear order.

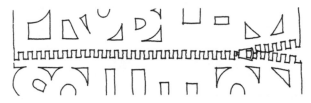

Each step in this linear *zippering* must be correct and consistent and must remain a part of the final overall congruence lest gaps develop which might reopen the entire closure. The *zipper* has a fixed beginning and ending and its narrow linear process solves difficulties in the process by backing up linearly and then forcing its way through them. Lateral entanglements, as when the facing material becomes caught in the *zipper,* are to be avoided at all costs.

The complementary model of the design process is the random whip-stitching used in sewing two pieces of fabric together or darning a sock. This kind of closure sews the problem to the solution in a series of actions which rely more on the skill developed by experience (akin to Levi-Straus's bricolage) than on any formalized method. While successive *stitches* are to some extent determined by earlier *stitches,* the order is never precious and the entire pattern of *stitches* may include unnecessary or even incorrect *stitches*. Unlike the

zipper, lateral movements are the most valuable, and the first *stitches* are not anchored on the problem side of the seam, as most linear models of the process seem to imply, but arise from some intuitive hunch or feeling about a possible solution. This is because the environments which we inhabit and from which we gather the experience or knowledge we bring to any problem are made up entirely of solutions. We probably only understand design problems in terms of design solutions we know about. The problems for which the solutions were generated are never seen and can only be inferred from the world of solutions we experience. The first *stitches* arise and are anchored on the solution side of the seam we are sewing, and always seek a part of the problem which fits, or can be made to fit, their insight.

The *zipper* is an efficient management tool, but creativity occurs in spite of it, not because of it. Our creative insights occur as disorderly lateral *stitches* across the gap in our problem-solving, and the pattern they make in joining any problem to its solution is unpredictable, inefficient and only barely manageable, but infinitely more beautiful and human as a patterned whole than any *zipper*.

LOGICAL LANGUAGE

When we are called upon to explain our design process to a colleague or client, our linear language and our cultural indoctrination assure that we will describe our actions as having been a flawless logical process: a *zipper*. In our culture this habit begins very early, with parents' demands that children use the language they are just learning to produce logical explanations for their actions. "Why are you so late coming home from school?" or "Why did you get your shoes all muddy?" imply that even such ad hoc behavior is to be logically explained. The child hasn't the slightest idea why she got her shoes all muddy except as the unanticipated and incidental result of actions in which she was completely and intensely involved. The pretense that muddy shoes are the result of logical action is absurd, but children and environmental design students learn early that parents, teachers and society in general expect them to be able to offer rational explanations for their actions.

Thomas Kuhn points out in his *The Structure of Scientific Revolutions* (1962), that the history of science is described in textbooks as a smooth linear process—a *zipper*—leaving out the dead ends and misdirected efforts of whole groups of scientists because their mistaken "*stitching*" is now an embarrassment to the linear logical model. Much of the recent writing about the design process has been dominated by *zipper* advocates who would model all design activity as a linear process. The word "process" itself tends to carry this implication. It sounds suspiciously like that symbol of our technological age, the production line, and the inflexible standardization implied by such a process and its products is boring and inhuman. There is some indication that the motivation or act of writing about creativity or problem-solving, or our language itself tricks authors into describing the activity as a logical procedure.

THE HITCH

From Osborn to Archer the literature is full of verbal descriptions which gloss over the crucial *hitch* in the process when the design idea is formed. I will call this period CONCEPT FORMATION although psychology has already appropriated that phrase for a slightly different purpose. The period during which the design concept is formed is the most significant point in the so-called process because it signals a profound change in design activity. In my experience *stitching* always starts the process and continues until

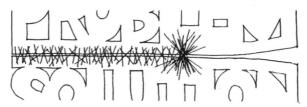

one *stitch* or series of *stitches* sews the problem to the solution in a way that feels uniquely right and promises to be a solid anchor for the *zippering* which will systematically extend the idea and develop its logical rationale. The feeling of correctness is preverbal and may occur as a recognition of a certain congruence which appears in the exploratory drawings or diagrams between the form of solution and the continual restatement of the form of the problem.

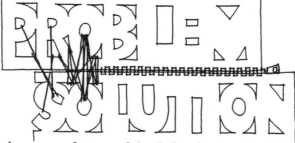

Any complete model of the design process must include both the *stitching* and the *zippering,* as well as that crucial *hitch* when the design concept is formed. Concept formation involves a commitment to a particular idea or collection of ideas capable of organizing the subsequent design activity. It represents a change in behavior from searching to testing, or from intuition to logic, as well as from insights into the various individual parts of the problem, to an attempt to deal with the problem and its solution as a comprehensive whole. I don't mean to imply that this concept formation and the transition from *stitching* to *zippering* occurs only once in the process. It may recur many times and the model of the overall design process for any complex problem will be more like a multiple exposure than a single picture.

THE COMPOSITE MODEL

We now have a composite model of the design process which represents both *stitching* and *zippering* as well as the connecting transition, and on such a model we can understand the disparate description of the design process in our literature.

CREATIVITY

Authors such as Maslow, Koestler and deBono are examples of theorists who are mostly interested in the first part of the process, represented by the *stitch* end of the composite model. Such authors concentrate on the kinds of attitudes, activities and thought patterns which preceed creative ideas, assuming that creativity consists mainly of discovering or generating a unique idea and ending with the birth of that idea. The creativity theorists tend to leave the testing or evaluation to others or to assume that the quality of the idea is entirely and immediately apparent. They also tend to view the implementation of any idea as being rather automatic, uncreative and mostly a matter of technique.

DESIGN METHOD

The design methodologists, on the other hand, like Jones and Archer, come directly from scientific method as expressed in Karl Popper's writings. This point of view *begins* with a hypothesis and is not interested in how the idea came to exist—which it regards as unknowable—but in its systematic criticism and refinement. Design methodologists are mostly interested in the *zipper* end of our composite model of the design process. They assume that ideas just happen or that they already exist in the form of rather obvious alternatives, and what really counts is the application of rigorous testing and criticism to determine the correctness and best form of the idea, or the systematic evaluation of the available alternatives.

Real practicing designers and people of recognized creativity in all fields have been curiously silent about how they do what they do. Maslow found evidence that they may not even know how they do it because they are so "lost in the doing" that the cooly detached phenomenological management advocated by Jones in his "designers as self-organizing systems" may not be possible. Another reason designers have seldom tried to describe their personal design processes may be that they know the process must be self-made to be of any value, and they have little desire to convert other designers to their way of designing. They might consider such evangelism arrogant and ill-mannered.

Scientists, on the other hand, have as their goal the logical explanation of the universe. Science sets out to describe how the world works, including creativity, so that verbal or mathematical explanation can be seen as the very essence of science. Further, science is not satisfied with personal speculation or insight, but aims for verifiable principles of universal application.

Viewed in this way it is ironic that artists are usually the ones accused of ego-tripping, when all they ever offer is the personal witness of their individual experience of the world. Artists seldom seek any universal acceptance of what they do, for they know that whatever value is found in their work springs from its individuality and subjectivity.

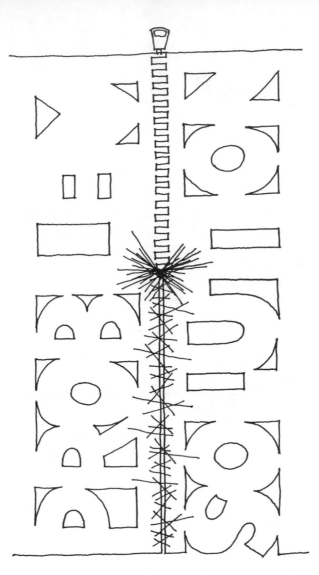

One other explanation for the lack of testimony from the *stitch* end of the process is that doing and saying are fundamentally different, having different goals, rules and values. The doing of art is equivalent to the saying of science. The artist may find the request for explanation superfluous because the work itself was intended to communicate something about the artist's experience, and when the communication fails it can only be the fault of the artist or an insensitive observer.

While designers may not go around telling people how they design, or seem to exhibit a great consistency between what they say and what they do, most of them try very hard to understand and control what they do when they design. They make a personal model of the process, if not at the conscious intellectual level, then in perhaps a more meaningful way by their actual behavior. Their dilemma, or as I prefer to believe, their good fortune is that they stand uncomfortably astraddle of the art/science, *stitches/zipper* continuum. Their responsibility is to maintain the traditional illogical balance they have inherited by talking, when they must, like scientists, but behaving, as they must, like artists.

The implications of the *stitches* and *zipper* analogy for drawing depend on which end of the model you adopt as being most representative of the design process. All the drawings can become valuable *stitches,* from the most mysterious personal doodles and diagrams, to the many graphic techniques illustrated in Paul Laseau's *Graphic Problem Solving* (1975), to tentative perspectives, sections and plans. *Zipper* drawings are more formal and tend to be more quantitative than qualitative. There is no place in the *zipper* for the expressive, exploratory or experimental drawings which give us those sideways glances so valuable to the early *stitching.* The mandatory drawings of the *zipper* end of the process conclude the process and record its results with eyes fixed steadfastly to that goal. They tend to be the more refined plans, sections and elevations necessary to establish and relate the various physical aspects of the design, take off its quantities and instruct its builders. The more detailed implications any model of the design process holds for drawing must be considered on the basis of what role in the process it assumes for drawing.

THE ASSUMED ROLE OF DRAWING is usually implied in the model of the design process which designers either subscribe to intellectually or demonstrate when they design. In the earlier chapter on CONCEPTION, I offered six different concepts of the relationship of drawing to the design process, depending on whether a designer believes or behaves as if:

- drawing persuasively sells the product—indicating full color perspective renderings;

- drawing neutrally prints out the results of a mental process that occurs separately, privately and previously—indicating graphs, charts, matrices, sections, elevations and plans;

- drawing communicates the process—indicating networks and critical path diagrams;

- drawing participates in the process—indicating all forms of drawing including any new ones that can be invented;

- drawing leads the process—indicating all sorts of exploratory drawing during which concepts are expected to appear;

- drawing is the process—indicating drawings which provoke other drawings in a chain reaction.

In the chapter on CONCEPTION I described the first two roles as excluding drawing from the process, but I saved the discussion of the various participatory roles drawing can have for this chapter.

THE COMMUNICATIVE PURPOSE of any drawing varies according to its succession in the process. The most simple polar way of thinking about drawing in relation to its communicative role in the design process is to categorize the drawings designers make as being either open or closed; open, exploratory, input-seeking questionnaires; or closed, persuasive, convincing commercials. Drawing alternates between these poles during the design process and only generally progresses from open to closed over the entire process.

Along the way there are several other kinds of drawings but most of them may be thought of as either opening or closing the process.

Any successful design process must be a dialogue in which the roles of communicator and listener alternate frequently, as well as gradually shift in response to the overall form of the process. The pattern below indicates the course of any cycle in the design dialogue.

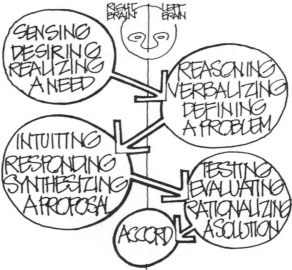

The entire dialogue may take place in the privacy of the designer's consciousness, as a conversation between the right and left cerebral hemispheres. In a strongly intuitive designer the sequence may short circuit down

the intuitive side without bothering to rationally define the problem or logically test the solution. The need to communicate, rationalize or defend the solution however, which is always necessary with a client, assures that the pattern will become a true dialogue.

The pattern may also be repeated as a communicative cycle between designer and client or between designer and consultant regarding a particular issue, or may be seen as the overall form of the design process.

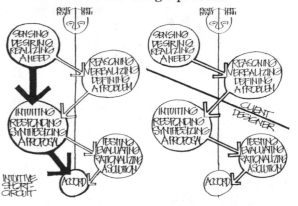

The pattern of the dialogue may be restated in terms of communication as the initial cycle in the design dialogue, in which the designer gains information from the client by questioning, listening and confirming a correct understanding of the problem. In the second half of the cycle the direction of the communication switches as the designer responds to the information gained in the first half of the cycle with some sort of designed synthesis.

Drawing can participate in any such dialogue by recording or translating the input into graphic notes, or it may lead the process by making drawings which are graphic question marks, which solicit input like a questionnaire. After the transfer of information has been completed, drawing can confirm the correctness of the designer's understanding by synthesizing the information graphically—

as a secretary furnishes a set of minutes for approval.

The role of drawing in the second half of the cycle is more familiar. Here drawing represents a proposed solution or conceptual response to the problem and will be altered until it pleases both the client and the designer. The client's approval completes the cycle and the proposal may now be tested.

The testing may be an inner self-dialogue by the designer which follows a similar form to the client-designer dialogue. Further testing may be by a consultant or other member of the design team, in which the form of the dialogue is again similar with only the names changing. Now the designer has the apparent problem and the consultant has the potential solution. Later in the process the designer may have the apparent problem (not able to satisfy the clients' needs within the budget) and the clients may have the potential solution (reducing their needs).

After a great number of similar cycles in the dialogue, with various participants filling the two roles, the overall process begins to become closed to the client and the dialogue shifts to the design team. During this time of testing, improving and refining the concept, the communication follows an overall script developed by the design team from experience in many such previous processes, and the communicative purpose of any drawing shown the client is more like journalistic reporting of the now linear process which is being *zipped* closed.

Finally the process becomes *zipped* tight, fully closed and the only communicative purpose remaining is that of persuading others—bankers, buyers or building officials—of the quality of the product.

The drawings which record or lead the design dialogue must themselves be carefully designed so that their focus and content is appropriate to their purpose. To continue the *stitches* and *zippers* analogy, the kinds of drawings which fulfill the various communicative purposes during the process may be thought of as:

OPEN DRAWING

Opening Drawings—designed to prevent premature solutions, open up the design space and establish the designer's credibility by asking questions and posing tentative alternative choices—directionless exploration of the design space;

Clearing Drawings—designed to remove various kinds of blocks, misunderstandings and preconceptions by drawing and confirming alternative syntheses of the problem statement;

CLOSING DRAWING

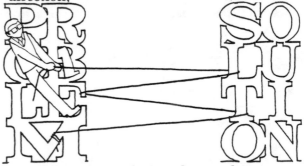

Stitch Drawings—designed to make trial closures between the problem and a solution by drawing tentative piecemeal solutions to specific parts of the problem—searching for direction;

Hitch Drawings—designed to anchor a particular conceptual solution to the problem by drawing various organizing concepts—establishing direction;

Zipper Drawings—designed to test, develop and rationalize the solution's relationship to the problem by drawing representations which study all the aspects of the solution and their relationship to one another in search of the best final form for the solution—integration of the solution in the established direction;

CLOSED DRAWING

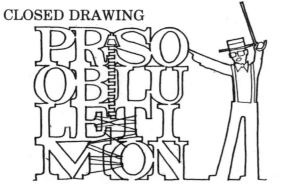

Zipped Drawings—designed to convincingly present the solution by drawing its most flattering views—extolling the destination reached.

Designers must be effective communicators and skill in communication depends not just on convincing logic, persuasive oratory or even sensitive poetry, but also on skill in asking questions, patience in listening carefully and perseverance in trying to understand the answers. While the design dialogue will gradually close, it should never do so without the help and understanding of all those involved in the process.

KIND OF PROBLEM OR SOLUTION should affect the relationships the various drawings have to the design process. Although we lack agreement as to what constitutes a proper typology for design problems, this very lack indicates the complexity of establishing such a typology because of the range of problem types and the way the range transforms itself depending on the designer's point of view.

Even if it is decided that for a particular problem the best way to proceed is to begin with plan drawings, it is quite different to start with bubble diagrams which emphasize adjacency or separation vs. diagrams which emphasize circulation and sequence vs. structural framing plans which emphasize framing direction and modular bays.

All beginnings are also strongly affected by the confidence a designer feels with successive stages of the process and the progression of drawings that are appropriate for the later stages. It is quite different to begin with certain drawings out of fear or incompetence—because they are familiar and easy—vs. beginning with the same drawings out of conscious deliberate choice.

The conventional sequence of drawings made during the design process is: plans, sections, elevations and perspectives. As Edward deBono's writing has made clear, the choice of entry point into any problem and the sequence in which information is processed is extremely important because without deliberate choice or random variation we wear a perceptual/conceptual rut which becomes increasingly difficult to avoid.

There are kinds of problems which suggest beginning with drawings other than plans. The vertical circulation sorting required in airports or stadia indicates sections as the first drawings. Filling in an empty site on a historic street or square might suggest elevation studies as the first drawings. Buildings in which the quality of the interior space is paramount, as in churches or restaurants, might lead a designer to begin with interior perspectives; while buildings which are to occupy beautiful natural sites might demand exterior perspective sketches as the first conceptual drawings.

The conventional construction drawing sequence of plan, section and elevation represents the sequence in which a building is built and is basically a construction order—a logical *zipper*. The conceptual drawings which make the random *stitches* which initiate the design process should be related to the kind of problem being solved. Experienced designers know that it is just as possible to make the plan fill in a concept which begins as an exterior perspective or arrive at a plan as the rotation or extrusion of a conceptual section as it is to always make the plan be the generator of the design.

Even after the holistic *hitch* which anchors the organizing concept of any solution, I believe the first *zipper* study drawings should be based, not on the construction order, but on the characteristics of the particular solution. There are kinds of solutions which suggest beginning the necessary testing and refining with drawings other than the plan. Solutions based on level changes, sight lines or earth integration should be studied first in section. Solutions which are based on the way natural light is brought into the building or on a particular palette of interior finishes or spatial sequence would demand interior perspectives as the first study drawings. Solutions based on relationships to an urban context might indicate street elevations as the first drawings, while solutions based on scale, materials and articulation of the overall form of the building should be studied first in exterior perspectives.

If we become sensitive to the benefits of varying the drawings we choose to draw in response to the kind of design problem or to the kind of solution with which we are working, we will also become more sensitive to what we expect to be shown by the various drawings.

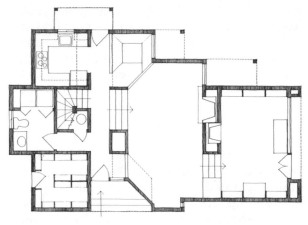

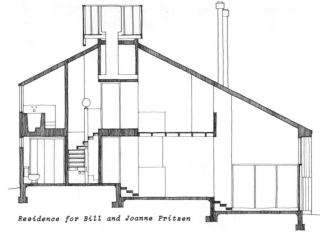

Residence for Bill and Joanne Pritzen

CHOICE OF DRAWING in the design process is the final variable and the bottom line in relating drawing to the design process. The deliberate choice of the kind of drawing to make at any particular point in the process, and in what level or detail, must be based on the preceding variables and a thorough understanding of what kinds of information can be included in the various drawings.

While plans, sections and elevations are very questionable as representations of the experience of an environment, they are difficult to beat as conceptual drawings. They allow an abstraction or distillation that focuses on the basic relationships of spaces and architectural elements which is not possible in perspectives.

The content of the various drawings in relation to the process is most important to the choice of drawing, but equally important is the appropriate level of detail for the chosen drawing at any particular point in the process. Plans may be the correct choice for a series of opening drawings early in the process because of the zoning or sequential circulation they show. The plans should be left sketchy and ambiguous, however, because their purpose is to solicit input and open up options, and above all to communicate the open tentative character of the process at that point.

A brief listing of the potential for each kind of drawing and some examples of the levels of detail and finish should serve to indicate the range of each drawing's form and content.

PLANS CAN SHOW:
Horizontal Functional Sorting—zoning, adjacency, separation and interpenetration;
Horizontal Circulation—pattern and arrangement of the corridors, vestibules, entries and exits;
Horizontal Functional Adequacy—scale, shape, and appropriateness for the functions being accommodated;
Horizontal Formal Arrangement—point, line or matrix generated geometries;
Vertical Architectural Elements and Openings—characteristics and arrangements of columns, walls, windows and doors;
Horizontal Orientation and Inflection to the larger context—wind, sun, view, topography, and adjacent or distant responses to the built environment;
Furniture Arrangement and Floor Materials—and other levels of detail;
Roof and Floor Framing;
Horizontal Distribution of mechanical, plumbing and electrical elements;
Horizontal Integration of all the above—as in the relationships between the spatial subdivisions and the structural module or between the human circulation and the mechanical distribution.

SECTIONS can show:
Vertical Functional Sorting—stacking, separation and interpenetration;
Vertical Circulation—pattern and arrangement of the stairs, ramps and elevators;
Vertical Functional Adequacy—scale, shape, and appropriateness for the functions designed for;
Vertical Formal Arrangement—stacked, staggered, stepped or clustered geometries;
Horizontal Architectural Elements and Openings—characteristics and arrangements of spandrels, slabs, parapets, overhangs, stairwells and atria;
Vertical Orientation and Inflection to the larger context—the building's relationship to the site—buried, raised, adjacent and distant response to the built environment;
Natural Lighting and Wall Materials and other levels of detail;
Wall, Floor and Roof Construction;
Vertical Distribution of mechanical, plumbing and electrical elements;
Vertical Integration of all the above—as in the relationships between stairs and elevators and the mechanical chases or between the column spacing and the stacking of the spaces.

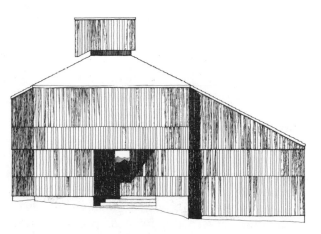

ELEVATIONS can show:
Pattern, Scale and Proportions of Facades— openings, articulations and overall composition of a building's facades;
Contextual Relationships to the adjacent natural and built environment;
Shadow Patterns and Wall Materials on the building's faces.

INTERIOR PERSPECTIVES can show:
Experience of the Enclosed Environment— the combination of all the perceptions which can be cued or predicted by our visual sense, including the tactile or kinesthetic experience of touching or walking through the environment.

EXTERIOR PERSPECTIVES can show:
Experience of the Building as an Object— the combination of all perceptions which can be cued or predicted by our visual sense, including the tactile or kinesthetic experience of touching or walking around any object.

The distinction between the conventional construction drawings and perspectives can perhaps be best understood by recognizing the complementary but essential kinds of syntheses they show. Plans, sections and elevations show a holistic synthesis of the entire building as a built object—a synthesis that can never be experienced directly, but which has always been held to be important to great architecture, and that is essential to the logical consistency involved in constructing the building.

Perspectives on the other hand, even in unlimited numbers, can never show the building as a total object like the set of plans, sections and elevations. What they can show, however, is the synthesis of what can be experienced in one place at one time, and that experience includes the prediction of the further experience of the adjacent spaces. Perspectives are indispensable in testing the success of the ideas generated in the other drawings. They show how many or how few of the designer's intentions for relating the various design elements will actually be perceived when the environment is built.

There is nothing fixed in the preceding list of variables. They are no more than a framework for a changing set of relationships, but designers should keep these relationships alive by thoughtfully choosing as many as possible in the design process and by continually developing their drawing ability so that the breadth of choice continues to expand. The choices of the drawings we make and the order in which they are made are very important because, although we seem to process visual information simultaneously, the order in which we show ourselves separate drawings will never be without influence. The earlier drawings will always be the more influential ones, for they become our point of entry into the problem. The relationships which can be shown in the drawings we choose to make first are assured their share of our design attention. The relationships which we never see because we can't or won't make the drawings which would show them, however, are excluded by a kind of self-imposed censorship that we wouldn't accept if it were applied by any other person or institution in our society.

Most of the recommendations of those who have written about thinking, creativity or problem-solving can be related to the *stitches* and *zipper* analogy suggested earlier, and the rest of this chapter will be devoted to discussing in some detail the various ways drawing can manifest those recommendations. The rest of the chapter is divided into the categories used earlier to describe the various communicative roles drawing can fulfill along the *stitches* and *zipper* model. What follows, however, does not limit drawing to the role of communicating with others, but includes

that intense self-communication between the left and right halves of the brain, when drawing completes the *eyemindhand* loop that allows the holistic use of all our conceptual abilities; when, to the observer of design behavior, drawing *becomes* the design process.

All the following tactics are worth mastering. A premature closure may result in a clumsy seam. The lack of adequate clearing may result in strange lumps sewn into the seam, and the inability to find a *hitch* to anchor the *zipper* may not secure the time needed to develop the design in a consistent direction. The failure to convincingly rationalize the closure may result in doubts and questions which undo the entire effort.

The mastery of the various tactics should also maintain a certain balance. An overemphasis on opening tactics, for instance, may drive the problem and solution so far apart that closure is literally inconceivable for a beginning designer. An overemphasis on the abilities at the *zipper* end of the process may just as easily result in the entire creative effort being spent on closed, persuasive drawings and a polished rationale designed to make superficial solutions acceptable to clients who have been closed out of the process.

DESIGN EDUCATION'S IMBALANCE
The ability to form concepts depends on a balanced use of the various opening, clearing and closing techniques. Design education is often guilty of an imbalance in the direction of opening techniques. Some design teaching consists mostly of pointing out a more and more comprehensive list of design criteria—loading the student with a massive burden of responsibility in the form of problems and concerns, and an equally long list of alternative solutions.

This teaching method often drives the problem and solution as far apart as possible and then simply walks away, leaving the student with only a threatening deadline as a mechanism of closure. We should spend more time teaching clearing and closing techniques, for human reasons as well as design reasons. Students' confidence in their conceptual ability or in the humanity of the profession they are entering is hardly helped by a shattering crit session two days before a deadline.

If we return now to the *stitches* and *zipper* analogy we will find that any and all drawings may be valuable in the opening, clearing and stitching phases if they are kept open, sketchy and ambiguous so that they invite input and interpretation. The *hitch* drawings and the first *zipper* drawings must be perspectives, however, if the hoped for perceptions of the solution's qualities as an environment are to be truly tested. After this playback potential has been rigorously verified in perspective, the process can return with confidence to the logical integration of the building as a built object promoted by the orthographic drawings.

OPENING DRAWINGS

designed to suspend judgment, prevent premature solutions and open up the design space.

If design can be thought of as the activity of joining a problem to a solution, then the space between the two belongs to the designer. The extent and quality of such design spaces are extremely variable, and designers must often fight to open up an adequate space to work in. The design space may be almost closed by a number of forces or circumstances, and its premature closing may catch the designer like a vise. One of the handiest tools with which to hold the jaws of the vise open is your pen or pencil. Drawing ability can be a great help in prying apart and propping open any narrow design space.

The opening required may be of two kinds: opening the client's and others' minds and opening the designer's mind. The opening may further be divided into: pushing back the solution side of the space, or pushing back the problem side.

The first thing designers should do is take a very careful look into the design space in which they will have to work—the space between the presumed problem and its suggested solution—and ask themselves if they really want to be there.

Clients who tell you, "We know what we want, we just need someone to draw it up"; or "I've built three of these developments in California and I know what sells"; or "I just need a set of plans to get through the building department" are also telling you that the design space is virtually closed.

Clients are not the only "others" who restrict a designer's moves. Mortgage bankers, government agencies, laws and society in general all prefer narrow design spaces because they need standard, conventional ways of looking at what, to designers, are opportunities for creativity.

A careful look into any design space should tell you whether there is going to be room for you or not. Younger designers tend to be optimistic about any design space, while older heads are extremely wary of, or resigned to, tight design spaces.

What is needed most is an accurate evaluation of the opening potential. It may be a matter of educating the others to an understanding of the design possibilities, or to an appreciation of your abilities; and if you are going to enter the design space at all, design tradition demands an initial flailing about, just to discover how tight the space really is.

If you make a serious and skillful effort in your first attempts to open the design space, that effort will show in your drawings; and the narrow-minded client or jaded building official will respect your effort, your skill and your spirit.

Designers themselves often leave precious little room for perceiving a problem freshly or conceiving its solution freely. The limitations of their own experience and their cultural or professional indoctrination may also make the design space narrow indeed. This narrowness is one of the reasons designers need to read, travel and broaden their education in every possible way. Thankfully, in most designers, preconception is balanced by a healthy procrastination, so that even though they seem to sense a perfect solution right away, they seldom get around to doing anything about it until other, better ideas have begun to occur to them.

The motivation to become a designer and the indoctrination of most design education arouses a certain stubborn openness, or persistence in finding an unusual or imaginative solution. A designer's openness may be distinctly one-sided, however, coming from the designer's application of a preconceived formal solution to the next problem that comes along, whatever it is. In such cases the designer demands a completely open problem side, allowing a drastic restatement of the problem, or an ignorance of certain parts of the problem in order that it can accept a rather rigid preconceived solution, which the designer brings from another, perhaps quite dissimilar problem.

The designer's preconceptions may come from several sources:
- over-familiarity with the problem type
- admired solutions to similar problems
- personal preference for certain formal solutions.

Openness, for the designer, may be more a problem of *balancing* the design space; of pushing the solution side open and holding it open, while exploring the problem side with a careful analysis of the particular problem and an understanding of how it differs from similar problems.

Many of those who have written about thinking, creativity or problem-solving have recognized the problem of premature closure. John Dewey, *How We Think* (1909), stated the problem as early and as clearly as anyone.

> The essence of critical thinking is suspended judgment; and the essence of this suspense is inquiry to determine the nature of the problem before proceeding to attempt its solution.

Tactics for opening the design space are all designed to suspend judgment, and most of the recommended behaviors aim at concentrating the designer's and others' attention on the problem side of the design space, so that preconceived or premature solutions may be avoided. Most of the activities are verbal, mathematical, logical, analytical, left-brained operations. Meanwhile the uninvited, uninvolved holistic right-brain may impose its preconceived solution out of utter boredom and frustration.

A far more successful approach, and one of the ways in which drawing can be helpful, is to involve the right-brain in *designing* and

drawing alternative ways of seeing the problem, the site, the function or the context—to make a design problem of the problem side of the design space. The solution side of the problem is thus pushed back by a splitting of the problem side and a relocation of the design space.

While most of the kinds of drawings which follow seem concerned with the problem side, or with the relocated design space, they indirectly hold or push back the solution side of the original problem by both extending the range and variety of potential solutions and deepening our understanding of the specific, mandatory criteria for any acceptable solution.

DRAWING THE PROBLEM
The displacement of the design space *within* the problem allows the designer to involve both sides of the brain , both intuition and logic, in designing the problem to be solved. This makes clear the difference between concept attainment and concept formation, discussed earlier in the chapter on CONCEPTION. In concept attainment the problem side is always *given,* with no opportunity for changing it and what is needed is simply a one way *compliance* of the solution with this rigid problem statement. In the concept formation involved in design, the problem side is always extremely variable, depending on the client, the context, and the

experience, ability and resources of the designer; and what is sought is a *congruence* between the problem and a solution, in which both are developed simultaneously or alternately.

Drawing the problem, then, really becomes *designing* the problem and involves a congruence *within* the problem side. Clients and/or users should be involved in the establishment of the congruence because this will apply the opening tactics proposed here to all those involved in the design process. This involvement in the opening phase will also assure that the congruence reached will reflect a consensus and will be shared by all those involved in the process. This agreement on the problem to be solved is essential, and should be addressed up front in the open.

There may be difficulties in including the client in this opening of the design space. Clients may not understand the need to pay you to waste time exploring what to them seems an obvious and straightforward problem or in questioning assumptions they have already made and criteria they have already established. Sensing this, the designer may choose to ignore the clients' or users' closed-mindedness and hope to smuggle in an imaginative solution later on in the process after a rapport has been established. You will certainly have to use your own judgment and sensitivity in estimating any client's prejudices, but the earlier you can test the limits of the design space, the better.

One very helpful technique is to frame the opening techniques as a series of questions which you ask the client. The questions should be designed to inquire about aspects of the problem they haven't thought through. The designer then becomes the recorder and synthesizer of this information, while the client is asked to find the information or evaluate alternatives. The designer is thus the innocent questioner, apparently not unduly influencing the process and obviously not spending great amounts of time at the client's expense.

There are at least six categories of such exploratory "opening" questions which can help open both the clients'/users' and the designer's minds.

1. WHAT ALTERNATE GRAPHIC PROBLEM-SOLVING LANGUAGES SHOULD BE CONSIDERED? Such a question usually involves a choice between verbal/logical, mathematical or visual languages, but in a book on drawing, and based on the arguments I have made for the visual thinking drawing promotes, the question is limited here to *drawn* languages. There are more alternate graphic languages than you might think, and they are rather easily combined and mutated to make entirely new languages.

The traditional drawings will form the base of most problem-solving languages. Bubble diagrams, for instance, have a strong relationship to the horizontal links and separations of plan views. There is tremendous potential, however, for plans of various kinds, which show relationships which are impossible to see in conventional mass/void plan drawings. I have argued earlier (*Drawing As a Means to Architecture,* 1968) that we become prematurely satisfied with our building designs when the formal patterns of the walls, openings and columns are ordered, because those are the images we work with. Our evaluative *eyeminds* may never see the actual functional patterns involved and these more important patterns may remain confused and chaotic.

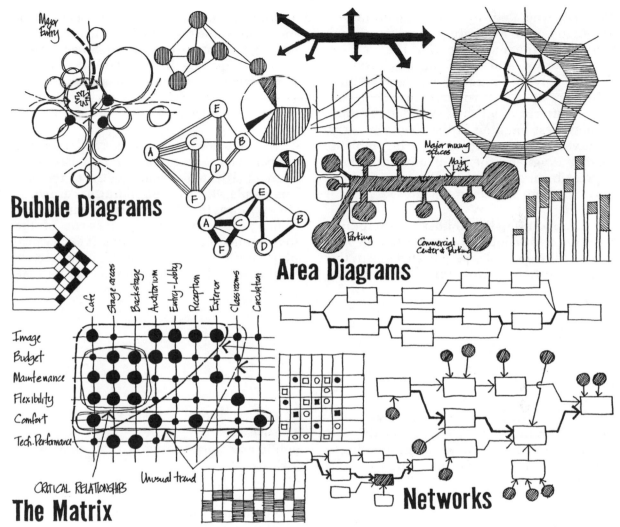

From GRAPHIC PROBLEM SOLVING FOR ARCHITECTS AND BUILDERS by Paul Laseau

Beyond the traditional drawings lies a range of other graphics which, while not directly translatable into buildings, represent crucial patterns and relationships involved in the design of any environment. Area diagrams, matrices and networks are examples of this kind of graphics and they indicate comprehensive, ideal relationships, and decision-making and operational sequences in time which must be considered in the design process.

Paul Laseau's *Graphic Problem Solving for Architects and Builders* (1975), presents and carefully explains the various uses of bubble diagrams, area diagrams, matrices and networks. These basic graphic tools can be further enriched by establishing a meaningful color code for the particular problem. Most problems offer a potential for further inventions of graphic languages which can be used to represent various parts of a particular problem.

207

We often waste our *eyemind's* potential for perceiving and evaluating complex visual images. If the meanings for the various colors, forms and lines in any graphic problem-solving language are clearly established, our *eyeminds* will be able to deal with visual patterns of much greater density than we may first imagine. If the clients or users are involved in developing a special problem-solving language they will have a built-in interest in understanding the relationships that language can communicate.

It is disappointing that the design disciplines have never developed a commonly accepted functional color code. I suggested one in the original edition of *Drawing As a Means to*

Architecture (1968), but changed it to black and white in the revised edition in an effort to keep the cost of the book down. Since there is no hope of keeping the cost of this book down, let me expand that color code and generalize it so that it can apply to most built environments.

With such a color code it is easy to represent the behavioral patterns in a proposed environment. If the movement paths of the various people who use the building are drawn in the appropriate color, and in a proportional volume, the real activity patterns of the environment become apparent. It is now possible to see how the various colors meet or conflict and their patterns may be manipu-

lated to either segregate certain kinds of circulation, or to control and increase the opportunity for meetings and interaction in appropriate places.

The establishment of meanings for a language of symbols like those variations for zones, points and lines suggested by Laseau and the color code proposed here and demonstrated in the succeeding sections will greatly enhance your and your client's understanding of the functional *structure* of the problem. If the specific graphic language or languages can be established early in the process they can be used in all the graphic notes, precept and concept diagrams—*all* the design drawings made during the process.

VIOLET • BLUE • GREEN
Main inhabitants of the environment:
the staff in a commercial or public building—hospital, school, restaurant, family in a residence.

VIOLET
top of the hierarchy:
boss, management, doctors, principals, maitre d', parents;

BLUE
middle of the hierarchy:
managers, tellers, nurses, teachers, chefs, waiters, older children;

GREEN
bottom of the hierarchy:
janitors, errand boys, custodians, busboys, younger children, live-in in-laws.

RED • ORANGE • YELLOW
Those served:
public, customers, patients, students, drivers, visitors.

RED
top of the hierarchy:
most important, largest depositors, most critical, oldest;

ORANGE
middle of the hierarchy:
ordinary, average;

YELLOW
bottom of the hierarchy:
least important, least critical, youngest, nuisances.

BLACK • GRAY • BROWN
Service:
deliveries, pick-ups, garbage, utilities (water, electricity, gas, sewer, telephone).

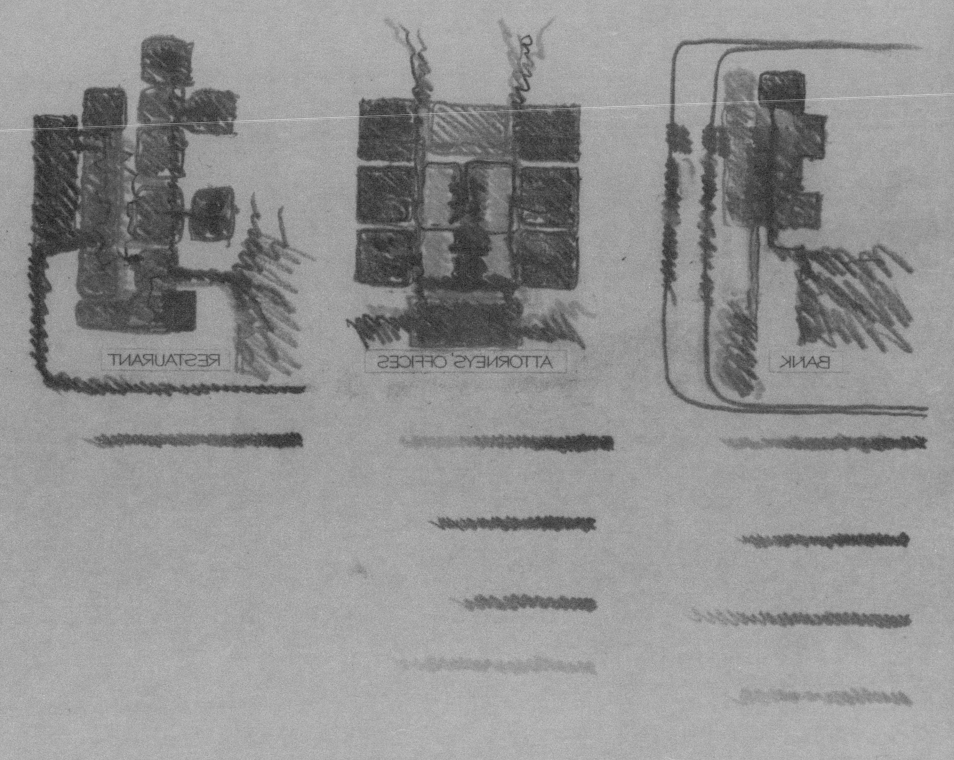

RESTAURANT

ATTORNEYS OFFICES

BANK

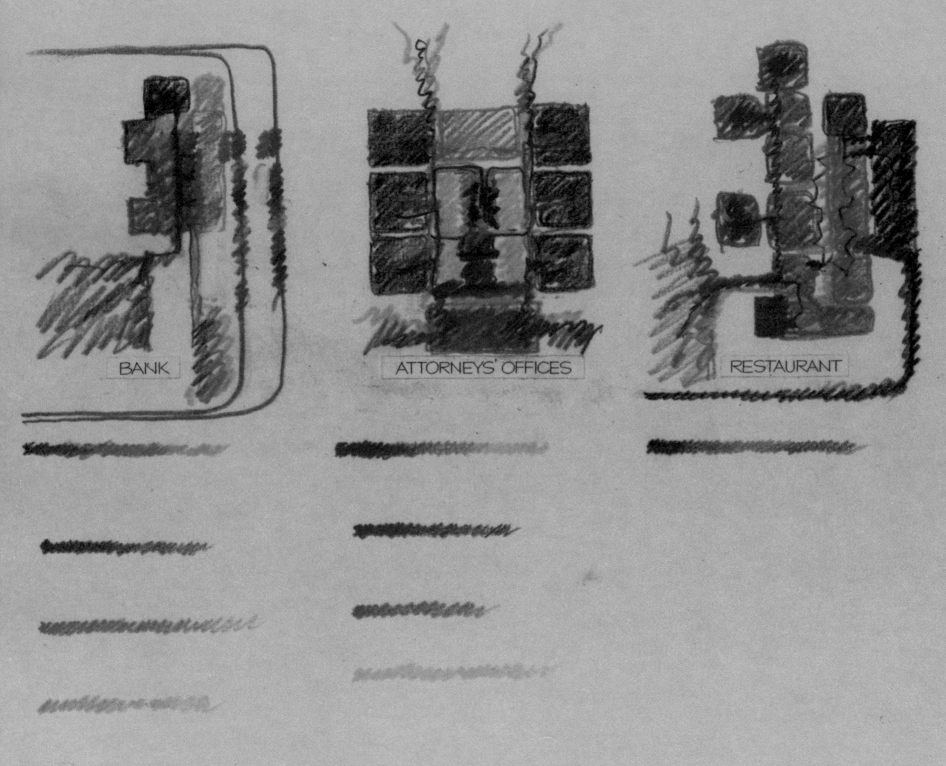

BANK

ATTORNEYS' OFFICES

RESTAURANT

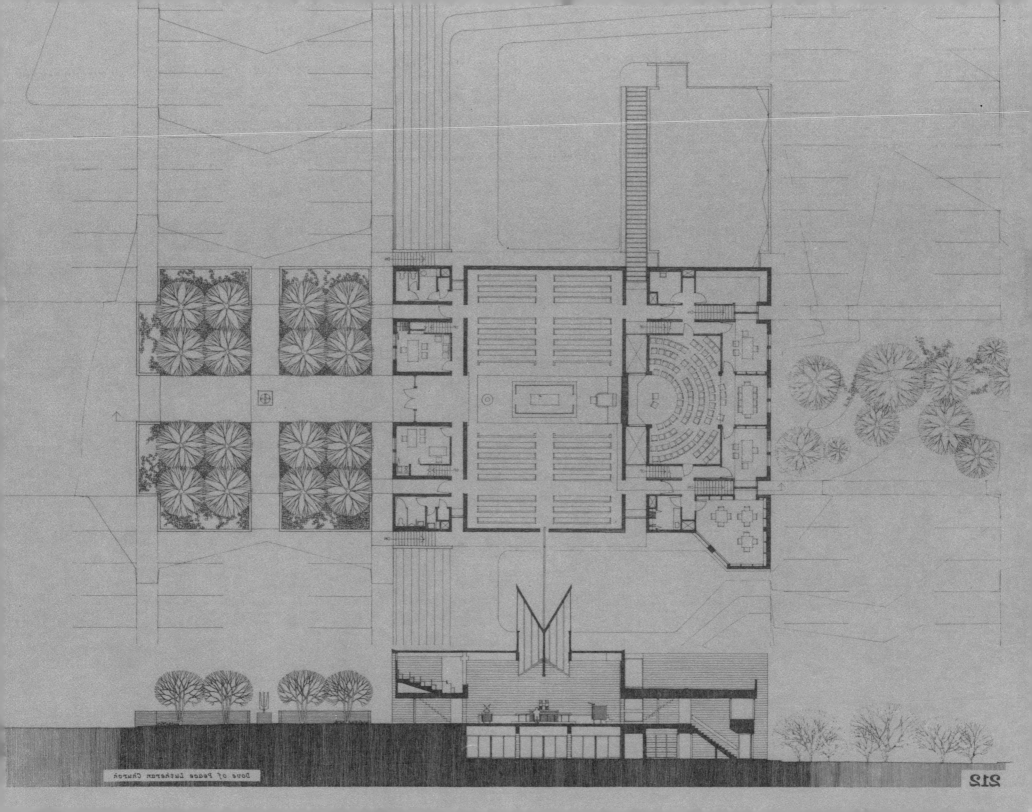

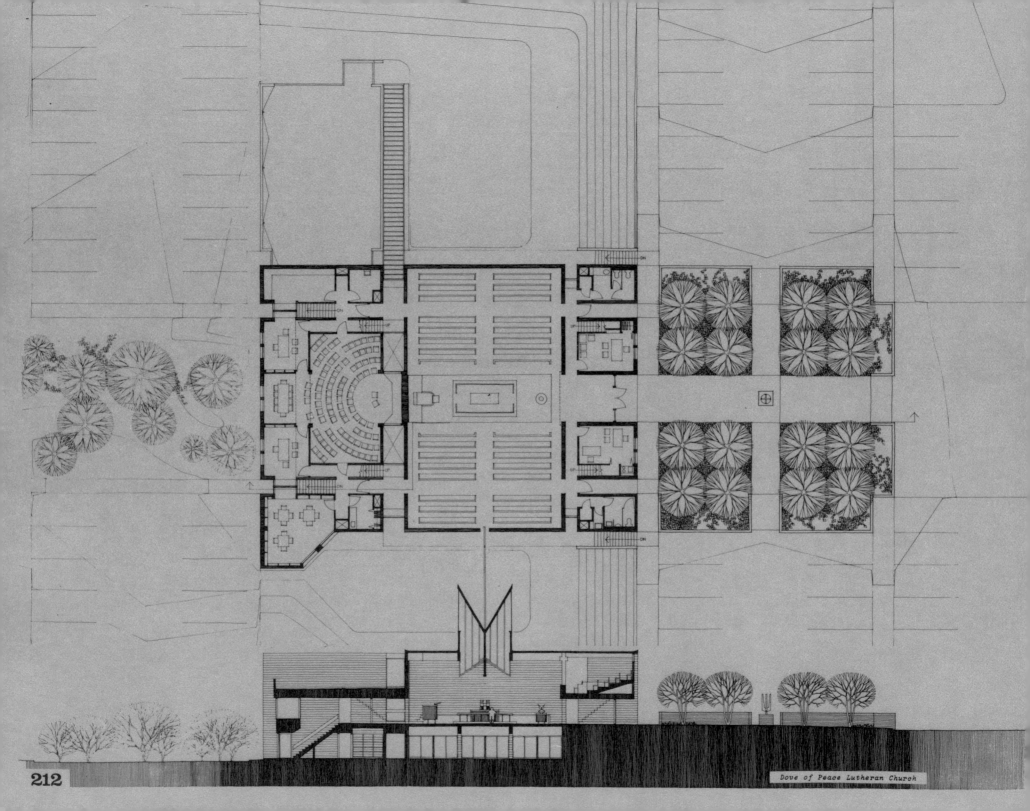

Dove of Peace Lutheran Church

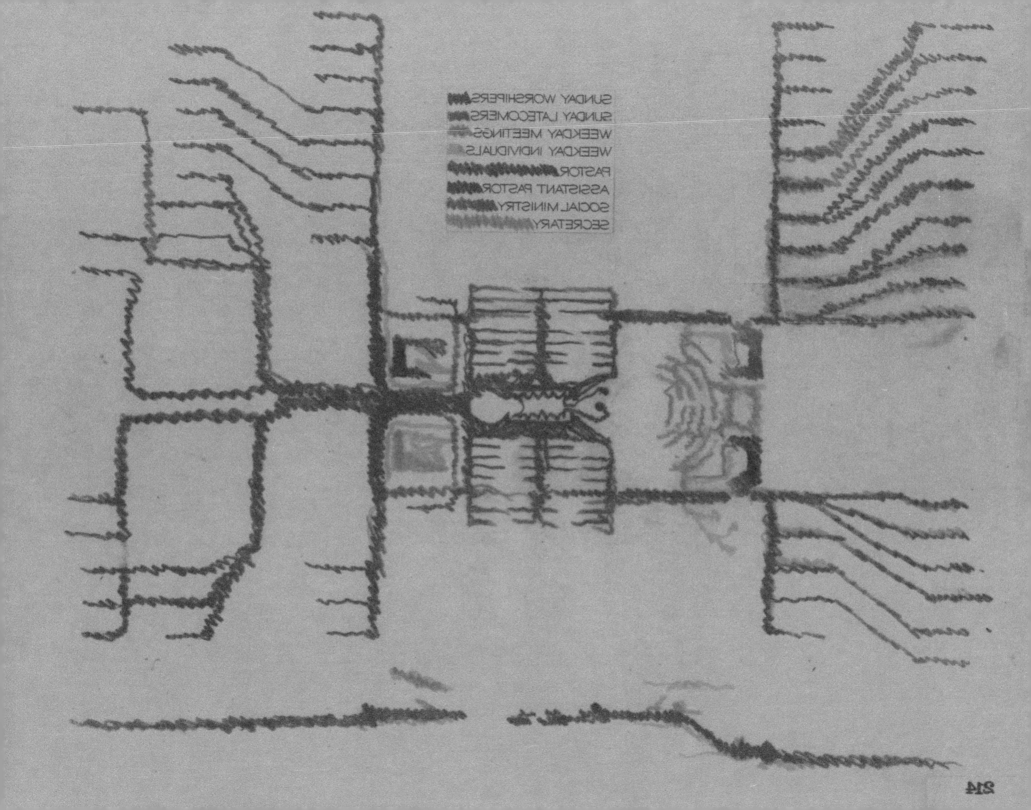

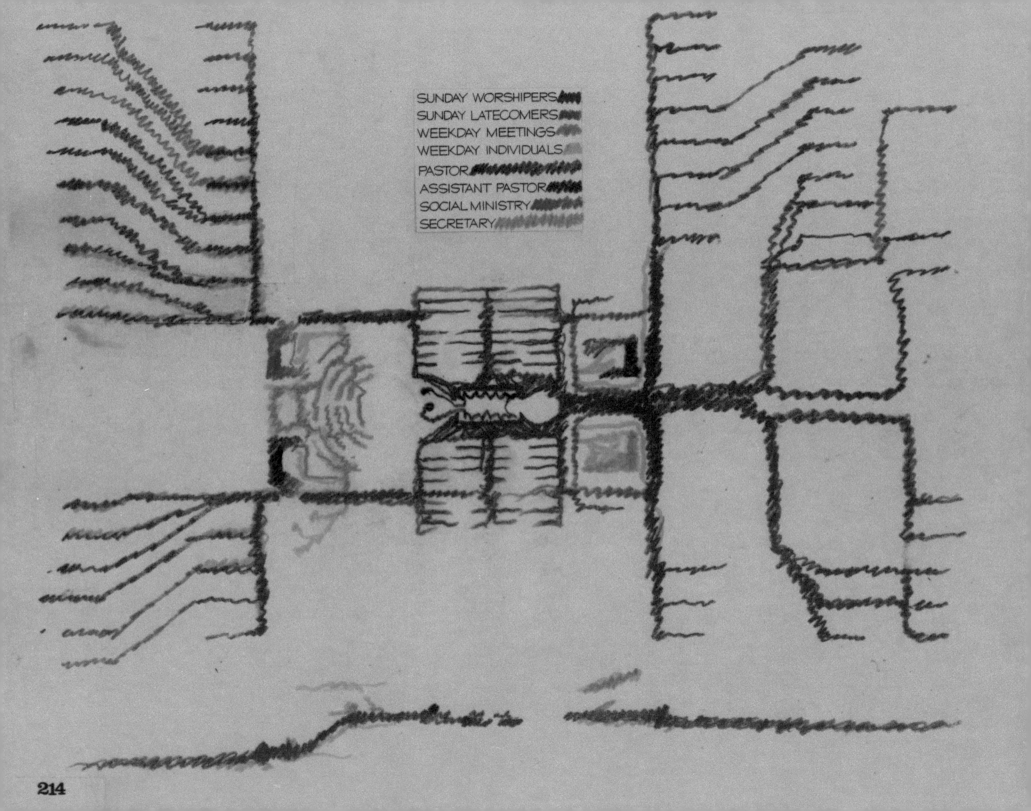

SUNDAY WORSHIPERS
SUNDAY LATECOMERS
WEEKDAY MEETINGS
WEEKDAY INDIVIDUALS
PASTOR
ASSISTANT PASTOR
SOCIAL MINISTRY
SECRETARY

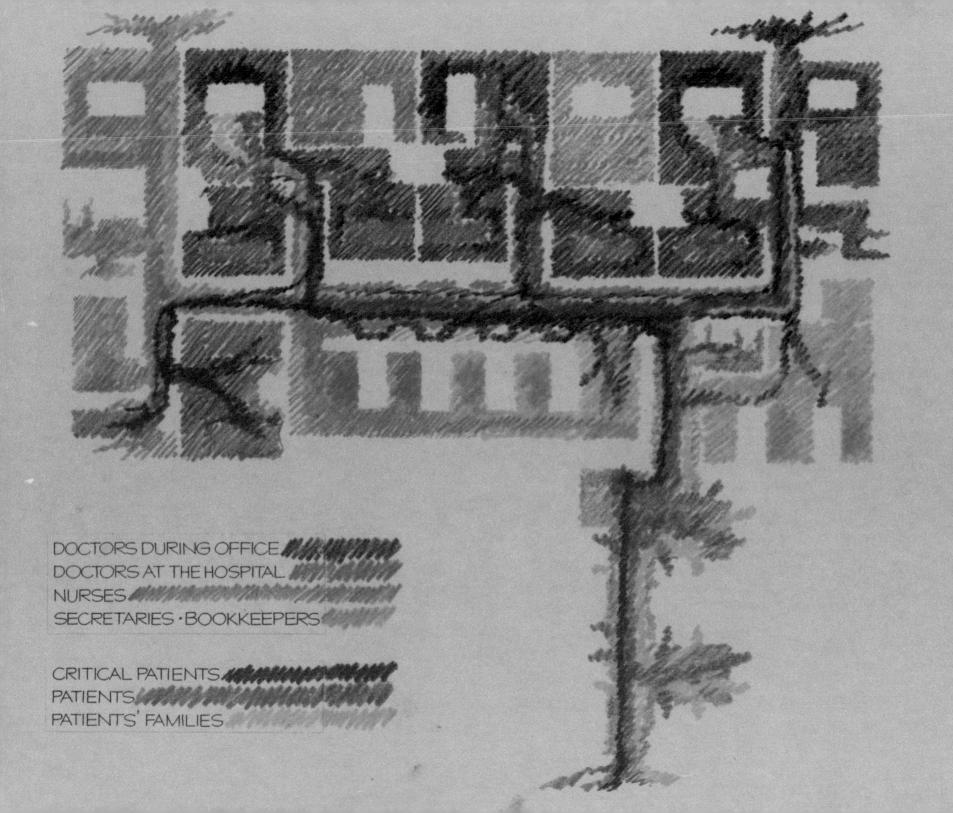

DOCTORS DURING OFFICE
DOCTORS AT THE HOSPITAL
NURSES
SECRETARIES · BOOKKEEPERS

CRITICAL PATIENTS
PATIENTS
PATIENTS' FAMILIES

215

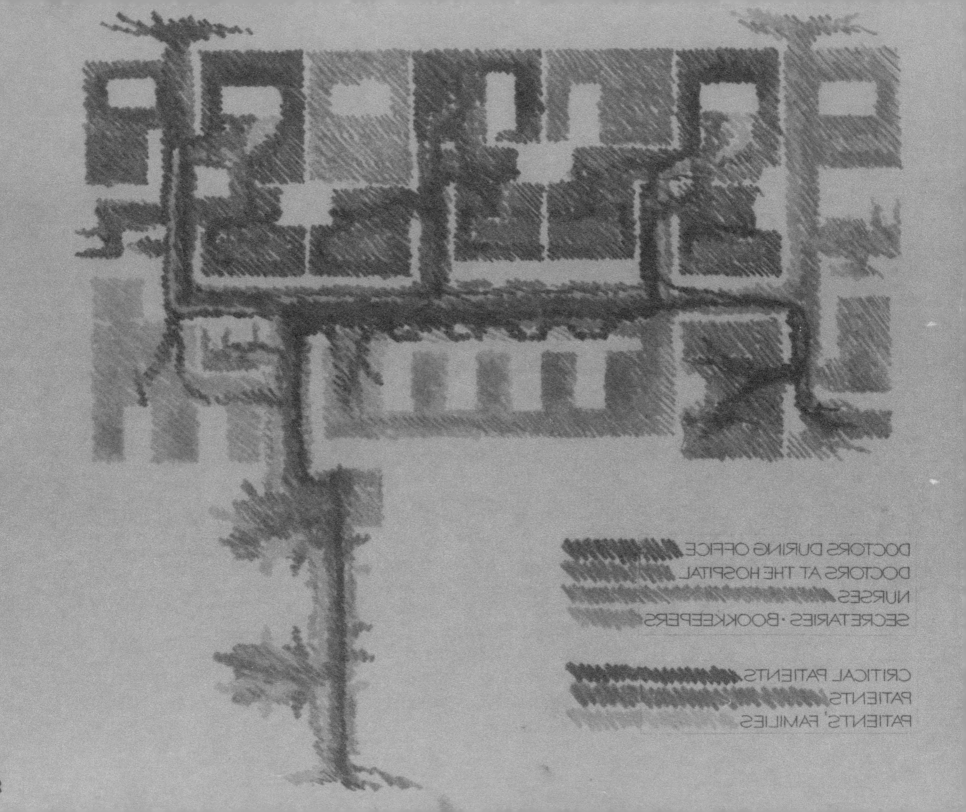

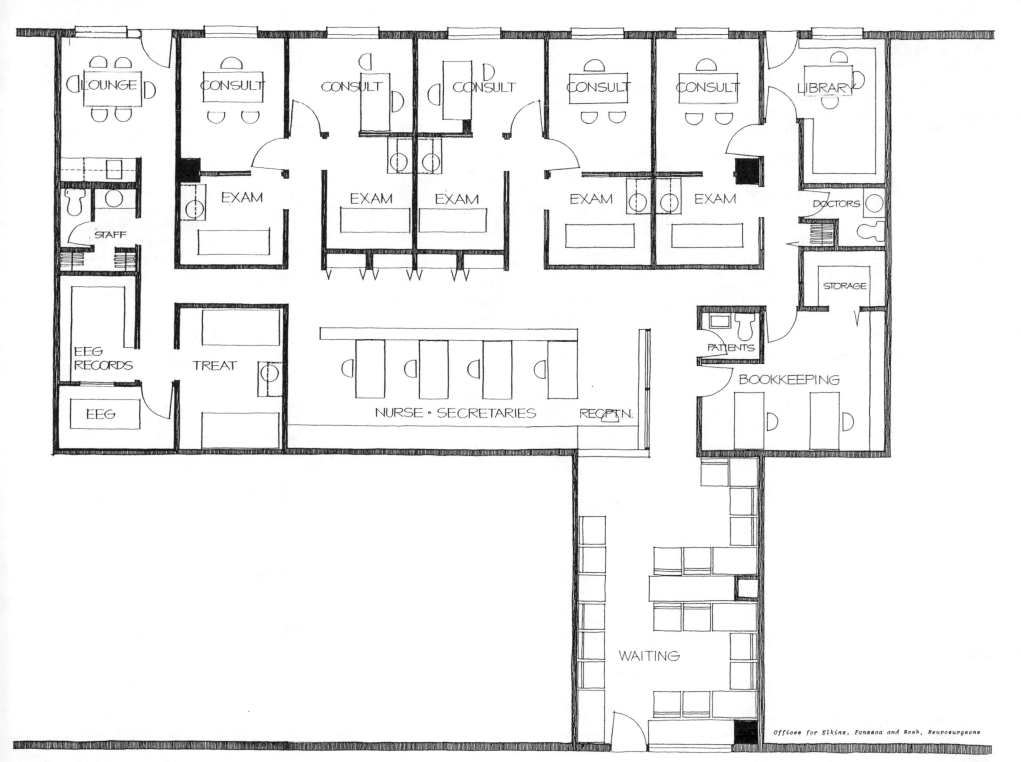

LOUNGE

CONSULT CONSULT CONSULT CONSULT CONSULT LIBRARY

STAFF

EXAM EXAM EXAM EXAM EXAM

DOCTORS

EEG
RECORDS

TREAT

NURSE · SECRETARIES RECPTN.

STORAGE

PATIENTS

EEG

BOOKKEEPING

WAITING

Offices for Elkins, Fonseca and Nash, Neurosurgeons

217

2. WHAT ADDITIONAL INFORMATION CAN BE FOUND ABOUT THIS AND SIMILAR PROBLEMS?

One of the most obvious ways to open the design space and assure that judgment is withheld is to actively seek further information about the function being designed for, the site and existing solutions to similar problems. This is one of the roles of programming described in Edward T. White's *Introduction to Architectural Programming* (1972):

> ...Briefly, in terms of the design paradigm mentioned, programming finds, selects and organizes pertinent facts and translates them from VERBAL to GRAPHIC expression so that they may, in turn, be tanslated into a physical expression....

The facts that need to be collected are of several kinds. White identifies "traditional" facts as those which are conventionally used by environmental designers and are not arguable. Even these traditional facts must be evaluated for their relevance to the problem at hand and that relevance should be a matter of consensus among all those involved in the process.

White lists nine categories of traditional facts:

1. Similar projects and critical issues
2. Client
3. Financial
4. Building Codes
5. Planning by related organizations
6. Function
7. Site
8. Climate
9. Growth and Change

Each of these major categories may contain an extensive list of subcategories. For example, under 6. Function, White identifies these subcategories:

a. operational systems—including links beyond the building
b. critical issues in insuring success in systems' operation
c. needs which are supporting to operation (lounge, waiting, toilet, janitor)
d. main operational sequences—"feeder sequences" which support main sequence
e. divisions or departments in the system
f. general departmental relationship affinities
g. number and type of people involved (task categories)
h. operations performed by each type of person
i. systems of people movement
j. systems of information movement
k. systems of material movement
l. work nodes (stations where work is performed)

and as an example of the further subdivision of these subcategories, k. systems of material movement:

(1) points of origin and destination (including delivery and pick up)
(2) frequency and pattern (continual or intermittent)
(3) degree of urgency
(4) role in overall operation
(5) form (size, weight)
(6) special considerations (fragile)
(7) operations performed on material (including unpacking and disposal of waste)
(8) storage implications
(9) peak loads

What White calls "non-traditional" facts will be dealt with next under CLEARING tactics. The clients and users must provide much of the information involved in the previous outline of "traditional" facts, or certainly participate in its collection. The designer's task is to record and collect the information into categories and translate it into more usable graphic form. Such a document is the beginning of a program; in fact the left hand side of the design space, which we have been calling *problem* could be called *program*. The major objection I have to that change in the analogy is that most programmers assume that the program is a rigid antecedent to the solution, and instead of the concept formation involved in a simultaneous congruence between the problem and a solution, we have regressed to the concept attainment involved in the compliance of a solution to a fixed program.

3. WHAT ARE THE ALTERNATIVE WAYS OF CATEGORIZING THE PROBLEM?

This activity is one of the most crucial in the design process and also one of the most potent as a technique for opening the design space. As discussed earlier in the chapter on CONCEPTION, categorization involves at least three relationships as a member of a contextual hierarchy, each of which provokes a number of questions.

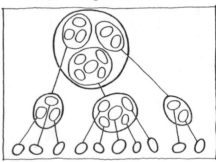

As a part, the problem should relate to the larger physical whole of the neighborhood, city and region and to the larger temporal whole of its period in time.

• What responsibilities does the design have to the larger system?
• Should the design blend in with the larger environment or stand out as different? to what degree?
• What should the design's response be to the larger climatic systems of sun, wind and rain?
• How can the design avoid adding unnecessarily to traffic congestion or air pollution?
• How can the design preserve and extend existing amenities? bike paths? landscaping features like street trees?

As a whole, the problem will be composed of various parts, and this subdivision should be explored as alternate ways of taking the problem apart.

- What are the alternative ways in which the problem can be subdivided? functionally? contextually? sequentially? structurally?
- What are the advantages and disadvantages of the various subdivisions?
- Should these subdivisions remain in the constructed design? Would they be meaningful in understanding the environment when built?

As a sibling, the problem will have relationships to similar environments, designed by others or, perhaps, by yourself.

- What relationships should the design have to similar environments? should it look newer? larger? more expensive? more imaginative? more traditional?
- Should it share certain characteristics? be identifiable as a member of a set? restaurant, bank, etc.?
- How should it be different?

It may be difficult to get a client or user to accept alternative ways of categorizing a design problem, because the categories in which we see the world are the stronghold of conventional wisdom. This conventional perception is perhaps even more likely in clients who can afford to commission a professional architect, landscape architect or interior designer since that very fact demonstrates their success in the conventional world, and they are perhaps more likely to be enmeshed in conventional categories and values than others. If you can persuade them to see one or two alternative ways of categorizing the problem, however, it will be worth the effort.

4. WHAT ALTERNATIVE ANALOGIES CAN BE DRAWN FOR THE PROBLEM?

Analogies are well established as creative links in problem-solving, and they are equally useful in terms of understanding the problem to be solved. They can help in the categorization of the problem, just discussed, by clarifying the relationships of the problem and its various parts to other kinds of problems. Alternate analogies are especially helpful in posing choices of ways of looking at the problem.

- Is the problem of designing a shopping mall like designing a vending machine or a carnival midway?
- Is a new building on an older street like a blood transfusion or an uninvited guest?
- Is the problem of designing for a multiple client like making a stew, offering a smorgasbord, or serving a very safe, bland dinner?
- Should the problem of designing on a very limited budget be approached like designing a denim muu-muu or a mink bikini?
- Is the problem of the interior design of an office suite like designing the company's letterhead or letting each employee make a nest?
- Should the landscaping of a patio be thought of as a collection of specimen pieces or as functional furniture which gives shade and adds visual interest?

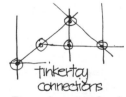 tinkertoy connections

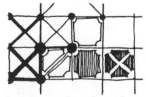

Drawing analogies may seem redundant but they are useful in the extension of the likeness they provide. Analogies often contain unsuspected depth that can't be appreciated verbally, especially in the details that make up their physical form.

5. WHAT ALTERNATIVE ENTRY POINTS CAN BE ESTABLISHED INTO THE PROBLEM?

Edward deBono, (*Lateral Thinking,* 1970) has made it clear that the order in which we gain information in solving a problem has a great influence on the solutions we reach:

> ...Because of the nature of the self-maximizing memory system of the mind the entry point for considering a situation or a problem can make a big difference to the way it is structured. Usually the obvious entry point is chosen. Such an entry point is itself determined by the established pattern and so leads back to this. There is no way of telling which entry point is going to be best so one is usually content with the most obvious one. It is assumed that the choice of entry point does not matter since one will always arrive at the same conclusions. This is not so since the whole train of thought may be determined by the choice of entry point. It is useful to develop some skill in picking out and following different entry points....

Usually the common entry points to any problem are the function and the context. One of the simplest ways to vary the entry point is to imagine initiating the design process by looking at the problem from the points of view of some of the people who may be involved;

- the owner
- the user, if different
- the builder
- the unfamiliar visitor
- the next designer
- the larger community
- the building official
- the mortgage lender
- the critic
- the fire chief

or to approach the design from one of the narrower concerns which follow:

- structurally
- economically
- maintenance-wise
- formally
- security
- accessibility
- esthetically
- mechanically
- for future growth & change
- color, texture
- energy conservation
- traditionally

6. WHAT ALTERNATIVE DESIGNS FOR THE DESIGN PROCESS ITSELF SHOULD BE CONSIDERED? This is an excellent opening technique because it allows you to communicate clearly to your clients or users the general form of the design process and the roles played by the various participants in the process. It also provokes you to consider alternate ways of proceeding based on this particular problem. The range of options may be suggested by a list of questions.

- In what phases, over time, should the process be conceived? Is there a standard professional description of the designer's services which will be followed?
- Whose participation and approval should be sought and when? Where are the critical decision points in the process in terms of commitment to a particular design?
- Which aspects of the problem seem most critical? What are the most important decisions to be made? from the clients' or users' standpoint? from the designer's standpoint?
- How can a desirable flexibility or contingency be built into the process?
- What will be the most effective ways of communicating during the process? frequent short meetings? infrequent in-depth meetings? memos? drawings?
- Which parts of the process promise to be most profitable in terms of the designer's creativity? early overall conceptualizing? or later critical details?
- Which parts of the process will be most critical for client/user participation? initial goals and criteria? or are they so well established that participation can be concentrated on later detailed development of the concept?

Taking time to design the process and record it graphically is always worthwhile, even for design projects in school. Planning the way we will use any period of future time, like an appointment calendar, or a critical path bar chart, helps guide our efforts and recognizes that getting finished is always part of the problem. The participation of those involved, in designing the process, also tends to commit them to the successful completion of the process they have helped design.

THE DESIGNER'S CREDIBILITY
In opening the design space, designers may also establish their credibility as problem-solvers and demonstrate the breadth and depth of their knowledge and creativity. When this establishment of credibility is necessary it is generally better done graphically because a designer's graphic ability is usually impressive. The graphic advantage which most designers have over the general public results not so much from our great skill as from the lack of the general development of graphic skills in our culture's educational system. Drawing skill is one of the few communicative advantages we enjoy over most clients and we should use it whenever we need to be impressive.

In my experience the intelligent and skillful use of drawing can open the design space and involve clients in the continuing dialogue of the design process. Abstract plan and section diagrams and sketchy perspectives are excellent for this opening role. The drawings should be like graphic questionnaires or conversation pieces, deliberately ambiguous and subject to alternate interpretations so that they provoke discussion and contribute to the opening of all the minds involved in the process. If you can produce a profusion of these drawings, indicating alternative ways of seeing and solving the problem, you will also communicate that the decision-making process is open to your clients and users and that you welcome and expect their participation— their company in the design space.

CLEARING DRAWINGS
designed to remove various kinds of blocks, misunderstandings and preconceptions— breaking the conventional categories in which we think about a problem—clearing the design space.

Clearing is the other kind of open drawing and can be thought of as describing tactics for clearing up misunderstandings and removing obstructions and residue which may make the eventual closure of the problem to the solution difficult or awkward. Clearing may overlap with opening and several of the opening tactics just discussed may help in clearing the design space. In the analogy we are using, however, we may assume that the opening techniques have helped us achieve an acceptable congruence on the *problem* side and we have now resumed our station in the original design space.

Clearing tactics may consist of brief exercises in breaking the categories in which the problem is understood, or the clearing may involve a profound conversion of the way a client or a designer looks at the built environment or the world in general. The main technique in clearing conceptual blocks is simply learning to recognize them.

In many design processes there is no time or need to get involved in rethinking everything about the problem. The problem may be simple and familiar and the designer's efforts may be better concentrated on some other part of the process. On the other hand, if the problem is too familiar, or if either the client or the designer is seeking an especially innovative solution, then a thorough clearing of the design space may be necessary.

Most clearing tactics can be thought of as category-breaking, or what deBono has called the breaking of "cliche patterns." As Bruner, Goodnow and Austin made clear in their *A Study of Thinking* (1956), the categories in which we perceive or conceive the world at once allow and limit all our cognitive activity. If in designing a house we accept the conventional spatial categories of living room, dining room, bedrooms and bathrooms, our design will be limited to an arrangement of those categories. If we deliberately break those categories, however, and make ourselves consider other ways of classifying the spaces of a dwelling, we might find several interesting alternatives.

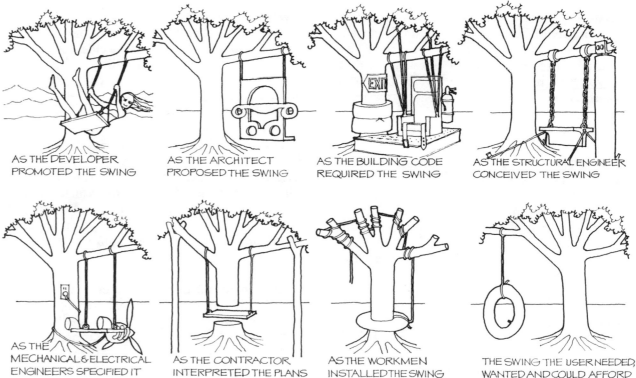

AS THE DEVELOPER PROMOTED THE SWING

AS THE ARCHITECT PROPOSED THE SWING

AS THE BUILDING CODE REQUIRED THE SWING

AS THE STRUCTURAL ENGINEER CONCEIVED THE SWING

AS THE MECHANICAL & ELECTRICAL ENGINEERS SPECIFIED IT

AS THE CONTRACTOR INTERPRETED THE PLANS

AS THE WORKMEN INSTALLED THE SWING

THE SWING THE USER NEEDED, WANTED AND COULD AFFORD

A more meaningful way to think about residential spaces might be in terms of several polar continuums: public/private, waking/sleeping, noisy/quiet, light/dark, hard/soft, adult/children or individual/communal. The subcategories into which we take any design problem apart will absolutely limit the ways in which we reassemble it as a whole.

Two other ways to rattle the conventional categories might be either to undercategorize or overcategorize. Undercategorization would be accomplished in the house by assuming that all functions *could* happen in one undivided space, and then gradually and deliberately adding categories and spatial subdivisions in a carefully considered order.

Overcategorization can be accomplished by taking each space and subdividing it further, as you might categorize the bedroom into

sleeping, sitting and dressing areas; or the kitchen into storage, preparation, cooking and serving areas. Either variation makes clear that the conventional categories are arbitrary and should not be accepted as necessary.

Category-breaking in some form is recommended by most of those who have written about the *stitch* end of the design process.

In addition to the preconceived categories in which we may frame any problem statement, the design space may be cluttered with various blocks. James Adams' excellent *Conceptual Blockbusting* (1974) discusses an extensive list of Perceptual, Emotional, Cultural, Environmental, Intellectual and Expressive blocks. Adams proposes that the first step in clearing conceptual blocks is learning to recognize them. He suggests both

conscious and unconscious ways of clearing conceptual blocks. Consciously, Adams recommends the use of various checklists, conscious questioning and striving for fluency and flexibility; for unconscious blockbusting he recommends the techniques of Brainstorming (Osborn), Synectics (Gordon) and Self-Actualization (Maslow).

Drawing might be used to clear out three such blocks simultaneously: the perceptual block Adams calls "stereotyping—seeing what you expect to see"; the cultural block he describes as "problem solving is a serious business and humor is out of place"; and the perceptual block he calls "inability to see the problem from various viewpoints." By deliberately drawing a set of humorous stereotypical solutions to the problem, as seen from the viewpoints of the various people involved in the design process or who will experience the environment when built, we may clear out a great many of our preconceptions. If we are honest enough to include ourselves as designers in this gallery of stereotypes, and brave enough to show the collection to the other participants in the process, we may have an excellent start toward clearing the design space.

Drawing can help in understanding and clearing many such blocks, and the inability to use drawing as a problem-solving language is one of the kinds of Expressive blocks Adams discusses. Fluency with various languages and the flexibility to translate from one language to another, including drawing, is central to any design process.

Two other of the blocks Adams has identified (the emotional block of "fear to make a mistake, to fail, to risk," and the perceptual block of "tendency to delimit the problem area too closely") might be loosened by deliberately drawing the most outrageous extensions of the problem we can think of.

And one last graphic effort might simultaneously clear the blocks Adams calls "preference for judging ideas rather than generating them" (emotional) and "taboos" (cultural). Here the idea, recommended by several other writers on creativity, would be to set ourselves a quota of alternative concepts, several of which include obvious cultural taboos, and delay evaluating them or eliminating objectionable or apparently ridiculous ideas until we had generated and graphically recorded the full quota.

Drawing is particularly helpful in these clearing operations because the actual, physical making of the drawing, and the drawing's physical manifestation of the ideas purges our consciousness at a deeper level because it engages the *eyemindhand* triad.

If we broaden clearing to include *clarification* we can further our understanding of the problem and prevent premature closure of the design space by the programming technique of collecting and screening what White calls "non-traditional" facts. These facts will require more discussion and negotiation because there will be conflicting and antithetical facts brought by various participants in the design process. The disagreement is caused by the relational, contingent quality of this kind of information and because, unlike the earlier "traditional" facts, "non-traditional" facts do not lie within one particular participant's area of expertise.

A typical example of a contradiction in "non-traditional" facts is the "fact" that people value well-designed, well-maintained environments and respect them in their behavior vs. the "fact" that people are not to be trusted and if there is any way that an environment can be vandalized or littered, it will be. Because of the controversial nature of such "non-traditional" facts, it is important that during the clearing phase, disagreements and misunderstandings be cleared up as much as possible.

The best I can do is to quote Tim White, (*Introduction to Architectural Programming,* 1972), with whom I taught for many years at the University of Arizona:

NON-TRADITIONAL FACTS
A. There is no clearcut division that can be made between traditional and non-traditional architectural facts. The classification of a fact as one or the other will depend upon the degree of programming and design DETAIL required for the building type in question, the UNIQUENESS of the building type and the depth and breadth of the KNOWLEDGE of the designer. What is non-traditional for one building or designer may be very common for another.

These "non-traditional" facts will have to be screened for relevance, and made graphic as White suggests, and their inclusion and arrangement into categories and a hierarchy of importance will always be a matter of discussion and consensus among all the participants in the process. Designers and others probably always harbor a covert set of their own "non-traditional" facts which they will try to smuggle into the process, but these are always better acknowledged openly and graphically up front and agreement sought for their inclusion in the documented *problem* statement.

CLOSING TECHNIQUES
Closing techniques are not given the attention they deserve in most works on creativity. This lack of attention to closure may come from a hesitancy to suggest conscious, deliberate closing techniques and may carry vestiges of the traditional myth that concepts are *given* not *made* and are beyond coaxing; and the best that can be done is to open the mind, clear away the blocks, and then just wait patiently. After the "problem-solver" follows the prescribed opening and clearing techniques, she or he is described in the moment of solution as variously "seeing the solution," "arriving at the solution," or "discovering the answer" or as coolly choosing between various alternatives.

My memory of those moments as a designer, or as a thinker, is not of any kind of instantaneous seeing, arriving, discovering or choosing. I would describe the beginning of the closure more as seeing, usually in the drawings, a way to make a promising first *stitch* across the design gap, and the feeling of anticipation or confidence that other reinforcing *stitches,* only vaguely sensed at the beginning, will then become possible.

STITCH DRAWINGS

designed to make trial closures between the problem and a solution by drawing tentative piecemeal solutions to specific parts of the problem—searching for direction.

Stitches are the first tentative attempts at closing the design space. These first attempts at closure cannot always be delayed through the opening and clearing phases discussed earlier. They happen. Designers cannot *not* have ideas about how to join parts of the problem to parts of the solution; they surface through the cracks in our consciousness and are comforting evidence of the futility of ever being able to control human behavior, especially human thought. Methodological robots might be able to march through the design process with never a sideways glance, or without ever breaking stride into a skip or a dance, but human designers always behave anticipatorily, peeking behind the curtains of whatever model of the design process they say they follow.

The literature on thinking, problem-solving, programming and creativity varies widely in its recommendations for ways of closing the design space that separates the problem from a solution: from Adams' counsel to "relax, incubate, and sleep on it"; to Synectics' search for various analogical links to similar problems and solutions in other fields; to deBono's many suggestions for different ways of perceiving and manipulating the

problem; to White's methodical development of a detailed program of facts and precepts. As if the range weren't wide enough already I'd like to extend the range on the incubation end by adding what might best be called "managed procrastination."

I have found that, after an intense initial effort to understand the problem, the deliberate avoidance of working or even thinking about the problem for extended periods of time is, for me, a very useful technique. Perhaps my tendency to use procrastination as a creativity technique increased after I read that procrastination was the *sine qua non* of creative people; I know it increased with my conceptual confidence and my drawing skill; or perhaps I have some Hopi blood in me. The Hopi see no necessary relationship between how dilligently they work in , say, weaving a basket, and how soon the basket is finished. They are simply helping the basket become a basket, which it will do when it is ready, or when the time is right. Most design students are potential Hopis, so that the procrastination technique must be controlled by very careful and confident management, because getting finished is always part of any design problem.

Despite the wide variety of advice on how to *stitch* the problem to a solution, there is broad general agreement that the most successful *stitches* are made by those who have a solid set of conceptual skills, including drawing, a good basic knowledge of existing solutions and who have made an intensely concentrated attempt to "get their heads around" the problem. Beyond this initial agreement the range of suggested techniques quickly diverges and we can only sample it here.

Synectics (1968), by W. J. J. Gordon proposes four specific classes of analogies which are very clearly illustrated in Paul Laseau's

excellent *Graphic Thinking for Architects and Designers* (1980):

Analogies

In his book *Synectics: The Development of Creative Capacity,* William Gordon described four types of analogy: symbolic, direct, personal, and fantasy.

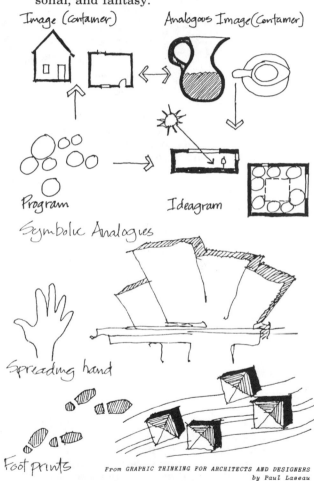

From GRAPHIC THINKING FOR ARCHITECTS AND DESIGNERS
by Paul Laseau

The example of the pitcher and the house as containers is a *symbolic analogy,* a comparison between general qualities of the two objects. Other symbolic analogies might be made between the spread of a hand and the extensions of a house or between footprints and canopied pavilions which loosely constitute the house.

223

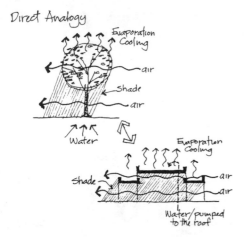

Direct Analogy

Direct analogy compares parallel facts or operations. In the above example, the house is designed to have the same cooling characteristics as a tree: shade, evaporation, and air movement.

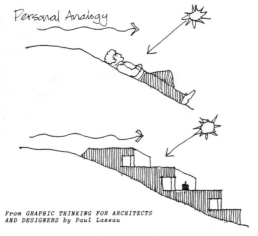

Personal Analogy

From GRAPHIC THINKING FOR ARCHITECTS AND DESIGNERS by Paul Laseau

In a *personal analogy,* the designer identifies himself directly with the elements of the problem. Assuming that the prime consideration for this house is warmth and comfort on winter days without large uses of non-renewable energy sources, the designer might imagine himself to be the house. To make himself comfortable, he might lay close to the ground below the ridge so the cold wind can pass over his head. This can be translated into a low-profile, house below the ridge with trays of space covered by sloped glass skylights to admit the warm rays of the sun.

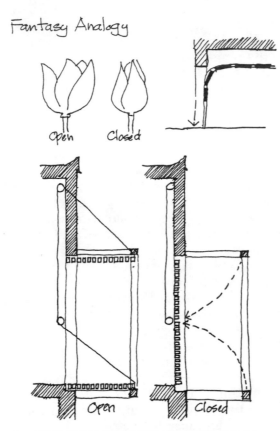

Fantasy Analogy

Open   Closed

Open   Closed

From GRAPHIC THINKING FOR ARCHITECTS AND DESIGNERS by Paul Laseau

The fourth type, *fantasy analogy,* uses a description of an ideal condition, desired as a source for ideas. In the case of our recreational house, the designer might fantasize a house that opens itself up when the client arrives on the weekend and automatically closes up when the client leaves. It could be compared to a tulip that opens and closes with the action of sunlight, or the automatic garage door, or a puppet that comes alive when you pick up the strings. The decks and the roofs over the decks could be like the leaves of the tulip. But how do they open and close? A motor is another energy consumer; is there another way? How can the puppet strings help? The final solution uses ropes and pulleys to raise and lower the flaps. The system is balanced so that the weight of a person on the decks can pull up the roofs, and the drooping of the roofs could pull the decks back up. The decks and roofs would be held in both open and closed positions by spring latches.

The ability to see similarities, to make relationships, to make relationships, to draw analogies or make metaphors is perhaps the most valuable creative mechanism. To be able to see how one thing is like another allows designers to *stitch* ALL they know or have experienced to their current design problem, not just what they may know about architecture, landscape architecture or interior design.

Edward deBono's *Lateral Thinking* (1970), suggests many techniques for getting out of the rut of what he calls the "vertical thinking" of conventional logic. I have referred to some of deBono's suggestions earlier but a few of his techniques are especially appropriate in *stitching*:

THE REVERSAL METHOD

Unless one is going to sit around waiting for inspiration the most practical way to get moving is to work on what one has. In a swimming race when the swimmers come to turn at the end of the pool they kick hard against the end to increase their speed. In the reversal method one kicks hard against what is there and fixed in order to move away in the opposite direction.

In the reversal method one takes things as they are and then turns them round, inside out, upside down, back to front. Then one sees what happens. It is a provocative rearrangement of information. You make water run uphill instead of downhill. Instead of driving a car the car leads you.

In Aesop's fable the water in the jug was at too low a level for the bird to drink. The bird was thinking of taking water out of the jug but instead he thought of putting something in. So he dropped pebbles into the jug until the level of water rose high enough for him to drink.

In lateral thinking one is not looking for the right answer but for a different arrangement of information which will provoke a different way of looking at the situation.

The purpose of the reversal procedure

Very often the reversal procedure leads to a way of looking at the situation that is obviously wrong or ridiculous. What then is the point of doing it?

- One uses the reversal procedure in order to escape from the absolute necessity to look at the situation in the standard way. It does not matter whether the new way makes sense or not for once one escapes then it becomes easier to move in other directions as well.
- By disrupting the original way of looking at the situation one frees information that can come together in a new way.
- To overcome the terror of being wrong, of taking a step that is not fully justified.
- The main purpose is provocative. By making the reversal one moves to a new position. Then one sees what happens.
- Occasionally the reversed approach is useful in itself

The reversal method suggests several possibilities for design drawing:

- Graphic figure/field reversal is often useful in helping the designer see the problem in a new way. The conventional dark/light, mass/void indication can be reversed so that the space is drawn as black and the walls or structure as white.

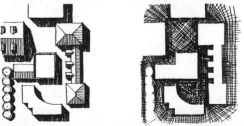

- It might also be interesting to briefly draw up the *worst* solution for the problem you can imagine. This effort might help you see what would constitute the *best* solution, by contrast.
- It might be interesting to draw what you consider to be the *least* important aspect of the design, and give it your undivided design attention for just awhile.

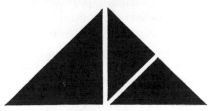

From LATERAL THINKING: CREATIVITY STEP BY STEP by Edward de Bono

Another technique recommended by deBono (*Lateral Thinking,* 1970) has to do with the importance of the point of entry into any problem:

ENTRY POINT

The choice of entry point is of huge importance because the historical sequence in which ideas follow one another can completely determine the final outcome even if the ideas themselves are the same....

Divide a triangle into three parts in such a way that the parts can be put together again to form a rectangle or a square.

The problem is quite a difficult one since the shape of the triangle is not specified. You first have to choose a triangle shape and then find out how it can be divided up into three pieces that can be put together to give the square or rectangle.

The solution to the problem is shown opposite. It is obviously much easier to start with the square instead of with the triangle which was suggested as the starting point. There can be no doubt about the shape of a square whereas the shape of a triangle (and to a lesser extent of a rectangle) is variable. Since the three parts have to fit together again to form a square one can solve the problem by dividing up a square into three parts that can be put together again to give a rectangle or a triangle. Two ways of doing this are shown opposite.

In many children's books there is the sort of puzzle in which are shown three fishermen whose lines have gotten tangled up. At the bottom of the picture a fish is shown attached to one of the lines. The problem is to find which fisherman has caught the fish. The children are supposed to follow the line down from the tip of the fishing rod in order to find which line has the fish at the end. This may involve one, two or three lines. It is obviously much easier to start at the other end and trace the line upwards from the fish to the fisherman. That way there need never be more than one attempt.

Choice of entry point is easily translated into a useful design drawing technique by beginning the *stitching* with drawings which normally come much later in the process, say, a reflected ceiling plan, a window detail or an interior perspective. Such unaccustomed graphic beginnings can have the same beneficial effects which deBono describes in geometric puzzles and verbal thinking:

RANDOM WORD STIMULATION
This is a practical and definite procedure in which the true random nature of the input is beyond doubt. If one is a purist one can use a table of random numbers to select a page in a dictionary. The number of a word on that page (counting down the page) can also be obtained from the table of random numbers. With less trouble one can simply think of two numbers and find the word that way. Or throw some dice. What one must not do is to open a dictionary and go through the pages until one finds a likely looking word. That would be selection and it would be useless from a random stimulation point of view.

The numbers 473—13 were given by a table of random numbers and using the Penguin English Dictionary the word located was: 'noose'. The problem under consideration was 'the housing shortage'. Over a timed three minute period the following ideas were generated.

noose—tightening noose—execution—what are the difficulties in executing a housing programme—what is the bottleneck, is it capital, labour or land?
noose tightens—things are going to get worse with the present rate of population increase.
noose—rope—suspension construction system—tent like houses but made of permanent materials—easily packed and erected—or on a large scale with several houses suspended from one framework—much lighter materials possible if walls did not have to support themselves and the roof.
noose—loop—adjustable loop—what about adjustable round house which could be expanded as required—just uncoil the walls—no point in having houses too large to begin with because of heating problems, extra attention to walls and ceilings, furniture etc—but facility for slow stepwise expansion as need arises.
noose—snare—capture—capture a share of the labour market—capture—people captured by home ownership due to difficulty in selling and complications—lack of mobility—houses as exchangeable units—classified into types—direct exchange of one type for similar type—or put one type into the pool and take out a similar type elsewhere.

Random word stimulation is directly analogous to randomly selecting a page from Ching's *Architecture: Form • Space & Order* (1979), and beginning with the plan or section patterns you find there, or randomly selecting a page from a book on architectural ornament or a book of photographs of electron microscopy and working with the patterns you find there. Gyorgy Kepes (*The New Landscape in Art and Science,* 1956) makes the very interesting point that artists and designers, who once had direct access to all the visual stimulation of the world are no longer seeing the incredibly stimulating visual patterns that are available to scientists. Today there are privileged people peering into micro- and macro-worlds through powerful microscopes, telescopes and various other lenses, and we can only envy the random visual stimulation they enjoy.

If the problem is small in scale or scope, *stitch* drawings may quickly become the holistic *hitches* which synthesize entire solutions and anchor the rest of the design process. That kind of complete closure may still be premature, however, and one of the advantages of the deliberate piecemeal approach of programming is the suspended judgment it enforces by its careful consideration of as many aspects of the problem as possible.

The great virtue offered by programming is that the precept diagrams which correspond to the *stitches* in the present analogy begin to translate the verbal program statements into visual or graphic form. This initial translation and the visual verification of the precept is necessary if the final design is to fulfill the goals expressed by the precept. Neither the owner nor the designer can give guided tours through most environments when they are built, or except in rare cases, write guidebooks explaining the intricacies of the design. The designed environment will have to speak for itself and one of the ways to begin to test what it may say is to begin translating verbal programming ideas into precept diagrams.

To quote once again from Edward T. White's *Introduction to Architectural Programming:*

> The organization of data is the essential process for bridging the gap between the PROBLEM STATEMENT and the SYNTHETIC OPERATION that will result in a solution. It is the point where client needs and their relationships with the other facts gathered, analyzed and evaluated are TRANSLATED into the language of the designer.

> Needs and other facts at the gathering stage are largely VERBAL concepts. As architecture is a PHYSICAL (visual) expression of the solution to the problem statement it is of value to express as much of the program GRAPHICALLY and DIAGRAMMATICALLY as possible. This diagrammatic translation of the programming facts is the start of the formation of the physical building, as diagrams have DIRECT implications on physical building form.

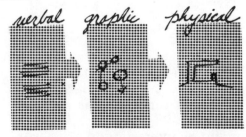

The programmer's ability to design visual, graphic communication of programming data will largely determine the extent to which all the programming NEEDS are met in synthesis.

Example organizational operations are:

1. SORTING and GROUPING of facts into categories based on qualities identified in analysis and according to criteria established by the programmer (sequence of use, relative importance).

2. Sorting and grouping of the EFFECTS on the design of individual building aspects implied by the program data.

3. Establishing a HIERARCHY of determinants which will direct the sequence and intensity of the designer's attention in synthesis.

4. Writing DEFINITIVE precepts describing individual conclusions about the data and proposals about what the final design should accomplish.

   a. Precepts should be SHORT, CONCISE, deal with only ONE issue at a time and be expressed GRAPHICALLY.

   b. Precepts should identify the UNIQUE-NESS of the problem. The extent to which general or "universal" precepts are written down and contained in the document depends on the PURPOSE of the document. OBVIOUS precepts may need to be included when EDUCATING the client.

   c. Precepts should deal with issues involving building SECTION and ELEVATION as well as plan. This will help to avoid the "extruded plan" difficulty.

   d. An important role of precepts is that of EVALUATORS of directions taken in the conceptualization stages of synthesis. By checking alternative design directions against the precepts, the development of INVIABLE concepts can be avoided. Precepts help SCREEN and EVALUATE design alternatives.

   Theoretically a comprehensive establishment of precepts at all levels of design synthesis (schematics, development) will result in a CONVERGENCE to the most viable solution to the problem. Hence, the statement, "the solution is contained in the statement of the problem."

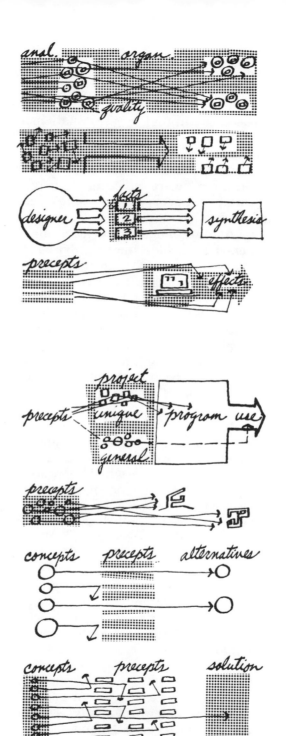

From *Introduction to Architectural Programming* by Edward T. White

e. The use of precepts can help identify POTENTIAL CONFLICTS in the design problem. This is most clearly illustrated when two precepts COMPETE for a response from a particular building aspect or element where a response to one EXCLUDES the possibility of responding to the other.

f. PATTERN LANGUAGE (Alexander) is closely related to the precept model. Essentially it proposes synthetic solutions to sub-problems which can be used in designing many different building types. The RESOLUTION of conflicts in the patterns and the SYNTHESIS of them into a whole is left to the DESIGNER.

5. Identifying the ALTERNATIVE CONCEPTS for the design of the building SUGGESTED by the precepts.

6. Putting all the analyzed, evaluated and organized data into USABLE form (presentation). This task has special implications where the program is to be published or where data is to be fed to a computer for sorting or grouping.

Most of the techniques which are recommended in the literature on creativity can be applied to environmental design, and most of them can be applied graphically, but their value in design drawing tends to be limited to the opening and clearing phases of the design process. When it comes time to begin *stitching* the design space together most experienced designers have little patience with analytical or analogical drawing. They will continue to use the analytical, analogical and manipulative techniques in their *eyeminds*, but what they draw will be sketchy doodles and diagrams based on the traditional representational drawings of their design disciplines. Unless they have deep blockages or hangups about externalizing their ideas in drawings, they begin to draw *stitches* which directly join parts of the problem to parts of the solution.

227

Stitch drawings are usually plans and sections because those two views of any designed environment show its internal relationships most abstractly and efficiently. These diagramatic plans and sections are usually followed closely, and at times may even be preceeded, by thumbnail exterior aerial perspectives which show the three-dimensional form of the design, and interior eyelevel perspectives which predict the experience of the environment when it is built. *Stitch* drawings also usually include sketches of relatively minor details and many verbal notes. Paul Laseau (*Graphic Thinking for Architects and Designers,* 1980) has summed up their characteristics:

1. There are many different ideas on one page; his attention is constantly shifting from one subject to another.
2. The way da Vinci looks at problems is diverse both in method and scale; there are often perspectives, plans, details, and panoramic views on the same page.
3. The thinking is exploratory, open-ended; the sketches are loose and fragmented, while showing how they were derived. Many alternatives for extending the ideas are suggested. The spectator is invited to participate.

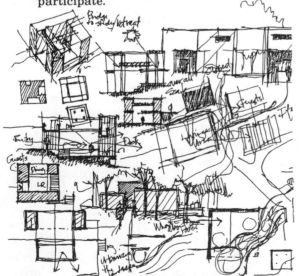

From GRAPHIC THINKING FOR ARCHITECTS AND DESIGNERS by Paul Laseau

Stitches have an undisciplined freedom to range over all our experience and knowledge—of the natural world, of the other arts and sciences, and all of human knowledge—anywhere we can find or make relationships to the problem we are trying to solve. *Stitch* drawings are characterized by wild variations and alterations of scale and focus, as if the designer were looking through a microscope / telescope / x-ray / time-machine of infinitely variable magnification and focal length. At one moment the focus may be lengthened to include the neighborhood, urban area or region, and the next be shortened to considerations of the shape and finish of the doorknobs. In addition to their range and flexibility, *stitch* drawings should have a certain ambiguity, low in specific information and capable of a variety of interpretations. This kind of drawing may be described as a kind of open expectant doodling, pregnant with possibilities.

A shift in the analogy we have been using may synthesize what I have to say about the *stitch* phase of the design process. If we lay the vertical design space which separates the problem from a solution down, horizontally, and fill it with water we have a river which separates one bank called the "problem" from another called the "solution." And if we bend the river we have substituted for the design space around a central castle we will have a moat. If we call the castle the "solutions" and the surrounding land the "problems," the designer's task becomes building ways of joining the problem to the solution by crossing the moat.

The conventional image of this analogy is that we assault the castle with the catapults of reason, the arrows of analysis, feigned withdrawals, and the whole range of methodical siege and assault weapons which we can marshall from the problem side of the moat.

The difficulty with this view of the analogy is that we have it backwards. We are on the other side of the moat, imprisoned in the castle of the solutions we know about. We designers do not march up to the moat from the land side to storm the castle—we are already its prisoners! We sally forth into problem-solving land across the drawbridges of our design abilities to relate the solutions we know about to the problems on the other side of the moat. And one of the longest and strongest drawbridges we can cross over on is drawing.

Analysis and programming may extend the abutment which the drawbridge has to reach or scatter stepping stones into the moat leading toward the castle, in the hope of reducing the creative leap to an easy step, but the moves which finally cross the moat (the *stitches* from the previous analogy) must come from the solution side, because that is where we live.

If we strip the analogy down to simply standing on an island of the solutions we know about, separated by a moat from the surrounding problem, we can summarize and illustrate the various *stitch* techniques we have been discussing:

- The analogies of *Synectics* broaden the solution island on which we are standing by adding *all* the solutions we know about, from any field of knowledge or experience.
- deBono's reversal method means doing an about face and viewing the problem shoreline 180° from the conventional view; his choice of entry point means deliberately examining through the 360° of problem shoreline for the most promising entry point; and his random stimulation means randomly probing the bottom of the moat in the hope of finding a ford that can be waded.
- The precepts of programming are stepping stones extending out into the moat from the problem shore.

All techniques are potentially helpful, but in all cases the first plunge into the moat must come from solutions we understand.

HITCH DRAWINGS

designed to anchor a particular solution to the problem by drawing various overall organizing concepts—establishing direction for the subsequent zipper.

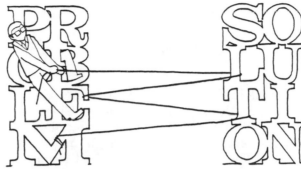

We have reached the most crucial and controversial point in the *stitches* and *zipper* analogy for the design process. Many of those who have written about creativity regard this as the moment of primary creativity—*the creative leap;* while many of those who have written about design method discount its importance, and some deny the need or even the desirability of any overall concept or big idea.

THE FORMAL IMPERATIVE

One point of confusion which needs clearing up is that, in the design professions, organizing concepts, those ideas which are capable of ordering the entire design and the remainder of the design process, must be visual, graphic or spatial. They must have a physical reality. They cannot be a verbal statement or a mathematical formula, which is secondarily translated into some three-dimensional form. While it is true that needs and wishes may initially be expressed verbally and be translated into graphic precept diagrams, or *stitch* drawings, the translation is the designer's responsibility—in all likelihood the reason he or she enjoys the activity—and the generation of a specific

physical form or pattern in response to any design problem is the core of design responsibility.

The recent denigration of "formalism" and "formgiving" is perhaps justified by the abuses of those designers who have littered our environment with strident, self-conscious, formal "statements." We probably don't need many more "form-givers." We have plenty of forms already, but we will always need sensitive designers to apply and recombine the rich formal heritage of the design professions.

Words and numbers may be necessary to the understanding of a problem and useful as description or rationalization, but they cannot be design ideas. *There is no such thing as a verbal design idea, only verbal descriptions of design ideas.* Organizing ideas in environmental design are formal patterns, not necessarily innovative, axial or even geometrically regular; but in order to have any ability to organize an environment they must have a memorable pattern *that can be drawn.*

Frank Ching's *Architecture: Form • Space & Order* (1979) is a beautiful collection of historic and contemporary organizing patterns for architecture. One brief look at the richness and variety of these organizing ideas makes it clear that we needn't strain to invent too many new patterns.

Tim White's *Concept Sourcebook • A Vocabulary of Architectural Forms* (1975) is another excellent source of more abstract, less traditional organizing ideas for buildings.

In the past, organizing concepts for additions to the built environment have lasted for centuries, with builders content to repeat the traditional way of building, constrained by an unquestioned cultural conformity and limited by material and technological necessity. The very notion that each problem should have an innovative solution is relatively new. It may be the product of our cultural and technological freedom, and the *raison d'etre* of the design professions, but it certainly is also one of the reasons for the visual chaos of our built environment.

Today's lack of cultural conformity and the technological freedom we enjoy necessitate an anchor point in the design process, however, whether we view it as an opportunity for radical creativity or merely as a deliberate choice of which formal vocabulary to follow. The formation or selection of such an overall organizing concept is also necessary for design teamwork, where a common goal must be clearly understood by several different people.

THE POPCORN ANALOGY

If you will permit me another simple-minded analogy, the individually conceived piecemeal closures of parts of the problem to parts of a solution—the *stitches*—can be thought of as individual popcorn kernels. Once a certain conceptual temperature has been reached such individual ideas can be popped off with relative ease. Undisciplined designers and their clients can soon be up to their knees in popcorn without any notion of how to organize the profusion of separate ideas.

Real popcorn can be strung, bagged or balled, and these three ways of organizing popcorn illustrate three kinds of organizing concepts. The popcorn string is an analogy for design method as an organizer, while bagging or balling popcorn are analogous to the kinds of organizing ideas sought for in *hitch* drawings.

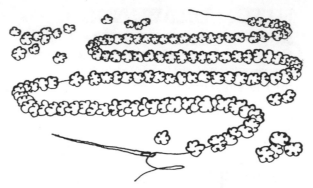

The stringing of individual kernels into a popcorn chain used in trimming Christmas trees is much like the serial string of operations recommended by design methodologists. The organization achieved is more a product of the linear logic of the method—the needle and thread—than of any overall compositional idea. The popcorn chain is not really an anchoring *hitch* in the process, but is an analogy for the whole process, with the design method being the organizer.

The collecting of selected popcorn kernels into a bag is analogous to the traditional exclusive notion of architectural unity. The bag unifies a certain set of ideas by taking them within an exclusive boundary. This kind of organizing idea uses the bag as a discriminatory boundary, concentrating on how the included individual ideas are superior to the excluded ideas, rather than how they are related to one another. This can be demonstrated by shaking the bag, which may drastically rearrange the internal relationships of the selected kernels without changing the outward appearance of the bag. Bags of popcorn are quantitative organizers because any such selective boundary has a limited capacity.

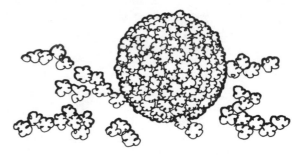

The making of popcorn balls is analogous to an inclusive way of organizing individual ideas. The unifying element in this case is the caramel or syrup, which can be thought of as an inner structure or affinity the ideas have for one another. This basis of inner integrity rather than an outer boundary sets no limit on the size of the resulting popcorn ball, and while the outward appearance changes with each additional kernel, the inner integrity remains. This kind of organizing idea is more qualitative than quantitative and inclusive rather than exclusive.

Traditionally, organizing concepts are based on characteristics of the problem or the various sub-concepts or *stitches,* not on any particular method or procedure. The *stitches* and *zipper* model of the design process assumes this traditional view.

Another difference in the description of this *hitch* or anchor point in the design process is whether such organizing concepts are, or should be, thought of as selected, discovered, revealed or made. (Discovered and revealed ideas were discussed earlier in the chapter on CONCEPTION. Selected ideas are a contribution of design method.)

The *selection* of an organizing idea presumes that the alternative ideas are known and broadly shared. If organizing ideas must be *discovered* the presumption is that, although they exist they must be searched for in unexpected places. *Revealed* ideas can only come in moments of inspiration, which may be hoped for but never acquired by direct effort. The *making* of organizing ideas may include a little of all the foregoing, but assumes that organizing ideas should be the result of an active synthesizing effort, unique to every problem, for which the designer is responsible.

Much of the testimony as to how creative ideas actually occur holds that they surface into our consciousness unbidden, at times when no direct effort is being made. This would seem most like the revealed or inspired view of creativity, but this may be misleading because the seemingly innocent occurrence of the idea comes only after periods of intensely concentrated conceptual effort and only to persons who have a certain mastery of the subject matter area.

The selecting or finding of organizing concepts also has a validity, in that there is a legacy of such ideas in the design disciplines which is endlessly mined and reinterpreted by successive generations of designers.

Whether organizing concepts are bags or balls, or whether they are selected, found, revealed or made, they can appear in the drawings we make when we are designing. There is nothing magical about their appearance, although one of the great advantages of drawing is that it legitimizes the participation of the unconscious, that great well of wisdom and experience which is normally closed off to verbal or mathematical inquiry.

To say that organizing ideas "appear" in our drawings is to say that if we have taken the trouble to build an extensive knowledge of such organizing patterns, so that we can recognize one when we see it; and if we habitually make exploratory drawings, patterns will indeed "appear."

To return to the self-model suggested in the chapter on CONCEPTION, there is no chance whatever of your recognizing a potential organizing pattern, even if it should happen to come out the end of your pen, unless the perception of a similar pattern is lodged somewhere in your experience. You'll never get it out if you didn't put it in.

You may never have consciously studied such a pattern. You may have walked it or seen it in a book, without ever having brought it to your conscious attention; but it must be a part of your conscious or unconscious experience if you are to have any hope of recognizing it when it "appears."

Such appearances are characterized by their holistic nature—their ability to take over whatever pattern we are working on, whether it be a plan, section or functional diagram. While we might have been considering only one aspect of the design task, the organizing concept allows or demands that we begin to work with the entire problem, as a whole. The comprehensive synthesis which is realized in the *hitch* drawings is always beneficial. Too often in design education there is only time for one of these syntheses in the days or hours before the deadline. The many details and relationships which appear for the first time in drawing up such a synthesis leave the designer an extensive list of unresolved problems to be worked out during the series of successive syntheses involved in the *zippering* phase which follows.

Those who have written about creativity characterize such moments as occurring when individuals suddenly see how the problem is like something normally not associated with it ("bisociation", Koestler 1964) and the experience is usually a profound conversion in their perception of the problem. Others believe that Koestler's "bisociation" and the examples he cites like Kekule's dream—discovery of the benzene ring (*The Act of Creation,* 1964) are too pat and simplistic. Howard Gruber (*Darwin On Man, A Psychological Study of Creativity,* 1974) believes the overall structure of the process is more important than the individual insights within it:

As for problem solving, it takes place in a diverse train of activities: reading and observation, imagination and memory, argument and discussion. For all we really know of it, focused problem solving may be a comparatively rare event. The very act of taking up a problem crystallizes a long history of development.

Given a problem-solving process, we may find reflection, sudden insights, and gradual improvement through trial and error. Even the groping trials are not blind or random: they emerge from the problem solver's perception of the structure of the problem as he has come to recognize and understand it from his own particular vantage point. Thus, the sudden insight in which a problem is solved, when it is solved suddenly, may represent only a minor nodal point, like the crest of a wave, in a long and very slow process—the development of a point of view.

Although it is presumptuous to compare the process of designing an environment to the development of Darwin's theory of evolution, which is what Gruber is referring to in the preceding quotation, most design processes have more in common with his description than with the examples in most of the literature on creativity. Examples from science seem to dominate most of what has been written about creativity, limiting creativity in what Kuhn (*The Structure of Scientific Revolutions,* 1962) calls "normal science" to *concept attainment.* The *concept formation* of environmental design is complicated by several characteristics which are fundamentally different from what Kuhn calls the "puzzle-solving" of normal science:

- There are no fixed, verifiable answers to the problems of environmental design as there are in science.
- There is not even agreement as to what the problems are, or which problems should be solved, as there is in science.
- Unlike science, both the definition of the problems and forms of the solution must be synthesized and will remain openly arguable: and the congruence of a problem and a solution should reflect a consensus of all those involved in the process, toward which the designer must persuade.
- Unlike science, quantification, mathematics, reason and logic are only one set of the tools needed in achieving and defending the congruence of a problem and a solution.
- Unlike science, environmental design always occurs within the real constraints of time and money. The design process is committed to deadlines and budgets which must be met. There is no possibility of *not* solving the problem.

In the design process of mature designers the *hitch* occurs most often as the recognition of

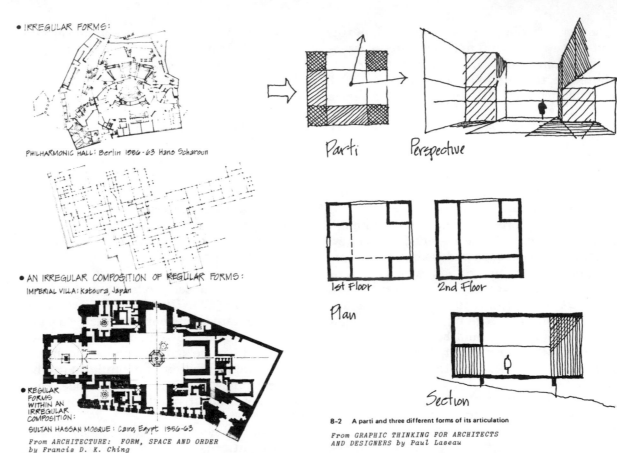

● IRREGULAR FORMS:

PHILHARMONIC HALL: Berlin 1956-63 Hans Scharoun

● AN IRREGULAR COMPOSITION OF REGULAR FORMS:
IMPERIAL VILLA: Katsura, Japan

● REGULAR FORMS WITHIN AN IRREGULAR COMPOSITION:
SULTAN HASSAN MOSQUE: Cairo, Egypt 1356-63

From ARCHITECTURE: FORM, SPACE AND ORDER
by Francis D. K. Ching

Parti   Perspective

1st Floor   2nd Floor

Plan

Section

8-2   A parti and three different forms of its articulation

From GRAPHIC THINKING FOR ARCHITECTS
AND DESIGNERS by Paul Laseau

a pattern or potential pattern—a potential congruence with a pattern that is part of our conscious or unconscious experience. Unfortunately beginning design students are often asked to produce environmental designs with little or no introduction or exposure to the amazingly rich and stimulating heritage of patterns with which other designers have already ordered parts of the built environment. This practice suggests that one of the major tasks of environmental design is to invent its organizing patterns from scratch, in response to each new problem.

The cataloguing of these patterns has been traditionally the province of historians and critics who have revealed the collection

chronologically in history courses or stacked the deck of examples to rationalize some particular theory. *Architecture: Form • Space & Order* (1979), by Francis D.K. Ching is a refreshingly different kind of collection of these organizing patterns. The examples range over all of history, including buildings as recent as 1978, and all over the world, including hemispheres and cultures often ignored by the bias of many architectural histories; the collection is also categorized on a neutral abstract basis in several ways which directly emphasize the formal patterns involved; and the entire book is *drawn* which makes the patterns much more usable to the design student because they are presented in the same medium which the student will be using in the design process.

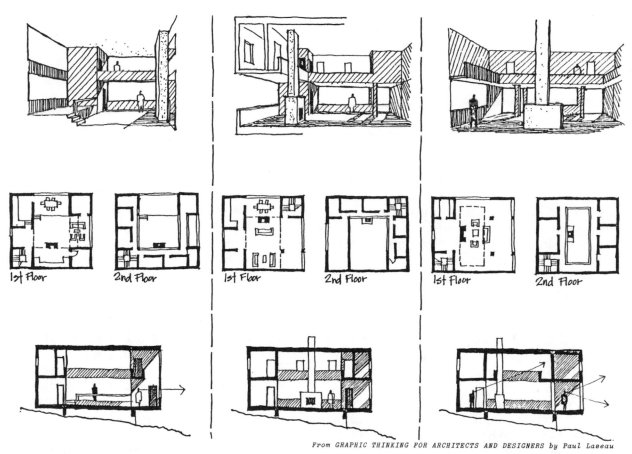

1st Floor   2nd Floor   1st Floor   2nd Floor   1st Floor   2nd Floor

From GRAPHIC THINKING FOR ARCHITECTS AND DESIGNERS by Paul Laseau

ceptual patterns: *the commitment of the designer and the remainder of the design process.* This commitment is evidence of the inner congruence between the organizing concept and the designer's goals, wishes and hunches described in the chapter on CONCEPTION, and may occur in the face of the initial resistance and rejection of other participants in the process. The organizing idea gives meaning to such criteria as integrity and consistency, and allows a sorting of the accumulation of piecemeal ideas that may have preceded it. All ideas may now be seen as supporting or diluting the main organizing idea.

The commitment of the designer to a particular organizing concept is an exercise of free will. There is nothing "natural" or "necessary" about any of this and the commitment to a design concept is simply another of those existential choices made "in fear and trembling." Design is always to some degree the imposition of the designer's will on the environment, and in mature designers the range of organizing ideas is usually severely prescribed by certain formal prejudices they have developed over the years.

In addition to the holistic, yet incomplete, character of such organizing ideas, and the designer's commitment to them, perhaps their most surprising characteristic is that the *recognition, the testing and the commitment are usually preverbal.* The profound conversion of the perception of the problem, the intense preliminary working out and testing of the idea and the complete commitment may occur in the absence of any verbalized rationale. The potential of *hitch* ideas are sensed in that covert, inner congruence discussed earlier in the chapter on CONCEPTION. The quality or correctness of the organizing idea is seen or felt, not reasoned.

When such a potential pattern is sensed, drawing *becomes* the design process, because there is now a sensed goal or direction and the drawings are immediately manipulated to see if the congruence can be accomplished—to see if the pattern can be realized.

This need to be confirmed or worked out gives us the second characteristic of the anchoring *hitches* in the design process: *they are never completely resolved at the moment of recognition.* They are only recognized potentials— a betting on the come—and they usually provoke intense design activity. The activity provoked by such potential pattern recognition always includes a certain testing of this crucial *hitch* which will anchor the rest of the

design process. Like testing the security of a knot you've just tied by tugging at it, or setting the hook after a fishing strike, the organizing concept must be tested in two ways: as an object, and as an environment.

A quick turning of the idea through the orthographic drawings (plan, section and elevation), will evaluate its integrity as a built object, but the testing must include eyelevel perspectives if the environmental experience of the concept is to be measured. Paul Laseau's *Graphic Thinking for Architects and Designers* (1980) offers several excellent examples of this kind of testing.

If the organizing pattern passes these tests, it achieves a third characteristic of such con-

233

Hitch drawings signal a profound change in design activity. Instead of the random, aimless wandering of the previous *stitching* phase, there is now an established direction, a sensed goal. The difference can be dramatically illustrated by the word association games that can be played around a table. If the game is begun with a word and the only criterion is to name a new word which has a relationship to the initial or previous word, there will be an interesting progression of associations. Succeeding players can move up to more generic categories, down to subcategories or sideways to siblings or opposites. The relationships may be imaginative or dull as they move over the hierarchy of verbal meanings we share, but their movement will be a directionless odyssey much like the *stitches* of the previous phase. If the rules of the word game are changed, however, so that two words are given, an initial word and a goal word, with the objective being to build a series of transitional words which "get to" the goal word, the whole character of the game changes. With just a little practice, the goal word can be reached with only a few or even a single transitional word.

The anchoring *hitch* in any design process always includes a sensed direction. Unlike the analogy of the word game, the direction is not a fixed destination. The goal is only generally sensed, it is never a direct copy of an existing solution. The direction established for the *zipper* which will close the problem to a solution may be better understood as a set of "rules of the road" which are included with any proper *hitch*. Interestingly, these rules can be read in the designed environment after it is built. It is as if the designer wrote the rules and then played the game according to those rules, for all to see. The built design stands not just as the product of some mysterious process, but to the trained perception of

critics and other designers, as the record of a design process.

Once the anchoring *hitch* for a potential solution is secure and the designer begins to represent and evaluate the various forms the solution might take, the most useful drawings will be suggested by the solution itself. If the concept is to provide any particular kind of spatial or kinesthetic experience, then the representative drawings must be eyelevel perspectives. Concepts which are based on some desired relationship to the physical context must be represented in perspectives of that context if their success or failure is to be evaluated. Concepts which are based on particular relationships to the human figure might be best represented in sections which show those relationships. Any design solution is best studied and evaluated with those drawings which best show the success or failure of its conceptual basis. Sometimes the concept is, indeed, primarily a plan concept, and the conventional order of drawings has the best relationship to the design synthesis. To always follow the conventional order of drawings, however, will in time narrow designers' conceptual range to plan concepts, or mislead them into believing they can adequately evaluate, in plan, concepts which have their basis and best representation in other drawings. Preoccupation with plans will limit functional articulations to *horizontal* separations—like sorting nails, when the best way to sort the functions may be *vertically*.

Wherever the design synthesis begins and whatever drawings the designer uses to represent its first stages, the playback potential must be judged at the level of human experience. This means that as quickly as possible the synthesis must reach a stage where this playback of the designer's inten-

tion can be tested with eyelevel perspectives which show the experiential qualities of the design. Experienced designers reach this stage within hours or minutes of the first conceptual synthesis. As soon as the concept is externalized in some graphic form or pattern, there is an irresistible compulsion to test "What it will look like" in reality. Inexperienced designers or those who have difficulty drawing perspectives, often deliberately avoid this experiential testing. They may be offended by their own drawing ability or they may have come to dread this phase because of their ability relative to some of their peers who draw better.

Design teachers often find it more stimulating to spend their time talking to those students who can, confidently and quickly, roll the representational drawing wheel through all the drawings. The design is more real for both student and teacher and it is exciting to talk about new directions or subtle changes in the direction of the rolling wheel. I believe the more basic responsibility of the design teacher is to help the student pump up the flat places on the wheel so the student can confidently roll it through all the representational drawings. If the student does not draw sections well, or avoids perspectives, the teacher's time should be spent helping correct that inability. Eventually the choice of direction for the rolling of the wheel should be, and will be, the student's; and the responsible teacher will spend as much time lubricating and balancing the wheel as in heady discussions as to where it should roll.

There is seldom only a single *hitch* in any design process. There are usually several false *hitches*, each of which at its moment of conception seems uniquely promising. The unsuccessful *hitches* may be abandoned for several reasons: some of them will be rejected by clients or others involved in the process; part way down the *zipper* some will appear dull, simplistic, naive or inappropriate; others will be beyond the designer's *zippering* capability at the moment, and will be reluctantly put aside for use in some future process.

One of the hallmarks of designers is their regenerative ability to come up with *hitch* after *hitch,* with equal enthusiasm and optimism, sure that *this* one will be the answer. The primary creativity involved in synthesizing the ideas which are capable of organizing the solution to a complex design problem is essential, but no more important than the so-called "secondary" creativity required to follow the rules established by that anchoring *hitch* in the *zippering* which must close out the design process.

ZIPPER DRAWINGS

designed to test, develop and rationalize the best final form for the solution—integration of the solution in the established direction.

After the commitment to any organizational idea, that idea must be fleshed out and made to work. This kind of activity is normally defined as *secondary* creativity, but the abilities involved require great experience and craftsmanlike skill, and are, of all the designer's abilities, perhaps the most difficult to acquire. Beginning designers can often come up with ideas for solutions which have great potential, but they botch, dilute or abandon these ideas because they can't work them out.

Abraham Maslow in *The Farther Reaches of Human Nature* (1971), describes the danger of overlooking the ability needed in this phase of the process as:

> . . . a tendency to deify the one side of the creative process, the enthusiastic, the great insight, the illumination, the good idea, the moment in the middle of the night when you get the great inspiration, and of underplaying the two years of hard and sweaty labor that then are necessary to make anything useful out of the bright idea.

> In simple terms of time, bright ideas really take a small proportion of our time. Most of our time is spent on hard work. My impression is that our students don't know this. . . .

One of the romantic myths which clings persistently to design is that good designs evolve naturally and inevitably, with elements effortlessly falling into place and relating to one another in an utterly convincing way. We are taught to abhor designs which leave any indication of having been forced or contrived. While it may be true that good designs look natural and inevitable, and seldom seem forced or contrived, they are often the products of massive willful manipulation by some of the cleverest of forcers and contrivers. It is the skill with which it is done that makes all the difference.

The skill involved in working out the potential which is promised in the *hitching* we have just discussed is misleadingly glossed over in most of the writing about problem-solving and creativity and misunderstood by beginning designers. The secondary creativity involved in working out a design is seldom described because it is completely different for each field or discipline and its intricacies would fill several books. The skills involved must be learned "on the job" because when they are separated from the real context in which they are applied they lose their meaning. It is also much more interesting to write about the excitement of generating creative ideas and most authors wisely avoid boring their readers with descriptions of the tedious push and pull and give and take involved in getting those creative ideas to work, long after the flush of excitement from their generation has faded. The involvement and commitment required to value, and even be stimulated by, this working out of ideas can only come with years of experience and deeper levels of understanding. Perhaps the conceptual framework of this *zipper* phase can be outlined, however, without being superficially misleading or overly boring.

235

OVERLAID REFINEMENT

Much has been made over the potential of using computer graphics in the design process. The computer is a marvelous tool for repetitive tasks like education or for the analytical or computational tasks involved in material takeoffs or heat loss calculations, but at the present state of the art the invention of computers and their contribution to the design process can't compare with the development and usefulness of tracing paper! Simple, ordinary buff tracing paper allows a designer to compare alternate designs directly and simultaneously and improve the later one in relation to the earlier one. The ability to overlay design drawings is an incredible design tool. Wouldn't it be nice, for instance, to overlay your life, or your face and tinker with it just a little? You can always lift the overlay if it goes awry and leave the base drawing unaltered. Overlays are "play-like" as children say, "Let's play like...." The act itself is tentative imagining—not yet for real—what if??? The tentativeness, the relatedness, and the involvement of the *eye-mindhand* could hardly be a more appropriate symbol for the design process.

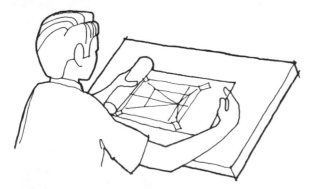

In many ways design begins when the beginning student picks up that first roll of buff tracing paper and overlays a drawing. The essence of the design process is the hopeful, expectant pursuit of a better idea which seems sure to be unrolled with the next over-lay. One of the ways you can tell the *zipper* of the design process is working is that the solution represented in the *zipper* drawings begins to change with each overlay.

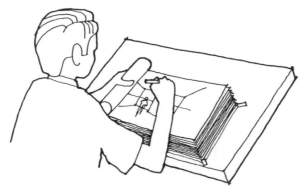

Designers should learn to visualize any design drawing, not as a single drawing, but as a potential stack of drawings progressing from a very crude sketch at the bottom to a very slick, detailed rendering at the top layer. When you have the disciplined ability to raise any rough sketch to these various levels, drawing becomes a matter of free choice, depending on the purpose of the drawing and the time available.

It takes awhile to develop the skill and confidence to refine a rough sketch and know where you're going with it ... and it's always tempting to try to make a drawing halfway up the stack without the supporting underlays. The drawing and placement of figures, trees and shadows always needs the benefit of overlaid refinement.

One of the mistakes many architectural graduates make is to fill the portfolios of their work which they take along to show prospective employers with laborious renderings. Most practicing professionals expect that graduate architects, landscape architects and interior designers, given *unlimited* time, will be able to make beautiful drawings. What these prospective employers may be very much more interested in is the kind of drawings their apprenticing professionals can make in *limited* time. Employers are usually comforted by the appearance of a few rough sketches in any prospective employees' portfolios as evidence that they can draw more ways than slowly.

At some time during the *zipper* phase of the design process most designers experience what has been called "analogue takeover," a phenomenon by which the representational drawings, which are analogues for the developing solution, *become* the design solution. This analogue takeover happens earlier with complex projects because their complexity cannot be held whole in the mind. In order to work on the whole problem and its interrelationships the designer must literally go where the drawings are. The only way to work with the solution to the problem after this point is to work with the representative drawings which have become the solution.

This is necessary because at home, after dinner, over coffee, in those relaxed moments when creative insights often occur, the designer simply cannot remember the relationships between the structural framing, the ductwork and the necessary clearances at a particular point in the building. This explains the habit many designers have of hanging up the representative drawings of a project all around their drawing board and spending hours seemingly lost in the contemplation of these drawings.

In spite of firm anchoring *hitches* and skillful *zippering* the precise direction and destination of any design process is unpredictable. In a sense the analogue takes over, the design becomes a separate part of Popper's World 3 (the products of minds) and strong enough to deflect the direction and affect the destination of the process. Although many designers have trouble accepting Louis Kahn's idea of a building's "existence will" or its "wanting to be," most anticipate and welcome shifts in the direction of any design process. In addition to shifts caused by the evolving concepts of the design itself there will be other shifts caused by unforeseen changes in the client's, the user's, the code's, or the lender's requirements which will affect the process and must be responded to. Confident designers *manage* these shifts rather than fight them, and their attitude is summed up by Abraham Maslow in *The Farther Reaches of Human Nature* (1971):

...a new kind of human being who is comfortable with change, who enjoys change, who is able to improvise, who is able to face with confidence, strength, and courage a situation of which he has absolutely no forewarning.

...what I'm talking about is the job of trying to make ourselves over into people who don't need to staticize the world, who don't need to freeze it and make it stable, who don't need to do what their daddies did, who are able confidently to face tomorrow not knowing what's going to come, not knowing what will happen, with confidence enough in ourselves that we will be able to improvise in that situation which has never existed before. This means a new type of human being. Heraclitian, you might call him. The society which can turn out such people will survive; the societies that *cannot* turn out such people will die.

THE SYSTEMS AND THEIR RELATIONSHIPS

The built environment is conventionally thought of as being made up of several subsystems which must be designed and related to one another. Most design environments include:

- Functional systems
- Spatial systems
- Enclosure systems
- Structural systems (may not be a concern of landscape architects or interior designers)
- Active environmental control systems (may not be a concern of landscape architects or interior designers)

and relationships to larger contextual systems such as:

- climate
- topography
- circulation systems serving the site
- neighboring built environment

The relationships which must be established between each of these subsystems is best understood as lying somewhere on the unity/diversity continuum we discussed in the chapter on CONCEPTION. We can perhaps state this more simply as the sameness or difference of the various systems. They may be virtually identical or tightly integrated, or they may be separated in such a way that their distinction has a meaning:

and each of these will have its own subsystems:

enclosure systems, for instance, will include:

- passive environmental control systems (waterproofing, heating, cooling, lighting)
- visual access systems (views in and out)
- physical access systems (entries, exits, service)
- materials systems (choices of building materials and their relationships)

The most typical sameness is that of the functional system and the spatial system. We usually articulate our environments functionally (dining, kitchen, etc.), but this is not always consistent. For instance, family room and living room are not so much clear functional distinctions as they are behavioral or cultural conventions concerned with intimacy and formality. We may eat, drink, read, converse, listen to music or watch TV in either space. The distinction is based more on with whom we do these things and at what times or occasions.

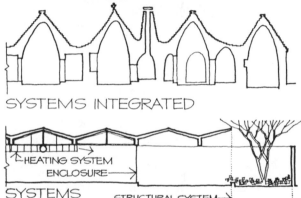

SYSTEMS INTEGRATED

SYSTEMS ARTICULATED

HEATING SYSTEM
ENCLOSURE
STRUCTURAL SYSTEM
SPATIAL SYSTEM

Difference in the systems often becomes apparent in the relation between the spatial system, the structural system and the enclosure system. They may have the satisfying match of the Trulli of Albarabello in which the spatial unit *is* the structural unit *and* the enclosure system. More often with the economy of today's structural spans the structural system is equated with the overall enclosure system, and the spatial system is a subdivision, a partitioning off, within this larger envelope. And in some buildings all three systems are different, with the structural system extending beyond the enclosure system and the spatial system sometimes extending with it to include exterior spaces and sometimes remaining as subdivisions within the enclosure system.

The active environmental control system may be integrated with the enclosure system in the form of automatically operated vents and louvers, or wall-integrated air conditioning units or mechanical ducts or chases. Alternately, it may be integrated with the spatial system in the form of individual room window air-conditioning units or fan-coil units above the ceiling. The mechanical system is also often tied to the functional system by following the distribution pattern of human circulation through the corridor system of a building. And, last of all, the environmental control system may express itself in an independent pattern of its own, in color-coded clarity.

These subsystems are potentially equivalent and competing siblings which make up the part of the larger environmental hierarchy which is being designed. A major part of the working out, the *zippering*, of any design is the establishment of the relationships among and within these subsystems. The relationships which the designer establishes may make the subsystems tightly integrated, distinctly separated or deliberately ambiguous.

The question of whether various parts of the built environment should be treated as being the same or as being different can be applied to virtually everything which is considered in the design process. Should the windows be made like the doors or expressed as being different? How are they the same (both openings in walls) and how are they different (one is for physical access, the other for light, ventilation and visual access) and to what extent can they be made alike or different? One curious application of this sameness/difference game is that the door hardware finish on the insides of toilet rooms is usually chrome, so that it matches the chrome of the toilet fixtures, rather than the bronze or brass of the

other hardware in the building. This distinction at least respects the integrity of the spaces separated by the door rather than the integrity of the door as an object.

OTHER SYSTEMS

Environmental designers traditionally make drawings which generate, test, and refine the relationships among what are conventionally considered to be the subsystems of whatever they are designing. The drawings with which they represent and study the relationships are biased towards the hardware of walls, columns, floors, roofs and beams while the software—the spaces and especially what happens in the spaces in terms of human movement and interaction, light, air circulation, etc., remains undrawn, unseen and largely unimagined. Environmental psychologists nag at us because our spaces prohibit or inhibit the human behavior they were designed for, yet this fault never appears in the drawings we make. Anything we mean to consider in the design process must be given graphic form, so that it is at least as well understood and habitually used as, say, a framing plan or a reflected ceiling plan. The design process consists of making and evaluating analogues for the congruence of the design problem and a design solution and if we don't represent and show ourselves certain relationships we literally never "see the problem." One of the responses to this failure from the methodological critics of design seems to be to talk us out of our drawings, but after some initial successes, that effort, thankfully, seems to be failing. The better solution would be to find a way to represent those concerns in the drawings by codifying the various unseen systems so they can be represented, evaluated and improved by manipulation in relation to the other systems which are graphically, visually *and therefore conceptually* in the process.

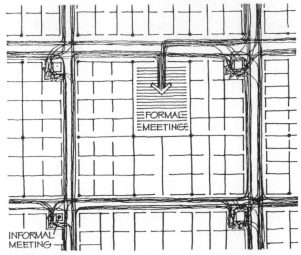

As an example of how the "behavioral system" might relate to the other systems—in most environments there are at least two kinds of meeting or gathering: one kind is the regular, formal kind that occurs at mealtimes, staff meetings, or seminars; the second kind is the informal, random, coincidental meetings of people whose "paths seldom cross." Both these kinds of meeting or gathering can be related to the enclosure system in the way such spaces are lighted, in the way they are textured or colored, or in what exterior views are provided from there. The formal meeting places might be distinguished by precisely matching the structural system at that point so that they occupied an even multiple of the structural bay and the structural spatial congruence could be revealed at that point by exposing the structure. The informal meetings that occur at crossings of the circulation system could be recognized and encouraged by responding with the spatial and enclosure system at those points in providing special spaces in which to extend the interactions and conversations that might develop from those meetings. These chance meetings could be further enhanced by an integration with the functional system by locating bulletin boards or mailboxes at those points.

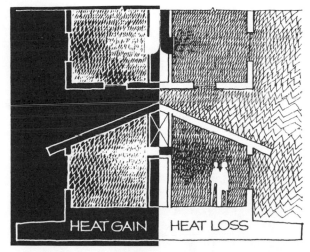

HEAT GAIN   HEAT LOSS

Energy conservation, with which we are all correctly concerned these days, is another of those unseen systems in the graphics with which we *zipper* the problem to a solution. When we draw the enclosure system certain characteristics concerned with energy conservation appear, but we must know what to look for, and we must know whether it is winter, spring, summer or fall. We do not have a comprehensive graphic system which shows the integration of the active and passive environmental control systems. Because of this, energy conservation is much more difficult to understand or "see" holistically in the conventional *zipper* drawings as compared to, say, the structural system, and therefore almost impossible to teach beginning designers.

The sameness/difference game, and many others, must be worked out during the *zipper* phase of the process while keeping the original goal that was foreseen in the *hitch* phase steadfastly in mind. The other burden which must be pulled along by the *zipper* is the logical verbal explanation which rationalizes the congruence between the problem and the particular solution. In addition to the clients, this rationale must now be clearly understood by consulting engineers, draftspersons,

and the expanding circle of user groups, building officials, mortgage lenders, and people who become involved in the *zipper* phase of the design process.

Most designers, after a few private trial tugs at the *hitch* with which they propose to anchor and set the direction for the *zipper,* seek approval of their clients, users and collaborators before entering the *zipper* phase of the process. Such consensus aproval of the anchoring *hitch* usually includes its initial logic, and successive presentations to clients, users and others whose understanding and approval are needed, must include a verbal explanation which is an extension of that initial logic. Many beginning students, after a brief exposure to open design reviews, conclude that success in having your design accepted is based on the eloquence of its verbal rationale. My perception of these moments in school and in practice is quite different. The rationale must be there, but the design's acceptance is more often based on the design itself as communicated in drawings and representative models; and after that, on the designer's commitment to and enthusiasm for the design and its rationale, often rather awkwardly or haltingly expressed in words. The sincerity of the commitment to a design, expressed most directly in the design itself, is usually more convincing than clever verbal salesmanship.

Zipper drawings are what the AIA description of services calls Design Development drawings. They are not yet rigid, drafted, working drawings—the construction patterns from which the design will be built. *Zipper* drawings are still design drawings and they are still exploratory, but disciplined now by a particular organizing idea. Their goal is to examine and resolve all the problematic relationships in the design—the trade-offs and compromises that must be

made between conflicting design criteria and budgets and building codes.

Because the goal of the *zipper* phase of the process must be to complete the joining of the problem to a particular solution, and its supporting rationale, one of the most helpful strategies is to repeatedly synthesize the whole design. The time has passed for piecemeal relationships, however elegant. The designer's attention space must expand to encompass the design as a whole, and oscillate frequently and evenly among the various parts. This means that *all* the drawings must be drawn and redrawn, *as a set,* so that the synthesis is kept continually current. The nauseously overworked phrase "getting it all together" describes these syntheses very well and the traditional "charettes" that precede such deadlines beneficially focus the attention of everyone involved in the process. Both creative and critical powers are heightened by the intense concentration involved, and the more of these conceptual closures that can be achieved in any process, the better.

While I spent a great deal of time, earlier, in knocking the conventional orthographic plans, sections and elevations as representations of reality or environmental experience, in this part of the process the orthographic drawings are indispensable. With the goal and its direction established by the previous anchoring *hitch,* the integrity, consistency and clarity of the design as a whole (as an object, if it is a building) can be tested with plans, sections and elevations. Although the experience of the environment will still need to be tested occasionally with eyelevel perspectives, and the three-dimensional quality of certain corners, joints and transitions will need to be studied in thumbnail perspective sketches, the patterns involved in this phase of the process are best seen and manipulated in the orthographic drawings.

CONVENTIONAL PLANS AND SECTIONS

Since the primary representational drawings of the *zipper* phase are plans, sections and, secondarily, elevations we should take a moment to understand the basis of these orthographic abstractions and how they are conventionally drawn.

Plan and section drawings show what would be seen if you cut through buildings or environments horizontally or vertically and removed the part of the building above or in front of the slice. These views also assume that we can look at the remaining building with a very large eye so that those lines and planes which would be perpendicular to the plane of the slice do not converge toward the single central vanishing point of a one-point perspective (as they would in reality) but can be seen as all being perpendicular to the axis of our vision. Perhaps a simpler way of describing this last phenomenon is to imagine that after the top of a building is cut away in a plan view, or the front of a building is cut away in a section view, we put the remaining building in some sort of giant press and compress it into a paper thin wafer. In a floor plan, the walls, kitchen counters, and furniture would all be mashed flat into the floor and drawn as if they were simply a pattern in the linoleum. A section would be similarly compressed into the back wall and any wall cabinets or furniture would be drawn as if they were so much patterned wallpaper on that wall.

LINE WEIGHT INDICATIONS

Those various parts of the building which are thus compressed are fundamentally different from one another and the drawing of them must somehow tell what they were before the compression. This indication of difference is made by the kind of line with which we represent them.

SPATIAL BOUNDARIES

The most important lines in any plan or section are the boundaries of the spaces which are cut through in removing the part of the building which allows the view. These lines indicate the boundaries of the volumes which make up any environment. The surfaces may also be thought of as walls, ceilings and floors, but it is much more sophisticated to conceive of them as the surfaces of the spatial volumes, the rooms or spaces of any environment—the surface of the living room, rather than the living room side of the wall dividing the living room from the entry. The importance of these lines is always indicated by their being the heaviest or thickest of all lines.

Sometimes plans are sections drawn in such a way that the walls, floors or roof structure appear as solid black. This is a much less sophisticated indication than those which indicate any wall, floor, or roof as consisting of two spatial boundaries, with an in-filling poché which indicates a thickness of separating material.

OBJECT OUTLINES

The next most important lines, and the next heaviest weighted lines, are those which indicate the outline of objects within the space of a plan or section which, before the compression described earlier, were positioned above the floor (in the floor plan) or in front of the back wall (in the section). These might be **attached counters, platforms or steps, or detached articles of furniture. Care should be** taken to indicate whether they are attached or not. The outline of a detached piece of furniture like a bed or table should be complete, and separate from the spatial boundary indicated by the line of a wall. Even a refrigerator has space behind it (as anyone who has cleaned behind one will discover), and its outline should not die into the wall line like that of a counter top or bathtub.

OBJECT DETAILS

Next in importance and line weight comes the set of lines which indicate details of an object lying *within* its outline. This kind of line would include the burners on a stove or the depressed bowl of a lavatory seen in plan, or the recessed panels of a door seen in elevation.

SURFACE LINES

The lightest lines are those which carry no spatial information, which just lie on the horizontal surfaces of a plan or the vertical surfaces of a section. This kind of line would include tile joints or other surface textural indications such as wood grain or carpet.

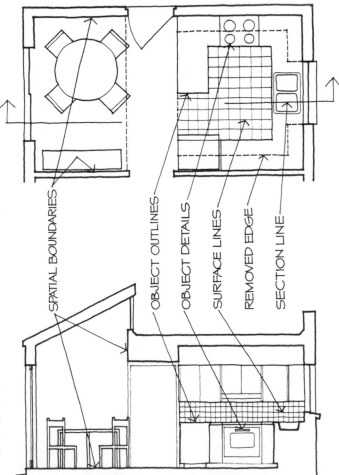

HIDDEN EDGE LINES and REMOVED EDGE LINES

There are two other kinds of lines which are sometimes shown and sometimes not shown according to traditional practice. Hidden edge lines are those which occur beneath or beyond the plane at which we are looking in a plan or section. In traditional practice these are only sometimes indicated, as in the hidden edges of footings beneath a working drawing foundation plan or the finished floor or ceiling lines beyond a working drawing section or elevation. Neither of these indications, especially the footing edges, are useful in design drawings.

Removed edge lines are those which occur in the part of the building which has been removed to take the plan or section. Of these, only the ones in plans are ever drawn, even in working drawings. The removed edges which are critical in plans are those which indicate the edges of overhanging planes, like roofs, balconies and upper cabinets. Both hidden edge lines and removed edge lines are indicated as dashed or dotted lines of the same medium weight as real edge lines.

SECTION LINES

The last kind of lines are those which aren't actually present in the environment at all but are abstractions which help the viewer understand and relate the drawings. The most important of these are the section lines which indicate where the sections are cut through the plan. These lines may also be used to mark where the plans are cut through the sections or elevations, but they are normally cut at such a standard height (somewhere between 4'-5' going above countertops, below upper cabinets and through all doors and windows) that there is no need to indicate their position.

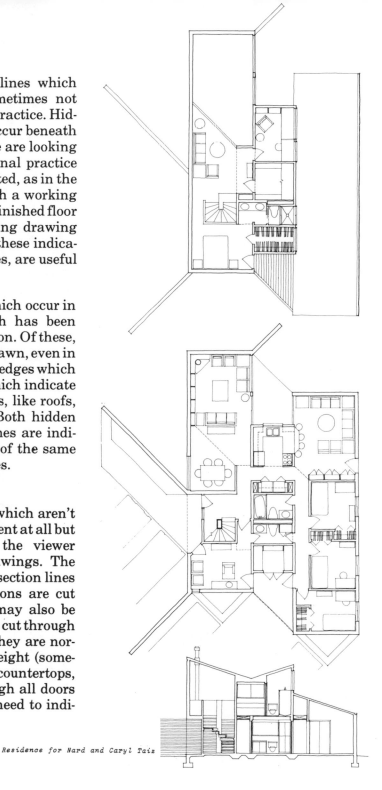

Residence for Nard and Caryl Taiz

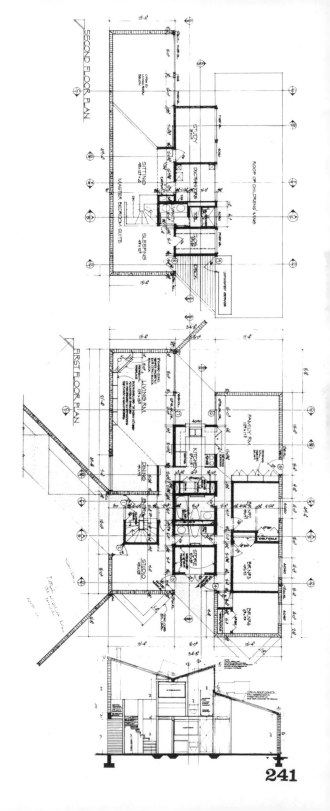

241

The crucial difference between *design drawings* and *construction drawings* can be seen clearly by comparing the drawings on the preceding page:

- *Construction drawings* describe the exact location, configuration, dimensions and inner physical structure and consistency of the *stuff* of which the walls, the floor and the roof are made.
- *Design drawings* describe the relative location, configuration, adequacy for human function and the pattern of interrelationships of the spaces which are formed within the walls, the floor and the roof.

The emphasis of *construction drawings* is on the *solids*, while the emphasis of *design drawings* is on the *voids*.

NON-CONVENTIONAL PLANS AND SECTIONS

We need to expand our use of plans and sections. I have already suggested a functional color code which would be helpful in understanding and organizing the patterns of use and circulation in any environment; and I have suggested a set of graphic conventions that might codify the behavior patterns we wish to encourage or inhibit. These two, at least could be made a part of our standard set of *zipper* drawings, so that we might require students in design schools to include a color-coded functional plan or a behavioral plan or section, just as we require other *zipper* drawings.

There will always be room beyond the standard set of drawings, however, even if we are able to expand the set, for innovative plans and sections which show qualities and relationships that are not normally drawn, or seen or thought of. The use of drawing in the design process offers at least as much potential for creativity as the design problem itself.

242

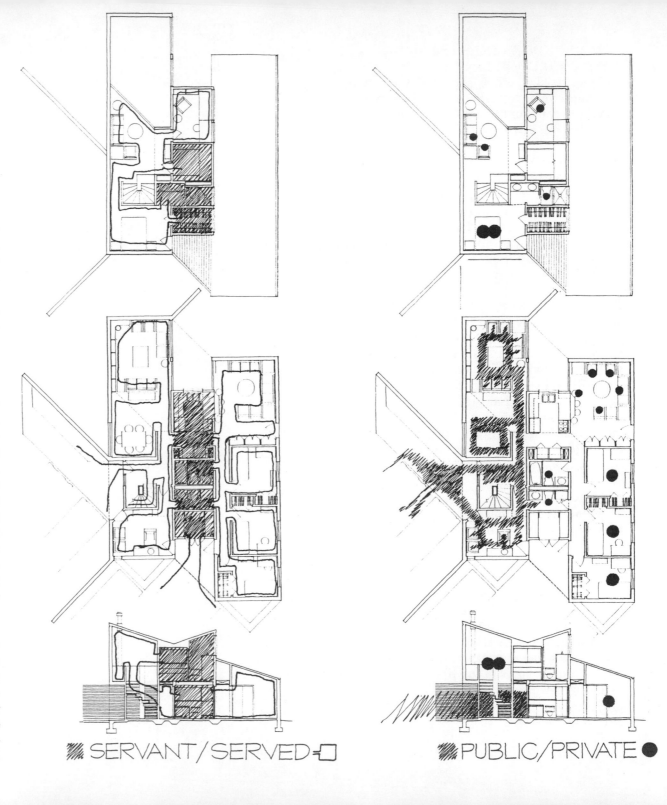

SERVANT / SERVED

PUBLIC / PRIVATE

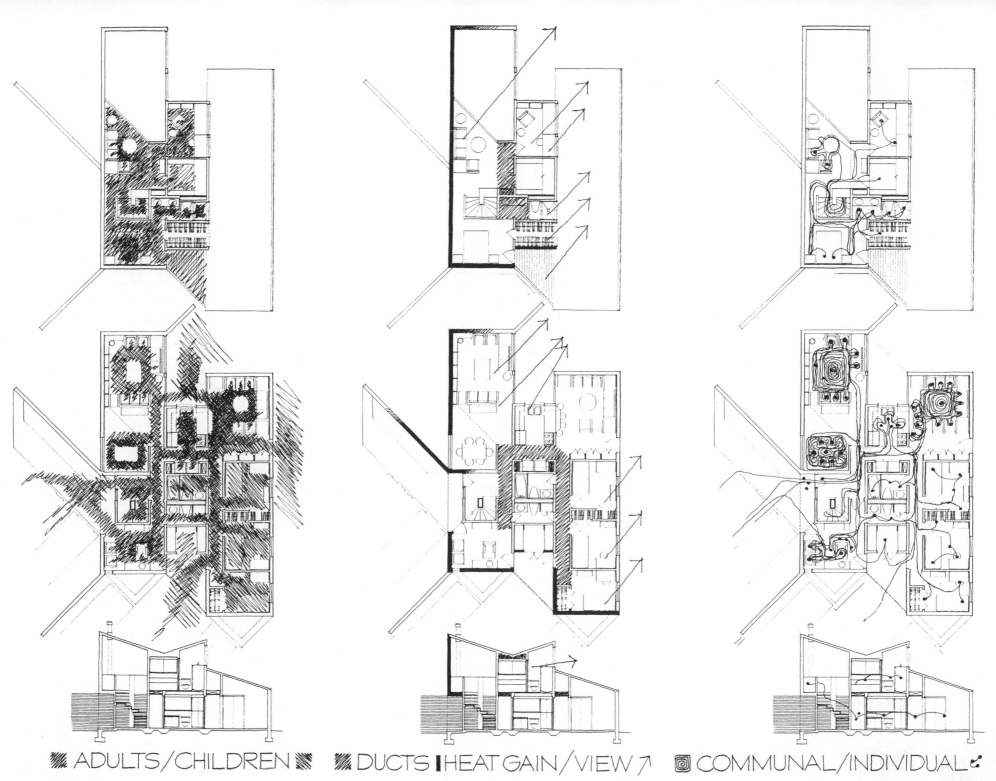

ADULTS/CHILDREN ⬛ ⬛ DUCTS ▮HEAT GAIN/VIEW ↗ ◎ COMMUNAL/INDIVIDUAL

243

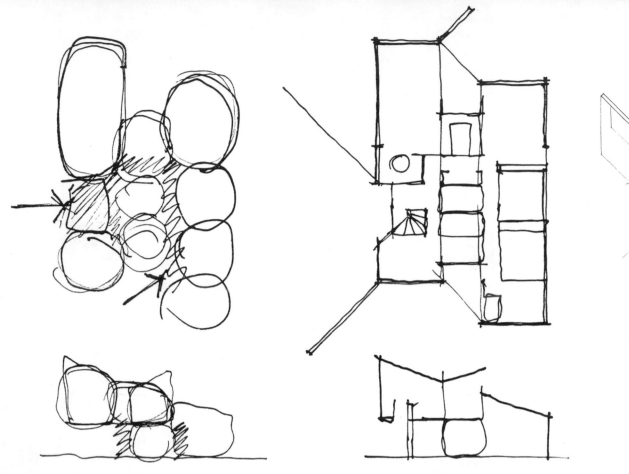

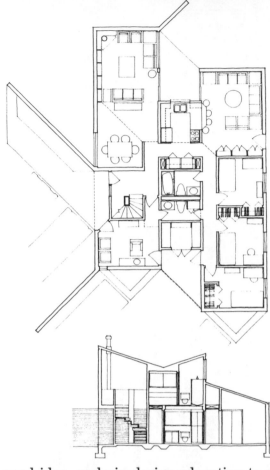

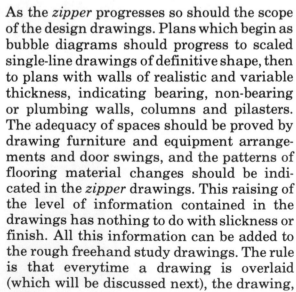

As the *zipper* progresses so should the scope of the design drawings. Plans which begin as bubble diagrams should progress to scaled single-line drawings of definitive shape, then to plans with walls of realistic and variable thickness, indicating bearing, non-bearing or plumbing walls, columns and pilasters. The adequacy of spaces should be proved by drawing furniture and equipment arrangements and door swings, and the patterns of flooring material changes should be indicated in the *zipper* drawings. This raising of the level of information contained in the drawings has nothing to do with slickness or finish. All this information can be added to the rough freehand study drawings. The rule is that everytime a drawing is overlaid (which will be discussed next), the drawing,

as well as the design, should be improved and the amount of information it shows the designer should be increased.

This increase in the density and detail of the design drawings is very important in the *zipper* phase of the process. It symbolizes and promotes the progress and closure of the process.

The final closing of any design process *zipper* is always difficult. By now the designer is so deeply involved in the congruence of the problem and its solution that the total resolution and articulation of that closure sometimes seems impossible. Time always threatens and frequently interrupts the complete closure. I've often thought it would be a

good idea, early in design education to give students a very simple problem and a ridiculously ample time to complete it; allowing them off whatever time remained after they completed the problem—just to experience deliberate self-closure. This ability to finally and firmly close the process is lacking in some otherwise creative people, but the control and command of this closure is impressive in strong, experienced designers. The levels of detail and consistency they can attend to and the range of relationships they can resolve near the end of the *zipper* is remarkable, and sometimes the most difficult thing for their families and friends to understand is that they find that kind of concentration and hard work extremely rewarding and enjoyable.

ZIPPED DRAWINGS

designed to convincingly present the solution by drawing its most flattering aspects—extolling the destination reached.

If the *zipper* has done its job well, the design space is now convincingly closed and the designer stands outside this masterpiece like a carnival barker, touting its excellence.

In order to design the drawings which will best communicate the solution to others, we must open a new design space within the solution side, leaving the problem closure alone. In this new design space we can now consider a new problem: that of persuading or convincing others that the closure we have made is the best possible.

The standard way of "selling" the final products of any design process to buyers, investors, mortgage bankers, boards of directors, stockholders or the general public is to order a professional full color rendering or a meticulously detailed model. While such efforts are always very impressive and make handsome adornments for corporate lobbies or boardrooms, they may tell very little about the building and the main organizing ideas of the design. While presentation drawings should certainly show what the final product will be like, especially experientially, those images will mean more to anyone trying to understand the building if there is some record of the process—some suggestion of the *stitches* and the *zipper*. A few conceptual diagrams, or a color-coded systems model or diagram, even analogical or precept diagrams can be extremely helpful in telling the story of the problem and the process as well as the solution.

Any designed environment will succeed or fail on its own, when built, without additional persuasive verbal or graphic explanations, but designers should never miss a chance to educate the public. We should marshall our clearest, most persuasive prose and our best graphic skills to communicate the process that produced the final design as well as the design itself. We should run through the *zippered* logic of the problem and its rationalized solution, and perhaps be open enough to allow some peeks at the illogical but creative *stitching* that anchored the process.

There is another very good reason for the development of a strong, clear verbal rationale for any designed environment. It should be part of a designer's responsibility to present such a rationale to any client, because long after the designer has gone on to other projects, the owners or users will have to repeatedly explain to others, who were not participants in the design process, why the environment was designed as it was. One of the great satisfactions in the design professions is to return to an environment you designed after many years, and find that the rationale for the original design has survived, and is now being passed on by people who weren't even involved in the original process.

Tim White's *Presentation Strategies in Architecture* (1977) is an excellent study of the factors involved in successfully communicating design ideas. White identifies five critical variables which apply to all kinds of presentations, including *zipped* drawings.

These are extensions of the five W's of journalistic reporting.

Usually the five "w's will be unequal in their IMPORTANCE to a presentation. We must determine which of these deserves the most EMPHASIS.

In planning the STRATEGY for a presentation, we must study the impact of the five "w's on the HOW.

From PRESENTATION STRATEGIES IN ARCHITECTURE by Edward T. White

The success of *zipped* drawings, like all successful communication depends on a careful analysis of, and response to, these factors.

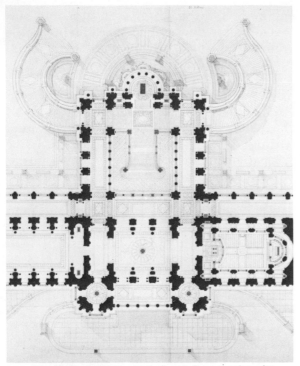

Brune. *L'Escalier principal d'un palais d'un Souverain.* First- and second-story plans.

Documents de l'Ecole Nationale Supérieure des Beaux-Arts, Paris

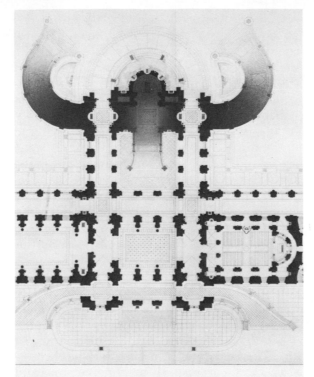

The classical example of *zipped* drawing, at least in architecture, is the traditional Beaux Arts presentation, named for the academic institution which formalized such presentations, the Ecole de Beaux Arts in Paris. "Beaux Arts" presentations collect all the architectural drawings which represent a design project into one grand composition. These presentations require great skill and hours of painstaking rendering— traditionally ink washes. They have been denigrated for their overemphasis on the supposedly superficial qualities of a design's formal and visual characteristics, and have been largely abandoned in architectural education and practice. They did have several advantages, however, especially in design education:

- they required designers to carefully compose the representative drawings which made the communication more clear and efficient and added another layer of design—the communication;

- they led designers to a deeper understanding of their designs as well as a deeper understanding of what the various drawings can show and how they best relate to one another.

To give you a simplified example of the kind of composition involved in such presentations, let me take the final problem we are using in the freshman drawing class at the University of Arizona. The problem is to take a given floor plan of a presumably manufactured or pre-cut vacation cabin, site adapt it and make a formal presentation using the essential representative architectural drawings. The resulting 20x30 boards are valued not only as rather satisfying compositions in themselves, but as an integrated way of having the students experience the characteristics of the various drawings and their potential relationships to one another.

When we analyze the representative drawings, we will find that, in any collective composition, some of them are happier in certain positions in the compositions than in others. When any such composition is displayed vertically, on the wall, it relates to gravity— it has a top and bottom. This makes those drawings which also have a top and bottom, like sections and elevations, want to "settle" to the bottom of the composition. This is especially true when we delineate the band of earth underneath them. Plans and perspectives "float" more successfully than sections and elevations and can be safely placed at the top of collective compositions of drawings.

The strongest relationships between drawings are between multi-storied plans, plans and sections, and plans and elevations, usually in that order. These relationships between the drawings are more essential than the preciousness of north being at the top of the sheet. A single prominent north

246

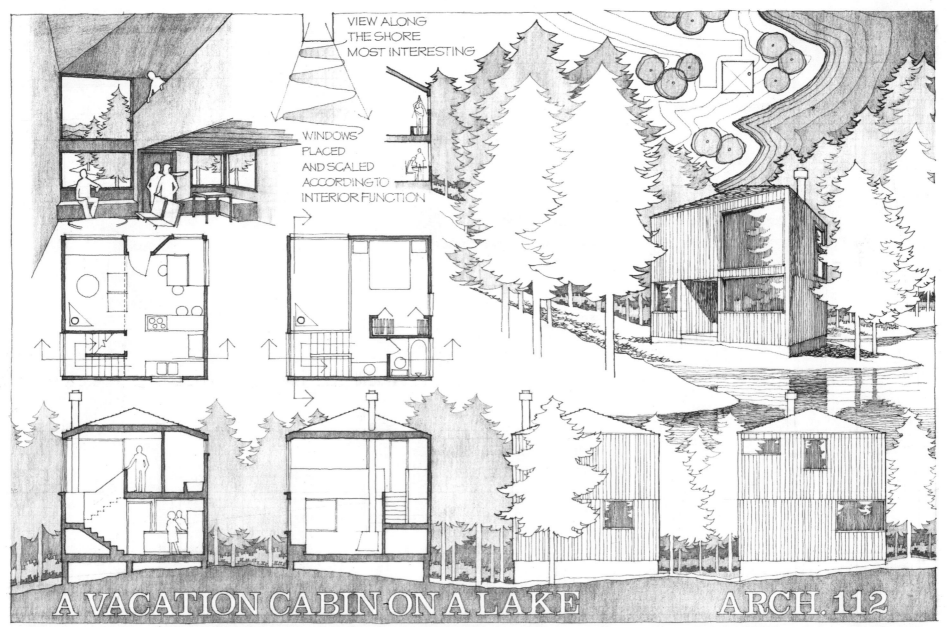

VIEW ALONG
THE SHORE
MOST INTERESTING

WINDOWS
PLACED
AND SCALED
ACCORDING TO
INTERIOR FUNCTION

A VACATION CABIN ON A LAKE   ARCH. 112

arrow can explain an unconventional orientation, but having to mentally rotate drawings 90° and relate them to another drawing on the other side of the composition in order to understand how a plan relates to a section or how the floor plan relates to the site plan will waste the attention span of anyone trying to understand your drawings.

Perspectives, especially interiors, are best positioned with the vanishing point near one side of the composition so that the space of the perspective opens up toward the rest of the composition. If perspectives can also be taken in a direction that relates to the orientation of a nearby plan, that is even better.

Major titles or lettering, because letter forms also relate to gravity, are more successful along the bottom of the composition, forming a base. Lettering should never call too much attention to itself, and for that reason, open, outlined letters are excellent because they can be an appropriate size without being overly important.

RADIO STATIONS—TUNING THE SET

One last requirement, and perhaps the most difficult one, is that the drawings should be consistent *as a set*. They need to look like they have received an equal amount of the delineator's attention, and they need to be drawn in the same media and technique. The best analogy I have been able to think of for this kind of consistency is that of tuning in a radio station. You may have heard Bill Cosby's imitation of the whistle, which, in early radios, used to rise in pitch on either side of any precisely tuned station. To eliminate such distracting whistles in your presentation drawings you must first be aware of several radio stations and their different positions on the dial, like the examples of pure "Drawing Techniques" discussed previously. You then will be able to identify the particular one you are seeking with your drawings. You should have a mental, or real "template" for the kind of graphic consistency you want, and then bring the whole composition up together—like turning up the volume knob satisfyingly once the station is precisely tuned.

If we mean to be persuasive with *zipped* drawings we must not forget a few things we know about the psychological behavior of human beings. The drawings which communicate the final designed environment should prominently show as many of the other participants' contributions to the process as possible. I am not suggesting that designs should simply be a hodge-podge collection of all the participants' suggestions, but it is also unrealistic, even undesirable, to pretend that the designer has been the sole source of all the contributions to any design. The participants will be looking for evidence of responses to suggestions they made during the design process.

The other rather obvious criterion is to present the environment as successful. If it is a shopping center or a restaurant, show it filled with eager consumers or convivial diners. If it is a school, show active children, exploring, enjoying, participating with the environment. Always show the design as you and your clients hope it will be.

The drawings which communicate the results of any design process should also be careful to preserve the correct emphasis. The emphasis should remain on the area of design responsibility—architecture, landscape architecture or interior design. One of the weaknesses of commercial renderings is that they often look more like fashion adver-

tisements or automobile brochures, or just virtuoso examples of commercial art than like design drawings. This is because their slickness can make them "opaque" as design drawings and because their beautiful people and automobiles can make us assume that they are a part of the ubiquitous commercial advertising with which we are so familiar.

During the design process correctly placed emphasis can focus designers' attention where it should be—on the area of design for which they are responsible; and it can thus avoid the dissipation of design effort into areas beyond their concern. In making *zipped* drawings at the end of the process, correct emphasis will similarly hold the viewer's attention where it should be—on what has been designed; and this kind of focus on what is most relevant offers the added bonus of taking less time to draw.

ARCHITECTURAL DESIGN

This drawing is intended to show what might be the correct emphasis for an architectural design drawing. Drawing effort, especially textural interest, is concentrated on the space-defining surfaces, emphasizing the structural elements and the architectural materials. The rendering effort is on the spatial container with the furniture and trees left as unrendered outlines, and placed carefully so that they never hide the volume-defining intersections of wall, ceiling and floor.

LANDSCAPE DESIGN

This drawing is intended to show what might be the correct emphasis for a landscape design drawing. Drawing effort, especially textural and figural interest, is concentrated on the exterior spaces, trees and plants. The furniture has little design character and is kept to a bare minimum and the architectural surfaces and the furniture are left as unrendered outlines.

INTERIOR DESIGN

This drawing is intended to show what might be the correct emphasis for an interior design drawing. Drawing effort, especially textural and figural interest, is concentrated on the interior space. The furniture, drapes, carpeting and accessories are selected and drawn with more design character, while the architectural surfaces and the exterior spaces are left as unrendered outlines. The interior furnishings are also given prominence in their placement, not hesitating to cover up architectural details or exterior spaces.

249

Perhaps the most profound change in the making of *zipped* drawings over the last thirty years has been the increasing use of models. The use of models during the design process and in final presentations has both advantages and disadvantages. The real three-dimensional presence of a model is much more quickly understandable *as an object,* and its reduced scales arouses a child-like fascination in most people like the miniaturization of doll houses, model trains and airplanes. These advantages are very worthwhile in the persuasion involved in presentations. The disadvantages are that the emphasis on the design *as an object* cannot tell us what it will be like to be inside the model—to experience the design *as an environment.* The miniaturization and the necessary simplification of materials in models also has a profound influence during the design process, because there is a tendency to choose materials which can be realistically modeled. This is one of the reasons we see so many buildings that look like cardboard models.

We should make another change in the traditional drawings with which we communicate the final products of our design processes. Instead of lavishing hours of time in futile attempts to make the orthographic abstractions (plan and section especially) look *realistic,* we should recognize them as abstractions, and use them to indicate the multiple realities of the environment being presented. We should develop a whole range of abstract qualitative drawings which could communicate the following kinds of information:

- the day/night, weekday/weekend, summer/winter use of the environment.
- the patterns and volumes of use, color coded to the various categories of users.

- the various zonings of the environment into servant/served, public/private, children/adults, noisy/quiet, staff/administration, dark/light, soft/hard.
- the potentials for flexibility, including variations in furniture and equipment arrangement, as well as future additions to the environment.

With such an array of alternative plan and section abstractions we could forget the traditional frozen, dead, empty moment in time shown in traditional presentation drawings and show the extended, cyclical, qualitative *life* of the environment which has been designed.

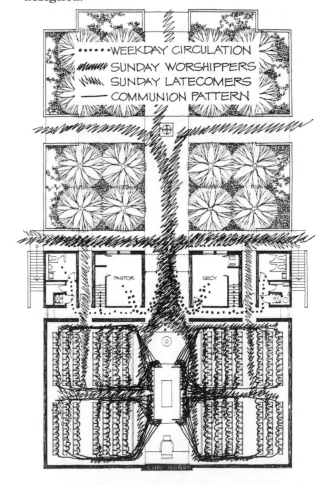

SPEED AND ACCURACY

Speed and accuracy in drawing are often thought of as being mutually exclusive criteria and seemingly in conflict, but professional designers need to be both accurate and quick—almost as much as professional gunfighters. You may be the West's most accurate marksperson, but if you can't get it out of the holster you'd better stay off the street. Similarly you may be the fastest gun in the West, but without accuracy you may also be the shortest lived. This dual demand on design drawing is one way to illustrate the relationships to experience and to the design process.

ACCURACY can be directly associated with the relationship to experience, and probably must come first in learning to draw. The criteria for accuracy must eventually lie with the designer. Designers must be able to draw with an accuracy that their *eyeminds* find acceptable. The representative drawings they make must look real to them and to others (teachers, boss designers or clients) with whom they must communicate. In the beginning, this acceptance requires a cold-eyed, objective assessment of your drawing ability and a desire to undertake its continual improvement. It also requires a lot of patience with your, perhaps, untrained hand, so you can accept your drawing ability, whatever it is at the moment, and see through it to whatever you are designing.

Generally, designers, as they mature, develop a very personal way of using drawings to represent their designs. In the beginning, they make detailed representational drawings of their designs and the development of their drawing ability helps them acquire the ability of seeing and holding more complex visual images in their *eyeminds*. The drawings which many mature designers make to represent their designs to themselves have become a curiously personal sketchy shorthand, but what they have learned to see and evaluate from this personal shorthand is as comprehensive and detailed as the representational drawings they made as fledgling designers.

Students should not be misled by mature designers' sketches into assuming this is as well as they can draw. Mature designers draw the way they draw out of intelligent deliberate choice, and they are no longer seeing the drawing—THEY ARE SEEING THE POTENTIAL REALITY OF WHAT THEY ARE DESIGNING.

The later design sketches of Kahn or le Corbusier (to choose two architect examples), are in this very personal, sketchy, graphic shorthand, but both men were excellent delineators in their apprentice days and came to draw in their own personal shorthand, not because it is the only way they could draw, but because it is the way they chose to draw.

SPEED is almost as directly associated with the relationship drawing has to the design process. In the continued spinning of the *eyemindhand* wheel through the representation phase, graphic representations must be presented to the designers' *eyeminds* at a pace which can keep up with their evaluation and continuing conception. Speed in drawing, in my experience, comes after accuracy and, rather than frenetic hand speed, is more a matter of confidence and wisdom. The confidence comes from knowing you can draw *anything* you need to accurately, in several techniques. the speed then comes from choosing the appropriate technique for the time available and knowing what *not* to draw. Speed in drawing is very much a matter of confidently and wisely using the full range of drawing abilities instead of letting your inabilities use you.

WISDOM AND EFFICIENCY
Although both wisdom and speed or efficiency are largely the products of experience, there are certain techniques which can hasten the development of these attributes. The management and flexibility which the LINE AND TONE technique allows, the use of tracing paper overlays to refine a drawing, the efficiency allowed by correctly placed emphasis and the various ways in which reproduction processes can supply technological tonal interest are worth knowing about. All these amount to a greater freedom of choice in the making of a drawing relative to the communicative purpose of the drawing and the time available. And freedom in drawing, as in other matters, comes from knowing what the options are and having acquired the skills to make them happen.

A part of the wisdom concerning drawing includes the insight that to hold efficiency too high as a goal is antithetical to the development of drawing ability because drawing

must first become, and remain, enjoyable, or it isn't worth doing at all. The paradox is that you will only learn to draw quickly by first learning to enjoy drawing slowly.

Beginning designers always want to know ways to make *quick* sketches. I can't recall ever being asked how to make a slow sketch. This is a little like a miler who wants to learn how to run a 4-minute mile, but isn't interested in how to first run 6, 5½, 5 or 4½ minute miles. It's as if an older designer were standing beside a stack of all the drawings she or he had ever made, and a beginning student walked up and asked to be taught how to make those last quick sketches on the top of the stack. The correct answer to the student's question, "How long did it take you to make those last two sketches?" is probably "Forty years."

TECHNOLOGICAL SHORTCUTS

Understanding and intelligent use of reproduction processes can also save you a great deal of drawing time. One of the most time-consuming tasks in drawing is the addition of tonal interest to a drawing. Any drawing technique requires hours to change a white sheet of tracing paper to the poster-like composition of tones on which strong tonal interest depends.

There are three ways you can use any OZALID or "blueprint" machine to produce broad tonal areas instantly.

UNDEREXPOSURE AND SUBSEQUENT COLORING. In this method, a tracing is run through an Ozalid machine at a faster-than-normal speed so that the light-sensitive print paper is underexposed. This underexposure results in an even tone all over the print (black, blue or sepia—depending on the paper used). The effect is very much like putting on a pair of tinted sunglasses; the normal tonal range of white-to-black is reduced to MIDDLETONE-to-black. What remains to be done is add the middletone-to-WHITE tonal range by coloring the sunlit surfaces with white prismacolor, exactly like rendering in the black and white on middletone technique discussed previously, and in detail in *Drawing As a Means to Architecture* (1968).

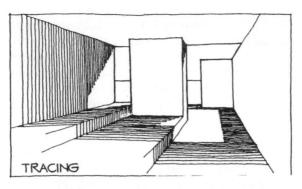

TRACING

PRINT

COLORED PRINT

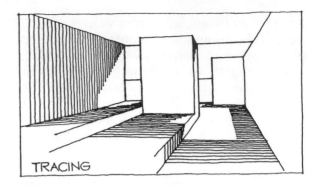

TRACING

MASK

PRINT

REDUCED COPIES ON VARIOUS OPAQUE MIDDLETONE PAPERS.

A more recent technological boon is the development of reducing copying machines which can print a really quality line reproduction on almost any lightweight paper, and add the benefit of infinitely variable reduction. This allows a designer to get a reduced copy of any line drawing on middletone paper *instantly* and *economically*, a process that used to be prohibitively expensive in time or money or

both—truly a "miracle" in the words of the little monk in the commercial. Such a transfer to an opaque middletone paper used to require trace-transferring by hand, and the reduction and printing of any line drawing on middletone paper was very expensive and time-consuming for small quantities. Economical copying on middletone paper opens up the full range and variety of black and white on middletone rendering by simplifying the most difficult step in the process.

MASKING. A second method of using an Ozalid machine to add tonal interest is to make one or several tracing paper overlays with cutout areas where you want the lighter tones. These overlay tracing paper "masks" are then taped to the original drawing at the corners. When this laminated stack of tracings is run through an Ozalid machine, the added opacity of the masks produces an even tone over all the areas of the drawing they cover.

252

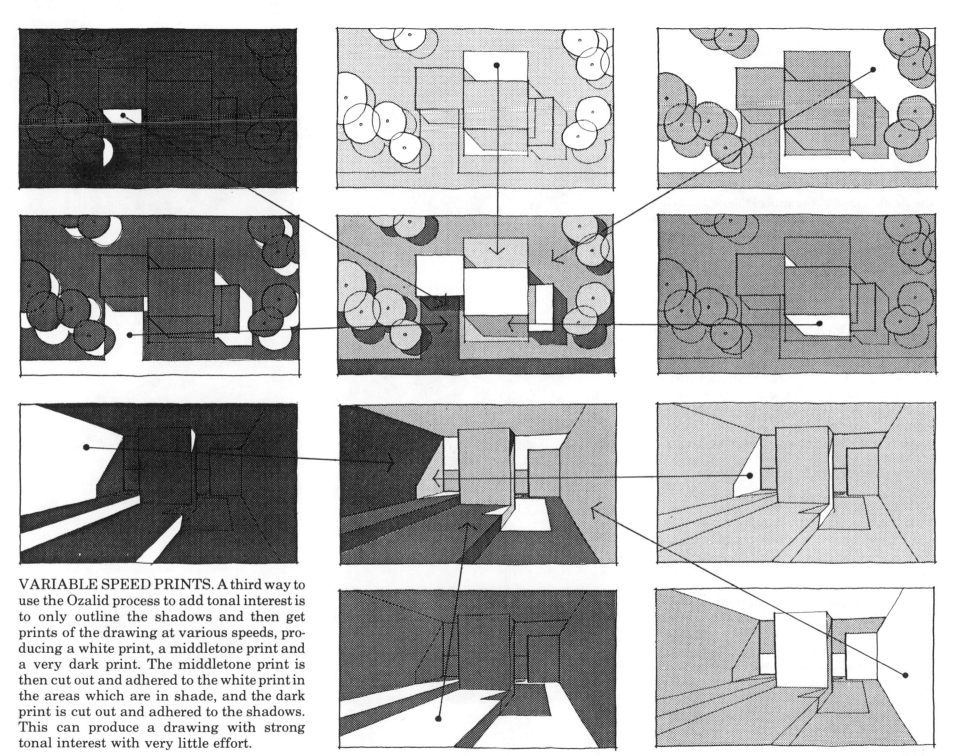

VARIABLE SPEED PRINTS. A third way to use the Ozalid process to add tonal interest is to only outline the shadows and then get prints of the drawing at various speeds, producing a white print, a middletone print and a very dark print. The middletone print is then cut out and adhered to the white print in the areas which are in shade, and the dark print is cut out and adhered to the shadows. This can produce a drawing with strong tonal interest with very little effort.

253

REPRODUCTION PROCESSES

Perhaps the most helpful knowledge in meeting drawing deadlines is that gained from the actual experience which allows a designer to visualize very clearly what must happen in the final stages of the process, how long each stage takes and the options that are available. These final stages often include the reproduction of the drawings for publication, and since the reproduction and publication of drawings offer so many opportunities and pitfalls those options must be considered very early in the process. It isn't a matter of completing the drawings and *then* deciding how they are to be reproduced. It is rather a matter of understanding how the drawings can, should, or will be reproduced and then making drawings of a size and technique that best suits that means of reproduction. Reduction, color, number of copies, time and budget available are just a few of the variables which must be considered *before* any drawing for reproduction is undertaken.

To illustrate one of the most basic options in the reproduction of drawings, let us consider the pitfalls in the *half-tone* reproduction of a TONE drawing and the *line-shot* reproduction of a TONE OF LINES drawing. The extremes of under-exposure and over-exposure are demonstrated in the reproductions at right. Generally, ink line drawings reproduce more dependably than pencil tone drawings in photographic reproduction. The *half-tones* required by pencil tone drawings are both more expensive and more subject to mistaken exposures than *line shots*. If you can arrange to walk the first drawing you make for photographic reproduction through the process, you will learn a great deal.

254

TONE

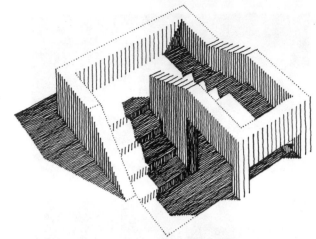

TONE OF LINES

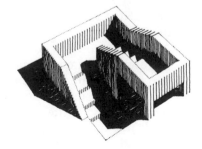

THE LONGER PROCESS

"Design process" usually refers to a series of activities that produces a designed product. There may be several of these processes going on simultaneously, but each one begins and ends with a specific design task. If we step back for a moment and look at the bigger picture, we can see that these individual processes may be seen as parts of a larger and longer process: that of becoming a designer or that of developing a better process, which is perhaps the same thing.

We have been discussing the relationships drawing may have to individual design processes, but the relationship drawing has to the longer process of becoming a designer is somewhat different. The development of this longer relationship lasts a designer's lifetime and is funded and shaped by the education and experience of that lifetime and the individual design processes that make up the designer's life's work. Drawing's relationship to the process of becoming a designer will inevitably become very personal and idiosyncratic, inseparably related to the way a designer works. The goal of design students should be to master as many ways of using drawing as possible so that the personalization of the relationship may be a matter of free choice, not an unquestioned inherited convention, nor the timid, habitual use of some single way of representing designed environments.

This larger or lifelong relationship of drawings to the design process generally shows another tendency which the conventional order and skill development of drawing

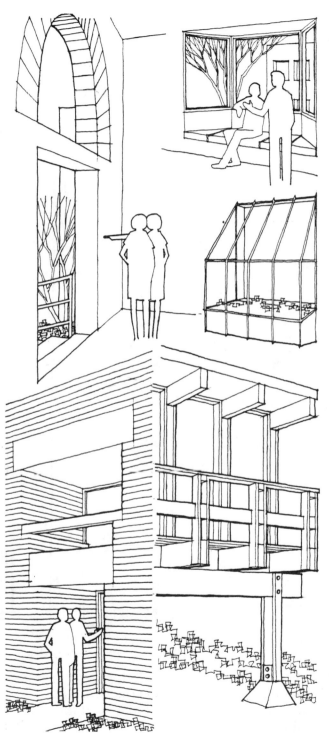

ignores. This tendency is the development of the designer's personal way of making environments. This way of making environments is more a matter of material choices, corners, connections, and articulations than of plan forms or section forms—and the range of choices that designers must be aware of before they can choose maturely or make their own way is much broader than can be represented by the orthographic abstractions (plan, section and elevations).

More than anything else, it seems to be this way of making environments that designers carry from one problem to another and continually refine and worry with. They then hang this personally developed way of making environments on various plan or section frameworks which suit the particular problem.

In design education and drawing education, we too often call attention to the plan or section, because these are the drawings we require, when the real character of the environment lies in the way the surfaces and elements are made and related to one another. Small "thumbnail" perspectives are the best representational drawings to develop this ability, for it is a matter of designing the three-dimensional qualities of windows, doors, steps, walls, the integration of structure, the relationships of roof to wall, and whether the approach to overall composition is volumetric or planar, additive or subtractive. The design of these characteristics of an environment is often the last ability to be mastered by designers, partly because these details are never drawn, studied or considered as a consistent three-dimensional set. It would perhaps be better to leave the plans and sections as diagrams and spend more time designing these three-dimensional characteristics of any environment.

255

DRAWING AS AN
INVESTMENT HIERARCHY

Earlier, under ZIPPER DRAWINGS,it was suggested that designers should visualize any drawing task not as a single drawing, but as a stack of potential drawings, progressing from a quick sketch at the bottom to a slick, detailed rendering at the top layer. This is one way of thinking of drawing as an investment hierarchy—as a choice of how much time and effort to devote to a particular drawing.

There is another way of thinking of drawing as an investment hierachy which is slightly different, based on the procedure for making any individual drawing. The idea is to invest your effort in the more important aspects of the drawing first. This is similar to the up front way journalists are trained to write newspaper stories. Journalists can never be sure how many column inches their stories will be given, so they cover everything of importance in the lead paragraph, with successive paragraphs filling in details in a hierarchy of importance. If you can learn to draw in this way your drawing effort will always be a solid investment even when you don't get finished.

As we learned earlier under DRAWING TECHNIQUES, the LINE AND TONE technique's flexibility make it ideally suited for such phased management.

One of the unique advantages of the line and tone technique is its open-endedness. Line and tone drawings can be made in a sequence which produces an acceptable drawing quickly, but then allows you to add detail in whatever time you have left. Beyond the first stage the drawing will never look unfinished (as other techniques would) and you can return to the drawing and improve it when you have time. This investment hierarchy is

best understood in terms of the drawing interest categories: spatial, tonal, textural and additional.

When a rough design sketch is selected to be made into a more finished drawing, it should first be given an accurate drafted framework,

256

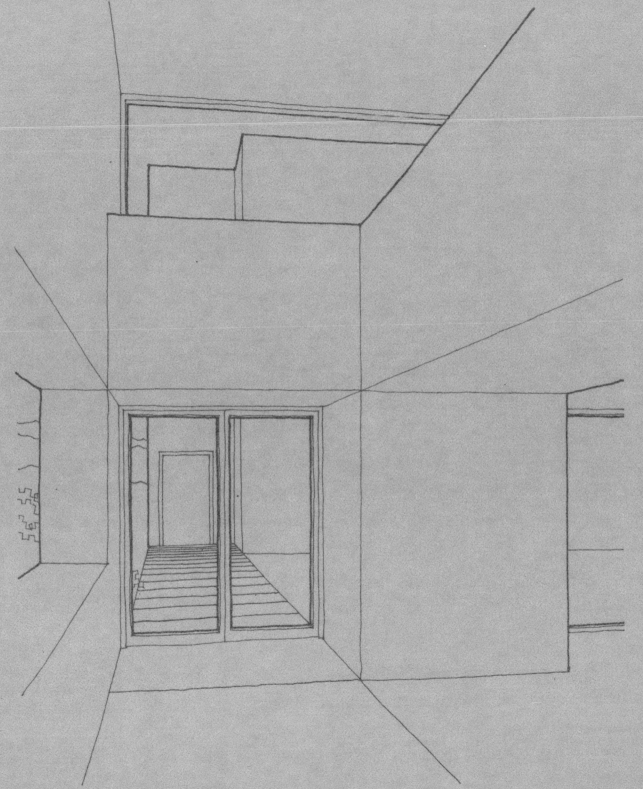

like the drawing on the preceding page. This accurate underlying spatial structure is always the first investment on which everything else will stand and should include possible shadow patterns, and the placement of figures, furniture and trees, so that they will have the benefit of refinement along with everything else.

SPATIAL INTEREST

The most basic category of environmental interest for designers is the interest offered by the spatial configuration of any environment. This kind of interest consists almost entirely of the number and variety of hidden spaces which will be progressively revealed as we move through any environment.

While it is valuable to be able to select or discover the perspective view which will have the most interest in its spatial layering, it is even more important to improve the spatial interest of a design based on what any perspective shows you. Spatial interest can never be reduced to a problem of clever selection of views, nor can its lack ever be adequately compensated for by overemphasizing the other interest categories. If the space looks dull in the drawing, it probably is dull, and represents a design problem as well as a drawing problem.

The spatial interest of any perspective will be enhanced by adjusting the view so that it shows a maximum number of spatial laps or layers, while hiding a minimum number of planar intersections. The configuration of the environment should be represented as interesting and promising the progressive revelations which movement through it will bring, but the view chosen should never be deliberately mysterious or confusing. Corners, intersections, edges, stairs and floor level and ceiling level changes should always be visible, never obscured by nearer elements.

like the drawing on the preceding page. This accurate underlying spatial structure is always the first investment on which everything else will stand and should include possible shadow patterns, and the placement of figures, furniture and trees, so that they will have the benefit of refinement along with everything else.

SPATIAL INTEREST

The most basic category of environmental interest for designers is the interest offered by the spatial configuration of any environment. This kind of interest consists almost entirely of the number and variety of hidden spaces which will be progressively revealed as we move through any environment.

While it is valuable to be able to select or discover the perspective view which will have the most interest in its spatial layering, it is even more important to improve the spatial interest of a design based on what any perspective shows you. Spatial interest can never be reduced to a problem of clever selection of views, nor can its lack ever be adequately compensated for by overemphasizing the other interest categories. If the space looks dull in the drawing, it probably *is* dull, and represents a design problem as well as a drawing problem.

The spatial interest of any perspective will be enhanced by adjusting the view so that it shows a maximum number of spatial laps or layers, while hiding a minimum number of planar intersections. The configuration of the environment should be represented as interesting and promising the progressive revelations which movement through it will bring, but the view chosen should never be deliberately mysterious or confusing. Corners, intersections, edges, stairs and floor level and ceiling level changes should always be visible, never obscured by nearer elements.

258

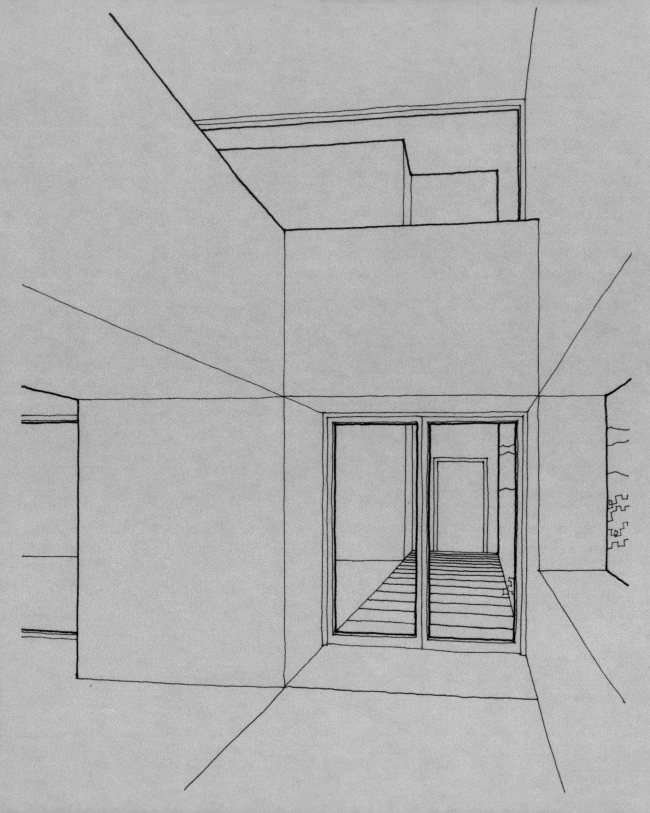

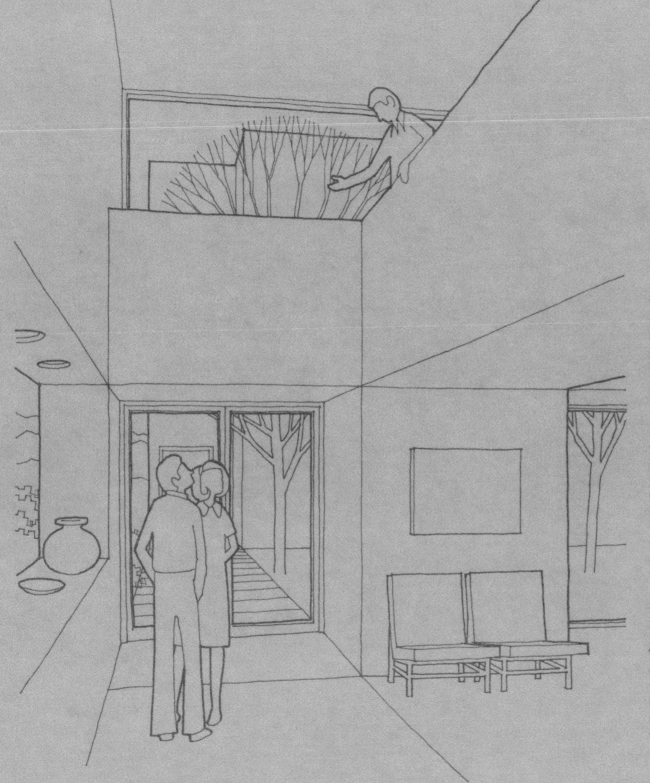

SPATIAL AND ADDITIONAL INTEREST

This spatially profiled open line drawing is the first stage of any line and tone drawing. It is very much like the simple line drawings in a child's coloring book, but everything is spatially defined, and it is a very committed, unequivocal drawing.

Spatial interest and the items of additional interest are tightly interrelated. The number of hidden spaces and spatial layers or laps should be maximized and objects of additional interest should demonstrate the space without hiding space-defining intersections (like the tree or the upper figure). The drawing communicates the environment while stopping short of the two most time-consuming interest categories.

What has been drawn is also a sound investment in the hierarchy because the time taken to make an accurate perspective framework and a studied integration with objects of additional interest will never have to be reinvested. If there is the need or opportunity to continue or return to the drawing, this solid initial investment will support the remaining interest categories which add tone and texture.

SPATIAL AND ADDITIONAL INTEREST

This spatially profiled open line drawing is the first stage of any line and tone drawing. It is very much like the simple line drawings in a child's coloring book, but everything is spatially defined, and it is a very committed, unequivocal drawing.

Spatial interest and the items of additional interest are tightly interrelated. The number of hidden spaces and spatial layers or laps should be maximized and objects of additional interest should demonstrate the space without hiding space-defining intersections (like the tree or the upper figure). The drawing communicates the environment while stopping short of the two most time-consuming interest categories.

What has been drawn is also a sound investment in the hierarchy because the time taken to make an accurate perspective framework and a studied integration with objects of additional interest will never have to be reinvested. If there is the need or opportunity to continue or return to the drawing, this solid initial investment will support the remaining interest categories which add tone and texture.

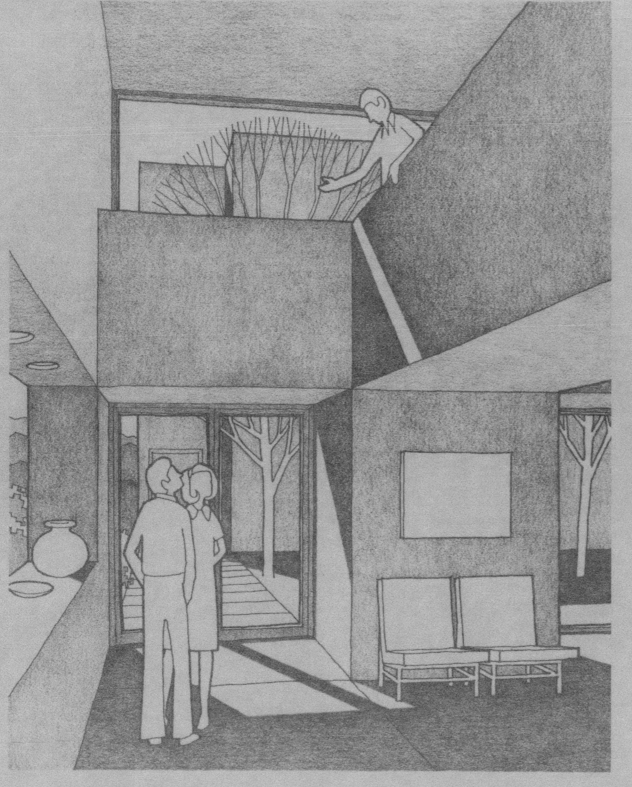

TONAL INTEREST

The two remaining interest categories are both very time-consuming. Tonal interest should be next because its main source—light—is not as arbitrary as the main source of textural interest—materials—and because tonal interest lends itself to various technological shortcuts.

Ozalid prints, drawing on middletone paper, mounting a tracing paper drawing on a black background and then coloring on the back with white prismacolor or mounting white paper cutouts beneath are some of the shortcuts.

In this technique the tones, including color, should be smooth, flat and characterless. Don't draw or render with the tone-making tools. All such rendering should be done with the pen. This will preserve the distinction between edge-indicating lines drawn with a pen and surface indicating tones drawn with a pencil or marker.

The pattern of the tonal interest—the shade and shadows—is also a matter of your choice and deserves careful study. It can do wonders to make a space read and it should be carefully integrated with figures etc.

TONAL INTEREST

The two remaining interest categories are both very time-consuming. Tonal interest should be next because its main source—light—is not as arbitrary as the main source of textural interest—materials—and because tonal interest lends itself to various technological shortcuts.

Ozalid prints, drawing on middletone paper, mounting a tracing paper drawing on a black background and then coloring on the back with white prismacolor or mounting white paper cutouts beneath are some of the shortcuts.

In this technique the tones, including color, should be smooth, flat and characterless. Don't draw or render with the tone-making tools. All such rendering should be done with the pen. This will preserve the distinction between edge-indicating lines drawn with a pen and surface indicating tones drawn with a pencil or marker.

The pattern of the tonal interest—the shade and shadows—is also a matter of your choice and deserves careful study. It can do wonders to make a space read and it should be carefully integrated with figures etc.

262

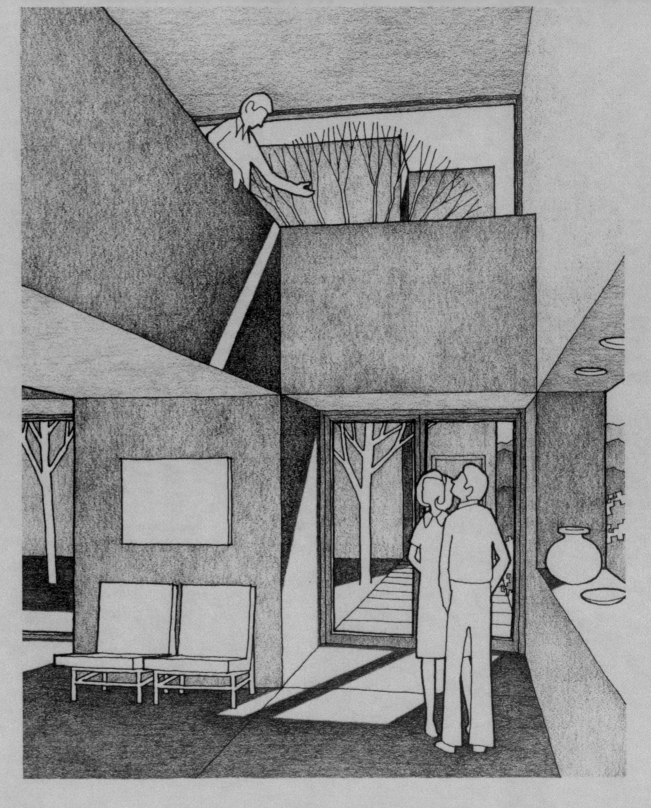

TEXTURAL INTEREST

In the hierarchy suggested here, textural interest is the last category to be added. This is because the addition of textural interest is very time-consuming and, unlike tonal interest, it must be applied by hand with no technological shortcuts. It also tends to be the interest category most subject to change since its main sources—materials—are often considered late in the design decision-making process and frequently are matters for adjustment in meeting the construction budget.

In line and tone drawings, textural interest should be applied only with a pen, and applied first to the space-defining surfaces beginning with the floor or ground plane. These surfaces should always be rendered continuously because intermittent texturing will destroy the perception of the surface as the continuous background with which all spatial perception begins. Objects standing in front of these textured surfaces should never be textured but remain open silhouettes, so that the viewer's perception always continues past them to the textured surface beyond.

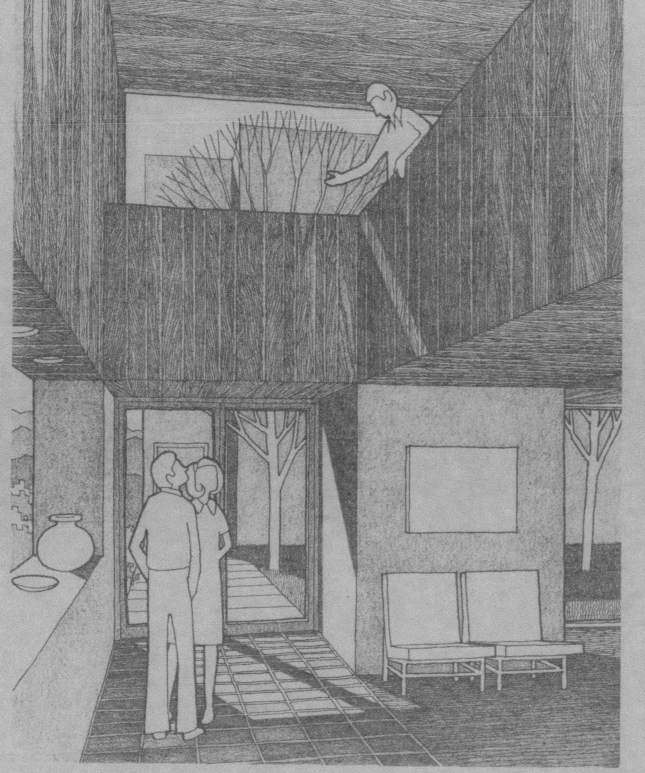

TEXTURAL INTEREST

In the hierarchy suggested here, textural interest is the last category to be added. This is because the addition of textural interest is very time-consuming and, unlike tonal interest, it must be applied by hand with no technological shortcuts. It also tends to be the interest category most subject to change since its main sources—materials—are often considered late in the design decision-making process and frequently are matters for adjustment in meeting the construction budget.

In line and tone drawings, textural interest should be applied only with a pen, and applied first to the space-defining surfaces beginning with the floor or ground plane. These surfaces should always be rendered continuously because intermittent texturing will destroy the perception of the surface as the continuous background with which all spatial perception begins. Objects standing in front of these textured surfaces should never be textured but remain open silhouettes, so that the viewer's perception always continues past them to the textured surface beyond.

The preceding *stitches and zipper* analogy was intended to be a model which could accomodate most of the opinions and recommendations as to what does or should occur during the design process, so that the various relationships that drawing has to the process could be discussed. Models are never innocent, and although I have tried very hard to deny the exclusive validity of linear models, even the *stitches* and *zipper* analogy winds up looking like a linear procedure. After several years of considering various frameworks for saying what I felt was important about drawing's relation to design I chose to stay with the so-called "process" and the so-called "problem" and "solution" because of their broad general acceptance and use in design education.

I must now add a brief but comprehensive disclaimer for serious readers. "Problem," "solution" and design "process" may be very misleading words, if they are taken literally. I would much prefer to replace "problem" with *perceived conceptual opportunity* or *PERCEPT*; to replace "solution" with *rationalized conceptual response* or *CONCEPT*; to replace "problem-solving" with *OPPORTUNITY-SEEKING*; and to replace design "process" with design *SYNTHESIS*. I decided, however, that what I had to say might be difficult enough for my limited writing skills and powers of persuasion without also trying to change the accepted vocabulary.

LIMITATIONS OF THE DESIGN PROCESS

Of all the misleading phrases commonly applied to design, "creative problem-solving" surely takes the cake. It belongs in that select class of oxymorons, alongside "jumbo shrimp," "postal service" and "military intelligence." Anyone who approaches whatever they do as "problem-solving" gives up creativity at the outset. Creativity is always what *else* you do, besides solving the obvious or conventional problems. "Creative problem-solving" implies that the problems are already known and that creativity is only needed in finding a solution for the fixed problem—the *compliance* of what I have called *concept attainment*. Real creativity includes seeking, understanding and responding to design opportunities that have been overlooked by others—the *congruence* of *concept-formation*.

The greatest danger of all linear methods or models of thought or creativity, even ones as loose as the *stitches* and *zipper* analogy, is that they might lead designers or thinkers to surrender their subjectivity. We are the products of two infinitely wiser processes: human evolution and the experience of our own lifetimes, and when our senses veto the products of our linear, rational processes or methods as "inappropriate" or "ugly" we should accept that judgment without question or apology.

Unlike the scales, distances and speeds of modern physics, which are beyond direct human experience, but whose techniques many design methodologists would emulate, the scale and complexity of the environments we design can still be represented quite adequately with traditional drawing and modeling techniques. The ultimate evaluation of the environments we design will be made by human beings like ourselves, with the same perceptual apparatus we have been using all our lives, and our best hope is still what it has always been: to develop our own individual sensitivity to our fellow human beings and to the built environment, and to consider our additions to that evironment very carefully, with accurate representational drawings and models so that the process is open to the evaluative perception of all those concerned.

To deny or censor the evaluation of the senses of our collective evolutionary and individual human history in favor of the pseudo-certainty of any ritual, however logical, mathematical or scientific, is a very serious mistake. To believe in any design method to the extent that we are prepared to let its results override our own subjective experience is to abdicate our role as environmental designers and our responsibility as human beings.

AFTERTHOUGHT

The oldest drawings we know about were design drawings. The cave paintings of southwestern Europe were not made as records of history or as art to impress or influence the viewer. They were made by torchlight in the most inaccessible parts of the caves and were often overlays of earlier paintings. They are not flat plans or sections, but remarkably realistic representations of reality.

Most experts agree that the drawings were intended to *influence the future*. Their makers believed that the act of making graphic representations of successful future hunts would help those future efforts be successful.

DESIGN DRAWINGS are the direct descendants of these prehistoric drawings. They have much more in common than either has with Art or Drafting. DESIGN DRAWING has precisely the same intention as these earliest drawings, without the magic. The drawing of alternative futures has more potential for synthesizing, evaluating and accomplishing those futures than either art or drafting.

Photograph by Douglas Mazonowicz. From PREHISTORIC ART by T. G. E. Powell

BIBLIOGRAPHY

The categorization of drawing books is a continuing problem, as you will discover from the shelving patterns found in any library. The categories of this bibliography are ordered according to the organization of the book, which seems appropriate for design drawing.

My greatest problem with the categorization is where to place my own previous books, *Drawing as a Means to Architecture* (1968) and *Design Drawing Experiences* (1973). Several books by others appear more than once in the bibliography, but since the categories are my categories, my books wind up in every category, or none. I have decided the latter choice is the more modest, and so you will find only *Design Drawing Experiences* listed under INTRODUCTORY BOOKS WITH EXERCISES. *Drawing as a Means to Architecture*, one of the first books which attempted to relate drawing to the design process, and the initiator of many of the ideas in this book, is so general that it fits all the categories and, therefore, no single category.

PERCEPTION

This is a very selective, basic list of books which directly relate perception to environmental design and drawing.

Arnheim, Rudolf. *Visual Thinking*. Berkeley and Los Angeles: University of California Press, 1969. Paperback ed. 1971.

Berrill, N. J. *Man's Emerging Mind: The Story of Man's Progress Through Time*. Paperback ed. New York: Fawcett World Library, 1965.

Bronowski, J. *The Ascent of Man*. Boston/Toronto: Little, Brown & Company, 1973.

Gibson, James J. *The Perception of the Visual World*. Boston: Houghton Mifflin Company, 1950. Reprint ed. Westport, CT: Greenwood Press, 1974.

Gibson, James J. *The Senses Considered as Perceptual Systems*. Boston: Houghton Mifflin Company, 1966.

Gibson, James J. *The Ecological Approach to Visual Perception*. Boston: Houghton Mifflin Company, 1979.

Gombrich, E.H. *Art and Illusion: A Study in the Psychology of Pictorial Representation*. The A.W. Mellon Lectures in the Fine Arts, 1965. Paperback ed. Bollingen Series XXXV 5. Princeton: Princeton University Press, 1972.

Gregory, R. L. *The Intelligent Eye*. New York: McGraw-Hill Book Company, 1970.

Hall, Edward T. *The Hidden Dimension*. New York: Doubleday and Company, 1966. Anchor Books ed. 1969.

Ittelson, William H., ed. *Environment and Cognition*. New York: Seminar Press, 1973.

McLuhan, Marshall. *Understanding Media: The Extensions of Man*. New York: McGraw-Hill Book Company, 1964.

CONCEPTION

The books which follow are selected to demonstrate the range of thought, most of it by nondesigners, which can be related to environmental design and drawing.

Adams, James L. *Conceptual Blockbusting: A Guide to Better Ideas*. 2nd ed. New York: W. W. Norton & Company, 1974.

Allport, Gordon W. *The Nature of Prejudice*. Reading, MA: Addison-Wesley Publishing Company, 1954. Garden City: Doubleday Anchor Books, 1958.

Arnheim, Rudolf. *Visual Thinking*. Paperback ed. Berkeley and Los Angeles: University of California Press, 1971.

Bruner, Jerome S.; Goodnow, Jacqueline J.; Austin, George A. *A Study of Thinking*. New York: John Wiley & Sons, 1956.

Bruner, Jerome S. *On Knowing: Essays for the Left Hand*. Cambridge: Harvard University Press, 1963. Paperback ed. New York: Atheneum, 1973.

Bruner, Jerome S. *Beyond the Information Given: Studies in the Psychology of Knowing*. Edited by Jeremy M. Anglin. New York: W. W. Norton & Company, 1973.

Churchman, C. West. *The Systems Approach*. Paperback ed. New York: Dell Publishing, 1968.

DeBono, Edward. *The Mechanism of Mind*. New York: Simon and Schuster, 1969.

DeBono, Edward. *Lateral Thinking: Creativity Step by Step*. New York: Harper & Row, Publishers, 1970.

DeBono, Edward. *New Think: The Use of Lateral Thinking in the Generation of New Ideas*. New York: The Hearst Corporation, Avon Books, 1971.

Foz, Adel Twefik-Khalil. "Some Observations on Designer Behavior in the Parti." Master's Thesis, Massachusetts Institute of Technology, 1972.

Gordon, William J. J. *Synectics: The Development of Creative Capacity.* New York: Harper & Row Publishers, 1961. Paperback ed. Collier Books, 1968.

Gruber, Howard E. *Darwin on Man: A Psychological Study of Scientific Creativity.* New York: E. P. Dutton and Company, 1974.

Kepes, Gyorgy. *The New Landscape in Art and Science.* Chicago: Paul Theobald and Company, 1956.

Koestler, Arthur. *The Act of Creation: A Study of the Conscious and Unconscious in Science and Art.* New York: The Macmillan Company, 1964. Paperback ed. Dell Publishing Company, 1967.

Koestler, Arthur. *The Ghost in the Machine.* New York: The Macmillan Company, 1967. Gateway ed. Chicago: Henry Regnery Company, 1971.

Koestler, Arthur. *Janus (A Summing Up).* New York: Random House, 1978. Vintage Book ed., 1979.

Kuhn, Thomas S. *Structure of Scientific Revolutions.* 2nd ed., enlarged. Chicago: The University of Chicago Press, 1962, 1970.

Koberg, Don, and Bagnall, Jim. *The Universal Traveler.* Los Altos, CA: William Kaufman, 1972.

Levi-Strauss, Claude. *The Savage Mind.* Chicago: The University of Chicago Press, 1966.

McKim, R. H. *Experiences in Visual Thinking.* 2nd ed. Monterey, CA: Brooks/Cole Publishing Company, 1972.

Magee, Bryan. *Karl Popper.* New York: The Viking Press, 1973.

Martin, William David. "The Architect's Role in Participatory Planning Processes: Case Study-Boston Transportation Planning Review." Master's thesis, Massachusetts Institute of Technology, 1976.

Maslow, A. H. *The Farther Reaches of Human Nature.* New York: The Viking Press, 1971. Viking Compass ed., 1972.

Newell, Allen, and Simon, Herbert A., *Human Problem Solving.* Englewood Cliffs, NJ: Prentice-Hall, 1972.

Ornstein, Robert E. *Psychology of Consciousness.* San Francisco: W. H. Freeman and Company, 1972. 2nd ed. New York: Harcourt Brace Jovanovich, 1977.

Pearce, Joseph Chilton. *The Crack in the Cosmic Egg: Challenging Constructs of Mind and Reality.* New York: Julian Press, 1971. Paperback ed. Simon & Schuster, Pocket Books, 1973.

Polanyi, Michael. *The Tacit Dimension.* New York: Doubleday and Company, Inc., 1966. Anchor books, 1967.

Prince, George M. *The Practice of Creativity.* New York: Harper & Row. Paperback ed. Collier Books, 1972.

Samuels, Mike, M.D., and Samuels, Nancy. *Seeing With the Mind's Eye: The History, Techniques and Uses of Visualization.* New York: Random House, 1975.

REPRESENTATION

DRAWING'S RELATIONSHIP TO EXPERIENCE

DRAWING TECHNIQUES

LINE

Bon-Hui Uy. *Architectural Drawings and Leisure Sketches.* Hololulu: Bon-Hui Uy, 1978.

Bon-Hui Uy. *Drawings, Architecture and Leisure.* New York: Bon-Hui Uy, 1980.

Parenti, George. *Masonite Contemporary Studies.* Chicago: Masonite Corporation, 1960.

Welling, Richard. *The Technique of Drawing Buildings.* New York: Watson-Guptill Publications, 1971.

TONE

Kautzky, Ted. *Pencil Broadsides: A Manual of Broad Stroke Technique.* New York: Reinhold, 1940, 1960.

Kautzky, Ted. *The Ted Kautzky Pencil Book.* New York: Van Nostrand Reinhold Company, 1979.

Oles, Paul Stevenson. *Architectural Illustration: The Value Delineation Process.* New York: Van Nostrand Reinhold Company, 1979.

TONE OF LINES

Guptill, Arthur Leighton. *Drawing with Pen and Ink.* New York: Reinhold, 1961.

White, Edward T. *A Graphic Vocabulary for Architectural Presentation.* Tucson: Architectural Media, 1972.

LINE AND TONE

Cullen, Gordon. *Townscape.* New York: Reinhold, 1961.

Jacoby, Helmut *Architectural Drawings.* New York: Frederick A. Praeger, Publishers, 1965.

Jacoby, Helmut. *New Architectural Drawings.* New York: Frederick A. Praeger, Publishers, 1969.

PERSPECTIVE

Burden, Ernest. *Architectural Delineation: A Photographic Approach to Presentation.* New York: McGraw Hill Book Company, 1971.

D'Amelio, Joseph. *Perspective Drawing Handbook.* New York: Tudor Publishing, 1964.

Doblin, Jay. *Perspective: A New System for Designers.* New York: Whitney Library of Design, 1956.

Ivins, William M., Jr. *On the Rationalization of Sight: With an Examination of Three Renaissance Texts on Perspective.* New York: Da Capo Press, 1973.

LIGHT

Doyle, Michael E. *Color Drawing.* New York: Van Nostrand Reinhold Company, 1981.

Forseth, Kevin, with Vaughan, David. *Graphics for Architecture.* New York: Van Nostrand Reinhold Company, 1980.

Oles, Paul Stevenson. *Architectural Illustration: The Value Delineation Process.* New York: Van Nostrand Reinhold Company, 1979.

COLOR

Doyle, Michael E. *Color Drawing.* New York: Van Nostrand Reinhold Company, 1981.

Oles, Paul Stevenson. *Architectural Illustration: The Value Delineation Process.* New York: Van Nostrand Reinhold Company, 1979.

Welling, Richard. *Drawing with Markers.* New York: Watson-Guptill Publications, 1974.

TAPES AND TEMPLATES

Burden, Ernest E. *Entourage; A Tracing File for Architecture and Interior Design.* New York: McGraw Hill Book Company, 1981.

Denny, Edward, and Terrazas, Patricia. *Bod File: A Resource Book for Designers & Illustrators.* Arlington: Inner Image Books, 1976.

McGinty, Tim. *Drawing Skills in Architecture: Perspective, Layout Design.* Dubuque: Kendall/Hunt Publishing Company, 1976.

Szabo. *Drawing File for Architects.* New York: Van Nostrand Reinhold Company, 1976.

Wang, Thomas C. *Plan and Section Drawing.* New York: Van Nostrand Reinhold Company, 1979.

White, Edward T. *A Graphic Vocabulary for Architectural Presentation.* Tucson: Architectural Media, 1972.

INTRODUCTORY BOOKS WITH EXERCISES

McGinty, Tim. *Drawing Skills in Architecture: Perspective Layout, Design.* Dubuque: Kendall/Hunt Publishing Company, 1976.

Lockard, William Kirby, *Design Drawing Experiences.* 4th ed., Rev. Tucson: Pepper Publishing, 1973, 1974, 1976, 1979.

Wester, Lari M. *Think and Do Graphics: A Graphic Communication Workbook.* Proof Copy. Guelph, Canada: Guelph Campus CO-OP, 1976.

DRAFTING

Ching, Francis D. K. *Architectural Graphics.* Paperback ed. New York: Van Nostrand Reinhold Company, 1975.

Forseth, Kevin, with Vaughan, David. *Graphics for Architecture.* New York: Van Nostrand Reinhold Company.

Martin, C. Leslie. *Design Graphics.* 2nd ed. New York: The Macmillan Company, 1968.

Patten, Lawton, M., and Rogness, Milton L. *Architectural Drawing.* Rev. ed. Dubuque: Wm. C. Brown Company, Publishers, 1968.

Ramsey, Charles G., and Sleeper, Harold R. *Architectural Graphic Standards.* 6th ed. New York: John Wiley & Sons, 1970.

DRAWING'S RELATIONSHIP TO THE DESIGN PROCESS

DESIGN PROCESSES AND METHOD

This list offers a collection of descriptions and prescriptions of what does or should happen during the so-called design process. Some of the methods exclude drawings from any meaningful role in the process, and so disagree totally with the basis of this book.

Broadbent, Geoffrey, and Ward, Anthony, eds. *Design Methods in Architecture.* Architectural Association Paper Number 4. London: Lund Humphries Publishers, 1969.

Broadbent, Geoffrey. *Design in Architecture: Architecture and the Human Sciences.* Chicester: John Wiley & Sons, 1973.

Jones, J. Christopher. *Design Methods: Seeds of Human Futures.* London: Wiley-Interscience, 1970.

Moore, Gary T., ed. *Emerging Methods in Environmental Design and Planning.* Paperback ed. Cambridge: MIT Press, 1970.

CONCEPTUAL DRAWING

This category addresses all the drawings involved in opening, clearing and closing the design space. No such books existed fifteen years ago and the growing list is encouraging.

Adams, James L. *Conceptual Blockbusting: A Guide to Better Ideas.* 2nd ed. New York: W. W. Norton & Company, 1974.

Ching, Francis D. K. *Architecture: Form, Space & Order.* New York: Van Nostrand Reinhold Company, 1979.

Hanks, Kurt, and Belliston, Larry. *Draw! A Visual Approach to Thinking, Learning and Communicating.* Los Altos, CA: William Kaufmann, 1977.

Hanks, Kurt, and Belliston, Larry. *Rapid Viz: A New Method for the Rapid Visualization of Ideas.* Exp. ed. Los Altos, CA: William Kaufmann, 1977.

Laseau, Paul. *Graphic Problem Solving for Architects and Builders.* Boston: CBI Publishing Company, 1975.

Laseau, Paul. *Graphic Thinking for Architects and Designers.* New York: Van Nostrand Reinhold Company, 1980.

McKim, R. H. *Experiences in Visual Thinking.* 2nd ed. Monterey, CA: Brooks/Cole Publishing Company, 1972.

Porter, Tom. *How Architects Visualize.* New York: Van Nostrand Reinhold Company, 1979.

White, Edward T. *Introduction to Architectural Programming.* Tucson: Architectural Media, 1972.

White, Edward T. *Ordering Systems: An Introduction to Architectural Design.* Tucson: Architectural Media, 1973.

White, Edward T. *Concept Sourcebook: A Vocabulary of Architectural Forms.* Tucson: Architectural Media, 1975.

PRESENTATION DRAWING

The books which follow are mostly collections of closed, persuasive drawings which come after all the design decisions have been made — what I have called *zipped* drawings. The most hopeful characteristic of this group is its great diversity and also the growing number of books which show in detail exactly how the drawings were made.

Atkin, William Wilson; Corbelletti, Raniero; and Fiore, Vincent T. *Pencil Techniques in Modern Design.* New York: Reinhold, 1953.

Atkin, William Wilson. *Architectural Presentation Techniques.* New York: Van Nostrand Reinhold Company, 1976.

Burden, Ernest. *Architectural Delineation: A Photographic Approach to Presentation.* New York: McGraw-Hill Book Company, 1971.

Doyle, Michael E. *Color Drawing.* New York: Van Nostrand Reinhold Company, 1981.

Halse, Albert O. *Architectural Rendering: The Techniques of Contemporary Presentation.* 2nd ed. New York: McGraw-Hill Book Company, 1972.

Jacoby, Helmut. *Architectural Drawings.* New York: Frederick A. Praeger, Publishers, 1965.

Jacoby, Helmut. *New Architectural Drawings.* New York: Frederick A. Praeger, Publishers, 1969.

Jacoby, Helmut. *New Techniques of Architectural Rendering.* New York: Frederick A. Praeger, Publishers, 1971.

Kemper, Alfred M. *Drawings by American Architects.* New York: John Wiley & Sons, 1973.

Kemper, Alfred M. *Presentation Drawings by American Architects.* New York: Wiley-Interscience, John Wiley & Sons, 1977.

Oles, Paul Stevenson. *Architectural Illustration: The Value Delineation Process.* New York: Van Nostrand Reinhold Company, 1979.

Pile, John, comp. *Drawings of Architectural Interiors.* New York: Whitney Library of Design, 1967.

Walker, Theodore D. *Perspective Sketches.* Paperback ed. West Lafayette, IN: PDA Publishers, 1972.

Walker, Theodore D. *Perspective Sketches II.* West Lafayette, IN: PDA Publishers, 1975.

White, Edward T. *A Graphic Vocabulary for Architectural Presentation.* Tucson: Architectural Media, 1972.

White, Edward T. *Presentation Strategies in Architecture.* Tucson: Architectural Media, 1977.

INDEX